Mastering
The Novels of Jane Austen

Palgrave Master Series

Accounting
Accounting Skills
Advanced English Language
Advanced English Literature
Advanced Pure Mathematics
Arabic
Basic Management
Biology
British Politics
Business Communication
Business Environment
C Programming
C++ Programming
Chemistry
COBOL Programming
Communication
Computing
Counselling Skills
Counselling Theory
Customer Relations
Database Design
Delphi Programming
Desktop Publishing
Economic and Social History
Economics
Electrical Engineering
Electronics
Employee Development
English Grammar
English Language
English Literature
Fashion Buying and Merchandising Management
Fashion Styling
French
Geography
German
Global Information Systems
Human Resource Management
Information Technology
International Trade
Internet
Italian
Java
Management Skills
Marketing Management
Mathematics
Microsoft Office
Microsoft Windows, Novell NetWare and UNIX
Modern British History
Modern European History
Modern United States History
Modern World History
Networks
Novels of Jane Austen
Organisational Behaviour
Pascal and Delphi Programming
Philosophy
Physics
Practical Criticism
Psychology
Shakespeare
Social Welfare
Sociology
Spanish
Statistics
Strategic Management
Systems Analysis and Design
Team Leadership
Theology
Twentieth-Century Russian History
Visual Basic
World Religions

www.palgravemasterseries.com

Palgrave Master Series
Series Standing Order ISBN 0–333-69343–4
(outside North America only)

You can receive future titles in this series as they are published by placing a standing order. Please contact your bookseller or, in case of difficulty, write to us at the address below with your name and address, the title of the series and the ISBN quoted above.

Customer Services Department, Macmillan Distribution Ltd
Houndmills, Basingstoke, Hampshire RG21 6XS, England

Mastering
The Novels of Jane Austen

Richard Gill
and
Susan Gregory

First published 2003 by
PALGRAVE MACMILLAN
Houndmills, Basingstoke, Hampshire RG21 6XS and
175 Fifth Avenue, New York, N.Y. 10010
Companies and representatives throughout the world

PALGRAVE MACMILLAN is the global academic imprint of the Palgrave Macmillan division of St. Martin's Press, LLC and of Palgrave Macmillan Ltd Macmillan® is a registered trademark in the United States, United Kingdom and other countries. Palgrave is a registered trademark in the European Union and other countries.

ISBN 0–333–94898–X

This book is printed on paper suitable for recycling and made from fully managed and sustained forest sources.

A catalogue record for this book is available from the British Library.

Library of Congress Cataloging-in-Publication Data
Gill, Richard, 1945–
Mastering the novels of Jane Austen / Richard Gill and Susan Gregory.
p. cm. – (Palgrave master series)
Includes bibliographical references and index.
ISBN 0-333–94898–X (pbk.)
1. Austen, Jane, 1775–1817—Criticism and interpretation—Handbooks, manuals, etc. I. Gregory, Susan, 1945 May 28– II. Title. III. Series.
PR4037 .G54 2002
823'.7–dc21 2002028683

10 9 8 7 6 5 4 3 2 1
12 11 10 09 08 07 06 05 04 03

Printed and bound in Great Britain by
Creative Print & Design (Wales), Ebbw Vale

For Pat and in memory of Ken

Contents

Preface

Many people read Jane Austen's work because they find her entertaining and invigorating. Jane Austen is funny, and her, at times, outrageous preoccupation with 'Mighty Aphrodite' gives her work energy and wide-ranging appeal. Jane Austen is one of the few authors whose novels students of English have read for themselves, and she features prominently in discussions of books by people who have no professional interest in literature. Jane Austen's tone is laconic, engaged, detached, amused, askance and angry by turns. Virginia Woolf observes that 'Sometimes it seems as if her creatures were born merely to give Jane Austen the supreme delight of slicing their heads off' (*The Common Reader,* 1st ser., The Hogarth Press, 1975, p. 176.

Moreover, Jane Austen's story lines are strong. Her style is witty, direct, elegant, above all supple. Her writing is robust and rigorous and it makes demands. It engages – and it defies – the reader. Jane Austen is strenuous in her moral awareness. Virginia Woolf traces her moral charge to her wit and to 'an exquisite discrimination of human values'. She continues:

> The wit of Jane Austen has for partner the perfection of her taste. Her fool is a fool, her snob is a snob, because he departs from the model of sanity and sense which she has in mind, and conveys to us unmistakably even while she makes us laugh. (*The Common Reader*, p. 177)

Sometimes Jane Austen is uncomfortably exacting; *Mansfield Park* is a novel that divides opinion, perhaps because readers feel the standards required – and not just the moral standards – make *too* many demands.

Exacting also are the claims upon the attention of the reader. This is not to say that Jane Austen's novels are difficult 'to get through'. The experience of generations is that they are not. But we are required to follow the implications of the texts. Readers have to look back, to make connections, to exercise their aesthetic, social and moral sense and to supply what is not there. Jane Austen invites us to collaborate with her. She makes novelists of us all.

The implications in the text are often concerned with characters. From the light sketches through to the richness of her central figures, Jane Austen`s men and women have the ability to provoke readers. Provoke, that is, to speculation. A dangerous and unscrupulous pursuit, according to most critics, who, honourably, wish students to contextualize, not fantasize. But one which the lay reader may find it difficult to resist.

Nevertheless, we would advise against speculation of the kind we occasionally engage in when it comes to public examinations. For this reason we signal carefully where we have permitted ourselves this indulgence. But we reserve the right, as countless readers have done before us, tentatively to plug some provocatively provided gaps. Readers may choose to play this game in their own way.

We have also found it rewarding to consider the occasional event which, by historical accident not connected with plot, may throw into yet sharper relief the profundity of Jane Austen's achievement.

Of course, at every turn, we shall have missed a great deal. Jane Austen wrote that her books were not for 'such dull elves / As have not a great deal of ingenuity themselves' (Letter to Cassandra Austen, Friday 29 January 1813). It is *the* challenge for all who encounter her to try not to be accounted one!

Jane Austen shares a quality with authors such as Shakespeare, Wordsworth and Dickens: her works are receptive to different interpretative approaches. This is not just a case of how amenable the novels are to structural or stylistic readings; they are, but so are all literary works. They also yield up satisfactorily when read in the light of history and politics.

It is perhaps not surprising that the novels have received interpretations based on the politics of feminism; each of them is female-centred. Fanny Price, valued by Sir Thomas Bertram for her `persuadableness` (vol. 2, ch. 10), resists male persuasion with the plain defiance of common sense: 'I think it ought not to be set down as certain, that a man must be acceptable to every woman he may happen to like himself' (vol. 3, ch. 4).

Political readings must have seemed impossible at one time – no mention of the French Revolution – but now, or, rather, since Alistair Duckworth and Marilyn Butler, it seems natural to read Jane Austen's books in the light of contemporary attitudes to women, tradition and innovation. The increased interest in political readings has naturally generated work on Jane Austen's relation to her own society. Roger Sales's work is of especial value in this area.

We have not sought to give a systematic reading of the novels from one critical perspective. Many of the issues dealt with have become part of the tradition of Jane Austen criticism. In terms of historical context, there is an emphasis upon her Anglicanism. The Bible, the Prayer Book, the sermons of Bishop Butler and the spiritual writings of William Law have an important, though tangential, place in her thinking. We have also shown that her work has links with the philosophers of the empirical tradition. When it comes to ethics, it seems to us that there is an implicit challenge to utilitarian thinking in the novels. Jane Austen's ethical code might be described as embracing the Christian virtues, with Conscience as our guide (see 15.10).

Much critical writing about Jane Austen must deal with substantive issues such as relations within families, attachments between characters, the etiquette of conduct, perception, the difficulties of judgement, the nature of the imagination, the place of intuition, the problems of self-knowledge and the adjustment of one class to another, while acknowledging Jane Austen's wider sense of a sociey that is undergoing change. Most studies also engage with formal matters such as narration, plot movement, grammar, and the conventions of the comic genre.

In addition, we have found it fruitful to ponder at least three other issues. The first is topography. Jane Austen has a sharp sense of the importance of place and space. Allied to this interest are the common themes of ejection, loss of home and the search for the 'right' home. It may be that, in her concern for the spaces of home, Jane Austen reflects the plight of women in a world which assigns them a domestic role but denies them control over the places in which their roles are exercised.

A third issue is a formal one: the nuances of her vocabulary. We have found it rewarding to look at the range of meanings open to Jane Austen by consulting Johnson`s *Dictionary*. Johnson, of course, is earlier, and, in addition, it does not follow that all the meanings of individual words open to Jane Austen are present when those words appear in her texts. All we are claiming is that the force of some passages is increased if we recognize some of the meanings that the words had in, or shortly before, her day.

A book on Jane Austen will never be 'finished'. She will ever stimulate, and elude. Virginia Woolf paid powerful tribute to this characteristic evasiveness:

> She wishes neither to reform nor to annihilate; she is silent and that is terrific indeed. (*The Common Reader*, p. 176)

RICHARD GILL
SUSAN GREGORY

Acknowledgements

We would like to thank the following friends who have helped us in various ways with our thinking about Jane Austen: Joan Allen, Judith Andrew, Doreen Avery, Don Ball, Pip Batty, Tania Benedictus, Paul Bowman, Tina Bowman, Alan Caine, Sarah Caine, Barbara Corlett, Pamela Cormack, Jane Clarkson, Dr Nigel Dadge, Justin Dill, Diane Edwards, Sheila Fahy, Richard Freeston, Judith Gibson, Mary Gill, Miriam Gill, Naomi Gill, Annie Goodger, Mari Green, the Green family, Richard Gregory, Edith Grossu, Mircea Grossu, Diane Hall, Antonia Harrison, Helen Harrison, Miranda Harrison, Nigel Harrison, Pamela Hinett, David Hopkins, Anne Hudson, Bob Jackson, Ian Jodrell, Joyce Jodrell, Dr Dinesh Khoosal, Roger Knight, Barbara Langley, Roger Langley, Kathleen Lea, Penny Luithlen, Elizabeth Mackenzie, Gabriella Maffioli, Bruce Moffat, Azreen Mussa, Susan Newman, Shelagh Petrie, Ed Price, Nancy Reid, Anna Revill, Bernard Richards, Alison Richardson-Jones, Kathleen Roberts, Neil Roberts, Ian Robinson, David Roe, Olivia Schelts, Helen Smith, Hilary Spanos, Elizabeth Stone, Michael Sweeney, Jan Todd, Stephen Turner, Hayley White, Fred Yarker, Vera Yarker. We would also like to thank Stephen Cranham for his illustrations and the anonymous readers of our original manuscript for their comments on an earlier draft of the book.

We have found the following books helpful and wish gratefully to acknowledge our indebtedness to the authors' scholarship:

Marilyn Butler, *Jane Austen and the War of Ideas* (Clarendon Press, 1975)
David Copeland and Juliet McMaster (eds) *The Cambridge Companion to Jane Austen* (Cambridge University Press, 1997)
W.A. Craik, *Jane Austen: The Six Novels* (Methuen, 1965)
Alistair M. Duckworth, *The Improvement of the Estate* (The Johns Hopkins University Press, 1971)
Roger Gard, *Jane Austen*'s *Novels: The Art of Clarity* (Yale University Press, 1992)
J. David Grey (ed.), *The Jane Austen Handbook* (Athlone, 1986)
D.W. Harding, *Regulated Hatred and Other Essays on Jane Austen* (Athlone, 1998)
Barbara Hardy, *A Reading of Jane Austen* (Athlone, 1979)
Claudia L. Johnson, *Jane Austen: Women, Politics, and the Novel* (University of Chicago Press, 1988)
Margaret Kirkham, *Jane Austen, Feminism and Fiction* (Athlone, 1997)
Oliver MacDonagh, *Jane Austen: Real and Imagined Worlds* (Yale University Press, 1991)
Ian Milligan, *Studying Jane Austen* (Longman, 1988)
K.C. Phillipps, *Jane Austen's English* (Longman, 1970)
Warren Roberts, *Jane Austen and the French Revolution* (Athlone, 1995)
Roger Sales, *Jane Austen and Representations of Regency England* (Routledge, 1994)
B.C. Southam, *Jane Austen: The Critical Heritage* (Routledge & Kegan Paul, 1968). Volume 2 (1987)
Tony Tanner, *Jane Austen* (Macmillan – now Palgrave Macmillan, 1986)
Claire Tomalin, *Jane Austen: A Life*, 2nd edn (Penguin, 2001)

Fay Weldon, *Letters to Alice on First Reading Jane Austen* (Coronet Books, Hodder & Stoughton, 1984)
Andrew H. Wright, *Jane Austen`s Novels* (Penguin, 1962)
Virginia Woolf, *Collected Essays, Volume II* (Hogarth Press, 1931)
Virginia Woolf, *The Common Reader*, First Series (Hogarth Press, 1975)

We have worked with the following editions: Penguin, Oxford University Press, Oxford World Classics.

Part I

Northanger Abbey

she is formally conducted by Dorothy the ancient housekeeper up a different staircase, and along many gloomy passages, into an apartment never used since some cousin or kin died in it about twenty years before." Northanger Abbey

Gothic

1 A consciously designed novel

1.1 Works of art

'... **for though she could not write sonnets, she brought herself to read them** ...' (vol. 1, ch. 1)

Northanger Abbey is the Jane Austen novel that contemporary readers may find the most immediate because it is the most youthful, exuberant and *consciously* literary. It is designed with the formality, complexity and playfulness of the sonnets that the young Catherine reads. It might be said to be about the nature of fiction. At the same time, while remaining a book, it claims for itself a 'reality' that draws attention to Jane Austen's lasting preoccupation with the relationship between life, nature and art.

A playful novel

The very writing of *Northanger Abbey* displays stylistic bravura. Its energy complements the impudence with which Jane Austen immediately establishes that she – and her heroine – are about to break the mould. There is flippancy and irony in the vigorous opening, in which it is established that Catherine Morland makes an unlikely heroine. The ironic tone seems inevitable in a writer who is determined from the start to question received wisdoms and the conventions of popular fiction. This determination gives the novel its scaffold. Jane Austen is constantly playing off her heroine against a traditional concept of what constitutes the heroic. She also subverts the glamorising tendency that more conventional fiction adopts towards the central character.

So Jane Austen preposterously presents a 'real' girl, very plain at least as a child and 'occasionally stupid'. Catherine's clergyman father and robust mother count against her heroic status. As an infant she has a taste for what is forbidden. She is noisy, wild and chaotic, drawing houses that look like chickens, loving rolling down hills and reading stories with 'no reflexion' (vol. 1 chap. 1). She is 'fond of all *boys'* plays' (our italics). This anarchic being – 'A heroine in a hack post-chaise' (vol. 2 chap. 14) – is chosen by Jane Austen as worthy of centre stage. This is subversive and humanitarian. If Catherine Morland, then any of us. Jane Austen claims the significance and centrality of every human life, probably from early in her writing career.

Reflexivity

Contemporary readers have become accustomed to thinking about literature as being about itself. The term 'reflexive' has proved useful when talking about those moments when a literary work draws attention to its own status as a work of art. Reflexivity is used of works that, for example, engage with the inspiration, writing and reading of books. They appeal to readers of a structuralist turn of mind. Sometimes critics talk about literature as being about its own processes; that is, the making of literature is a theme of the work that is being made.

Northanger Abbey is such a novel. It uses other novels, in particular *The Mysteries of Udolpho* by Mrs Radcliffe, to construct an alternative fiction to the kind its young people usually read.

Playing with contrasts

Contrasts hold great fascination for the author of *Northanger Abbey.* It is not only two distinctive kinds of fiction and two polarized notions of the feminine 'heroic' that engage her. The two men in Catherine's life – Henry Tilney and John Thorpe – are clearly contrasted, as are her two female friends – Eleanor Tilney and Isabella Thorpe. Catherine and her brother James, babes in the wood, are counterpoised between the other sibling pairs. Sometimes, chameleon-like, they adopt the colouring of Thorpes, sometimes of Tilneys. These 'brother-sister' complements intensify the novel's patterned quality.

Northanger Abbey is built upon such balances, contrasts and linkages. A novel with a binary structure, it provides a playground for polarities. To think of one element is to be aware of another, which contrasts and/or complements it.

Parody – the mocking, usually through exaggeration, of literary form and conventions – is by nature a binary phenomenon. The reader must have in mind the genre which is being parodied in order to enjoy the parodic text. Both the narrator and Henry Tilney indulge in parody. The heroine, and the kind of fiction that absorbs her, invites it.

Incidents are treated with a mischievousness that draws attention to telling parallels. For example, Catherine is rescued from John Thorpe by his being 'born off by the resistless pressure of a long *string* of passing ladies' (our italics), much as a horse, with which John Thorpe has far more affinity than with a woman, might similarly be swept along (vol. 1, ch. 10).

1.2 Locations

'Can you, in short, be prevailed on to quit this scene of public triumph and oblige your friend Eleanor with your company in Gloucestershire?' (vol. 2, ch. 2)

The two major settings

Northanger Abbey has two primary locations. Bath occupies the earlier part, and Northanger Abbey the latter. As the novel starts and ends in Fullerton, there is a neat locational pattern, with the scenes of Catherine's adventures bookended by the setting of her childhood home. The movement and design of the novel is orderly and symmetrical (see 3.11).

Moreover, the name of Catherine's childhood village suggests that, humble though that birthplace might be, it has more to offer of lasting value than either Bath or the now secular Northanger. The life of the parsonage, from which Catherine escapes with such delighted anticipation, is shown ultimately to be more fulfilling than both the city of 'ton' and the fine country mansion. Catherine, fittingly, will exchange, through marriage, one country parsonage for another, Fullerton for the durable-sounding and solidly based Woodston.

Journeying between locations

The journeys between the locations, in addition to being conventional emblems of moral progress, also work as patterning elements. We are implicitly invited to compare the language of Catherine's journey to neo-classical Bath, with its distinctly romantic frissons of 'Robbers' and 'tempests' denied (vol. 1, ch. 2), and the 'unceasing recurrence of doubts and inquiries' (vol. 2, ch. 14) that mark rational angst on the journey from 'romantic' Northanger to Fullerton.

Parallels between settings

The binary nature of the novel emerges through the parallels between the two major settings. Links between Bath and Northanger formally tie the two halves of the book together. Even so, some readers might feel that the structure of the novel – two such different locations with their own distinctive narrative material – is inherently weak. However, the two volumes artfully yield up reflections and contrasts which cement their thematic links.

- In Bath Catherine is dominated by the self-seeking Isabella, a creature of Gothic extravagance. It is at romantic Northanger that she benefits from a growing friendship with the sensitive, altruistic and rational Eleanor.
- In Bath, the architecture of which is based in classical reason, Catherine is driven by the reckless John Thorpe, but it is the careful Henry who drives her to Gothic Northanger. John's driving, like his wooing, never gets anywhere, while Henry brings Catherine safely to the Abbey, originally a female foundation, where she learns judgement.
- In architectural terms, Bath is neo-classical, but Northanger, at least in its original state, is Gothic (see 3.7). Yet the literature Catherine reads in classical Bath is Gothic. It is in the Abbey that she becomes disenchanted with romance. It is here that she reads laundry lists!

The ingenuity as well as the variety of the linkages prevents them from lapsing into formulaic predictability.

1.3 Plotting, themes and characters

'provided they were all story and no reflexion . . .' (vol. 1, ch. 1)

Comic writing, and all Jane Austen's novels are comic, is not commonly considered to be concerned with substantive issues to the extent that tragic works are. Yet in *Northanger Abbey*, preoccupations of literature – for example, acute awareness of language, sensitivity to what we might call the morality of style (see 1.4), and the balancing and counterbalancing of characters in the interests both of ethics and of craftsmanship – highlight a number of serious issues.

Self-expression

One of the ways in which *Northanger Abbey* sports with contrasts is through the characters' talk. Their idioms are revelatory of character and of moral capacity. For example, three young characters are inclined to say whatever comes into their heads. Isabella indulges in noncholant excess and John Thorpe's rattle manner indicates a man out of control. The plot reveals that neither has the least concern with an outer truth and reality. Their language is emotional pulp. In contrast, Catherine's spontaneity is part of her instinctive drive towards truthfulness. Her capacity to vocalize strong feeling shows a liberating integrity.

In this Catherine both contrasts with the more phlegmatic and cautious hero and is his match. For Henry *can* let his guard down: 'That gentleman would have put me out of patience, had he staid with you half a minute longer' (vol. 1, ch. 10).

Learning to read

In a novel about literature, 'reading' itself becomes a major preoccupation. Catherine's learning to be more discriminating provides the trajectory of the plot. Through Henry and through trial and error, she develops a capacity for a kind of literary criticism which she can eventually apply both to literature and to life (see 1.4). This is aided by a growth in her understanding of Henry Tilney's parodies. Wherever there is language, Henry's ear is cocked. He parodies Bath conversation, a young woman's journal, Mrs Ratcliffe's works, even the Catechism.

Catherine, compared with Henry, is conventional. This is signalled, in part, by her innocence of parody. The novel is constructed around the joke of the naïve Catherine's meeting with 'a most extraordinary genius'. (vol. 1, ch. 3). Or, for Henry has the intellectual detachment for self-mockery, with her being 'strangely harassed by a queer, half witted man…who distressed me by his nonsense'.

Either way, Henry, like his creator, and unlike Catherine, is knowing. Catherine, the plot demonstrates, is never going to catch up with them in this respect. But what the novel slowly reveals is her progress towards a closer approximation, Moreover, what she *comes* to see goes deeper than Henry's perceptions (see 4).

Northanger Abbey is about Catherine's improvement in social, moral and aesthetic literacy. First and foremost, Catherine must learn to read people and to act upon her insights. For example, when James appears in Bath, Catherine realizes that Isabella neglects her, but she does not fully recognize that she is being manipulated until she has it in writing; in the second volume she receives a letter from Isabella, begging her to intercede with James (vol. 2, ch. 12).

Catherine must learn to discriminate between the conventions of entertaining fiction and the responsibilities of living. She must learn, to put it in Henry's terms, the difference between the dreadful suspicions she harbours and the life of a Christian country. She has to come to terms with 'the common feelings of common life' (vol. 1, ch. 1). Northanger Abbey becomes the place in which the extravagances of the literature Catherine picked up in Bath are tested.

Promises

The Thorpes are casual about promises. The most serious promise in the novel is arguably the promise to marry. Isabella breaks off her engagement with James Morland without thought. Moreover, she and her brother, and James, press Catherine to break her promise to walk with the Tilneys.

In deliberate contrast Catherine recognizes the solemnity of promises. She talks of *engaging* herself with Miss Tilney for a walk. It is significant that Henry has already talked of his relationship with Catherine as a kind of engagement: 'We have entered into a contract of mutual agreeableness for the space of an evening . . .' (vol. 1, ch. 10).

Like Catherine, the Tilneys treat promises with the utmost seriousness. Though it is never formally stated, Henry might have ceased his courtship of Catherine precisely because she appeared to be casual about keeping promises.

1.4 False friends

'she was ashamed of Isabella, and ashamed of having ever loved her' (vol. 2, ch. 12)

James and John

The friendship between James Morland and John Thorpe typifies the kind of attachments that enjoy an ephemeral life in the whirligig of a university. James was probably swept into friendship, possibly assisted by John's good ale, with someone with whom he has little in common. Brought up quietly in a country parsonage, he appears susceptible to 'show', and, being a little more worldly than Catherine, is more open to moral taint. Lacking self-knowledge, and without the sense of his sister, James believes that John, in spite of a rough disdain for rationality, is 'as good natured a fellow as ever lived' (vol. 1, ch. 7). He is as taken in by John as he is by Isabella.

Isabella and Catherine

James's lasting capacity to be hoodwinked by John is contrasted with Catherine's gradual awareness of Isabella's perfidy.

To begin with Isabella sweeps Catherine up in the kaleidoscopic life of fashionable Bath. Jane Austen announces the friendship between Isabella and Catherine with an oxymoron: a 'sudden intimacy' (vol. 1, ch. 4). It is virtually a contradiction in terms to suggest that 'intimacy', with its connotations of trust, warmth and personal confidences, can be 'sudden'. The idea of 'intimacy' is further undermined by the girls' shallow topics of conversation: 'dress, balls, flirtations and quizzes'. The narrator shows that

Isabella does not so much form friendships as appropriate people whom she will find useful.

She might be said to 'make' friends in the sense that she shapes them for her own convenience. As with John, a friendship for Isabella must be 'serviceable'. (vol. 2, ch. 15). Appropriation takes tangible forms. Isabella takes possession of Catherine physically – they are soon arm-in-arm at her suggestion. She also impinges psychically, through hyperbolic language and demands on Catherine's attention. Isabella's language is immediately characterized as extravagant by her use of the words 'excessively like' (vol. 1, ch. 4). At the theatre, Catherine finds that much of her leisure is 'claimed' by 'returning the nods and smiles of Miss Thorpe' (vol. 1, ch. 5.)

Incarceration

This shows the novel's preoccupation with entrapment, another building block for its design. Instead of being forced 'away to some remote farm house' (vol. 1, ch. 1) by a rapacious male, Catherine is taken possession of in civilized Bath by a predatory *female.* (see 4.6). Isabella may accuse the Tilneys of swallowing up 'everything' (vol. 1, ch. 13), but she is the one with the voracious gorge. Later Catherine will entrap *herself,* metaphorically, in Northanger, enticed by her romantic expectations, and oblivious to the designing of the more conventionally unscrupulous male.

We are aware of the language of increasing control when Isabella's and Catherine's attachment is 'not to be satisfied' by walking arm-in-arm in the Pump room, but 'required' that Isabella keep hold of Catherine all the way home, followed by a 'lengthened shaking of hands' (vol. 1, ch. 4). Coercion later becomes explicit, when Isabella catches 'hold of one hand' and refuses to let go (vol. 1, ch. 13). She has captured Catherine to prevent her from running after her preferred hares, the Tilneys.

The idea of possession is further symbolized by Isabella's asking what Catherine will wear, because she is 'determined at all events to dress exactly like you' (vol. 1, ch. 6). Isabella's proposal that they look like twins is an attempt to deny Catherine her individuality. As Jane Austen is always interested in what makes a person singular, this is a bad sign. At the same time, Isabella reveals her superficiality: she sets store by consistency in appearance while ignoring consistency in those areas of life where it is important.

There is plenty of evidence that Isabella is false, self-contradictory, inconsistent. It is ironic that Catherine finds Northanger inconsistent – its drive is 'smooth' and 'level' (contrast 2.3 and the Latin root of 'horrid') – but not her false friend. So, for example, on the evening of James's and John's arrival, Catherine finds herself almost returned to the friendless state of her first evening in Bath, for 'James and Isabella were so much engaged in conversing together, that the latter had no leisure to bestow more on her friend than one smile, one squeeze, and one "dearest Catherine"' (vol. 1, ch. 8).

Catherine is also puzzled when Isabella claims to have scolded men for not admiring her friend, Miss Andrews. To Catherine's rational mind admiration is not a matter of moral judgement, so you cannot be rebuked for either admiring or not admiring. Her surprise is expressed by her exclamation 'Scold them!', and when she asks why Isabella scolds, Isabella answers by paying herself a compliment: 'I have no notion of loving people by halves; it is not my nature' (vol. 1, ch. 6). Isabella's language here is characteristically supercharged – 'no notion' and 'not my nature' – while elsewhere the hyperbole is wildly inconsistent, as when, after 'nearly five minutes', she has waited for Catherine 'at least this age', then 'these ten ages' and finally 'this half hour'. (vol. 1, ch. 6). If Catherine were more confident in reading other people, she would see that Isabella is capricious, hypocritical, erratic and fickle. This proves characteristic of jailers. With judicious patterning, and revelatory of Jane Austen's insight into tyrants, General Tilney turns out to be the same.

Scheming

Northanger Abbey is, in formal terms, a third-person narration. We are shown what Catherine or Isabella or Mrs Allen do or say. But in the case of Catherine, the narrator chooses to have access to what she is thinking and feeling as well. This type of narration, as so often in Jane Austen's work, obliges the reader to put together what other characters are up to. We join Catherine in her act of interpretation.

Given her naïvety, Catherine is initially less successful than we are, and we enjoy the suspense of waiting for her to catch up. There is something playfully testing in this form of narrative; will the reader be alert to the motives of characters who do not openly say what they are after? In a fiction about fictions, Jane Austen invites us to think as a writer does.

The narrator usually abstains from direct statement, leaving the reader to infer a character's motives.

Isabella's motive for friendship is present in the first words she speaks about Catherine: 'How excessively like her brother Miss Morland is' (vol. 1, ch. 4). Isabella pretends to have an interest in Catherine, while using her as a means of securing James. Although in terms of formal etiquette, as well as of morality, Isabella's behaviour is not as correct as it should be (she welcomes Captain Tilney's attentions while engaged to James), she is not willing to jeopardize her reputation by spending long periods of time alone with a young man. Besides, James is conventional – he would not suggest it. Therefore Isabella needs another woman about her to convey respectability while she fixes James.

Hence the friendship with Catherine is a grand scheme. We notice Isabella's vehement energy when Isabella and John force Catherine to break her promise with the Tilneys for the sake of going in the carriage to Clifton. Isabella's scheme is to use Catherine, the fond sister and indulgent friend, as a chaperone, as her predatory instinct tells her that she can focus on James and make a kill on the drive.

Scheming is central to Isabella and to the plot. As with her brother, life for Isabella is a series of fictions adopted for her own aggrandizement.

***Northanger Abbey* draws a distinction between fictive creations, like Henry's parodies, which illuminate life through laughter, and fictive desecrations such as the Thorpes' lies.**

It is appropriate that, in a work of literature about literature, 'plotting' is what the villains do. General Tilney is a schemer, like Isabella. That conscious designs are in the end subverted is also appropriate in a fiction that aims to subvert. The conscious design of *Northanger Abbey* works like a series of Russian dolls or Chinese boxes (see 2.1). In the end it arguably subverts its *own* expectations and its *own* plot (see 3.11 and 4.10). In a tightly constructed novel, with all the symmetry of the classical, Catherine eventually breaks bounds.

Isabella and the clergy

Within the big scheme of fixing James, Isabella has a range of lesser ploys. The Thorpes know that the rich are usually wary of fortune-hunters. Therefore, Isabella has to conceal her mercenary motives from Catherine. Her ploy is to suggest that she is drawn irresistibly to the clergy. She says that she 'must confess herself very partial to the profession' and adds 'something like a sigh' (vol. 1, ch. 5) to indicate a romantic dimension. Isabella is thorough: when she has secured the engagement, she drives the point home. 'I feel that I have betrayed myself perpetually; so unguarded in speaking of my partiality for the church!' (vol 1, ch. 15).

Isabella's ludicrous justification of love for James on the grounds that he is a clergyman is in contrast with Catherine's love for Henry Tilney, which is for himself alone. The fact that he is a clergyman is immaterial. (Pun intended.)

The General

The preying on innocence by experience is a complementary motif in the second half of the novel. General Tilney is as avaricious as Isabella. To be out for all one can get is shown to know no boundaries of age, class or gender, and the wealthy are as prone as the more necessitous fortune seeker. The General shamelessly exploits Catherine's sensibility just as Isabella does. He claims Catherine as a guest in the alleged interest of companionship for his daughter.

Morland gold

The Thorpes and the General complement each other in that both parties believe that the Morlands offer 'more'. The General is convinced by Thorpe's conviction. He does not bother to check the truth for himself.

The Morlands themselves, far from being 'a forward, bragging, scheming race' (vol. 2, ch. 15), are not after anything, in spite of their name. They do not speculate when Catherine is invited to the Tilneys. They trust to Mr Allen's assessment of the General's fitness to tend her, and rejoice at Catherine's pleasure. Mrs Thorpe is clearly a (rather subdued) party to her offsprings' greedy scheming and the General is incorrigibly hypocritical on the subject of what he wants: 'He told me the other day that he only valued money as it allowed him to promote the happiness of his children' (vol. 2, ch. 10). But 'it . . . never entered' the Morlands' 'head to suspect an attachment' between Henry and Catherine (vol. 2, ch 16).

Criticism and the language of life

Catherine's reception of a letter from Isabella, inveigling her into interceding with James, shows that she has now become a mature and insightful reader of Isabella's behaviour:

> Such a strain of shallow artifice could not impose even upon Catherine. Its inconsistencies, contradictions, and falsehood, struck her from the very first. (vol. 2, ch. 12)

'Artifice' shows Catherine's recognition of artistic form, and 'shallow' is the judgement of a moralist. In a novel concerned with the values and expectations that literature can promote, the language of Catherine's awakening to the truth about Isabella draws on the language of art. Catherine's criticism is very English; that is, it is in the tradition of Johnson. A criticism of style is inseparable from a criticism of morality. This is the kind of thinking that fuels the contention that there are no specifically literary values, because the language of literature, and therefore the language of criticism, is the language of life.

1.5 The true friend

'your fair friend' (vol. 2, ch. 2)

Friendship and writing

In Jane Austen's work writing of any kind is a strong indicator of character and theme.

One of the links between Isabella as the false and Eleanor as the true friend is that both are associated with correspondence.

Isabella's letter shows she is false, and Catherine, by overcoming her pride and agreeing to write to Eleanor after her ejection, confirms the truth of their friendship. 'Fair friend' is what General Tilney calls Catherine in his heavy invitation (vol. 2, ch. 2). The reference is primarily to Catherine's beauty, but Jane Austen might be anticipating other meanings of 'fair'. Johnson's tenth definition is: 'Not practising any fraudulent or insidious arts.' Catherine is a fair friend in the sense that she practises no subterfuge. She also reads correctly Eleanor's lack of complicity when the General ejects her and reads as sincere her desire to correspond.

Fixing men

When Eleanor is introduced to Catherine, the narrator says this:

> she seemed capable of being young, attractive, and at a ball, without wanting to fix the attention of every man near her, and without exaggerated feelings of extatic delight or inconceivable vexation on every little trifling occurrence. (vol. 1, ch. 8)

Eleanor is the anti-type of Isabella. The difference lies chiefly in their respective self-estimations and self-presentations. Eleanor's manners are not 'affectedly open'. Johnson defines affectation as 'The act of making an artificial appearance' and 'affectedly' as 'hypocritically'.

Another obvious difference is that Eleanor does not want 'to fix the attention of every man near her'. At the end of the novel, we are told enough to infer that when Catherine met her, Eleanor's heart is already engaged: 'Her partiality for this gentleman was not of recent origin' (vol. 2, ch. 16). Isabella's partiality for James dates from Christmas, but that does not prevent Isabella from setting off 'in pursuit of the two young men' (vol. 1, ch. 6). At the close of the novel Isabella, for all her pretty tricks and ploys, has secured no admirer, whereas Eleanor, who, we may assume, has attracted her suitor without design, is married. Isabella has, literally and metaphorically, got nowhere, whereas Eleanor is a viscountess, with a 'place' to match (see chapter 3).

Sisters and brothers

There is one respect in which Catherine in her relations with Eleanor resembles Isabella in her relations with Catherine:

both Isabella and Catherine want to promote a friendship with a sister because they are attracted to a brother.

This is not a matter that the narrator leaves the reader to infer. In the same chapter that presented Miss Tilney (vol. 1, ch. 8), the narrator says: 'Catherine, interested at once by her appearance and her relationship with Mr Tilney, was desirous of being acquainted with her'. The zeugma – one word referring to two further words ('interested' and 'appearance'/'relationship') – works to bring out the difference in the weight of the two ideas that are objects of a single word. Catherine is not interested in Eleanor's appearance in the same way in which she is interested in her being Henry's sister.

In addition, the pattern of sisters and brothers brings out an important point about the pursuit of love:

love is social as well as individual; to meet a beloved is to meet his family and being

at ease with his family assists the growth of love. To fall in love is to find a new family and society.

The place of the family in the promotion of love can lead to scheming (see 1.4). Here we see the importance of the first term in the zeugma; Catherine has an interest in Eleanor, which is not just her consanguinity with Henry. Isabella only fakes such an interest in Catherine.

Readers might wish to speculate as to what Eleanor says to Henry about Catherine. It is hard not to imagine her intimating to Henry that Catherine is very much taken with him; an understanding between brother and sister must have been a factor in Catherine's being invited to the Abbey.

What is certain is that Henry, though no doubt with more than one motive, thanks Catherine 'for her kindness in thus becoming her [Eleanor's] visitor' (vol. 2, ch. 5), because she 'was uncomfortably circumstanced – she had no female companion – and . . . was sometimes without any companion at all'. There is, therefore, more than romantic selfishness present in the interest that Catherine has in Eleanor, and Eleanor and Henry have in Catherine. Isabella's motives in befriending Catherine are entirely selfish.

The growth of friendship

Between Catherine and Eleanor there is no 'sudden intimacy'. The absence of anything dramatic is a suggestion of the potential of their friendship.

Tricks spoil a natural flourishing of fondness. Jane Austen has an aversion to tricks and a romantic notion of love and friendship. Like the hyacinth, a flower that Catherine "has just learnt to love" (vol. 2 chap. 7), friendship and love must be allowed to bloom as they will.

At the first meeting of Catherine and Eleanor, there was no 'very speedy intimacy', because, although Catherine 'readily talked...whenever she could think of anything to say', she did not always have 'the courage and leisure for saying it'.(vol. 1, ch. 8).

At their second meeting there is more opportunity for talk. In an implied contrast with Isabella's effusive artifice, the narrator dwells on the kind of language Eleanor and Catherine use. They make remarks that have been made in Bath many times before:

> yet the merit of their being spoken with simplicity and truth, and without personal conceit, might be something uncommon. (vol. 1, ch. 10)

The talk of Catherine and Eleanor is direct, sincere, unaffected. Catherine's artless language allows Eleanor to see the considerable interest that Catherine takes in Henry, and its guileless openness recommends Catherine to her.

Enjoying conversation

An important stage in the gradual growth of their friendship comes on the walk to Beechen Cliff. Here there is a parallel with Catherine's friendship with Isabella. The first full conversation between Isabella and Catherine starts with Isabella's asking Catherine: 'Have you gone on with Udolpho?' (vol. 1, ch. 6). Eleanor extends such conversation to other sorts of reading, something that Isabella is incapable of.

Catherine and Eleanor genuinely converse; questions are asked about what the other thinks; tastes, such as Eleanor's for history, are debated.

Mischievous reversals

The true friends yet contrast with one another in a way that demonstrates Jane Austen's ingenuity. A structural principle of the novel is the contrast between Gothic fiction and literature more firmly grounded in 'reality'. For those familiar with Gothic fiction the contrast between Eleanor and Catherine is delightfully unexpected.

Catherine has a liberal father, who does not lock his daughter up in a country parsonage, yet Catherine's imagination is replete with Gothic fantasies. Eleanor, whose oppressive father metaphorically incarcerates her in a Gothic abbey, has a strongly grounded sense of actual life. It is the pragmatic Eleanor whose mother lacked constitutional robustness and died, thus causing Eleanor to experience the clichéd lot of the romantic heroine. But Catherine, who has been in training for such a role, disconcertingly has a sturdy mother who keeps producing children!

There is also an almost comic reversal in their appearances: Catherine, with her sallow skin and dark hair, looks something like the prevailing stereotype of the Gothic heroine, whereas Miss Tilney would not be out of place in a parsonage.

These contrasts act as a critique of Gothic fiction: there is no necessary link between a Gothic environment, albeit a subdued one, and the kind of events and characters found in the pages of Gothic romance.

1.6 Love and lovers

'But I had ten thousand times rather have been with you.' (vol. 1 chap. 12)

Wooing: design and fortune

John Thorpe, albeit with comic ineptitude, acts by design. He comes to Bath so that James can meet his sister. No doubt he also anticipates that Catherine might be a suitable spouse.

Henry has already entered her life, but in quite a different way. It was the role of the Master of Ceremonies in the Lower Rooms to make introductions, thus he 'introduced to her a very gentlemanlike young man as a partner – his name was Tilney' (vol. 1, ch. 3). This 'partner' is brought to Catherine by 'fortune', a word that still had as one of its meanings 'The power supposed to distribute the lots of life according to her own humour' (the first definition in Johnson). The reader should see that a lover allotted by fortune is a brighter prospect than one who acts by design. Catherine is of this view. She 'felt herself in high luck' (vol. 1, ch. 3).

Men and novels

John Thorpe and Henry Tilney are also contrasted in their attitudes to novels. Jane Austen has already paved the way for an implied denunciation of Thorpe by her vigorous defence of the novel (vol. 1, ch 5). John cannot discuss books. He never reads novels unless they are prurient or bawdy. His commendation of Mrs Radcliffe's novels is that there is 'some fun and nature in *them*' (vol. 1, ch. 7). Yet he does not recognize Mrs Radcliffe as the author of *The Mysteries of Udolpho*.

Henry, on the other hand, endorses the narrator's elevated opinion of the novel. He has read novels by the hundreds, deeply relishing Mrs Radcliffe's work. Thus he not only shares the heroine's enthusiasm but endorses it. Henry confirms Catherine in the courage of her convictions, whereas Thorpe undermines her independent judgement and her sense of self-worth.

John and his sisters

John and Isabella hunt together, though, ironically, she is more committed to a love chase than her brother, who prefers the literal kind. John, with his friend Sam Fletcher, had plans to 'get a house in Leicestershire', the heart of the hunting country (vol. 1, ch. 10). John is sufficiently close to his sister to bring James to Bath, but they cannot be called affectionate. He is insensitive towards the rest of his family. He 'vowed he would not drive her [his sister Anne] because of her thick ankles' (vol. 1, ch. 15). His crass boorishness throws Henry's tender concern for Eleanor's welfare into sharper relief.

Dancing

John Thorpe is both insistent and negligent. At their first meeting he engages Catherine to dance. Yet when the evening comes, he is late in claiming her as his partner, and when they dance talks of 'the horses and dogs of the friend whom he had just left, and of a proposed exchange of terriers' (vol. 1, ch. 8).

The following Thursday Catherine succeeds in avoiding the sight of John Thorpe for long enough to allow Henry to propose a dance. When John finds her, he claims that her avoidance of him is 'a cursed shabby trick'. Noticing Henry, he asks: 'What chap have you there?' Catherine answers in a single word: 'Tilney'. John's reply is revealing: 'Hum – I do not know him . . . Does he want a horse?' (vol. 1, ch. 10).

John Thorpe feels no pain! He is not up to being an unrequited lover. (In contrast Henry Tilney clearly *is* capable of jealousy.) It is hard to see John Thorpe as a dangerous man, who will distract, deceive or test Catherine (a common function of a Jane Austen villain).

Henry Tilney: the lover in conversation

The young clergyman is a conversationalist with a strong sense of style. Upon their first meeting, Catherine observes that 'He talked with fluency and spirit and there was an archness and pleasantry in his manner' (vol. 1, ch. 3). The archness (Johnson defines 'arch' as 'waggish, mirthful') and pleasantry emerge in his parody of a polite Bath conversation, which he treats as if it were the *Catechism of the Church of England.*

Henry's conversation is one of the features that distinguish him thoroughly from John Thorpe. His medley of styles might even be called 'postmodern'; it is as if he relishes variety and feels easy about choosing and mixing. He can talk seriously and, for Catherine, illuminatingly, in the language of picturesque landscape (vol. 1, ch. 14). He can explore an emblem – dance as representative of marriage – with the ingenuity required of a metaphysical conceit or a heroic simile (vol. 1, ch. 10). During his first conversation with Catherine, he engages in what now would be called literary criticism in his discussion of the style of men's and women's writing. This exchange allows Catherine to venture, with touching candour and an indication that she is not entirely happy with received opinion, her independent point of view. However 'strange' (vol. 1, ch. 3) she finds Henry, she can respond. With John Thorpe she 'is fearful of hazarding an opinion' (vol. 1, ch. 7).

The point of conversation

There is a point to all this verbal skirmishing. Married life among the (relatively) leisured classes allowed much time together in an evening, and if conversation is difficult the couple is deprived of one of the chief pleasures of marriage.

In Jane Austen's work love is inseparable from the business of finding a suitable marriage partner. Henry is finding out what kind of a conversation partner Catherine might prove. His requirements are subtle and complex. However, John's 'notion of things is simple enough' (vol. 1, ch. 15). 'Let me only have the girl I like, say I.' But what would he find to say to her? Any 'talk' he does have is entirely self-absorbed.

Henry and Eleanor

If Henry is to spend his evenings with Catherine, she must measure up to the other woman in his life – his sister. In Jane Austen's work, the sister/brother relationship is perhaps more important even than the one between husband and wife (see *Mansfield Park*, vol. 2, ch. 6). So John Thorpe fails miserably in his fraternal capacity as well as in all others.

We may surmise that being provocative has been a means of Henry's holding his own with his high-calibre sister. Conversation on the Beechen Cliff walk (vol. 1, ch. 14) assists Catherine to see how the mercurial Henry can be responded to. Eleanor helps Catherine to appreciate, and to an extent see through, Henry's style.

Eleanor clearly does not want Catherine to form an unfavourable impression of Henry. Isabella is shown to have no such concerns about the impression that *her* brother might make. Her complacent passing on (invention?) of suitably hyperbolic compliments is all, she believes, that is required to 'fix' Catherine.

Erotic engagement

Nowhere is there any indication that John Thorpe has any feeling for Catherine. He affords her a formulaic rendering of what he believes to be required, reserving his enthusiasm for horses and dogs.

On the other hand, when Henry draws an analogy between dancing and marriage, his feelings are clearly involved and his high moral tone is not without erotic force. Only a man excited by a young woman would talk so openly and so early of the rights and responsibilities of marriage. Jane Austen has been said to avoid writing about passion. In an obvious sense this is true. But passages such as Henry's 'emblem', playfully as he presents them, show that the judgement is false. His sheer exuberance is telling. Henry is obviously moved by feelings that can only be called passionate.

1.7 Meaning, manners and morals

'These manners did not please Catherine.' (vol. 1, ch. 7)

Nothing demonstrates more cogently the artfulness of *Northanger Abbey*'s design than the contrasting attitudes of its characters to meaning, manners and morals, each of which is subtly interconnected.

Proposal

It is common in Jane Austen's novels for a successful proposal to be referred to rather than fully presented. In the case of Henry's proposal, all the writer says is that 'his first purpose was to explain himself' (vol. 2, ch. 15).

In contrast, John Thorpe is shown in the act! One of the reasons why a reader might not find John Thorpe too threatening a figure is that, as a suitor, he is so inept. When in volume 1, chapter 15 he calls to bid Catherine farewell, he makes what the reader sees is a kind of declaration. Having quoted from the old song 'Going to one wedding brings on another', he suggests 'we may try the truth of this same old song'. Catherine does not understand, replying, unpromisingly, that she never sings. However, in a letter he writes to Isabella, John shows that he believes (through obtuseness and conceit) that Catherine 'gave him the most positive encouragement'. (vol. 2, ch. 3).

Meaning

John Thorpe can neither make himself clear nor bother himself with the meaning of others. His confused talk has already alarmed Catherine. On the drive to Claverton Down he says that James's gig 'is the most devilish little rickety business' but then assures her that it is 'safe enough'. Catherine has difficulty in reconciling 'two such very different accounts'. (vol. 1, ch. 9). She considers seeking clarification, but shows she has the measure of John when she perceptively reflects that 'he did not excel in giving those clearer insights, in making things plain which before had been ambiguous'.

He is very different from Henry, whose linguistic exactitude and concern to maintain the stability of meaning make him witty if, occasionally, pedantic. Henry calls into question the modish carelessness of Catherine's use of the word 'nice' and points to the confusion that results from a failure to make distinctions. It is the characteristic move of a philosopher in the English tradition: unless we observe distinctions between words we shall empty our common language of meaning.

Manners

The maintenance of stable and therefore consistent meanings is an aspect of good manners. Good manners require, among other things, that we mean what we say. The General's discourse is unreliable. When he expresses a wish that Eleanor, Catherine and he should visit Woodston, he says 'There is no need to fix' (a time) and then fixes the time of arrival precisely. Catherine reflects that such behaviour makes people unintelligible: 'but why he [the General] should say one thing so positively, and mean another all the while, was most unaccountable! How were people, at that rate, to be understood?' (vol. 2, ch. 11).

Both the General and John Thorpe are ill-mannered, because both are careless about meaning.

Morals

Making one's meaning clear is something that a person *ought* to do. Meaning and manners are therefore related to morality.

Considerate manners and the reciprocity of exchange that depends upon stable meaning scaffold the moral life.

Mrs Thorpe and Mrs Allen talk 'both together, far more ready to give than to receive information, and hearing very little of what the other said' (vol. 1, ch. 4). The witty use of the Biblical injunction that it is better to give than to receive shows that being receptive is morally central. If it is not, then meaning is lost.

John Thorpe is the comical embodiment of what happens when meaning, manners and morality drift apart. When Catherine resists the Clifton plan on the grounds that she has a prior engagement, his language becomes bullying: 'she *must* and *should* retract' (vol. 1, ch. 13). It is both moral and good manners to keep a promise, and to insist that one *must* go back on one's word is to show that one does not understand what the word 'promise' means. John does not listen actively and he does not engage with what he hears. That John's language choice is as lax as his morals is borne out by his summary of his dishonourable initiative when he postpones Catherine's arrangement with Eleanor as 'A pretty good thought of mine, hey?' (vol. 1, ch. 8).

John lies, and once the lie is in being, he embellishes it. He not only claims that he saw the Tilneys driving up the Lansdown Road but adds that Henry was hallooing to a man 'that they were going as far as Wick Rocks' (vol. 1, ch. 11). His lies become dangerous when, talking to the General, he grossly exaggerates Catherine's financial prospects, and then, resentful at Catherine's refusal and the failure of his attempts to reconcile Isabella and James, he represents the financial and moral standing of the Morlands to the General in an unfavourable light. So much for James' good-natured fear that 'his [John's] honest heart would feel so much' (vol. 2, ch. 10) at the failure of Isabella's and James's engagement. The truth is that to the end John displays with increasing malevolence the ill-mannered, contradictory and chaotic discourse of the morally bereft.

2 Fiction

2.1 Just like a book

'This is just like a book.' (vol. 2, ch. 5)

Critical interests

Contemporary academic critics who interest themselves in what is sometimes called narratology – the classification and study of the intricate and multiple strategies authors employ in their writing – would no doubt remark on what a highly literary novel *Northanger Abbey* is (see 1.1).

The literariness of 'Northanger Abbey'

Northanger Abbey is literary in two closely related and straightforward senses. First,

the business of reading and writing is one of the novel's topics.

Second,

fiction – the creation of and response to an imagined world – is one of the subjects of the novel.

But what appears at first to be straightforward soon yields up many questions concerning living, artistry and what we 'make' of experience.

For example, the narrative of *Northanger Abbey* raises the issue of what fiction really is. Is it make-believe or even lies, such as John Thorpe's (or Isabella's?) claim that Catherine encouraged him when he spoke of marriage (vol. 2, ch. 3)? Or is it, as the narrator claims in volume 1, chapter 5, 'some work in which the greatest powers of mind are displayed' – writing that challenges us, capable of revealing truths?

Parody

On the way to Northanger Abbey (vol. 2, ch. 5), Henry Tilney tells Catherine his parodic tale of how 'you' (this is an unusual story because it is told in the second person) are to spend a night in an abbey. 'To raise your spirits', Dorothy, 'the ancient housekeeper', relates that this part of the abbey 'is undoubtedly haunted' and that no servants are 'within call'. The fictionalized Catherine (that is what she becomes in Henry's story) discovers there is no lock to her door. Overcoming 'your *unconquerable* horror of the bed', Catherine sleeps, but on a later night, awakened by a storm, she sees 'a large, old-fashioned cabinet of ebony and gold'. The 'real' Catherine is on tenterhooks. Eagerly, she cries: 'Oh! Mr Tilney, how frightful! This is just like a book!'

Henry's tale is meant to be just like a book, just like the kind of fiction Catherine and Isabella Thorpe consume. Henry can 'write' in his head. The glory of his achievement is the way that he is *fantastically* weaving the 'real' Catherine's prospected experience at Northanger Abbey into a Gothic extravaganza, without being fully aware of Catherine's susceptibility *actually* to do the very same thing!

Catherine's response ought to tell her that there is a difference between the world within a book and the experience of reading it. The fictionalized Catherine is almost fainting; Catherine the 'reader' is agog!

The processes of fiction

So far the academic critic would enjoy the playful manoeuvres of the narrator:

***Northanger Abbey* might be judged to be about the workings of fiction on the page and on the reader.**

Catherine knows, for instance, that as a reader she will enjoy the 'uncommonly dreadful' thing that will shortly come from London (vol. 1, ch. 14).

The narrator, however, creates another kind of difference. The 'real' Catherine arrives at Northanger Abbey and is shown to a room which *does* contain an old chest. Moreover, its contents have nothing of the glamour of fiction about them.

***Northanger Abbey* works by observing a distinction between the fictional and the 'real'.**

Yet the academic critic might come back and say that although the novel purports to deal with a distinction that relates fiction to something which is not fictional – the actual world – it does so only in terms of fiction itself. This cannot be denied.

Northanger Abbey remains a book, but in that book the reader is invited to play with a number of distinctions. For example, what is fictional is *apparently* distinguished, by fictional means, from what is not. However,

like all art, the work only poses questions for those who sample it. It does not answer them.

Craft

Allusions to art and craft metaphorically extend the author's preoccupation with fiction *within* fiction and her interest in how literature is 'made'. Henry and Eleanor discuss landscape in terms of how it can be transformed into pictures with reference to the picturesque. Henry imagines a fictional Catherine discovering 'a division in the tapestry so *artfully* constructed as to defy the minutest inspection' (vol. 2, ch. 5; our italics).

That division in a tapestry (which turns out not to exist) is like the way into a fictional world from the individual construct that each of us calls life. Within Henry's imagination within a 'real' (though exaggerated) bedchamber within a 'real' abbey is a hair's-breadth divide. It is to be found within what has itself been crafted – a tapestry. This leads to a locked door that Catherine breaches to 'pass through . . . into a small vaulted room'. Within the room, a cabinet: within its 'folding doors' within a drawer a secret spring reveals an 'inner compartment' within which – rolls of paper, containing 'many sheets of manuscript', containing . . . ? It is like a spyhole into a dream.

But in 'reality' these manuscripts are not what they seem. They lack the magic of 'fiction'; they are mundane; they are 'real'. So Jane Austen conjures and conjures again, paradox within paradox, with all the craftiness for which she is so enthusiastically enjoyed.

2.2 On being a heroine

'But from fifteen to seventeen she was in training for a heroine.' (vol. 1, ch. 1)

The opening sentence

Catherine's infancy was such that anyone who saw her would not have expected her to grow up to be a heroine. Throughout the first chapter, the narrator plays on the connotations of 'heroine' and 'heroic'; these words have literary meanings.

What emerges from their usage is that Catherine is not the kind of character we would expect to find in the kind of novel she reads.

The only feature remotely complementary to the Gothic imagination is Catherine's hatred of confinement: female incarceration is a stock Gothic device.

Journeys

One of the purposes of the journeys in the novel is to bring out the differences between a Gothic heroine and Catherine Morland. On her way to Bath there are no lecherous 'noblemen and baronets as delight in forcing young ladies away to some remote farm-house' (vol. 1, ch. 2). Yet she *is* in danger from the unGothic John Thorpe, who, when he is driving her in his gig, 'laughed, smacked his whip, encouraged his horse, made odd noises, and drove on' (vol. 1, ch. 11). As the language of driving is metaphoric of sexual domination, are there latent sexual connotations in his inarticulate outburst?

The word 'heroine'

Three meanings of the word were available to Jane Austen. It is the third, the literary definition, which dominates: the principal female character in a poem, story, or play. Catherine does not do those things which the heroine of a novel is expected to do. It is true that in her buoyant impulsiveness she shows herself to be a young woman of feeling, but not in the exalted mode of the literary heroine. It is in her cricket rather than her devotion to dormice that her spirits are most evident. Within the fiction of the novel, Catherine is distinguished from the kind of character usually encountered in a fictional world.

Catherine's reading

It is, however, probable that when 'she read such works as heroines must read' (vol. 1, ch. 1) she was consciously preparing herself to live the life of a fictional character.

What she has to learn is that there is a difference between fiction and actuality. In the novel's characteristic mode of setting up binary oppositions, Catherine has 'to be a heroine' amid 'the perverseness of forty families' who are far from heroic. The irony of 'heroine' works against Catherine, who must discover the gap between the imagination and common life, in which there are no romantic foundlings and no lords: 'no – not even a baronet' (vol. 1, ch. 1).

In working against her fictive expectations, the novel also militates against the works that have fed Catherine's mind (vol. 1, ch. 1). In a novel about literature, the reader might expect that the literary works featured have more than an incidental importance. What then is to be made of Catherine's early experience of books?

'The Hare and many Friends'

Amongst her earliest achievements is repeating 'The Beggar's Petition' and 'The Hare and many Friends'. The latter, one of John Gay's fables, might have an emblematic significance. The subject of the poem is friendship. The hare is friends with everybody, but in practice every body actually means nobody. When danger comes, the hare is abandoned. According to the conventions of the fable, Gay supplies a moral; those

> who depend
> On many, rarely find a friend.

To whom might the moral apply?

A character who is distinctly in danger of being a 'hare' is Isabella, the false friend (see 1.5). Isabella, who has no true conception of what it is to be a friend, ends up without one.

2.3 Readers

'she sat quietly down to her book' (vol. 1, ch. 9)

In this self-consciously literary book

many of the major characters are readers

A reading list

Isabella and Catherine discuss Mrs Radcliffe's *The Mysteries of Udolpho.* They both appreciate that the pleasure of this book lies in its capacity to induce suspense; Isabella will not tell Catherine what lies behind the black veil, and Catherine 'would not be told on any account' (vol. 1, ch. 6).

In the same scene Isabella provides Catherine with 'a list of ten or twelve more of the same kind'. One might observe that in a novel about education, Catherine is being given her reading list! (see 1.3.) Isabella reads out the names: 'Castle of Wolfenbach, Clermont, Mysterious Warnings, Necromancer of the Black Forest, Midnight Bell, Orphan of the Rhine, and Horrid Mysteries.' Catherine asks: 'Are you sure they are all horrid?' (vol. 1, ch. 6).

Catherine's language choice is judicious: 'horrid' means hideous and dreadful. As K.C. Phillipps points out, Catherine's meaning is closer to the Latin original 'horridus' – prickly, rough and shaggy, and so, by extension, capable of making one bristle with fear. By contrast, Jane Austen disapprovingly makes Isabella's 'an amazing horrid book' (her judgement of *Sir Charles Grandison*) a less exact expression of distaste (*Jane Austen's English*, Longman, 1970, pp. 18–19).

Catherine the reader

Our amusement at Catherine should be tempered by our recognition that she is a potentially insightful reader. Her aversion to history is not unjust. She recognizes that 'a great deal of it must be invention' (vol. 1, ch. 14) – and feminist critics will relish her recognition that it is *his*-story – 'and hardly any women at all'. She is wiser than she knows. History *is* invention, but not just in Catherine's sense that the *speeches* 'must be invention'. History is not just one event after another; it is seeking causal links that will convincingly explain what went on.

Catherine's insights are sound, but what she needs is teaching where she lacks knowledge. In some scenes Henry performs the teaching role. This is what happens with regard to her 'reading' of the picturesque qualities of landscape at Beechen Cliff (see 4.4).

An unconscious satirist

At one point Henry points out that, quite unintentionally, Catherine has satirized contemporary conversation. She says, somewhat regretfully, that 'I cannot speak well enough to be unintelligible', to which Henry responds with 'Bravo! An excellent satire on modern language' (vol. 2, ch. 1). His enthusiasm for her remark stems from what it tells him about Catherine's character. She sees through pretence and artifice. Impressively fashionable talk often turns out to be without substantive sense. There is an appealing freshness in Catherine's confession that unintelligibility is beyond her!

Henry the reader

Earlier, on the walk round Beechen Cliff, Henry tells Catherine that he has read all of Mrs Radcliffe's works. Henry's reading is an indication that he is cultivated. It is also a metonymic sign: reading books stands for the exercise of all the critical faculties. In Henry Catherine has a useful interpreter.

Henry and the Gothic

Catherine has two exchanges with Henry about the Gothic. The first contains his entertaining burlesque (see 2.1). He knows his Gothic; his fanciful scene recalls one in Mrs Radcliffe's *Romance of the Forest* in which Adeline, the heroine, discovers a secret room – and its grisly contents – while staying in an abbey. Henry's manner is teasing yet scholarly (see 1.6).

The second conversation (vol. 2, ch. 9) occurs when Henry discovers that Catherine has been nursing Gothic imaginings about the death of his mother:

> If I understand you rightly, you had formed a surmise of such horror as I have hardly words to – Dear Miss Morland, consider the dreadful nature of the suspicions you have entertained. What have you been judging from?

He does not directly refer to Gothic novels, but he deploys the language of such works. His question about what she has 'been judging from?' tactfully implies that she has confused common life with Gothic fancy. In short, his judgement touches on those literary distinctions that are central to the novel. He is alluding to the implausibility of Gothic plotting.

2.4 Catherine's imaginary world

'Catherine sometimes started at the boldness of her own surmises.' (vol. 2, ch. 8)

Catherine is also presented as a kind of writer. Because she has read Mrs Radcliffe with an uncritical zeal,

she imagines life in terms of a Gothic novel.

Storms

There is a storm the first night she spends at Northanger Abbey, to which Catherine responds in the literary terms supplied by the language of Gothic fiction.

Although the writing is formally third-person, it functions as a first-person narration. Thus Catherine 'listened to the tempest with sensations of awe', and 'when she heard it rage round a corner of the ancient building' and 'close with sudden fury a distant door' she recollects 'a countless variety of dreadful situations and horrid scenes' (vol. 2, ch. 6). In literary terms, this dense, slightly over-written passage is akin to language such as this:

> Her imagination, wrought upon by these reflections, again became sensible to every impression, she feared to look round, lest she should again see some dreadful phantom, and she almost fancied she heard voices swell in the storm, which now shook the fabric. (Mrs Radcliffe, *The Romance of the Forest,* vol. 1, ch. 10)

Yet there is a difference; Mrs Radcliffe sees no ironic doubleness in 'she almost fancied'. Jane Austen would be aware that 'fancied' could allude to the faculty of literary invention.

Horrid suggestions

At one point, Catherine adopts the strategy of the novelist, who signals the inner torment of a character through troubled behaviour. When she hears that the General's wife died while Eleanor was away from home, 'Catherine's blood ran cold with horrid suggestions'. She observes the General:

> when she saw him in the evening, while she worked with her friend, slowly pacing the drawing-room for an hour together in silent thoughtfulness, with downcast eyes and contracted brow, she felt secure from all possibility of wronging him. (vol. 2, ch. 8)

We cannot know the actual state of the General's mind; we see that Catherine views him *as* a Gothic villain. She identifies him with the villain of *The Mysteries of Udolpho*: 'It was the air and attitude of a Montoni.'

Catherine the novelist

Volume 2, chapter 8 starts with the General's conducting Catherine and Eleanor round the Abbey. Catherine has already decided that the General is guilty of some dreadful deed, so neither his 'grandeur of air' nor 'dignified step' could 'shake the doubts of the well-read Catherine'. This is not just a piece of narratorial sarcasm; it is an indication of how Catherine's mind works.

What she sees derives from what she has read.

In the Beechen Cliff episode, the narrator refers to Fanny Burney as 'a sister author' (vol. 1, chapter 14). Catherine might be described as aspiring to be a sister of Mrs Radcliffe.

2.5 The Gothic novel

'but are they all horrid, are you sure they are all horrid?' (vol. 1, ch. 6)

As the Gothic novel is a central focus for *Northanger Abbey*, a reader should have some understanding of what it is. In English literature, genre is not a case of strict rules but rather a matter of works belonging together because they have some, though not necessarily all, features in common.

The Gothic world

The features that might be found in a Gothic novel include:

- a medieval or Renaissance setting, often in France, Germany, Italy or Spain
- a gloomy abbey or castle with secret passages
- a ghastly secret harboured in the castle or abbey, which is often brought to light through a dramatic discovery
- dramatic events which happen in the night and often during tempestuous weather
- an innocent young woman who is threatened by a powerful, corrupt and sometimes lecherous nobleman
- an eerie atmosphere and even actual ghosts
- sinister monks and nuns
- journeys through wild landscapes of forests, mountains and ravines

There are two stylistic features:

- the plots have a digressive, episodic movement
- the vocabulary is expressive of dread, fear and horror

Gothic imagining

Jane Austen expects the reader to be familiar with these features. Familiarity enables the reader to understand two things:

there are moments in the novel when the narration brims with Gothic possibilities;

the prospect of some events is likely to fill Catherine's mind with Gothic expectations.

Catherine's propensity to see the world in Gothic terms is a kind of prejudice. (As in *Pride and Prejudice*, there is a link between the uncontrolled imagination and prejudiced attitudes.) This Catherine eventually sees. What she had felt and done:

had been all a voluntary, self-created delusion, each trifling circumstance receiving importance from an imagination resolved on alarm.' (vol. 2, ch. 10)

This language shows that more is at stake than a mere burlesque of Gothic conventions. The language, as so often with Jane Austen, is concerned with mental faculties. Catherine has misread the world because her mind is not attuned to seeing the world as it really is. This is one of the occasions when within a fiction a distinction is made between what is and what is not fictional.

The imagination and Jane Austen

When Jane Austen wrote, the word 'imagination' was being amplified and enriched by contemporary writers, in particular the poets. Wordsworth is writing of the imagination when he says it is

> a sense
> By which he is enabled to perceive
> Something unseen before . . .
> (*The Prelude*, Book XII, lines 303–5)

The imagination enables discoveries; it engages with the world and reveals something which is true.

Jane Austen is much closer to Johnson in her assertion that the imagination can involve wilful self-delusion. Johnson's definitions include 'Contrivance; scheme'. Jane Austen's caution about the imagination is seen in the way Catherine has to wake up to the mistakes she has made. She recognizes that what lies behind her self-created delusion is 'the influence of that sort of reading which she had there [in Bath] indulged' (vol. 2, ch. 10).

The first night in the Abbey

Several of the features common to Gothic romance have potential parallels in *Northanger Abbey*: an abbey, a night scene, an innocent in a world that may well be corrupt.

The most developed expression of Catherine's propensity to regard her own life as if it were a narrative by Mrs Radcliffe comes in the passage which deals with her first night in the Abbey (vol. 2, ch. 6). Catherine no doubt sees the 'large high chest' in terms of one featured either directly in *The Romance of the Forest* or Henry's parody of it. Her consolation that she has 'nothing to dread from midnight assassins or drunken gallants' owes something to a passage in *The Mysteries of Udolpho.*

The comedy of Catherine's seriousness is the chief form of criticism in the passage:

while enjoying her wild surmises we see that she needs to test her expectations by canons of plausibility that are not drawn from the conventions of Gothic fiction.

What is at stake here is the meaning of words. The implicit insistence of the writing is that some language, be it literal or figurative, means what it says. For instance, Henry confirms that his father was 'truly afflicted by her [his wife's] death', so the truth of the language on her epitaph, doubted by Catherine who 'had read too much', about 'the inconsolable husband' *is* to be trusted (vol. 2, ch. 9). Catherine's deployment of Gothic categories to speculate about what has happened in Northanger Abbey's past does not disclose the truth of things.

A high, old-fashioned black cabinet

At one point the reader can recognize that Catherine is in a position to see through her own distorted imaginings. When she opens the drawer of the enticingly sinister cabinet, the narrator bluntly announces: 'It was entirely empty' (vol. 2, ch. 7). There is no dread secret, no coded message, no dying testimony, in 'many sheets of manuscript', of 'the wretched Matilda' (vol. 2, ch. 5). Had Catherine thought about it as the reader is implicitly invited to, she might have seen that emptiness is significant:

the fantasies of Gothic fiction are as empty as the cabinet.

And the cabinet is in reality black and yellow Japan, not, as Henry would have it, black and gold. Candlelight may gild it, but not the light of day. And the chest, which is shoved out of the way for practical, not sinister, purposes, contains a white, neatly folded counterpane. Catherine's lurid expectations are comically thwarted by the innocent, the orderly, the explicable, at every turn.

Yet, to anticipate, this is not a novel that endorses a flat realism; the Gothic can be helpful as a means of suggesting, through metaphor, the presence of real evil (see 4.10).

2.6 Gothic parody

'Henry was too much amused by the interest he had raised.' (vol. 2, ch. 5)

Genre and conventions

We can only laugh at the exaggerations which are the essence of parody if we see that a particular set of literary conventions are constitutive of a genre. Henry can spin his comical version of Gothic, because, as a critical reader, he understands it as a set of conventions. Catherine's problem is, in part, a literary one:

When she goes to the Abbey, Catherine is unable to regard Gothic as a literary genre. Catherine sees the Gothic as terrifyingly real.

Catherine's failure to recognize such a distinction is Jane Austen's way of enabling the reader to see that in *Northanger Abbey* the Gothic has a wider function than just the provision of humour:

Catherine's obtuseness and Henry's parody show that the Gothic is a structural principle.

The events of Catherine's visits to Bath and the Abbey are given shape and an increased depth of meaning by being paralleled by her innocent imaginings and Henry's knowing parodies.

Two ways of reading

As a result, the novel can be read in two different ways:

the reader may share the tensions (and pleasures) of Catherine's anticipations of horror

and

the reader may enjoy the events through the knowing jest of Henry's parody.

Both these ways of reading are available in the scenes set in Catherine's room in the Abbey.

Catherine adopts a somewhat heated rhetoric when, standing before the chest, she braces herself for what might, she rather hopes, turn out to be horrid: 'I will look into it – cost me what it may.' The reader can imagine an appropriately defiant posture and catch the thrill of her Gothic innocence. Of course, such defiance is amusingly at odds with what she says next: 'I will look into it – and directly too – by daylight' (vol. 2, ch. 6)

Amusement also comes from Henry's distancing perspective. Catherine reflects: 'Henry had certainly been only in jest in what he had told her that morning.' For a moment, Catherine glimpses the distinction between what is real and what is not as being a matter of tone and, more importantly, of conventions of language.

2.7 Fiction and actuality

'The visions of romance were over.' (vol. 2, ch. 10)

Waking up

The moment when Catherine sees the necessity of tempering her imagination and 'reading' reality should be understood as a counterpart to, and variation upon, what is usually a turning point in a Gothic plot. Gothic fiction makes much of the moment of horrific discovery. This moment becomes in *Northanger Abbey* what Aristotle calls *peripeteia* and *anagnorisis. Peripeteia* is reversal, the point at which the plot turns round, and *anagnorisis* is recognition, the realization by the central character of the real nature of what has been happening.

Catherine's moment of reversal is when Henry finds her emerging from his late mother's bedroom. What is reversed is Catherine's Gothic fantasy that the General is incarcerating his wife. Henry offers an all too real account of what happened, including the profound effect his mother's death had on his father.

The metaphor, now so conventional as to count as a dead one, is that of waking up. Catherine discovers her 'dreams' were her fond imaginings. Now she must be rational and see things as they are (something some of Jane Austen's heroines never find easy).

Three times in the course of the novel Catherine betrays the probable – in her anticipation of the contents of the chest, the cabinet and Mrs Tilney's room. On three separate occasions, however, Catherine begins to appreciate the actual. First, she wonders, as Mrs Allen has often done, how all the work of a Gothic edifice can be accomplished 'by two pair of female hands at the utmost' (vol. 2, ch. 8). Second, she who 'had so longed to be in an Abbey' begins to feel that 'there was nothing so charming . . . as the comfort of a well-connected parsonage' (vol. 2, ch. 11). Third, the night spent before she leaves the Abbey is even more disturbed than her first night of fearful imaginings. But her disquiet is now 'how mournfully superior in reality and substance! Her anxiety had foundation in fact, her fears in probability' (vol. 2, ch. 13) (note the chapter number). It is Catherine herself who turns out to be 'injured and ill-fated' (vol. 2, ch. 2).

2.8 The double crisis

'The anxieties of common life began soon to succeed to the alarms of romance.' (vol. 2, ch. 10)

Crises of realization

The binary structure of *Northanger Abbey* (see 1. 1) is evident in the way the book has a double crisis. Both of these crises are ones of realization:

in volume 2, chapter 10 Catherine sees through her 'horrid imaginings', and in volume 2, chapter 12, she learns of Isabella's treachery.

Both crises involve the two locations of the novel and are concerned with different kinds of reading.

The first crisis – learning how to understand Gothic romance – happens at the Abbey, but Catherine's error was fuelled by her reading of Mrs Radcliffe in Bath. The second crisis concerns her life in Bath and occurs when she receives letters from James and Isabella, while she is staying at the Abbey.

An inbalanced novel?

There is an argument that *Northanger Abbey* is an unsatisfactory novel, because there is a disparity between the significance of the two crises. How can the important discovery that an apparently devoted friend is shallow be compared with the commonplace discovery that fiction is not real?

Comparing the crises

A possible way of resisting this argument is to show that the rejection of Gothic romance and the discovery of Isabella's falsehood are not very different. The proximity of the two crises in the text may be taken as an invitation to see the similarities between them:

Catherine's fascination with the Gothic arises from her failure to see that it is essentially a fantasy out of touch with human reality. But Gothic fiction is not the only fantasy to which Catherine succumbs. She accepts the friendship of Isabella and is therefore in danger of being deceived into believing that Isabella's protestations of affection are true.

The phenomena of Gothic romance, of ardent but untested professions of friendship and of an expectation that we shall continue to be adored regardless of how badly we behave demonstrate the same human desire to imagine that the world is as we hope. It is ironic that

Isabella's world is even more unreal than Catherine's. She is out of touch with reality in a way that Catherine, even in the extravagance of her reading of the General, turns out, in a fundamental sense, not to be.

Isabella does not entangle herself in a web of Gothic imaginings. But it is a kind of fantasy that leads Isabella to think that she can snare any man, and that a man who has been hurt as much as James will cast himself adrift once more after the same siren. And, of course, Isabella does not wake up.

Isabella and the Gothic

A further link between the two awakenings is that Isabella introduced Catherine to Gothic fiction. Romance – a lie, an extravagant fiction – is introduced to Catherine by the false friend. At first, Catherine is unable to 'read' either the book or the friend.

Moreover, Gothic romance works by allowing the reader vicariously to experience terrors without any of the danger of their reality. Friendship which is professed but never tested allows the one who professes to enjoy all the reciprocal feelings of an attachment without any of its responsibilities.

2.9 The interplay between fiction and actuality

'such words could relate only to a circulating library' (vol. 1, ch. 14)

Fiction or history

Northanger Abbey plays with the multiple relationships between what is fictional and what is actual. At one point the confusion between fiction and actuality is debated.

On the Beechen Cliff walk (vol. 1, ch. 14), Catherine darkly says that she has 'heard that something very shocking indeed, will soon come out in London'. She expects 'murder and every thing of the kind'.

Catherine, of course, is talking of a Gothic novel, but Eleanor Tilney takes Catherine's words as an almost sibylline anticipation of public disorder. She trusts the authorities will cope. Henry (in his most supercilious manner?) clears up the confusion. He describes what Catherine has been talking about. 'nothing more dreadful than a new publication which is shortly to come out'.

Making sense of the horrible

Three things should be noted about the conversation between Catherine and Eleanor and Henry's speech.

The first is that something in Henry's tone might have alerted the reader to the shortcomings of his thinking. There must be a way of recognizing novels' fictional status without dismissing their achievement.

The second is that the confusion between Catherine and Eleanor arose because the language habitually used to talk about fiction is close to the language used in daily life. There are no separate words for, respectively, murders in novels and in life.

The third point is that what follows is yet another of Henry's parodies. The parody is part of the style of this very literary hero, part of his, in Eleanor's words, 'odd ways'.

In this case, however, he may be laying *himself* open to irony. He offers a fictional account of a London riot. When Catherine spoke of 'expected horrors in London', Eleanor, he says,

> 'immediately pictured to herself a mob of three thousand men assembling . . . the streets of London flowing with blood . . . and the gallant Capt. Frederick Tilney, in the

moment of charging at the head of his troop, knocked off his horse by a brickbat from an upper window.'

The irony is that such civic disturbance *had* happened. The historian Warren Roberts, following discussions by Walton Litz and Alistair Duckworth, asks whether what Henry fancifully pictures is based on the Gordon riots of 1780, when people did gather in St George's Fields. Alternatively, the picture has something in common with mass gatherings in the 1790s, during one of which, in 1792, both the Bank and the Tower were fortified against a possible attack (see *Jane Austen and the French Revolution*, Athlone, 1979, pp. 24–7).

Within the fictional world of a novel the relationship between what is made up and what refers to a real world is one of subtle interplay.

Henry's fiction is supposed to convince his sister that they do not live in a world of riot and disorder, but the light of contemporary history focused by the novel shows that London (and England?) is less secure than he imagines.

The irony lays bare an important aspect of the book; the 'real' world is also less secure than *Catherine* imagines (see 4.6). She has to be disillusioned of her child-like conviction that 'it cannot really happen to me' (vol. 2, ch. 5).

2.10 Thinking about novels

'some work in which the greatest powers of the mind are displayed' (vol. 1, ch. 5)

The narrator's praise of novels

If the impassioned discourse on the nature of the novel (vol. 1, ch. 5) is not to be regarded as an irrelevant digression, we have to ask ourselves about its place in a novel which deals with the potentially misleading nature of fiction.

This passage is bound to solicit the question: what kind of novel fits the description of the novel's potential? That question provokes this answer:

the kind of novel the narrator approves of is the kind she is writing.

The justification for giving this answer is that it is in accord with the conclusion to which Catherine herself comes:

> Charming as were all Mrs Radcliffe's works, and charming as were all the works of her imitators, it was not in them perhaps that human nature, at least in the midland counties of England, was to be looked for. (vol. 2, ch. 10)

Certainly, the Gothic novel has 'charmed', cast a spell over Catherine. Once she is freed, she is in a position to see that Gothic romances do not usually show 'a thorough knowledge of human nature' nor do they have much in the way of 'wit and humour'.

In contrast, in its presentations of Isabella and the General, *Northanger Abbey* does show something of the darkness of the human heart (see 4.6). It is at the same time funny. Henry, though sometimes irritatingly patronizing, provides the kind of distancing wit that Gothic novels lack. (If we find ourselves amused when reading Gothic fiction, this is often because the work has failed to engage us in the intended way.)

Jane Austen only writes about what is probable and plausible, yet in representing the

monotonies and minor excitements of the everyday, she reveals the perennial interest of human life. She also laughs at humanity's vaguaries.

What Catherine comes to appreciate is the nature of genre writing. When a work of fiction strays a long way from a recognizable society it becomes a romance.

2.11 The fiction-like nature of human life

'she returned downstairs with the volume from which so much was hoped' (vol. 2, ch.15)

Questioning dichotomies

Jane Austen's novels should not be reduced to neat polarities. Her writing often tempts us to indulge in dichotomies which the movement of the plot later dissolves.

***Northanger* Abbey invites us to move beyond a fictionality of easy make-believe and invites us to see that there are connections between life and art.**

Mrs Morland's recommended reading

When Catherine returns to Fullerton, her mother thinks that the elevated company of the Abbey has rendered her dissatisfied with home life. Accordingly, she recommends helpful reading: 'There is a very clever Essay in one of the books up stairs upon such a subject, about young girls that have been spoilt for home by great acquaintance' (vol. 2, ch. 15).

The surprises of fiction

But while Mrs Morland searches for the right *volume*, something with the surprise of fiction happens. Into the humdrum life of home steps the right *man*. Mrs Morland returns downstairs 'with the volume from which so much was hoped'. We can enjoy the conjunction of an improving essay, conventionally rated above a novel, with an event that is highly novelistic but recognizable from real life – the unexpected impact of a longed-for person.

With the volume of *The Mirror* in Mrs Morland's hand and the one called *Northanger Abbey* in ours, we can see that Henry's arrival is a real event that has the quality of fiction, occurring in a work of fiction. Perhaps there is an implied question: which of the two books – the improving essays or the novel – is the more effective at *mirroring* life? (Jane Austen has anticipated the answer in the swipe that she takes at 'compilations', following her spirited rebuke of criticisms of the novel.)

Jane Austen has suggested to the reader that there are reliable and unreliable novels, yet in no way denies that a Gothic romance may be a good read: 'I remember finishing it in two days, my hair standing on end the whole time' (vol. 1, ch. 14).

In the course of her pondering the nature of novels, she reminds us of the fiction-like tenor of everyday human living. She shows us that one of the features of a good novel is that it directs us to the kind of lives we lead, but that life, like fiction, is ever open to interpretation and it springs its surprises. The boundaries between what is romance and what is real will always remain blurred.

3 Spaces and places

3.1 Locations

'Northanger Abbey! – These were thrilling words.' (vol. 2, ch. 2)

The places of the novel

Two of Jane Austen's novels – *Northanger Abbey* and *Mansfield Park* – are named after houses. The titling of a novel after the name of a particular dwelling may be taken as an invitation to explore the significance of place and space.

The German philosopher Heidegger argued for the importance of space. For him dwelling is what all people seek to learn: 'mortals ever search anew for the nature of dwelling, that they *must ever learn to dwell*'. ('Building, Dwelling, Thinking', *Poetry, Language, Thought,* Harper & Rowe 1971, p. 161). Jane Austen's concerns are not those of the German philosopher, yet it might be said that one of the pervasive concerns of her books is what it is to have security in a place (see 3.6).

Topographical exactitude

Northanger Abbey is topographically exact; its writing about buildings and landscape is scrupulously accurate. Even some of the conversations are placed exactly.

Volume 1, chapter 6 begins with social and architectural specificity: 'The following conversation took place between the two friends in the Pump-room one morning'. The Pump-room was a large, spacious and elegant building, where the fashionable of Bath could meet and talk.

Our appreciation of what is happening is heightened by a knowledge of the topography of the city and the interior of its most popular public building.

3.2 The reader and Bath

'They arrived at Bath, Catherine was all eager delight; her eyes were here, there, every where, as they approached its fine and striking environs' (vol. 1, ch. 2)

Knowing Bath

The precision of the presentation of the city makes *Northanger Abbey* an early example of a novel that makes much of actual localities. Dickens's London and James Joyce's Dublin are rich developments of the tradition that makes setting part of the atmosphere and meaning of a novel.

Catherine's walk

The emotionally fraught and not unsymbolic scene in the Crescent (vol. 1, ch. 13) in which Catherine tears herself away from the Thorpes works with greater power if the reader knows the streets of Bath.

Catherine has her differences with the Thorpes, because they want her to go to Clevedon. Catherine is both angry and distressed when she learns that John Thorpe has lied to Eleanor. The topographically crucial passage is:

> Thorpe told her it would be in vain to go after the Tilneys; they were turning the corner into Brock-street, when he had overtaken them, and were at home by this time.

Catherine walks away in 'great agitation' and once she gets beyond the Crescent, which (it is Sunday) would be crowded with promenading parties, she 'almost ran over the remaining ground till she gained the top of Milsom-street'.

Bath's planning is subtly intimate. It is not a city of many long streets. (An exception is Pulteney-street, where Catherine stays.) Bath may be elegant and neo-classical, but its spaces are decidedly English rather than, say, Roman or French. It is a city of short views and glimpses. Brock-street, into which the Tilneys have turned, is short and narrow. A person approaching Brock-street from the Crescent can see very little of it. The Tilneys, therefore, would be out of sight once they had turned out of the busy Crescent.

Catherine would hurry along Brock-street till she came to the Circus, where she would turn right into Gay-street and then left into George-street, before another right brought her into Milsom-street. Her journey is an anxious one. Catherine is 'fearful of being pursued' and so 'could not be at ease'. The reader acquainted with the streets of Bath will also appreciate that not being able to see the people after whom she is running will have contributed to her agitation.

What the reader recognizes is that the anxiety of her walk is related to another anxiety – that Catherine might miss out on the company she most desires, possibly altogether. Miss Tilney says she was 'greatly surprized' when she was told that Catherine had withdrawn from an arrangement she had only just made.

Blaize Castle

Another moment when the reader is expected to supply what is absent in the text is the discussion of Blaize Castle (vol. 1, ch. 11). We need to supply a knowledge of literature and architectural history.

Catherine almost immediately represents Blaize to herself as 'an edifice like Udolpho'. Udolpho is irregular, lofty and bristling with towers and turrets. The reader is expected to know that Blaize Castle (usually spelt Blaise) is a folly, built in 1766 (only thirty years before Mrs Radcliffe's novel); it is not, as John Thorpe claims, 'The oldest in the kingdom' with towers 'By dozens', but small with stumpy, earnestly Gothic towers and embarrassingly large windows. Catherine must learn that, like so much she encounters, Gothic is not always what she imagines.

3.3 Landscape and seeing

'a lecture on the picturesque immediately followed, in which his instructions were so clear that she soon began to see beauty in every thing admired by him' (vol.1, ch. 14)

What characters know

Jane Austen often makes the same demands of her characters as she does of her readers. This is the case with topography. In the way that a reader should, so to speak, know where he or she is, so a character should be aware of place. Consequently,

there are moments in *Northanger Abbey* when characters are judged by their awareness of and responsiveness to places.

Catherine's lack of worldliness is emblemized in her journey home to Fullerton when 'she had been indebted for the post masters for the names of the places which were then to conduct her to it; so great had been her ignorance of her route' (vol. 2, ch. 14).

Catherine is an innocent abroad, but John Thorpe is actually found wanting. He is often on the move but takes no notice of the places through which he passes so swiftly. Jane Austen expects us to see that movement for its own sake is meaningless.

Picturesque landscape

In contrast with the heedless John Thorpe, the Tilneys appreciate their surroundings. They are capable of standing still and looking. They have learnt the language of the picturesque – the art of seeing landscape in terms of pictures – and this enables them to articulate what they observe.

Perhaps the Tilneys are too fixed in what proved to be a passing aesthetic fashion. Nevertheless, those who learn to see must, at least initially, be dependent on prevailing fashions in aesthetic appreciation. In any case, the fact that the Tilneys appreciate what is around them is what matters.

***Northanger Abbey* is about seeing and judging correctly.**

This is something that some people are better at than others. In most cases, it is something that we can learn to do.

Looking and judging

The ability to see a place, be it landscape or townscape, is analogous to the perception required to judge people properly.

An aspect of Catherine's growth towards judgement is her growing awareness of the physical world about her.

Therefore, we can say that

in a novel about learning to perceive people's true natures, a topographical responsiveness is the spatial equivalent of insight and discrimination.

Judgement and the novel

The writing of the novel itself may also be an enactment of the criticism that finds fault with Catherine for her thorough-going Gothic fantasies. One who imagines that an English folly is like a rambling pile from Mrs Radcliffe needs to be delivered from the confines of her ignorance. The way of deliverance is by looking at how things actually are. This is what the novel, in its topographical exactitude, does. Therefore

the topographical exactitude of *Northanger Abbey* acts as a criticism of Catherine's Gothic make-believe.

Judgement and spaces

One of the ironies of the novel is that, in spite of her wild imaginings, Catherine is sensitive to and sound in her judgements of architecture. Just before her embarrassing meeting with Henry as she emerges from his late mother's room, she has already perceived that her fantasies have been invalidated, because, in addition to their inherent implausibility, she realizes that the room gives no support to her suspicions (vol. 2, ch. 9).

Catherine is not only awakened to the invalidity of Gothic romance by Henry's clear statements about what is probable in Christian England. It is the room itself which clarifies her judgement. She eventually recognizes it as being part of the modern block of the Abbey. On Catherine's realization that the room is of recent construction the edifices of her imagined horror crumble.

3.4 The places of the plot

'In the Pump-room, one so newly arrived in Bath must be met with.' (vol. 1, ch. 9)

The social spaces of Bath

Characters meet to gossip, divulge confidences and discuss books in the richly detailed and specifically located places of Bath: the Assembly room, the theatre, the Crescent, Brock-street, Edgar's Buildings, Milsom-street, Pulteney-street and, on the edges of the city, Beechen Cliff and Claverton Down. It helps to have a map when reading *Northanger Abbey.*

This specificity of location draws attention to

the distinctiveness of Bath's social life. The spaces of Bath are social and communal, but they are organized to allow for convenient degrees of privacy.

To someone such as Catherine, brought up in a parsonage in a quiet village, the public spaces of Bath must feel very different. The novel recognizes that there is an experience which might be called Bath space.

Public and intimate

Catherine goes to the Lower Rooms, where she is introduced to Henry Tilney by the Master of Ceremonies. The etiquette of such introductions reveals a generous balance between publicly sanctioned meetings and pairings, such as those promoted by the

Master of Ceremonies, and an unusual freedom of association. Catherine and Henry can dance and take tea before Mrs Allen appears. The spaces in which Bath's social life takes place are both public and intimate. This has great appeal for young people. The intimacy of its spaces makes private conversations possible, yet these conversations happen in the public view and maintain respectability.

In volume 2, chapter 3 Catherine arrives in the Pump-room and is invited by Isabella 'to a secret conference'. Catherine is led to a seat. The next passage indicates the private/public nature of Bath's spaces:

> 'This is my favourite place,' said she, as they sat down on a bench between the doors, which commanded a tolerable view of every body entering at either, 'it is so out of the way.'

Isabella is clearly being disingenuous; she is placing herself so she can see and be seen. In particular, she is awaiting for Captain Tilney. (This is the dark side of Bath; its social spaces allow scope to the speculator and the seducer.) Isabella's command of space is indicative of her character and outlook. Isabella is literally and metaphorically keeping her eye open. Her position allows her to survey her options, and it allows others to include Isabella in theirs.

Nevertheless, it is possible in such a position for Isabella and Catherine to have a private conversation. Earlier in the novel, Catherine discovered the conveniences of Bath space; the Pump-room, she learnt is 'admirably adapted for secret discourses and unlimited confidence' (vol. 1, ch. 9).

The theatre

Like the Pump-room, the theatre is both public and private. It is a place of viewing not only plays but Bath life. One went to the theatre to view and to be viewed.

The theatre has a special place in *Northanger Abbey* because it is a place where fictions are acted out.

Again, we are reminded of the importance of viewing in the novel.

The fictions played out at the theatre, as might be expected in a novel that is preoccupied with the literary quality of everyday life, are not confined to the stage.

John Thorpe has little idea about fiction and, perhaps a related feature, has a weak grip on the actualities of everyday life. Appropriately, then, it is at the theatre that John Thorpe tells the General that the Morlands are even 'more wealthy than his vanity and avarice had him believe them' (vol. 2, ch. 15). (This is because he 'pretty well resolved upon marrying Catherine himself'.) The General, rather like an unscrupulous lover contending with a rival, 'almost instantly determined to spare no pains in weakening his [John Thorpe's] boasted interest and ruining his dearest hopes'.

The General believes John's 'story'. He is as gullible about fictions (lies) in the real world as ever Catherine is about Gothic fiction. He seizes the world as he wants it, without checking its truth.

3.5 Power, spaces, hosts and guests

'safely lodged in perfect bliss' (vol. 2, ch. 2)

On being a guest

When Catherine is invited to stay at Northanger Abbey her spirits 'are elated to rapture'; she has 'Henry at her heart, and Northanger on her lips' (vol. 2, ch. 2). We should note the religious resonances of the language: 'elated', 'rapture', 'heart' and 'lips'. 'Rapture', for instance, has a quite specific meaning in religious language: the act by which the soul is taken out of the body into the presence of God.

The use of words that, potentially, have religious meanings does not mean Catherine's stay is in a precise sense a religious event, but it does suggest that the status of host and guest can be understood as establishing a bond that is strong enough to be spoken of in religious terms. The Bible has many stories about the entertaining of guests, in which the duties of the host are underlined.

The power of the host

Being a guest and a host arouses primal feelings. The guest trusts the host, and the host recognizes duties of protection.

The link created by this most ancient relationship is acted out in rituals of welcome; guests wash, hosts receive gifts. A host is expected to be warm and welcoming; the guest, freely to relocate words from the text, should feel 'safely lodged in perfect bliss' (vol. 2, ch. 2).

To be a guest is to enter another's space.

It is a space over which the guest does not have authority. Therefore,

space entails power, so space is political.

To be a guest is to submit, even if notionally, to another's power.

In Northanger Abbey, Catherine is subject to the power of the General.

Awareness of his power is conveyed in spatial terms: he decides where she can and cannot go.

Her tour of the Abbey is suddenly concluded when the General prevents Eleanor from passing through the folding doors: 'the heavy doors were closed upon the mortified Catherine' (vol. 2, ch. 8).

Doors

Catherine often disregards boundaries. At the conclusion of her run through Bath, she rushes through the open door of the Tilney's Milsom-street lodgings. She is not defiantly rude but she does not await permission; she enters the house 'with only the ceremony of saying she must speak to Miss Tilney that moment' (vol. 1, ch. 13).

Here Catherine trespasses to set the record straight. She has no time for fictions that are lies in real life.

At the Abbey, she convinces herself that the General has incarcerated his wife. She even imagines the spaces through which the drugged victim was taken: 'Down the stair-case she had perhaps been conveyed in a state of well-prepared insensibility.' According to the Gothic conventions that determine her judgement (she probably has a scene from Mrs Radcliffe's *A Sicilian Romance* in mind), it would be wise for her to wait till after midnight before making her investigations: 'when the clock had struck twelve, and all was quiet, she would, if not quite appalled by darkness, steal out and look once more' (vol. 2, ch. 8).

The 'proposed examination of the mysterious apartments' (vol. 2, ch. 9) will be a transgression of the General's territory.

Catherine acts out her highly wrought fancies of his Gothic wickedness by physically trespassing upon the General's space.

(We might pause to ask whether the Gothic is a trespass on the probable. This is Henry Tilney's view, but see 4.8.)

For Catherine to transgress the boundaries established by the owner of the house, because she believes she has discovered a guilty secret, is also another kind of trespass – a trespass on the General's good name.

She is not turned out of the Abbey for acting upon her suspicion, but had the General known what she was thinking, he might well have dismissed her. This Catherine recognizes.

3.6 Ejection

'to have you driven out of the house, without the considerations even of decent civility!' (vol. 2, ch. 13)

Invitation and ejection

Ejection is the reverse of invitation. Jane Austen encourages us fully to appreciate the enormity of the former by establishing links between the scenes that contain each. For instance, Catherine's hope immediately after she learns that the Tilneys are to leave Bath is that Eleanor 'might introduce a desire of their corresponding' (vol. 2, ch. 2). She is invited to stay instead. The ironic reversal of this happens when, at the moment of her ejection, it is Eleanor, who is desperate for a correspondence: 'You must write to me, Catherine.' (vol. 2, ch. 13).

When the invitation is made (vol. 2, ch. 2), Eleanor begins 'in an embarrassed manner', but 'The entrance of her father put a stop to the civility'. There then follows the comedy of the overbearing father, who tells Eleanor 'to proceed by all means' but 'continued, without leaving his daughter time to speak'.

Catherine is ejected on his order but it is Eleanor who has to deliver the message (vol. 2, ch. 13). Poor Eleanor is like those messengers in Shakespeare who fear they will suffer because they bring unwelcome news. In both the business of invitation and ejection Eleanor indeed plays the role of a servant.

It is perhaps worth remarking that it is women who carry out the inviting and the ejection of Catherine (though in the latter case reluctantly so). As a prelude to Eleanor's inviting Catherine to the Abbey, Mrs Allen has been responsible for inviting Catherine to Bath in the first place. It is ironic that a woman of stifling conventionality, whose only concern when Catherine calls on her to confirm the veracity of her emotions is fear that she will 'tumble my gown', is nevertheless responsible for the crucial widening of Catherine's horizons. She is, no doubt ironically, said to be 'probably aware that, if adventures will not befall a young lady in her own village, she must seek them abroad' (vol. 1, ch. 1). It is the independent-minded Eleanor who is forced by filial duty to *limit* Catherine's horizons, both physically and emotionally. She, who so desires a match, is the means of cutting off Catherine both from Northanger and from Henry.

Severing the bond between host and guest

The ejection is the wilful severing of the bond between guest and host. As such it brings out the politics of space. The outrage can be felt in Catherine's anguished thoughts:

> Turned from the house, and in such a way! Without any reason that could justify, any apology that could atone for the abruptness, the rudeness, nay, the insolence of it. (vol. 2, ch. 13)

The way Catherine tries to find words adequate to the violation of a host's role shows that the ejection is more than a breach of good manners: the General outrages our deep and only rarely expressed feelings of the importance (even sacred importance?) of hospitality and safety.

When we remember that Catherine is turned out on a Sunday, the day when Henry will be reading Matins at Woodston, the shades of the event darken further.

No ritual of rejection

There are no rituals as there are in a welcome, because ejection marks the rupture of a relationship. Would it be too extreme to say it is a disjunction more starkly final than death, because with death there is a ritual of remembrance, whereas an ejection signals the end of an association?

The General expresses the finality of the severance by providing no travelling companion for his sometime guest. This pain is felt by Catherine and his loving and hospitable daughter: 'but a journey of seventy miles, to be taken by you, at your age, alone, unattended' (vol. 2, ch. 13).

Parting and losing

The parting of the two friends is painful, particularly for Catherine, who must know that ejection from Northanger Abbey is the end of all her hopes. All that can be left of Henry and of Eleanor for Catherine is her remembeance.

Departure

The actual moment of departure comes in the next sentence, and it concludes the chapter:

> But with this approach to his name ended all possibility of restraining her feelings; and, hiding her face, as well as she could with her handkerchief, she darted across the hall, jumped into the chaise, and in a moment was driven from the door. (vol. 2, ch. 13)

As her ejection corresponds to a moment of horror in a Gothic novel, it is not surprising that there are subversions of Catherine's former favourite genre. Instead of the black veil (see vol. 1, ch. 6), Catherine covers her face as well she can with her (white) handkerchief. She is the General's innocent victim.

The actual ejection is represented in language that is essentially domestic: it is a 'house' she leaves and her thoughts are for the one with whom she would like to dwell.

Crossing the hall

When we can see the ejection as an abrogation of the duty of protection we can appreciate the emblematic force of the space Catherine passes through on her way to the carriage. She darts 'across the hall' as if it were hostile territory. It must feel alien and cold, haunted by the very real emotions of resentment and indifference rather than by the ghostly presences which had proved illusory. The hall is no longer the place where the rituals of welcoming take place. On her arrival 'her friend and the General were waiting to welcome her'. Her friend is there at her ejection to witness what is now no longer an imagined 'future misery' (vol. 2, ch. 5).

Ejection in Jane Austen

The motif of ejection occurs in each of Jane Austen's novels. The repeated presence of this motif suggests that Jane Austen regarded the security of home as a necessary requirement for living a civilized and therefore good life; to be ejected from a house or home threatens a character's whole being and reveals the ejector as cold, unfeeling and even wicked. Ejection is an emblem of instability and evil. It is the females in the novels who are prone to it.

3.7 Gothic space

'a narrower passage, more numerous openings, and symptoms of a winding staircase' (vol. 2, ch 8)

The other abbey

A reader of *Northanger Abbey* who is familiar with Bath might be aware of a curious absence in the text. Had Catherine, when she left the Pump-room with Isabella, glanced to her right, she would have seen the soaring west front of one of the most important Gothic buildings in England – Bath Abbey.

Had she stopped and looked at it she would have seen two ladders carved out of the stonework, busy with ascending and descending angels. The angels are not inappropriate emblems of the state Catherine should aspire to – the reception of that illumination which descends from above. (A ladder is better than a winding staircase!) But Catherine never looks.

In a novel about a Gothic abbey, the one eminent abbey is invisible. Why? The answer must be that Bath Abbey is not Catherine's sort of Gothic. It does not have a grisly past nor is it a ruin. Above all, it is the wrong kind of Gothic. Bath Abbey is late English Perpendicular. Its radiance, the sense of visible rationality in its construction, would hardly appeal to Catherine.

Catherine's Gothic

Gothic to Catherine is an image, a picture, a literary creation. (She constructs her Gothic 'idea' in the way that the Tilneys construct their picturesque.) Gothic buildings are rambling and ruinous with musty, enclosed spaces. The pleasurable dangers of Northanger Abbey easily take root in her imagination:

> Its long, damp passages, its narrow cells and ruined chapel, were to be within her daily reach, and she could not entirely subdue the hope of some traditional legends, some awful memorials of an injured and ill-fated nun. (vol. 2, ch. 2)

The spaces Catherine imagines are confining ones, and her imagination is confined by dwelling on such places. By contrast, Perpendicular Gothic allows the mind, arguably most itself when it lives by the light of reason, space enough to fulfil itself in a light-filled church.

3.8 Popular Gothic

'with a frontispiece to the first, of two tomb-stones and a lantern' (vol. 1, ch. 14)

Eighteenth-century Gothic

In formal terms, Gothic is the style of architecture which has pointed arches, doors and windows. It is usually built of small stones, and its large interior spaces are divided by columns with carved capitals, from which arches spring. Gothic buildings are often long, and many of them, in particular churches, are subdivided or have additions – porches, chapels, sacristies. The plan of a Gothic building is often irregular.

Eighteenth-century taste found the Gothic appealing. This was a matter of mood and atmosphere. Observers began to find an interest in the rough textures of decay and the dark, brooding, mysterious light which suffused interiors in which the windows were small. These qualities constituted what we can call popular Gothic.

When Catherine is shown round Northanger Abbey, she cannot 'overcome the suspicion of there being many chambers secreted' (vol. 2, ch. 8).

The language of Gothic atmosphere

The eighteenth century gradually fashioned a language for the expression of Gothic atmosphere. Such a language can be found in the writings of Thomas Warton (1728–90) – historian, Professor of Poetry at Oxford and Poet Laureate. In 'The Triumph of Isis', a poem in defence of Oxford University, he strikes a representative note in talking of 'Gothic gloom'. Warton celebrates qualities that are found in Mrs Radcliffe's representations of ancient buildings.

'Gloom' is a quintessentially Gothic quality, and buildings are imagined to be many-towered, rough in texture and festooned with the ancient heraldry of chivalric enterprises.

In 'The Pleasures of Melancholy' Warton imagines such a Gothic scene:

> Beneath yon ruin'd abbey's moss-grown pile
> Oft let me sit, at twilight hour of eve,
> Where through some western window the pale moon

Pours her long-levell'd rule of western light;
While sullen silence reigns around,
Save the lone screech-owl's note, who build his bower
Amid the mouldering caverns dark and damp,

Or let me tread
Its neighbouring walk of pines, where mused of old
The cloister'd brothers: …
As on I pace, religious horror wraps
My soul in dread repose.

(lines. 28–34, 37–39 and 41–42)

It is a feature of the language of popular Gothic that it deals with the feelings aroused in the subject as well as what the location looks like. Gothic happens in the mind.

Mrs Radcliffe's language

The book Catherine does read – *The Mysteries of Udolpho* – uses a similar language. When Emily, the heroine, arrives at Udolpho (vol. 2, ch. 5) she 'gazed with melancholy awe upon the castle', seeing' its mouldering walls of dark grey stone, [which] rendered it a gloomy and sublime object'. Her 'heart sunk'. Murder preys on her mind:

> The sentiment was not diminished , when she entered an extensive gothic hall, obscured by the gloom of evening, which a light, glimmering at a distance through a long perspective of arches, only rendered more striking.

The architecture in Mrs Radcliffe is very similar to that of Warton. The subjective response to it is different, though. Religious horror wraps Warton, but what his soul feels is 'dread *repose*' whereas Emily is constantly oppressed, and her heart sinks.

Gothic feeling in 'Northanger Abbey'

When Catherine re-creates the General as a Gloucestershire Montoni, she asks about his incessant pacing:

> What could more plainly speak the gloomy workings of a mind not wholly dead to every sense of humanity, in its fearful review of past scenes of guilt? (vol. 2, ch. 8)

Catherine has no warrant for knowing that the General is gloomy. Gothic language is not finely nuanced enough to express the relative significances of experience. This is like Catherine herself who has not the knowledge of human nature yet to realize that the General's reluctance to have the memory of his wife activated is not proof of his indifference but quite the reverse.

The scene from *The Mysteries of Udolpho* in which Emily arrives at the castle is a source of Henry's parody. The fictional Catherine is conducted 'along gloomy passages'. On arrival, Catherine herself is disappointed; instead of large, clear panes in the windows, her imagination 'had hoped for the smallest divisions, and the heaviest stone-work, for painted glass, dirt and cobwebs' (vol. 2, ch. 5).

Catherine is at one with the late eighteenth-century fashion of imagining that

Gothic space is either vast or confined, its atmosphere is gloomy and its planning is rambling and uncoordinated.

3.9 Northanger's spaces

'Yet this was an Abbey. How inexpressibly different in those domestic arrangements from such as she had read about.' (vol. 2, ch. 8)

Arrival

What exactly are the spaces of Northanger Abbey like?

Her first entry reveals to Catherine that the Abbey is not what her 'fancy had portrayed'. The furniture has 'the elegance of modern taste' (vol. 2, ch. 5), and every pane of glass in the windows is 'so large, so clear, so light'. Furthermore, there are even very modern conveniences; the Rumford fireplace, an efficient form of heating, was new in 1796.

The General's tour

The tour conducted by the General confirms that

Northanger Abbey no longer looks or, perhaps more important to Catherine, feels Gothic.

'Yet this was an Abbey!' (vol. 2, ch. 8). Understandably, Catherine is disappointed. Ironies are built into the text: Catherine is quite unaware that the General assumes that the elegance will impress her. Another irony is that

the interiors of Northanger Abbey are very similar to the elegant spaces of neo-classical Bath.

Catherine is now aware that Northanger is not like a location in Mrs Radcliffe. Her arrival and the tour might have been occasions for her to wake up to the differences between how things are and how she would like them to be.

Had Catherine realized that the spaces of Northanger Abbey are no longer Gothic she might have woken up sooner to the truth that the life of the General is not exactly that of a Gothic villain.

How Catherine views the Abbey

In her early days at the Abbey, Catherine is prevented from awakening because what she does *not* see before her – the world of Radcliffean Gothic – is more potent than her own perceptions of her surroundings:

***Northanger Abbey* is about the capacity of the imagination to shape perception.**

In the words of a twentieth-century philosopher (Ludwig Wittgenstein), *Northanger Abbey* is about 'seeing as': that is, it is about how we arrange what we see. Catherine sees Northanger *as* something out of a Gothic romance. She sees it as a literary creation.

3.10 Perception and imagination

'Eleanor's countenance was dejected, yet sedate; and its composure spoke her enured to all the gloomy objects to which they were advancing.' (vol. 2, ch. 9)

Perception

The cultural world in which Jane Austen wrote was deeply engaged with the issue of perception. Writers such as Blake, Coleridge and Wordsworth insisted that we are, in part, the architects of what we see. The effect of this is to blur the distinction between what is actually there and what we make up (see 2.5).

Consistently in her novels, Jane Austen presents such a blurring as dangerous. Is, for instance, Eleanor really 'dejected'? Implicit in what Jane Austen writes is the view that

a true understanding of human life requires the tempering of the self-centred imagination and the strengthening of clear perceptions as to the actual nature of things.

In Catherine Jane Austen ponders our capacity to create taking over from our capacity to see. She implicitly takes issue with an age that was in danger of subsuming sight into fancy. Perhaps the topographical exactitude of the novel is a way of reminding the reader that we occupy real spaces.

3.11 Gothic and neo-classical

'All that was venerable ceased here.' (vol. 2, ch. 8)

The literary spaces of 'Northanger Abbey'

The notion of space can be applied to literary form; the way a book is organized and shaped is the equivalence of space. We may ask what kind of space the novel called *Northanger Abbey* is. To do this it is necessary to have an idea of what neo-classical architectural space is like.

Neo-classical architecture

The neo-classical architecture of Bath is symmetrical and formal; each building is designed to look complete, so additions, particularly those to the front, are almost impossible; they would disturb the rhythms and balances of the design. It is clear that General Tilney's tastes are neo-classical. At Woodston, he confesses that one of his aversions 'is a patched-on bow'. (vol. 2, ch. 11). By contrast, Gothic architecture can accommodate additions and extensions. The internal spaces of a Gothic building are likely to be asymmetrical and ranging.

The Gothic novel is the concomitant of the architectural spaces of a Gothic building:

like a castle or abbey in Mrs Radcliffe, Gothic novels are usually digressive and rambling.

The first third of *The Mysteries of Udolpho* is taken up with long journeys through a vast landscape. Emily does not get to the castle itself till the second volume.

Catherine's imagination is Gothic.

The plot she builds out of her own imagination is capable of having many additions tacked on to it.

Once she sets the foundations of her plot – the General as a Gloucestershire Montoni – she erects elaborate additions with the inventive zeal of a medieval stonemason. First, she pictures the circumstances in which, the children being absent, the General does away with his wife. Then, as it were, she re-designs her whole edifice by imagining him keeping her immured in some remote part of the Abbey.

The architecture of the novel

At this point we have to remember what was said in 1.1 about the design of the novel. The binary structure allows for a number of parallels between the characters, actions and settings. The novel is clearly 'constructed'. It might therefore be said that

the balanced design of *Northanger Abbey* is neo-classical in that it achieves a structual symmetry.

Such a design is at odds with two things.

The first is Catherine Morland's imagination. When she is shaping and reshaping her fantasies about the General, the novel supplies, in parallel with Catherine's imaginings, mundane, and not untrue, explanations of the General's behaviour. For instance, the General actually says he has 'many pamphlets to finish', but so compelling are her imaginative prejudices that nothing 'could win Catherine from thinking, that some very different object must occasion so serious a delay of proper repose' (vol. 2, ch. 8). The irony is that there *is something* Gothic (evil) about the General. Is he plotting other ways of aggrandizing family fortunes as he paces up and down?

There is a neo-classical symmetry about the way the true and false explanations – and indeed the neo-classical and the Gothic – are balanced in the fabric of the text.

The second is the selfish infidelity of Isabella. Her mercenary husband-hunting distorts the shape of social life. Her behaviour is, metaphorically speaking, Gothic, not classical. Her engagement to James in no way constrains her behaviour. The point can be made in Kantian terms; if all acted solely according to their individual whims, society would collapse because no one's behaviour could be relied on.

The design of *Northanger Abbey,* as elegant as the architecture of Bath, might be read as a critique of moral and aesthetic indulgence:

the shape of the plot is in itself a criticism of the digressive nature of most Gothic writing, and as such it is also a criticism of the infidelities of Bath, the General's mercenary scheming and Catherine's rambling, romance-shaping imagination.

Escaping at the edges

It might be said, though, that Catherine herself breaks the novel's symmetry towards the end. Just as she disregards boundaries when it suits her, so it could be argued that she escapes from her narrator and from the plot. (As a child she ran wild, always hating confinement.)

Catherine has an appeal for the reader *which goes beyond the control of the narrator.*

The lightly parodic tone which the narrator adopts does not allow Catherine the moments of angst, soul-searching and doubt which she has proved herself entitled to.

The *reader*, however, provides them.

So the neo-classical design of the novel is an aesthetic and moral key to its meaning, but it is also, even if unwittingly, subverted.

Catherine experiences a depth of feeling that is more Romantic than classical and points us towards a world that is more mysterious than the tone of the novel concedes.

This sense of a mystery and a suffering that far outstrip the laughable excesses of the Gothic and its legitimate, rational parody is one that increases in Jane Austen's work.

4 The education of a heroine?

4.1 Learning

'her resolution formed, of always judging and acting in future with the greatest good sense' (vol. 2, ch. 10)

A mistaken heroine

A heroine who is mistaken makes demands upon us. The plot of *Northanger Abbey* is the history of Catherine Morland's mistakes and the opportunities those mistakes provide for learning. Catherine's overactive imagination leads her into unthinking prejudices, from which she emerges with a knowledge of her 'own sense of the probable' (vol. 2, ch. 9).

In formal terms, learning becomes the main business of the novel. The plot of *Northanger Abbey* is so designed that its movement leads the reader to expect a turning point in which the protagonist becomes aware of her mistakes and thereafter seeks enlightenment.

In fact, the originality of *Northanger Abbey* lies in the surprise that things do not turn out exactly as the plot design leads the reader to expect (see 1.4, 3.11 and 4.10).

The language of learning

It is not only the design of the plot that leads the reader to think that this is a novel about the education of the heroine.

A change in Catherine is signalled by the language used by her and about her, confirming that she has needed to learn.

When she is contemplating the 'manuscript' she finds in the Japan cabinet, excited questions, abrupt and breathless, trouble her:

> The manuscript so wonderfully found, so wonderfully accomplishing the morning's prediction, how was it to be accounted for? What could it contain? To whom could it relate? By what means could it have been long concealed? And how singularly strange that it should fall to her lot to discover it! (vol. 2, ch. 6)

Catherine's language, urgent but vapid and wayward, indicates a lack of linguistic control and, consequently, an imprecision of thought.

The language of her awakening to Isabella's duplicity is also energetic, but its pithy assurance demonstrates a firm grip on argument:

> She must think me an idiot, or she could not have written so; but perhaps this has served to make her character better known to me than mine is to her. (vol. 2, ch. 12)

We should also contrast Catherine's neat encapsulations here with the continued excesses of Isabella's language about Catherine. Catherine's is now the language of someone who in future will endeavour to act with 'the greatest good sense' (vol. 2, ch. 10).

4.2 The pains of learning

'Thank God! I am undeceived in time!' (vol. 2, ch. 10)

Key observations

To endeavour to see life as it is becomes necessary because clear vision, insight and sound judgement are what constitute maturity. Henry points the way to Catherine: 'Consult your own understanding, your own sense of the probable, your own observation of what is passing around you' (vol. 2, ch. 9). Catherine is benighted metaphorically as well as physically when she over-enthusiastically snuffs the candle in pursuit of Gothic mysteries and 'Darkness impenetrable and immovable filled the room' (vol. 1, ch. 6).

Northanger Abbey goes further, though, than eighteenth-century rationalism, as do all Jane Austen's novels. To understand life is to recognize that it runs too deep for formulaic understanding.

A general need of education

Because Catherine is so clearly presented as the kind of heroine who needs to learn, readers might overlook the fact that incapacity to see straight is not a failing confined to her alone. Basic to the leading of the good life is the recognition that you cannot just make it up! Some characters still need to learn the basics by the end. Where is there any indication that John Thorpe is less of a liar?

Isabella and the General

Two characters who do not seem to have learned, though one has made an accommodation, are Isabella and the General. The fact that Isabella has lost both James and Captain Tilney and failed to fix any man might have brought home to Isabella that her posings can be seen through and that she has proved as gullible as James. Her letter to Catherine, asking her friend to help mend the breach between her and James, shows that Isabella, for all her worldliness, has not imagined that Catherine may have learnt. And to the last the General does not appear to see that there is more to a good marriage than status and wealth.

The deception of James

Both Catherine and James are deceived in and misled by Isabella and John Thorpe. Isabella embodies the glamour of Bath. To the innocent and essentially rustic Catherine, 'friendship' with Isabella offers a welcome entrance to Bath's diversions. When, therefore, Catherine meets her brother, the reader is in a position to understand the warm concurrence with which Catherine would have received James's words about Isabella: 'she is just the kind of young woman I could wish to see you attached to; she has so much good sense, and is so thoroughly unaffected and amiable' (vol. 1, ch. 7).

Perhaps because he does not wish to give too much away, James' question about Isabella is preceded by one about Isabella's brother, John. Catherine's words, though not her initial thoughts, are positive, and James responds with an easy piece of Oxford praise: 'He is as good-natured a fellow as ever lived.'

The Thorpes not only deceive Catherine and James but cause deception between them. Catherine, so pleased to see James, says with artless sisterly affection: 'how good it is of you to come so far on purpose to see *me*'. James, to his credit, is embarrassed so he 'qualified his conscience' by affirming 'with perfect sincerity, "Indeed, Catherine, I love you dearly."'

Catherine and James on John Thorpe

Because at the beginning of the novel, Catherine is presented as naïve, the reader might be inclined to regard the chief importance of the conversation between James and her in volume 1, chapter 7 as the display of her too credent innocence.

But this would be to overlook her unexpressed thoughts on John Thorpe. She has listened to him on gigs and girls, and she does not like him. However, she replies as she discerns James wishes.

Catherine, seventeen and out in the world for the first time, is more perceptive than her undergraduate brother. If men had a central position in Jane Austen's novels, James's painful passage towards knowledge of deceptive siren songs would have been a central matter. As it is, James is demonstrably more deceived than Catherine.

James's uninformed enthusiasm for Isabella is balanced both formally and thematically by Henry's catechisms. Henry's parody of Bath conversation might have alerted Catherine to how conventional and undiscriminating is the praise that James confers on Isabella and her vulgar brother.

4.3 What Catherine gets right

'"Thank you," said Catherine, in some distress, from a doubt of the propriety of accepting such an offer.' (vol. 1, ch. 7)

Recognizing nonsense

John Thorpe is the first person whom Catherine gets right. Listening to John the rattle accompanied by the rattle of his gig she cannot help but form a judgement:

> and unfixed as was her general notions of what men ought to be she could not entirely repress a doubt . . . of his being altogether completely agreeable. (vol. 1, ch. 9)

At the end of the chapter, she receives news that, while she was being driven by John, Mrs Allen had met the Tilneys walking in the Crescent. Disappointment forces a firm judgement: 'John Thorpe himself was quite disagreeable.'

Distress and propriety

The quotation at the head of this chapter is the second thought Catherine has about John Thorpe. (The first is that she is pleased to hear that because 'poor Freeman wanted cash', John Thorpe did not haggle over the price of a gig (vol. 1, ch. 7). This alleged generosity deceives her.)

'Doubt' is pertinent in a novel about learning and the snares that the ignorant can fall into. The issue is, broadly speaking, one of correct behaviour. Plenty of guides were available (they were called conduct books), but Catherine thinks and feels her way through the propriety of driving with John Thorpe on her own.

Writing about moral decisions in Jane Austen's work sometimes requires a vocabulary which might be called pre-cognitive; we speak of moral *feelings*, of *intuitions*.

The issue of driving with John recurs in volume 1, chapter 13, when Catherine eases her mind by mentioning 'the half-settled scheme' when Mr Allen is present.

Catherine is shrewd to mention what troubles her to Mr Allen. He is careful not to be too critical, asking her first whether she intends to accept the invitation. When she tells him she means to keep her promise to the Tilneys, he first commends her and *adds*, 'These schemes are not at all the thing'. Catherine does not congratulate herself on being right; it is up to the reader to see that her instinctive judgement has been vindicated.

4.4 Taste

'her attention was so earnest, that he became perfectly satisfied of her having a great deal of natural taste' (vol. 1, ch. 14)

Natural taste

At one point in the Beechen Cliff scene, Henry and the narrator seem to be at cross-purposes. The narrator, in the tones of a wry worldly wisdom, talks of the advantages of ignorance to a young girl being courted by an educated man. Catherine declares 'she would give any thing in the world to be able to draw' (vol. 1, ch. 14), and the sophisticated Henry responds with a lecture on the picturesque. Catherine learns quickly: 'his instructions were so clear that she soon began to see beauty in every thing admired by him'.

Here Henry proves himself less consciously 'clever' (perhaps even less cynical) than the narrator, for he sees that Catherine has 'a great deal of natural taste'. If propriety is largely something that she has sensed for herself, the same might be said of her aesthetic sense.

The Northanger gardens

One of the ironies of *Northanger Abbey* is that Catherine is more perceptive than she thinks she is.

Her initial reactions to John Thorpe turn out to be right, but at seventeen she has not the confidence to act upon her judgement. So it is when she first looks at a landscape. Yet she turns out to be sensitive to the gardens of Northanger Abbey. At first she does not feel up to the challenge of viewing the grounds:

> If Henry had been with them indeed! but now she would not know what was picturesque when she saw it.

The very next paragraph opens:

> She was struck, however, beyond her expectation, by the grandeur of the Abbey, as

she saw it for the first time from the lawn. The whole building enclosed a large court; and two sides of the quadrangle, rich in Gothic ornament, stood forward for admiration. The remainder was shut off by knolls of old trees, or luxuriant plantations, and the steep woody hills rising behind to give it shelter, were beautiful even in the leafless month of March. (vol. 2, ch. 7)

Catherine has acquired the essence of the picturesque. Unlike the more learned Henry, she (refreshingly?) does not speak in terms of 'fore-grounds, distances, and second distances' (vol. 1, ch. 14), but she responds with real appreciation. In one sense, Henry is no longer needed.

4.5 Understanding Isabella and the General

'Have I offended the General?' (vol. 2, ch. 13)

Catherine and the General

Catherine's response to the General is one of the main preoccupations of the second volume. The plot movement invites the reader to be amused at the sad mistake she makes about the fate of his wife and anticipates her awakening to her error.

Catherine is not at ease in the General's presence. On the morning they leave Bath, she finds his attentions to her comfort disconcerting. There is both comedy and pathos here. The General, so intent to make her feel at home, only succeeds in reminding her that she is a guest. Poor man, we might say; he tries so hard.

Yet with hindsight we know that he is mercenary. Believing the fictions of John Thorpe, he thinks Catherine is an heiress. She cannot know that, but she is uneasy with his attentions.

Might it be that Jane Austen is suggesting that her heroine who saw through John Thorpe and had a natural sense of propriety and taste is sensing that the General is not all that he appears to be?

The General has all the propensity to gush of Isabella. He is as capable as she is of producing 'a page full of empty professions' (vol. 2, ch. 16). Catherine seems inherently to sense and distrust this in the General, whereas she fails to in her friend.

Isabella and the General

One of the most significant pairings of characters is Isabella and the General; she dominates the first volume and he the second. They never meet.

Isabella's initial hold over Catherine stems from her personal charm and the exciting prospects she opens up. Her familiarity with the joys of Bath constitutes her 'powers': Catherine admires them, but eventually they are proved, compared with the General's, pitifully weak.

The General exercises power through impatience and his insistence on soliciting from others the required response. Like Isabella, he complains about being kept waiting. Niggling about time is a sign of selfishness, though in the case of the General the irritation is at least authentic (Isabella's protests make it difficult to know what she experiences) and might be put down to the effects of army discipline.

The oppressiveness the General generates is only fully registered when it is removed. When, for a few days, he leaves the Abbey, Catherine and Eleanor engage their time as they choose. Such pleasurable indulgence made them 'thoroughly sensible of the restraint which the General's presence had imposed, and most thankfully feel their present release from it' (vol. 2, ch. 13). The General does not physically hold Catherine as Isabella does (see 1.4) but the weight of his control can be felt in the physical connotations of the language. The meaning behind the sense of oppression that Catherine feels in the presence of the General is something that she has to try to come to terms with.

4.6 Gothic danger

'the violence of such noblemen and baronets as delight in forcing young ladies away to some remote farm-house' (vol. 1, ch. 2)

A victim

Catherine is a victim of Isabella and the General. One of the ironies of *Northanger Abbey* is that this pair – a beauty and a beast – are horribly alike in their desire to acquire and sustain status. Isabella wants James for his money, while the General looks upon Catherine as a promising acquisition, a potential Tilney commodity, like his pretty Staffordshire breakfast china, only far more valuable.

Isabella's literary antecedents

Isabella introduces Catherine to Gothic fiction and in one respect Isabella plays a Gothic role. An aspect of her being a false friend is that she is a seducer of female innocence. To what assumptions about behaviour might Catherine have been subject had she and Isabella caught up with the two young men they were pursuing up Milsom-street? In this sense Isabella functions in a manner analagous to the Lamia figure of nineteenth-century literature – the beautiful young woman who is in fact a snake (see *Lamia* by Keats).

The snake-woman is akin to the faery woman who, appearing to be human, seduces the unwary. Keats's 'La Belle Dame sans Merci' is a kind of succubus, a demon who takes a female form and destroys men through sexual intercourse. She is a literary descendant of Helen of Troy in Marlowe's *Doctor Faustus*, a figure who appears to be the most beautiful woman of all time but is in fact a spirit who, in intercourse with Faustus, ensures the latter's damnation.

What is interesting about the parallel with Isabella is that she deceives both a man and a woman. James is misled over her love and Catherine over her friendship. The dangerous spirit in the form of an alluring woman more often seeks victims among men. But the narrative of *Northanger Abbey* concentrates chiefly on the threat to Catherine.

There is at least one major work in the Gothic manner that shows a predatory female spirit latching on to a young woman – Coleridge's 'Christabel'. Coleridge wrote 'Christabel' in the same year that Jane Austen was writing *Northanger Abbey.* However, as the poem was not published till 1816, the year before Jane Austen's death, there can be no issue of a direct influence. Instead, we have two very different authors who were interested in one female destroying the innocence of another. Remarkably, the plots are almost identical: 'Christabel' features a Gothic building, a fierce father figure, the themes of hospitality and corruption (in this case vampiric or lesbian?), and two females, one innocent (Christabel), one predatory (Geraldine).

Isabella is entirely real, a flesh-and-blood adventuress. She does not, until her final letter, present herself, as Geraldine does, as a victim, yet she manipulates Catherine. We should understand that only her interest in Eleanor and Henry prevents Catherine from being fully exposed to the poison of Isabella's values. Nevertheless, Isabella plays out the role of a Geraldine; she is alluring and dangerous.

There is in the presentation of Isabella an implicit criticism of Gothic fiction: the real evils of the world are to be found in the moment by moment actuality of the everyday world. Corruption can be encountered in the assembly rooms of Bath and in a country mansion, regardless of whether it is an abbey or not.

Isabella as victim

There is irony, though, and a moral lesson, in the way that Isabella is eventually hoist with her own petard. For all her alleged determination to put down over-inflated members of the opposite sex, the self-styled independent Isabella becomes a martyr to men. She ends up wearing purple as an act of self-flagellation – 'I know I look hideous in it, but no matter – it is your dear brother's favourite colour' (vol. 2, ch. 12). In this she again contrasts with Catherine, who can always find in a good book an acceptable substitute for any man. This final ironical presentation of Isabella emblematically represents her as not nearly the threat that the General is. Her inner impoverishment at all levels corresponds with her financial status. It is a rich male, not an indigent female, who, in his genuine power, poses the greater threat.

The evil of Northanger

The evil that Catherine finds at Nothanger Abbey, the narrative insists, is not the kind that she imagines from her reading. Nevertheless, Northanger should be thought of as a place where evil lurks.

The heroine as victim is a feature of Gothic romance. The General has some of the characteristics of the Gothic nobleman – he lives in an abbey, he lures Catherine to it, and lustful desires of a kind – material and mercenary – drive him.

The reader may ask:

has Jane Austen presented the General in this way to show that it is not implausible that Catherine, given her Gothic reading, should make the kind of mistakes she does, or is it that Catherine is not wrong in seeing him as in some sense a villain?

Another way of putting the question is to ask: what kind of evil does Catherine encounter at the Abbey?

The only time when the narrator, independent of Catherine, gives a Gothic twist to the language describing the Abbey is when speaking of its transformation from 'a richly endowed convent', harbouring female spirituality, to a family home: 'its having fallen into the hands of the Tilneys on its dissolution, of a larger part of the ancient building still making a part of the present dwelling though the rest was decayed' (vol. 2, ch. 2).

'Fallen . . . dissolution . . . decayed.' This was the Abbey's fate under a monarch with all the appetite of a Gothic hero. This remains its fate under contemporary patriarchal authority. When the General quits the Abbey, the tranquillity of its original purpose is restored, as two virtuous women enjoy the company of their own sex undisturbed. Slowly Catherine will come to appreciate why life is tranquil without the General. For a long time she cannot embrace the possibility that he is responsible for the oppression that she feels in his presence.

4.7 Catherine's doubts

'in spite of all her virtuous indignation, she found herself again obliged to walk with him, listen to him, and even to smile when he smiled' (vol. 2, ch. 7)

Trust and insight

Catherine discovers that Isabella is unworthy of love and trust. The reader is to regard this as an important insight.

In the case of the General, after first giving him the benefit of the doubt, Catherine becomes very much his accuser. The General, she imagines, was a cruel, maybe even a wicked, husband. Hence she finds it difficult to walk with a man who has committed atrocities. The very preposterousness of Catherine's surmises renders them laughable. Consequently, so the argument runs, we cannot take this aspect of the novel as seriously as that which deals with Isabella's bogus friendship (see 2.8).

Inexplicability

If for a moment we resist the dichotomizing structure of the plot, the effect of which is to play up the gap between Catherine's wild imaginings that General Tilney is a Gloucestershire Montoni and the touchingly familiar reality of his grieving for his wife, we shall be able to see that Catherine does more than imagine his vices.

Catherine finds the General's conduct unaccountable.

Reference has already been made to his apparently casual requests to Henry concerning the visit to Woodston. His playing down of the importance of dinner is like a code. Catherine does not understand that 'you are not to put yourself out in any way' actually means 'I want you to provide me with a sumptuous meal'. Catherine frames the issue in the following way:' the inexplicability of the General's conduct dwelt much on her thoughts' (vol. 2, ch. 11). The reverse in standard syntax draws our attention to Catherine's bewilderment. We sense that this is not prejudice, but vision.

Henry and his father

Is this vision of the General's inexplicable behaviour shared by Henry? He has learnt to understand the General's code.

But in learning to read his father's behaviour, has Henry become blinded to just how disturbingly strange it is?

The answer lies in the fact that Henry eventually has to take a clear stand against his father, for Catherine's sake and for his own. His 'filial disobedience' carries the day. Henry can afford it, in every sense of the word, where Eleanor cannot.

4.8 Trusting her judgement

'And all this by such a man as General Tilney.' (vol. 2, ch. 13)

The General himself

Catherine is not merely bothered by a logical inconsistency. What troubles her is the General's conduct and, a deeper matter, the man himself. In the General, Catherine has come up against the fact that there are depths in people which are not open to a rational understanding. Furthermore, when such inexplicability is allied to despotic power, there is danger.

Catherine defers to Henry's judgement. As in her meeting with John Thorpe, she thinks that the man knows best. The irony is that

Catherine is wrong because she prefers Henry's judgement to her own.

It is wiser to be confounded by the inexplicable than to accommodate oneself to the unaccountable whims of a powerful person.

Incomprehensibility

That Catherine's strong sense of the General's strange behaviour is a central feature of the second volume is born out by her agitated reaction to the news of her ejection.

> And all this by such a man as General Tilney, so polite, so well-bred, and heretofore so particularly fond of her! It was as incomprehensible as it was mortifying and grievous. (vol. 2, ch. 13)

It is important to see that

we do not view Catherine's bewilderment as being completely satisfied by the explanations Henry offers of how John Thorpe's vanity and spite had misled the General.

Henry explains why his father was angry, but

his explanation does not account for why the General turned Catherine out so precipitantly. Nor does it explain the fundamental irrationality of a man who, already in possession of so much, yet craves more.

The fact that the General's yen for ever-accumulating riches appears to be a universal phenomenon, and one to be encountered throughout Jane Austen's work, does not make it any the more accountable, either to Catherine or to the reader.

Catherine's anguished representation of her situation to herself goes unanswered:

> Turned from the house, and in such a way! Without any reason that could justify, any apology that could atone for the abruptness, the rudeness, nay, the insolence of it. (vol. 2, ch. 13)

Should we resist the acuity of Catherine's insight, her sensible parents unknowingly lend support: 'General Tilney had acted neither honourably nor feelingly, neither as a gentleman nor as a parent' (vol. 2, ch. 14).

4.9 A Gloucestershire Montoni?

'Eleanor was called back in half a minute to receive a strict charge against taking her friend round the Abbey till his return.' (vol. 2, ch. 7)

The General's character

The character of the General is very carefully drawn. There is a richness in his complex of characteristics that exceeds even that of Henry. Most of his traits are unpleasant. Perhaps his best point is the pride he takes in his gardens, yet even here there is dissimulation. We might respond to 'He loved a garden' but he is not telling the truth when he says that 'Though careless enough in most matters of eating, he loved good fruit' (vol. 2, ch. 7).

Inflexibility at the table

Eating together, which in so many novels is a sign of communion, is difficult in the presence of the General. He is a stickler for punctuality. When Catherine joins the family for dinner, he is peremptory in his demands – he 'pulled the bell with violence, "Dinner to be on table *directly!*"' (vol. 2, ch. 6).

Impatience

His insistence upon punctuality is allied to his impatience. When he decides to leave Bath, Eleanor says he cannot be persuaded 'to give the waters what I think a fair trial' (vol. 2, ch. 2). His tetchy precipitance is at its most extreme when he stipulates the circumstances in which Catherine is to leave the Abbey.

Authoritarianism

Catherine's ejection is the grossest instance of the General's brutal power. What lies behind the exercise of that power – his authoritarianism – pervades all aspects of life at the Abbey.

It emerges that he decides, after the charade of a consultation, to show Catherine round the gardens before he exhibits the Abbey because, as Eleanor explains, 'he always walks out at this time of day' (vol. 2, ch. 7). Is there a hint of his frustration at not being able to exercise complete power over nature in his 'great vexations' that he 'could not always secure the most valuable fruits' from his garden?

When it is time to return to the house, he gives Eleanor a 'strict charge' not to show Catherine round the Abbey. He has no obvious reason for this; he gives orders because orders are what he gives.

At Woodston there is a troubling instance of his despotism. When Catherine praises the view of the cottage from the parsonage, he gives orders: 'You like it – you approve it as an object; it is enough. Henry, remember that Robinson is spoken to about it. The cottage remains' (vol. 2, ch. 11).

Such whims determine the fates of tenants. Clearly, the General had plans to demolish the cottage, but even if provision would have been made for the occupant, demolition would still have entailed the loss of the tenant's home.

Pride and Materialism

The General takes pride in his improvements to the Abbey. (Catherine, on the other hand, has the instincts of the true conservationist when she laments the destructive hand of General Tilney's father.) In the drawing-room 'all praise that had . . . meaning, was supplied by the General'. We can also hear his self-congratulatory voice in the improvements to the kitchen. He might represent his improvements as being for the benefit of the cook, but we have to remember how the master for whom servants work regards food.

Anger

The General can control inanimate objects and servants. He tries to control his children and Catherine. When he fails to fulfil his will he becomes angry. The General's anger is often in excess of what has caused it. Tony Tanner drew attention to the pun in the name of the General's home when he called his chapter on *Northanger Abbey* ('Anger in the Abbey' in *Jane Austen*, Macmillan, 1986).

It is Catherine who is the object of the General's fiercest anger. When Henry, returning to Northanger, meets his father, he is told of Catherine's ejection. Henry recounts the incident to Catherine:

> On his return from Woodston, two days before, he had been met near the Abbey by his impatient father, hastily informed in angry terms of Miss Morland's departure, and ordered to think of her no more. (vol. 2, ch. 15)

The General believes he has the authority to dictate his adult son's consciousness and conscience. When Henry refuses to go into Herefordshire and resolutely declares his intention of proposing to Catherine, 'The General was furious in his anger' (vol. 2, ch. 15) Catherine's failure to understand the extent of the General's passions confirms the depth of her moral sensibility. The General is inexplicable in his irrationality. So is evil (see below).

The General's children

The General, then, is inflexible, impatient, fussy, authoritarian, proud, self-congratulatory, materialistic and given to uncontrollable anger. Perhaps because they are accustomed to it, neither Henry nor Eleanor puzzles over his conduct, and therefore they underestimate his capacity for evil.

Because in some regards the General is entirely predictable – over time, meals and contradictory discourse – his children view him as a demanding norm. It takes Catherine in her insistence that he is Gothic in spirit to point out how abnormal he is. The moody, emotionally capricious General is not to be accounted for.

He is cruel like Mrs Norris (see 15.10). That is why he is dangerous. Catherine is the only character in the book fully to sense this.

4.10 Catherine: the model of true judgement

'Catherine attempted no longer to hide from herself the nature of the feelings which, in spite of all his attentions, he had previously excited; and what was terror and dislike before, was now absolute aversion.' (vol. 2, ch. 7)

Design and theme

The subtlety of *Northanger Abbey* is that the reader is eventually obliged to read the book in a way which is at odds with its design and thematic structure.

The effect of all the parallels and balances in the plotting is to give the impression that the book is about Catherine's hard-earned insight into her early folly. *Northanger Abbey,* it appears, is an 'education' novel, the plot of which shows that Catherine learns through her mistakes until she is enlightened. In Bath Isabella deceives her, and in Northanger she deceives herself about the General's past. She therefore has to come to a double awakening. It has the form of a chiasmus, the double awakening being in reverse order from the deceptions: first an awakening from the visions of romance and next a realization that Isabella is false.

The patterning is neat so long as it is accepted that Catherine is wrong about the General. But is she? In a trivial sense she gets the facts wrong: General Tilney neither murdered nor incarcerated his wife. Nor is the plot of the novel *quite* a Gothic one of an innocent young girl threatened by a wicked nobleman in a remote abbey.

What Catherine gets wrong is the *form* of her suspicion. It is her language, her means of representation that lead her astray.

In a literary novel, Catherine's mistake is appropriately literary: instead of taking the language of Gothic as a metaphor for potential evil, Catherine takes it literally.

Eventually horror for Catherine is not secret passages, blood-stained knives or ancient manuscripts – not the trappings of the Gothic; it is the peremptory order to leave the General's house.

But although Catherine's ejection is not portrayed in the unsubtle codes of the Gothic, this *is* an encounter with the evil of the world.

The word 'evil' might seem extreme, yet it is one that occurs in the text twice. Catherine's mind is 'occupied in the contemplation of actual and natural evil' the night before she leaves the Abbey (vol. 2, ch. 13) and the word recurs in a passage about the differences in mood between Catherine setting off and returning to Bath:

> It was not three months ago since, wild with joyful expectation, she had there run backwards and forwards ...free from the apprehension of evil as from the knowledge of it. (vol. 2, ch. 14)

The language suggests that Catherine suffers a kind of fall: in what appear to be a rustic girl's innocent Eden, she tastes the fruit of the tree of the knowledge of good and evil (and we know the General sets much store by his fruit!). Her ejection has some of the characteristics of an evil: it is ultimately inexplicable, in excess of that which has provoked it, arises from personal animosity, and the effect of the act causes immense suffering.

Confirmation

Catherine has already recognized the villain. Consequently, she 'attempted no longer to hide from herself the nature of the feelings . . . he had previously excited' (vol. 2, ch. 7).

Irony?

The reader must be careful when reading passages such as the one quoted above in which Catherine is so sure that she has seen through the General.

They present themselves as irony, but the real irony is that they are *not* ironical.

When Catherine listens to Henry's account of the General's anger, she feels vindicated. We are tempted into smiling at yet another example of the fanciful Catherine's naïvety, but in fact the irony is self-cancelling:

> Catherine, at any rate, heard enough to feel, that in suspecting General Tilney of either murdering or shutting up his wife, she had scarcely sinned against his character, or magnified his cruelty. (vol. 2, ch. 15)

Her Gothic fancies might have distorted her vision, but they did not exaggerate the General's capacity for evil. Catherine and the reader should have trusted the feelings of unease she experienced throughout her acquaintance with him. Catherine is shown to be right.

Catherine and literary criticism

Catherine's too easy adoption of a Gothic vision can be seen as a subtle exercise in Jane Austen's literary criticism. What Catherine gets wrong is the appropriate means of literary representation, of a suitable mythology or set of symbols.

***Northanger Abbey* implicitly asks what means of representation *would* have been fitting, and the answer is the one given in volume 1, chapter 5: the kind of novel that concentrates on achieving a penetrating perception and evaluation of a familiar world.**

Northanger Abbey is such a novel (vol. 1, ch. 5). It is the kind of novel that might have prompted Catherine Morland to trust her essentially acute powers of perception and judgement from the start. In 'making' her story Catherine is 'writing' exactly the sort of novel that her mother might have handed to her for her benefit. Or her narrator is. Indeed, the question might be asked: does Catherine even escape from, and do better than, her narrator (see 3.11)?

This brings us back to the point from which we set out: *Northanger Abbey* is the kind of novel that appeals to the current literary mind because it plays with the terms of literature itself. Moreover, it has a plot which undermines itself:

***Northanger Abbey* is a self-subverting narrative because the reader is led to think that it is a novel about a heroine in need of education when, we learn at the climax, its subject is the substantial reliability of Catherine Morland's judgement.**

Catherine copes with evil in real life. She refuses to be side-tracked in her pursuit of the good – true friendship and true love. Intuitively and rationally she recognizes both evil and good. She holds out against the one and she embraces the other. She *deserves* to be a heroine.

Part II

Sense and Sensibility

5 Sensibilty

5.1 Sensibility and the plot

'Marianne's abilities were, in many respects, quite equal to Elinor's.' (vol. 1, ch. 1)

Design

Sense and Sensibility is, as Marilyn Butler observes, a contrast-novel. She further points out that the contrast-novel has a didactic purpose: the reader is being taught about the nature of human thought and action. A novel written in this way 'compares the beliefs and conduct of two protagonists – with the object of finding one invariably right and the other invariably wrong'. Such novels seem to have been fashionable in 1795–6 (*Jane Austen and the War of Ideas,* Clarendon Press, 1975, p. 182).

Yet perhaps Jane Austen set out to write a contrast novel only to find that a more complex novel – one engaged in genuine debate – was emerging. In a novel where intrusion and breaching are important (see 8.12), rogue ideas encroach upon the central thesis, and fundamental questions are raised, such as 'how should women behave?'

So *Sense and Sensibility* is ambivalent and in some ways tentative: it poses many questions, and leaves them hanging in the air. As Claire Tomalin points out:

> Austen is considering how far society can tolerate openness, and what its effect on the individual might be. The question was keenly debated in the 1790s as part of a wider political discussion, with radical writers like William Godwin and Robert Bage favouring the complete openness practised by Marianne, conservatives insisting that the preservation of the social fabric requires an element of secrecy and hypocrisy. *Jane Austen: A Life,* Penguin Books, 2000, p. 155)

Sense and Sensibility shares both its form – a plot built on contrasts – and its manner – the didactic approach to conduct – with contemporary fashion – but ultimately it proves broader in its scope and in its irony.

Parallels and polarities

Sense and Sensibility and *Northanger Abbey,* both novels of the 1790s, are marked by the decade in which they were written by their preoccupation with binary structures (see 1.3):

both *Sense and Sensibility* and *Northanger Abbey* are built upon parallels and polarities.

These emerge in the movement of the plot. The full significance of many scenes depends upon the reader linking them with previous episodes. For instance, on the last evening the Dashwood women spend at their family home, Norland, Marianne wanders in the grounds, bidding farewell to the trees (vol. 1, ch. 5). When in volume 3, chapter 6 Marianne wanders, heedless of her health, in the garden of Cleveland, there is the disturbing suggestion that she is not only bidding farewell to a life of happiness with Willoughby, whose country estate is in the same county, but, perhaps wilfully, bidding farewell to her own life.

5.2 The sisters

'*Your* competence and *my* wealth are very much alike.' (vol. 1, ch. 17)

In accordance with the kind of plot Marilyn Butler presents as typical of the contrast-novel, the most important of the plot linkages are those concerned to establish parallels and contrasts between the elder two of the Dashwood sisters.

The quotation above neatly encapsulates the working of parallels and polarities: the sisters' thinking about money is paralleled, indeed it is very alike, as far as actual sums of money are concerned, but what to Marianne is a 'competence' is to Elinor 'wealth'.

Common experiences

The novel invites the reader to dwell on the differences in outlook and behaviour between Elinor and Marianne.

We are not allowed to forget the thematic insistence of the novel's title.

The differences between Elinor's sense and Marianne's sensibility are evident in the contrasting ways in which the sisters bear up under experiences that are essentially similar.

The movement of the plot, particularly in the early part, invites the reader to compare the responses of Elinor and Marianne.

Elinor has fallen in love with Edward before the novel opens; Marianne takes a tumble on the topsy-turvily named Highchurch Down and meets her romantic 'preserver', Willoughby. Elinor is not presented, as Marianne is, as undergoing the experience of enjoying for the first time the tumultuous feelings of a strong affection.

Elinor is parted from the man she loves, and, after a very rapid romance, Marianne is also separated from Willoughby. Elinor discovers the apparently fatal impediment of Edward's prior engagement, and Willoughby causes devastation when he becomes engaged to another.

The elder Elinor undergoes the experience of loss first, so the reader is prompted to measure Marianne's responses against Elinor's.

In the comparative responses of the sisters we can see the novel apparently declaring for a set of values which have moral, aesthetic and even political implications.

Each sister thinks the other sister's behaviour is incomprehensible. In this ambiguous novel, the sisters show us truths about life; for example, the unfair directness of Marianne and Elinor's cautious equity, taken together, sum up the paradoxical nature of human honesty.

5.3 Two men

'He was the only person in the world who could at that moment be forgiven for not being Willoughby.' (vol. 1, ch. 16)

The person who could be forgiven for not being Willoughby is Edward Ferrars. That Marianne hopes to see Willoughby but that it is Edward who arrives is in part an expression of the way in which the novel parallels the two men. It also nudges Marianne to recognize what Elinor has already acknowledged – that life is not always what we want it to be.

Two men contrasted

The men whom Elinor and Marianne love are very different in their attitudes and morals, but, in order to explore those differences, the plot affords parallels in their actions and situations.

Both men take a considerable interest in the sisters, but neither explicitly declares his love.

Because Elinor's is the central consciousness of the novel (a potential difficulty in a novel built on contrasts?), the inscrutability of both Edward's and Willoughby's behaviour is mediated to the reader through her mind alone.

Elinor is puzzled and pained by Edward's lack of spirits, but it is also Elinor who is troubled by Willoughby's intentions.

The behaviour of both men is mysterious. Why does not Edward declare himself, and has Willoughby proposed marriage to Marianne?

One of the purposes of the plot is to provide explanations. The plot is designed to reveal that both Edward and Willoughby have formed previous attachments, the discovery of which blights the happiness of the sisters.

The existence of prior love interests makes plot sense of the 'debate' about second attachments (vol. 1, ch. 11). This 'debate' between Elinor and Colonel Brandon helps to characterize Marianne's outlook and, in the resolution of the plot, provides material for some ironic reversals.

As is often the case in Jane Austen, affairs of the heart are not unrelated to the business of the pocket. Neither of the men is financially independent. Their security depends upon maintaining the favour of an older woman, in Edward's case his proud mother, and in Willoughby's his strictly principled relative, Mrs Smith, who exerts financial pressure for moral reasons. The monetary strictures governing the two young men focus attention on the part that economics play in the plot. The Dashwoods are ejected from Norland by an entail. Willoughby finally regards marriage as a matter of economics rather than romance. *Sense and Sensibility* is in part a novel about a society where the economic power of the old (and even the dead) ruthlessly constrains the young, and forces them to conform both to convention and unreasonably selfish whims.

Related to the financial uncertainty of their lives is the issue of how the young spend their time. Neither of the young men has a fixed occupation so they both have time on their hands, though neither uses it particularly profitably.

5.4 The plot and the Colonel

'Her's for me, was, I believe, fervent as the attachment of your sister to Mr Willoughby.' (vol. 2, ch. 9)

The Colonel's tale

The above conversation with Elinor starts with the Colonel's announcement that she will find him 'a very awkward narrator'. What follows has much in common with the overemphasized emotional contours of popular fiction. It is one of the teasing ironies of the novel that the extravagant utterances of Willoughby, the man of sensibility, turn out to be theatrical lies, whereas Colonel Brandon, as sensible as Elinor, has a story to tell which, for all its romance and melodrama, turns out to be true. He has contemplated elopement; like Marianne he has loved and lost; he fights a duel of honour and wins a wife eighteen years younger than himself.

The third man

The presence of Colonel Brandon first disturbs and eventually helps to resolve the plot. He plays a part in the lives of both the young women and the young men.

He has important links with the sisters. He is taken with both young women; he silently admires Marianne but, like Edward, he is in the not unfamiliar position of being able to talk more freely to the sister with whom he is *not* in love. He is also, like Edward and Willoughby, a character who generates mystery. His actions prompt the characters and the reader to seek for explanations. Like Willoughby he makes a dramatic departure. He is like Edward in that he is a character who has a past, which is the cause of present suffering.

The lost girls

The life of Colonel Brandon's ward, Eliza Williams, provides parallels and potential parallels with some of the other female characters. She is like a character from popular fiction. (Sixty years later she would have been the central figure in a 'sensation' novel.) She represents innocence betrayed – a young and inexperienced girl who is seduced by a dashing gallant.

The role Marianne avoids

For Colonel Brandon the pain of Eliza's fate lies partly in the way it unhappily parallels that of her mother. Both are guilty of sexual incontinence, both are ruled by excessive sensibility, and both are relegated to the margins of society, where both suffer. Colonel Brandon's account of discovering his first love 'in a spunging-house' (a house to which people were sent prior to their internment in a debtor's prison) is one of Jane Austen's rare visits to the criminal underworld.

The plot works by alerting the reader to the potential parallel with what might have been the fate of Marianne. It is up to the reader, prompted by the similarity between her and their cases, to reread the 'courtship' of Willoughby in a more questioning manner.

Marianne goes willingly to Allenham with Willoughby, without apparently realizing that she is placing herself in danger of being seduced. 'All this will be yours some day if only . . .'.

Even more suggestive is the incident reported by Margaret when Willoughby 'seemed to be begging something of her, and presently he took up her scissors and cut off a lock of her hair' (vol. 1, ch. 12). The literary parallel is with Pope's *The Rape of the Lock*, a playful mock-epic in which the cutting of a lock of hair is symbolic of the taking of virginity.

Marianne does not fall morally, though she takes a literal tumble down a hill. The importance of the incidents of her romance with Willoughby is that they indicate that others have fallen and Marianne might have done.

5.5 Relatives

'*You* are my cousins, you know, and they are my wife's, so you must be related.' (vol. 1, ch. 21)

Cousins, brothers and sisters

The world of *Sense and Sensibility* is peopled by relatives. There are two Jennings sisters, two Steele sisters and two Ferrars brothers. Colonel Brandon also had a brother. Sir John and Mrs Dashwood are cousins and Lady Middleton is cousin to the Steele sisters. Perhaps it is significant that the only family that has no relatives, except those acquired through marriage, is the Ferrars family.

Plot possibilities

With so many pairs, the reader can see that the possible resolutions through marriage are numerous. *Sense and Sensibility* has the plot design of a comedy; there are many characters, some of whom we feel are going to be paired, though exactly *how* is not clear.

We do not know how Elinor will be able to marry Edward, but the configuration of the plot prompts us to think she will. It is not entirely satisfactory that Robert Ferrars marries Lucy (as a Ferrars he is hardly likely to marry a penniless girl), but at least it gives a purpose to a character who appears to have little function apart from his concern for toothpicks!

Once the various pairings have taken place, there is a Shakespearean pathos (see the close of *Twelfth Night*) of characters who find no one to marry. As R. W. Chapman points out in his list of characters in his Oxford edition of the novel: 'Doctor Davies . . . did *not* marry Miss Steele.'

5.6 Design and theme

'"Elinor, can he be justified?"
"No, Marianne, in no possible way."' (vol. 2, ch. 7)

Questions about behaviour

The subject of this dialogue is the behaviour of Willoughby. Marianne desperately asks whether his conduct – his public rejection of her – can be (morally) justified.

It is not just in the case of individual characters that a moral is pointed.

The purpose of the novel

***Sense and Sensibility* is a novel with a case to make.**

Through an examination of behaviour it presents an interpretation of the moral and social aspects of human life. An ideology emerges in a number of ways.

Concepts

The text of *Sense and Sensibilty* is rich in concepts that work morally, psychologically and cognitively. This characteristic of the novel's language is evident from the start. In the first chapter of the novel we find the concepts of honour, generosity, ungraciousness, prudence, judgement, eagerness, reflection, attachment, integrity, exertion, forbearance and affliction.

Debate

Conversations which debate issues express the themes of the novel. *Sense and Sensibility* opens with a debate, even if it is only a parody of one. The grotesquely funny 'Dutch auction' in which Mrs John Dashwood persuades her husband not to share his inherited wealth with the Dashwood women burlesques the issues of duty and responsibility that are to be important in the novel. Elinor, for instance, has even the moral refinement to recognize that she has a duty to keep Lucy's disclosure secret at cost to herself.

The narrator

In the early chapters the narratorial tone is strongly didactic. It is very different from the vivacious, impudent and worldly-wise tone that marks the narrator's voice in *Northanger Abbey*. The narrator of *Sense and Sensibility* is often serious, decided, exact and, at times, slightly ponderous. She occasionally resembles aspects of Elinor's description of Marianne: 'she is very earnest . . . but she is not often really merry' (vol. 1, ch. 17).

5.7 The status of feeling

'if there had been any real impropriety in what I did, I should have been sensible of it at the time' (vol. 1, ch. 13)

Strong feelings

The reader should not be misled by the strong binary working of the plot into thinking that the novel passes a negative judgement on feelings.

***Sense and Sensibility* is not hostile to emotions.**

In the first chapter, the narrator says of John Dashwood that he 'had not the strong feelings of the rest of the family'. Because it is in the next chapter that he is argued, quite easily, out of his duty and charity, it may be assumed that the book

establishes a strong link between feelings and the moral life.

The narrator is careful that the reader should not misunderstand the novel's moral core – Elinor. The opening of the novel speaks of Elinor's 'strength of understanding, and coolness of judgement'. The next qualities that are singled out are 'an excellent heart; – her disposition was affectionate, and her feelings were strong'.

Insipid

The word 'insipid' is carefully used to characterize those whose feelings lack generosity and warmth. The narrator says that Lady Middleton displays 'cold insipidity' and is only stirred into any kind of life 'by the entrance of her four noisy children' (vol. 1, ch. 7). It is not surprising that, when they meet, there is a rapport between Lady Middleton and the selfish Fanny Dashwood.

5.8 Government

'her feelings were strong; but she knew how to govern them' (vol. 1, ch.1)

The language of self-control

The opening chapter makes it clear that Elinor and Marianne have much in common:both are intelligent (one of the first qualities of Marianne to be mentioned is 'sense') and both have strong feelings. Yet the opening chapter dwells on the crucial difference between them. This lies in a capacity that Elinor possesses and which is wilfully absent from Marianne's conduct:

Elinor controls her feelings, whereas Marianne displays and amplifies hers.

The distinction emerges in a conjunction: Elinor 'was deeply afflicted; *but* still she could struggle' (vol. 1, ch.1; our italics). The absence of that 'but' in Marianne's emotional life provides much of the material of the plot.

Elinor is presented in a vocabulary of strenuous self-control. At a crucial moment, as a result of Lucy's disclosure, her hope of Edward sinks but 'her self-command did not sink with it' (vol. 1, ch. 22).

The government of feelings

One of the most significant terms used of Elinor is 'government'. Government is a rich concept. One of its meanings is the (morally commendable) control of the self. Johnson's fourth definition is 'Regularity of behaviour'.

The government of the tongue

The word 'government' had been used by Bishop Butler (1692–1752), a significant figure in eighteenth-century thought. It is hard to imagine that Jane Austen's father, Revd George Austen, did not read Butler. Butler is cautious about feeling (he was an enemy of what contemporaries called enthusiasm in religion). In the sermon 'Upon the Government of the Tongue' he argues that 'true government' involves a subduing of 'that eager desire to engage attention'. Significantly, the word 'eager' is used of Marianne in the opening chapter. The sentence pivots on the important conjunction: 'She was sensible and clever; *but* eager in everything' (our italics)

Marianne is characterized by her refusal to govern her tongue. 'But' undermines those qualities the narrator starts off by valuing. Jane Austen makes 'government' thematically central to the novel.

Political implications?

There may be political implications in the word. To govern is to restrain and control. Political thinkers who had some sympathy with the American and French revolutions were suspicious of those who wished to regulate speech and behaviour. Opponents of revolutionary ideas saw the necessity of restraint in the personal as well as the public world.

Such restraint is typified in Elinor:

Austen sets out to present Elinor as the model of good behaviour, and to back her insistence on the social necessity of discretion and even lying. She speaks of the duty of 'telling lies when politeness required it'. (Claire Tomalin, *Jane Austen: A Life* Penguin Books, 2000, p. 155)

5.9 A criticism of feeling

'the excess of her sister's sensibility' (vol. 1, ch. 1)

The novelist's dilemma

One of the tensions in Jane Austen's work is that between her moral vision and her need to create plots. This is not a problem that is hers alone.

Many novelists who are also moralists find that what they wish to scrutinize critically is what they depend upon to provide the material for and the impetus of their plots.

In *Sense and Sensibility*:

the plot is the negation of the novel's central value.

The novel urges the government of feelings, but the incidents of the plot (and some would say its interest and life) derive from Marianne's refusal to learn restraint. It is not surprising that many who saw the film with the screenplay by Emma Thompson assumed that it was Marianne and not Elinor who is the central character of the book. It is impossible to dramatize Elinor's inner life on the screen. Yet perhaps the film does justice to the way that the novel in part eludes the didactic strictures of the contrast genre.

It is in the clash between an underlying moral message and the movement of the plot that an interesting debate emerges. It concerns authenticity (see 8.12). Elinor believes in concealment to protect herself and others. (This demonstrates her political conservatism.) Marianne is true to herself in her openness, even though this renders her vulnerable. Her capacity to be in touch with her feelings and her scorn of her sister for apparently tempering hers by her use of circumspect language makes Marianne appear (for good or ill) the more contemporary figure of the two.

The movement of the novel makes Marianne central:

in spite of the order of terms in the title, it is sensibility, not sense, that drives the plot.

There is, as is often the case in Jane Austen, a division in the reader's mind; criticism of the excessive indulgence of sensibility emerges in and through our enjoyment of those excesses and the dangers they bring. Moreover, our interest is stimulated by the complexities momentarily revealed when the attitudes of the two sisters are artfully juxtaposed. It is not surprising that the novel has divided critical opinion. Some will see in Elinor a pioneering heroine who rescues the novel from the stranglehold of sensibility, which has gripped it since the eighteenth-century novelist Samuel Richardson. Others will say that Jane Austen sets up an interesting situation in the two sisters without ultimately being prescriptive about either of them.

The relationship between morality and art, a relationship pondered deeply in *Mansfield Park* (the novel *Sense and Sensibility* most resembles), is a notoriously difficult one. In the former novel the reader sometimes feels that Jane Austen has deliberately abandoned some of those things that make art attractive, such as a lively hero and heroine.

Sickness

An author has to find ways of reducing the tension between art and morality by so shaping the plot that one serves the other.

The solution Jane Austen finds in *Sense and Sensibility* is to make Marianne a victim of her own emotional indulgences. Sickness eventually makes her incapable of taking an active part in the plot that she has hitherto driven by her unrestrained romantic aspirations.

The trajectory of the plot – Marianne's wilful descent into neglect and a life-threatening illness – not only graphically shows the dangers of neglecting self-command but makes her, for the first time in the plot, passive. There have been occasions before when she actually does nothing (as when, for instance, Willoughby leaves Barton) but she could dramatize her helplessness so as to make herself the centre of attention. Her eventual passivity enacts the narrator's morality: wilful indulgence in feelings results in conditions under which the subject can neither feel nor exert the will.

Yet one tends to feel that the novel is more ambiguous than that and that each sister has something to demonstrate – that judgement is important but so is true, authentic, sincere, original, fearless language. It is Marianne who fervently and intelligently takes issue with Sir John Middleton for using the insulting expression 'setting your cap at' (vol. 1, ch. 9).

Consequences

However, it must be said that because Marianne has both nursed and submitted to certain culturally fashionable postures, she has no way of coping when Willoughby abandons her. Because she has not learnt self-command, she has no way, in a crisis, of preserving self-respect, health and even life itself. This is in accord with contemporary understanding of sensibility which is never far away from oversensitivity, a disturbed nervous system, the sick room and even madness itself.

5.10 Romanticism

'her opinions are all romantic' (vol. 1, ch. 11)

Romantic literature

We cannot understand Marianne's ungoverned behaviour in isolation from that bundle of attitudes, beliefs and values that we now call Romanticism. The term is usually applied to literature written between 1780 and 1830. Thus, for instance, Blake, Byron, Clare, Coleridge, Keats, Shelley and Wordsworth are called Romantic poets and Sir Walter Scott a Romantic novelist. Jane Austen falls within this period.

Romantic subjects and ideas

Romanticism is not a tidy term. It certainly has a wider meaning than Elinor's remark about Marianne, where 'romantic' means something like emotionally supercharged and not very thoughtful.

Nevertheless, some subjects and concepts are felt to be characteristic of the period. Subject matter included children, trees, flowers, animals, wild scenery, the sea, outcasts, wanderers, rebels, the Middle Ages, ruins, legends and myths, and exotic settings. (This is not an exhaustive list.)

Romantic ideas were related to the subject matter: a preccupation with subjective experience; an interest in change and growth in both people and the natural world; a fascination with what is awesome and sublime in nature; a concern with the nature of human association and, in some writers, an interest in the nature of nature.

This led to broadly political concerns for ideal societies and an anger against oppression plus a desire for change, either by way of return to a previous state or in the creation of a different kind of community. There was, however, a tension between this desire for a better society and an absorption with and a confidence in the powers of the human mind. As more trust was placed in the individual, a sense of society as a group bound together by the common bonds of belief and law inevitably weakened.

Artists

The sort of mind that Romantic literature valued was imaginative, sharply conscious of itself and the world about it, emotionally receptive and creative. Artists (often regarded as heroic figures) were mental explorers, journeying into the outer edges of the mind and daring to find expressions for the mystery, and perhaps terror, of dreams, intuitions, visions and even disturbed mental states – fever, delusion and madness. What had only been extreme – madness, for instance – becomes central to Romantic literature.

Subjectivity

What informed both the subject matter and the concepts was a shift in matters of perception and thought from objectivity to subjectivity. This preoccupation with the nature of seeing and feeling led poets to regard what is external as expressions of states of mind. Keats's poem about the nightingale, for example, is an exploration of the imagination and the workings of art.

5.11 Romanticism in *Sense and Sensibility*

'Mrs Dashwood entered into all their feelings with a warmth which left her no inclination for checking the excessive display of them.' (vol. 1, ch. 11)

Sensibility

In *Sense and Sensibility*

sensibility is inseparable from Romantic subjectivity and individualism.

In Marianne and her mother, sensibility has two closely related characteristics: first,

the deliberate nurturing of strong feelings.

The grief at Henry Dashwood's death is 'voluntarily renewed', and they 'gave themselves up wholly to their sorrow, seeking increase of wretchedness in every reflection' (vol. 1, ch. 1).

Sensibility also involves

the public display of emotion to the exclusion of social propriety and the feelings of others.

When, after Willoughby has abandoned Marianne, Elinor asks her sister to show a 'reasonable and laudable pride' by not giving way to her misery, she replies: 'I must feel – I must be wretched' (vol. 2, ch.7). Marianne's 'must' virtually defines 'sensibility'.

A critique of Romanticism

In Marianne's behaviour – and that of her mother and Willoughby – can be read the narrator's sustained and imaginative critique of the cult of Romantic sensibility.

***Sense and Sensibility* is at its most didactic when dealing with the consequences of emotionally strong characters refusing to exercise self-command.**

The need to establish the dangerous error of an indulged sensibility can be seen in the way the lines of criticism are often graphically established in the early chapters. Having said that, the reader should do more than just criticize Marianne. At the beginning her sensibility is quite crudely portrayed. But Jane Austen gives Marianne interesting qualities and though she begins by mocking her, she appears to present her with increasing seriousness.

Marianne changes too. It is eventual awareness of her sister's suffering, as well as Willoughby the philanderer, that makes her change.

The will

Romanticism can be understood as an initial subjection of the will to the feelings, and a consequent assertion of the will when the feelings are strong. In the first chapter, the narrator tells us that Marianne is wilful. Elinor has acquired the 'knowledge' of how to govern her 'strong feelings', 'a knowledge which her mother had yet to learn, and which one of her sisters had resolved never to be taught'. The passage is almost embarrassingly indicative of how Marianne will behave. When Willoughby suddenly leaves Devonshire, 'she courted the misery which a contrast between the past and present was certain of giving' (vol. 1, ch. 16). 'Courted' trenchantly reveals the narrator's judgement: with no one to court her, Marianne turns those feelings intended for another upon herself.

Art

Elinor's art – drawing – requires attention to what is external to the self, whereas Marianne's art – music – allows for the expression of feeling. The narrator says that for Marianne 'taste' must entail a strong subjective response – 'rapturous delight' (vol. 1, ch. 4).

Marianne also values certain authors because of their effect upon her: 'these beautiful lines which have frequently almost driven me wild' (vol. 1, ch. 3). She is speaking of William Cowper, who, she asserts, deserves a more spirited performance than given by Edward, who read 'with such impenetrable calmness, such dreadful indifference'.

Marianne's literary alertness is attractive, yet we have to ask whether Marianne would be a good reader of Cowper. Her critical language is certainly imprecise: 'calmness' is not the same as 'indifference'. More importantly, is it inappropriate to read Cowper – a quiet, tender, contemplative and troubled poet – with what Marianne calls 'so little sensibility'? An emotionally tempered reading might allow the poet to speak for himself rather than have the emotional contours of his work obscured by the passion of the performer.

The pathetic fallacy?

Marianne is at her most Cowperesque when she wanders alone beneath the Norland trees, apostrophizing them in tones of melancholic sensibility (vol. 1, ch. 5). This valedictory lyricism is a style she has learnt (one of the ironies of the novel is that Marianne, the woman of strong feelings, is dependent upon acquired codes of behaviour). The poetic 'ye' and the regretful dwelling on decay and absence can be found, for instance, in some lines from Cowper's *The Task*, which Fanny Price quotes in *Mansfield Park*.

Marianne is giving vent to her feelings, and there is no doubt an element of indulgence in the fact that she is her own audience. Yet before we convict her of the pathetic fallacy (ascribing feelings to objects that cannot by their very nature have them) we might note that what she says is a good deal more intelligent than many effusive farewells. She knows that nature is not responsive to human feeling, that 'No leaf will decay because we are removed'. What she shows is sensibility *and* sense.

Unbridled talk

The only conversation we hear between Marianne and Willoughby in their whirlwind romance is one in which she says that Colonel Brandon 'has neither genius, taste nor spirit' (vol. 1, ch.10). This is clearly an occasion when she ought to govern her tongue.

What, in Marianne's view, Colonel Brandon lacks is what someone of a romantic outlook values.

The irony is that Marianne fails to see that Colonel Brandon *is* a man of taste and spirit. Moreover, her comments display a Romantic narrowness: are these the only important human qualities?

The narrator tells us of Willoughby's lack of restraint when his friendship with

Marianne begins. Elinor sees that he is like Marianne in his 'propensity of saying too much what he thought on every occasion, without attention to persons or circumstances' (vol. 1, ch. 10). The critique of Romantic sensibility discerns a connection between unbridled expression and selfishness.

Selfishness

Giving way, then, to the tug of feeling leads to selfish behaviour. Marianne's selfishness might be described as impersonal. She does not wish to hurt others; it is simply that a failure to exert self-command leads her to be oblivious of and to disregard the interests of others.

This is a recurring theme. When Marianne is overcome by Willoughby's public rejection of her, Elinor asks her to exert herself for the sake of her mother: "Think of your mother, think of her misery while *you* suffer; for her sake you must exert yourself." (vol. 2, ch.7)

Confidence in feeling

Those who govern their conduct place their trust in traditions of moral thought and conduct appropriate to that thought. In every period moral traditions take the form of rules.

Those such as Marianne who are of a Romantic sensibility shift the authority for what they do from external and publicly sanctioned rules to a private intuition of what is right.

When the outing to Whitwell is cancelled, Willoughby and Marianne ride off to visit Allenham. By any public rules of conduct, such behaviour is both imprudent and selfish. To rush off in a carriage is to put oneself in a position of being seduced (see 5.4), and what Marianne's and Willoughby's actions are effectively saying is that they look forward to the death of Mrs Smith, the present owner.

But Marianne recognizes no rules of public conduct. Thus when Elinor challenges Marianne, the reply is in terms of moral intuition:

> if there had been any real impropriety in what I did, I should have been sensible of it at the time, for we always know when we are acting wrong, and with such a conviction I could have had no pleasure. (vol. 1, ch. 13)

Rules, Marianne implies, are no guide to any real impropriety. There is a play here on 'sensible'. Marianne uses it to mean 'aware of', but the reader sees that she is not aware that her conduct is far from sensible. If we rely upon what our feelings tell us, morality becomes undiscussable. If no reason for or against an action can be given, there is nothing to say.

It might sound portentous, but such talk as Marianne's effectively abolishes society. A group of people who only act upon their privately ascertained feelings cannot understand each other and therefore can have nothing in common to bind them together as a group. The narrator shows us that only if morality is public can there be human society.

Sentimentality

Sentimentality is a misuse of feeling. It is a form of emotional casuistry that consists in playing up one's own or other people's feelings independent of the object that has aroused them. Willoughby becomes embarrassingly wistful on the evening when he sentimentally effuses about Barton cottage and with gusto attacks Mrs Dashwood for suggesting it should be improved. Elinor, the realist, points out that the stairs are dangerous and the kitchen smokes, but Willoughby waives such considerations. The cottage is valued solely for associations: 'this dear parlour, in which our acqaintance first began'. He accuses, albeit with gallant affection, Mrs Dashwood of wanting to 'degrade' the room by turning it into 'a common entrance' (vol. 1, ch. 14).

Words turn against the Romantic. It is Willoughby who is degrading the cottage by giving it no significance other than his pleasant memories.

Confounding meaning

Marianne overlooks the important distinction between what we do and what we think. Elinor has to spell it out: 'My doctrine has never been aimed at the subjection of the understanding. All I have ever attempted to influence is your behaviour.' Marianne must learn that because there is a distinction between treating 'our acqaintance . . . with greater attention' and adopting 'their sentiments', she can be considerate to others while refusing to 'conform to their judgement in serious matters' (vol., ch. 17).

Such behaviour is possible only to people, who, unlike those impelled to express all they feel, can make the distinction. Such a capacity, the narrator ironically points out, often works to the advantage of those who have it!

Childishness

When Annamaria is slightly grazed by a pin, the narrator tartly notes that Lady Middleton and the Steele sisters do 'every thing . . . which affection could suggest as likely to assuage the agonies of the little sufferer' (vol. 1, ch. 21). This sets the tone for what borders on being an allegoric or emblematic passage.

Kisses, lavender water and plums are bestowed upon the child, who responds with guile: 'With such a reward for her tears, the child was too wise to cease crying.' Ironically, it is Marianne who sees through the egocentric demands of a spoilt child and the affected concern of Lucy Steele: 'But this is the usual way of heightening alarm, where there is nothing to be alarmed at in reality' (vol. 1, ch. 21).

Marianne fails to see the similarity between Romantic expressiveness (bogusly present in Lucy who fakes sensibility) and the selfish demands of a wailing child.

Children, so often a Romantic emblem of innocence and spontaneity, are viewed here with the steady, unflinching vision of Christian orthodoxy. We are all fallen creatures, and not even the babe in arms, let alone the child who has learnt cunning, is exempt from the blight of original sin.

The passage is not just about children.

If **children can be selfish and demanding, how much more the adult who has acquired the polish of charm**.

Sensibility takes little stock of our capacity to corrupt ourselves and others. The suggestion that emerges from the passage is that this failure stems from the essentially childish nature of Romanticism. It is egocentric, manipulative and clamorous.

5.12 The trajectory of the plot

'my own feelings had prepared my suffering' (vol. 3, ch. 10)

Theme and plot

Marianne herself comes to recognize that the unhappy course of her life is due to the wilful augmentation of her feelings:

> I saw that my own feelings had prepared my sufferings, and that my want of fortitude under them had almost led me to the grave. (vol. 3, ch. 10)

Marianne recognizes the consequential aspect of morality. She is endearingly typical in choosing the word 'fortitude', with its literary associations of heroic resistance, to define the quality, the absence of which has endangered her.

Authentic feelings

An irony pervades the presentation of Marianne:

she despises behaviour which is merely conventional yet her own actions accord with the formulae of the Romantic code.

There is a humourously affectionate picture of her checking the rectitude of her behaviour against the Romantic image of a forlorn maiden:

> Marianne would have thought herself very inexcusable had she been able to sleep at all the first night after parting from Willoughby. (vol. 1, ch. 16)

The excess of 'very inexcusable' and 'sleep at all' expresses her earnest desire to be correct in the conduct of her feelings. Sensibility is a code.

Marianne cares not that she gives pain continuously to her mother and sister. The narrator expresses her disapproval sardonically when she says: 'Her sensibility was potent enough!' (vol. 1, ch. 16).

The narrator sees through the rhetoric of individualism. But there is one thing we should not doubt:

Marianne's behaviour is formulaic but the feelings that prompt her are entirely genuine.

Even when Marianne resolves to live in a disciplined manner, she does so in a characteristic way:

> I mean never to be later in rising than six, and from that time till dinner I shall divide every moment between music and reading. (vol. 3, ch. 10)

There is an authenticity and consistency about Marianne's emotional life. It was unwise of her to act as she did, but it is understandable that she should do so. It was partly the extravagance of youth, as Colonel Brandon recognizes. Her behaviour is, therefore, different – morally different – from those characters who choose to adopt the style of sensibility for reasons of personal advantage.

The distinction between the authentic sensibility of Marianne and the bogus feelings of Fanny and Lucy is evident to the reader though not to every character. Lady Middleton is taken in. From this there emerges a point larger than the impercipience of an individual character:

the code of sensibility makes it difficult to know whether professed feelings are genuine.

This uncertainty is crucial to the presentation of Willoughby. It is openly stated in the dialogue between Mrs Dashwood and Elinor on whether Marianne and Willoughby are engaged (see 7.11). Mrs Dashwood asks: 'Has he been acting a part in his behaviour to your sister all this time?' (vol. 1, ch. 15). The fact that the question can be asked at all shows how easily sensibility can be adopted and how it obfuscates the issue. It is a primary tool in manipulation. Is Willoughby acting in the sense that Marianne can be said to be, or is his behaviour an assumed role as it is for Lucy?

Seduction

Sensibility suits the seducer. By definition the seducer must be less emotionally involved than the one whom he or she hopes to undo. Willoughby admits as much to Elinor, when he declares that he used every means 'to make myself pleasing to her, without any design of returning her affection' (vol. 3, ch. 8).

Seduction is an art, a role adopted by design. An irony that may run through this scene is that although Willoughby is confessing that his actions were reprehensible, he may still be playing the same role. Elinor – 'poor Willoughby' (vol. 3, ch. 9) – could be his final seduction. Willoughby, who aptly heard of Marianne's dramatic plight when attending the theatre, may still be acting a part.

Of course, this is not the only possible reading. Claire Tomalin interprets Willoughby's extraordinary intrusion as being inherently sincere:

> The scene in which Willoughby and Elinor talk, he already married, Marianne lying ill nearby, has the surprisingness of art that has lifted entirely away from pattern and precept into truthfulness to human nature. (Claire Tomalin, *Jane Austen: A Life*, 2nd edn; Penguin Books, 2000, p. 158)

Whatever the reality of the matter, the softening of Elinor's feelings means that she does not ask two questions: is Willoughby telling the truth? And if he is, when did his change of heart occur? But even if Elinor had asked these questions, would satisfactory answers have been obtainable? The danger in the code of sensibility is that we have no way of reaching secure answers.

6 Sense

6.1 Valuing sense

'but exertion was indispensably necessary, and she struggled so resolutely against the oppression of her feelings, that her success was speedy' (vol. 1, ch. 22)

Theme and writing

Reading *Sense and Sensibility* involves the reader in a tension. The plot of the novel is largely driven by sensibility, and behaviour is evaluated by sense.

The subject of this chapter is the place of 'sense' in the thinking of *Sense and Sensibility,* its nature and its workings.

6.2 Poise

'Was his engagement to Lucy, an engagement of the heart? No; whatever it might once have been, she could not believe it such at present.' (vol. 2, ch. 1)

Reflecting

Those reflections of Elinor test both her head and her heart. She has to keep her own feelings about Edward and Lucy in control while she assesses the depth of Edward's feelings for Lucy. She can only reach an answer – a correct one – because she can recognize, using both sense and intuitive feelings, that Edward does not act like a person in love with any one other than herself.

Intellectual and emotional balance

Elinor is quite explicitly said to be a character with strong feelings, but sense governs and restrains her. It deals with what is potentially disturbing. The character who shows sense has balance and poise.

The reader first encounters Elinor in the first chapter, when her mother resolves to quit Norland immediately upon Fanny's insensitive arrival. What is at stake here is not Mrs Henry Dashwood's judgement of Fanny (the judgement is a true one) but how she responds to the indelicate intrusion.

The narrator tells the reader that Elinor is successful in preventing her mother from an imprudent departure, because she

> possessed a strength of understanding, and coolness of judgement, which qualified her, though only nineteen, to be the counsellor of her mother . . . She had an excellent heart; – her disposition was affectionate, and her feelings were strong

What the narrator wants the reader to see is the wholeness of Elinor's character:

the strength of Elinor's understanding and the coolness of her judgement are balanced by an affectionate disposition and strong feelings.

Perhaps the writing is too insistent, but the *meaning* and *value* of Elinor's behaviour are stated with unambiguous force. In the words of the novel's title, Elinor displays sense and sensibility. She is the kind of heroine who, unlike Marianne, does not appear to need to learn.

Two further things need to be said about this commendable balance in her intellectual and emotional constitution.

An unselfish sensibility

The first is that her sensibility is not like Marianne's; she does not nurture feelings for their own sake.

Because sense evaluates feelings, the sensible person knows when to give way to feelings and when to restrain them.

This government is beneficial to people other than the one who practises restraint. Elinor's control gains a few more months at Norland before a suitable future home is found.

Sense in the syntax

The second thing is that

the wholeness of Elinor's intellectual and emotional adjustment is enacted in the neatly balanced sentences of the narrator.

In the passage quoted above, two qualities of the head – strength of understanding and coolness of judgement – are neatly balanced by two of the heart – an affectionate disposition and strong feelings. The syntax further enforces this completeness by the careful placing of 'strength' and 'strong', which enclose the antithetical balance of 'coolness' and 'affection'. With the satisfying elegance of a chiasmus – a figure of speech which reverses the order of terms in two balancing clauses – the narrator establishes and implicitly praises Elinor in language that is fittingly expressive of her qualities.

Prudence and wisdom

Likewise, Elinor's exertion of self-control is wise. Not to tell her mother and sisters of Edward's engagement is prompted, in part, by a consideration for their feelings. It also allows her to escape their expostulations. Elinor has a strong sense of self-preservation.

6.3 Elinor's sense of humour

'Take care, Margaret. It may only be the hair of some great uncle's of *his*.' (vol. 1, ch. 12)

Pictures and locks of hair

Elinor makes this remark to the eager and romantic Margaret after she has had to remind her that her younger sister's romantic suppositions about Marianne and Willoughby have already proved false. The picture Marianne wears round her neck, which Margaret supposed was of Willoughby, turns out to be 'a miniature of our great uncle'. The lock of hair in Willoughby's pocket book could have come from a similar source!

A sense of the absurd

The passage shows that Elinor has a sense of the absurd. She knows it is ridiculous that a romantic figure such as Willoughby should wear a lock of his uncle's hair. What she enjoys, no doubt, is reducing to absurdity the social and literary expressions of ardent attachment. Even if the reader thinks that Elinor's humour is a defence against her worries about Marianne, it does not alter the fact that

Elinor, like Edward, is sardonic. The wit they share is born of sense.

The weight of seriousness

Elinor's wit is a welcome feature in a novel that sometimes feels burdened by the narrator's efforts to bring out significances.

There are moments when there is something of the heavy seriousness of Victorian fiction in *Sense and Sensibility.*

Elinor herself is not free from elements of earnestness. When Edward publicly states that he will stand by his engagement to Lucy, the narrator states that 'Elinor gloried in his integrity' (vol. 3, ch. 20). This is the kind of language that exactly ninety years later the oppressively pious and offensively priggish Mercy Chant uses in Hardy's *Tess of the D'Urbervilles* (1891): 'I glory in my Protestantism!' (chap. 40).

It is not easy to find that strenuous blend of religious adulation and moral grandeur attractive, even in Elinor Dashwood. But such writing is exceptional. In fact, it is Marianne who comes closest to the humorless striving from which Oscar Wilde's *The Importance of Being Earnest* rescued English culture. Elinor says to Edward that Marianne is 'very earnest, very eager in all she does' (vol. 1, ch. 17).

It would probably be inaccurate to describe Marianne's manner and tone as heavy. Her earnestness and eagerness are expressions of her ardent excess rather than of a crippling moralism. Nevertheless, Elinor's point is just: we might want to applaud Marianne (as when she sticks up for her sister in the presence of the appalling Mrs Ferrars) but do we laugh at her jokes?

6.4 Reasoning

'You must remember, my dear mother, that I have never considered this matter as certain.' (vol. 1, ch. 15)

The history of a word

By the time Jane Austen placed considerable semantic weight upon the word 'sense', it already had a long history in one of the traditions of British philosophical writing. This philosophical usage is not irrelevant to a novel such as *Sense and Sensibility*, which lays stress on issues of knowledge and the workings of the mind.

Empiricism

In the philosophical tradition called empiricism, our experience of the external world, mediated through the senses, is treated as the foundation of our knowledge. The empiricists further held that the mind works on the data of the senses, and the result of this working is knowledge.

Locke

When in his *Dictionary* Dr Johnson gave as one of the definitions of 'sense' 'the faculty or power by which external objects are perceived', he is accepting a usage that goes back at least as far as the seventeenth-century philosopher, John Locke. In *An Essay Concerning Human Understanding* (1690), Locke wrote that 'our senses . . . convey into the mind several distinct perceptions of things'. These form what he called *ideas*. In Locke's writing, 'ideas' is a wide category; it contains notions as diverse as 'yellow, white, heat'. Experience mediated through the senses and our awareness of the mind are 'the fountains of knowledge'.

Elinor's empiricism

Elinor can be said to stand in the empirical tradition to the extent that she reasons about what her senses disclose to her. Take, for example, Elinor's view of Lady Middleton: 'Elinor needed little observation to perceive that her reserve was a mere calmness of manner with which sense had nothing to do' (vol. 1, ch. 11).

The passage accords with the empirical paradigm: Elinor observes (the work of the senses) and exercises her mind so she perceives (the mind working upon its ideas). Her mind tries to come to terms with what her senses show her.

6.5 Perception and evidence

'The effect of his discourse on the lady too, could not escape her observation.' (vol. 3, ch. 3)

Observation

This quotation comes from the only passage in *Sense and Sensibility* which is not mediated through Elinor's consciousness. Mrs Jennings observes Colonel Brandon talking earnestly to Elinor and assumes that he is making a proposal of marriage. Though she is wrong, the mistake she makes is one that is consistent with the concerns of the novel:

***Sense and Sensibility* is about the problems of perception.**

This is also a broadly empirical concern. If knowledge is what our minds make of our experience, it is possible that our minds come to the wrong conclusions about what our senses have furnished us with.

It is therefore consistent with this empirical approach that several passages turn on the issue of what characters can legitimately make of what they see.

Elinor and observation

Throughout the novel

Elinor is associated with the language of observation and perception.

Elinor is presented as an acute observer. Colonel Brandon's partiality for Marianne 'became perceptible to her' (vol. 1, ch. 10) and she 'saw . . . the low spirits' of Edward (vol. 1, ch. 18).

True judgements

The above examples establish a point beyond that of empirical philosophy. Elinor's judgements arising out of her perceptions are true.

The implication is that they are true not just because she is observing a proper method of assessing the evidence of her senses but because she is concerned about the people about her.

It is characteristic of Jane Austen's irony that the working of the mind is often separated from the promptings of the conscience.

But in Elinor, perception emerges from and is assisted by a moral concern for her fellow human beings.

This even extends to one who has treated her badly – Lucy Steele herself (see 5.6). Elinor notices Lucy watching her in the scene where the three involved in the love triangle are embarrassingly present together. No doubt Elinor can see in Lucy's glances what her rival is up to. Elinor might also be able to imagine the uncertainties that Lucy is entertaining about Edward's regard for her.

There might even be wit in this, although it is the wit of the narrator rather than of Elinor. St Lucy is the patron saint of eyes, though Lucy Steele, who is frequently stealing glances at Elinor, does not employ her looking for enlightened purposes.

Evidence

Evidence matters to Elinor. This requirement gives some passages a decidedly philosophical thrust.

What is at stake in the discussion between Elinor and her mother about how things stand between Marianne and Willoughby is whether 'no probabilities' are to be 'accepted, merely because they are not certainties' (vol. 1, ch. 15). Such language is essentially philosophical, because what is at stake are distinctions in meaning. Probability admits doubt; certainty means no doubt is entertained.

Mrs Dashwood confirms that Elinor is something of a sceptic. The problem turns on what would convert a probability into a certainty. One answer would be strong, supporting evidence. This is not required by Mrs Dashwood; she easily fictionalizes

Willoughby's departure, explaining it in terms of Mrs Smith's disapproval of his connection with Marianne. She is aware that Elinor will have difficulties with her assurance that things between Marianne and Willoughby are as she has described them to be.

Mrs Dashwood finds Elinor's feelings 'incomprehensible' (vol. 1, ch. 15). The word 'feelings', of course, is crucial to Mrs Dashwood's view; Elinor, she implies, will not be able to accept that Willoughby has nothing to conceal, because her feelings make her 'rather take evil upon credit than good'. However, for Elinor it is not a matter of feeling but of proof. She says that she needs 'no proof of their affection' but only of their engagement. When asked whether their engagement can be doubted, Elinor points out that there is no evidence for it: 'every circumstance except *one* is in favour of their engagement; but that *one* is the total silence of both on the subject, and with me it almost outweighs every other'.

To Elinor, circumstances – the publicly *expressed* affection of Marianne and Willoughby – may strongly suggest that the supposition – that they are engaged – is correct, but this does not mean that nothing more is needed for confirmation. For an engagement to *be* an engagement, it has to be publicly *acknowledged*.

6.6 Elinor's testing

'this greatest exertion of all' (vol. 3, ch. 4)

The problem of being right

Sense and Sensibility appears to be didactic.

The strong narratorial judgement seems to be that Marianne needs to learn but that in essentials Elinor does not.

We should understand Marianne's sensibility and Elinor's sense in terms of the government of feelings: Marianne is without government, whilst Elinor exercises a government over feelings that are as strong as Marianne's. This means that

because the plot requires Marianne to change, readers might find more interest in her tough education than in the patience of Elinor.

Marianne must awaken, but the already alert Elinor is apparently not required to.

What the novel offers in place of the drama of an awakening is Elinor's quiet but intense suffering of disappointment.

Elinor is the first example of a kind of character who clearly interested Jane Austen: the central figure of a novel who nevertheless lacks many of the distinguishing features that novelists find vital in creating an engaging plot.

A character such as Elinor cannot undergo many of the experiences that make novels engaging to the reader:

Elinor cannot be wilful and adventurous, cannot make dramatic mistakes and cannot suffer the consequences of her folly.

So what can Jane Austen do with her? The answer is that

Elinor can be tested.

The secret engagement

Elinor is tested most severely by Lucy's disclosure concerning her secret engagement with Edward. Her other tests, such as directly informing Edward of Colonel Brandon's offer of the Delaford living, are only testing because of the existence of the clandestine engagement.

Plots about love often work by the lovers facing impediments to their happiness. In Elinor's case there are several. She has suffered under the strong disapproval of the Ferrars family over her attachment to Edward. She has also borne the doubts and uncertainties caused by his unaccountably low spirits. The discovery of the clandestine engagement disappoints her hopes. In addition, knowing that Edward cannot propose to her, Elinor has to suffer the, at times, resentful assumption of Marianne that she, unlike herself, is sure of her beloved's affection. Of course, Elinor is assured of it, but this is no consolation when there is no prospect of her marrying him.

Lucy's disclosure

Lucy's disclosure (vol. 1, ch. 22) and the subsequent dialogue engineered by Elinor (vol. 2, ch. 2) are made vivid by sharply focused moments of drama. The reader is intimately present in this scene of sly looks and overheard remarks. We feel exposed to Lucy's sideways glance at Elinor, and cringe at the inane yet acutely uncomfortable surmise from Miss Steele that 'Lucy's beau is quite as modest and pretty behaved as Miss Dashwood's' (vol. 2, ch. 2).

The test of self-command

The graphic quality of the writing is thematically significant:

the strain Elinor is under tests her powers of self-command.

The climax comes when Elinor can no longer believe that Lucy's story is false.

At this point, we are back with the issues dealt with in 6.4: reasoning and evidence. The evidence Lucy adduces convinces Elinor. The language shows a struggle between the two forces that the narrator has singled out as important for our understanding of Marianne – feeling and will:

> her heart sunk within her, and she could hardly stand; but exertion was indispensably necessary, and she struggled so resolutely against the oppression of her feelings, that her success was speedy, and for the time complete. (vol. 1, ch. 22)

Elinor shows a finely attuned adjustment of feeling and will. Her triumph is clear. (Perhaps too clear; some readers might find this passage too didactic: Marianne, take note!) Elinor remains upright, both in the moral sense of not giving away in public to feelings and in the physical sense of being able to stand. The physical sense is important. Because Elinor controls herself, she is able to carry the battle to Lucy when she returns to the issue of the engagement over the 'filigree basket for a spoilt child' (vol. 2, ch. 1). The struggle between them is conducted in the language of personal combat. Could this be Jane Austen's version of chivalry?

The test of sense

Lucy's disclosure is also a test of sense:

Elinor has to distinguish truth from what she would like to be the case.

It is the purpose of the passage of solitary meditation (vol. 2, ch. 1) to show Elinor's facing the unpalatable conclusion that though she might not in general trust Lucy, there are no grounds for doubting the existence of the engagement.

The language of this – the most sustained passage of reflection in the novel – can also be said to be philosphical: it is concerned with what is 'true', with what Elinor 'dared no longer doubt', because it is 'supported . . . on every side by such probabilities and proofs, and contradicted by nothing but her own wishes'.

Probability

Locke wrote of 'probability' as 'the proper object and motive of our assent', and in *The Analogy of Religion* Joseph Butler summed up his guiding intellectual principle in the words: 'But to us, probability is the very guide of life.'

And so it has to be for Elinor. It is improbable that even Lucy would invent 'a falsehood of such description'. Elinor, the one who struggled to make her body stand, has to confront 'such a body of evidence' as Edward's visits near Plymouth, 'his melancholy state of mind', 'uncertain behaviour towards herself' and 'the picture, the letter, the ring'. A metaphor of secure reasoning grows out of the 'opportunity of acquaintance in the house of Mr Pratt', which she sees is 'a foundation for the rest'. 'Foundation' is the kind of word used in philosophical debate.

The only thing that contradicts what Lucy says is of a quite different order from the evidence Elinor has seen – it is 'her own wishes'. This, once again, amounts to a critique of Romanticism. The Romantic insistence on the role of the subject, on how what we see is what we have half-created, gives prominence to the place in thinking of desire and wish, even to the point of supposing that, in the words of Shakespeare's Henry IV to his son, the 'wish' can be 'father' . . . to the 'thought'. (*2 Henry IV,* IV. iii. 221) Thus the world – reality, how things are, the substantial realm of things – gives way to the yearnings of what Iris Murdoch called the 'fat, relentless ego'.

Hope and reality

What emerges from a reading of Jane Austen is that perception and thought are not mere exercises of the mind; they are essentially moral functions in which the self escapes its own clamorous fantasizing to school itself in the actualities and limits of the real world.

Hope is a Christian virtue, but if it is untempered by clear vision it might lead to the fantasy of supposing that we can dream, as Keats claimed, and awake to find it true. Elinor is tested by the illusions of what she comes to see as an unrealistic hope when she 'found the difference between the expectation of an unpleasant event...and certainty itself' (vol. 3, ch. 12). The language is of a robust realism.

The language of discovery continues in a passage that deals directly with hope: 'She now found, that in spite of herself, she had always admitted a hope, while Edward remained single, that something would occur to prevent his marrying Lucy' (vol. 3, ch. 12).

To admit a hope that something might prevent Edward from marrying Lucy is a failure to exert the will. Marianne fails because her will prevents her from seeing the world from any other viewpoint than her own. Elinor must exert her will to overcome her hopes. In so exerting her will, she will see things as they actually are.

Perhaps the fact that there *is* actually hope (Edward, as it turns out, has not married Lucy) makes for a welcome dramatic irony in the novel's happy close. Or perhaps Jane Austen wants to draw attention to life's refusal to conform to a cut-and-dried moral formula. She enjoys scrambling the reader's expectations. Elinor, the embodiment of sense, is the only character allowed to win through to Marianne's romantic ideal of the fulfilment of first love.

The test of virtue

The novel makes it clear that to live according to virtue is not always to enjoy happiness or success. This is the difference between morality and prudence: in the former action is taken because it is right, in the latter because it is safe.

Elinor's chief suffering arises from Lucy's disclosure. Lucy tells Elinor about her engagement to warn Elinor off Edward at the same time as exacting a promise of secrecy.

Lucy's decision to impart her secret to Elinor is an exploitation of Elinor's honour. Elinor suffers because of her honesty and trustworthiness, and Lucy inflicts pain because she recognizes those good qualities in Elinor.

The wily Lucy knows that imparting the secret will hurt Elinor, hence the side glance. What she cannot have known, though might have anticipated, is that keeping the secret will continue to cause Elinor pain.

When Marianne says how easy it is 'for those who have no sorrow of their own to talk of exertion' (vol. 2, ch. 7), the irony is painful for Elinor and the reader. Lucy is the indirect cause not only of Elinor's suffering at this point but of Marianne's, when she discovers the burden her sister has been carrying for four months: 'and I reproached you for being happy' (vol. 3, ch. 1).

The test of goodness

We are accustomed to think that it is because of our weaknesses that we are tested. The glutton, for instance, is tested by the sight of food. In the case of *Sense and Sensibility*, however,

Jane Austen has so shaped the plot that tests come Elinor's way because of her virtues rather than her faults.

In so far as it is right to call her a victim,

Elinor is a victim of both her goodness and her self-control.

This is graphically evident in the passage in which Colonel Brandon, outraged by the way the Ferrars have treated Edward, asks Elinor to convey to the man whom she loves the news that will allow him to marry Lucy.

6.7 The faculty of sense

'She was stronger alone, and her good sense so supported her, that her firmness was as unshaken, her appearance of cheerfulness as invariable, as with regrets so poignant and so fresh, it was possible for them to be.' (vol. 2, ch. 1)

Making up one's mind

Exactly how Elinor makes up her mind is not explicitly explored in the novel. The issue, nevertheless, is an important one.

How the mind should reach a state of certitude is a question debated in the novel. If we exercise those faculties which we call intuition or imagination we adopt a Romantic reading of human experience. If, however, we exercise our capacity to reason, then we are truly creatures of sense. In *Sense and Sensibility*, the reader, because of the particular narrative mode, can discern how Elinor makes up her own mind and, also, how she comes to conclusions about other characters' minds.

The nature of the mind is related to another issue: how we know what other people are thinking and feeling. Where thought is concerned, we can listen to what people say. Is it any different with feeling?

The nature of feeling

Although there is much in the novel about secrecy,

the presumption of *Sense and Sensibility*, as in the rest of Jane Austen's work, is that emotions are primarily and essentially public.

Emotions are written in our actions and the expressions of our faces. When Colonel Brandon tells Elinor about his past and Willoughby's seduction of Eliza, Elinor knows what he is feeling from what he does: 'he could say no more, and rising hastily walked for a few minutes about the room' (vol. 2, ch. 9).

If emotions were not public, there would be no question as to whether it were possible to conceal them.

A criticism of sensibility

In this stress on the public nature of feeling, there is a subtle criticism of Marianne's dramatization of her emotional life. The implication of the writing about feelings is that Marianne, the one who values and nurtures her emotions, is actually mistaken about the nature of feelings.

If feelings, as Jane Austen shows, are essentially public, there is no need for Marianne, or any one else, to parade them, because the perceptive onlooker will be able to *see* what she is feeling.

Hence, when Willoughby appears at the assembly (vol. 2, ch. 6), Elinor knows what Marianne is feeling not by means of a shrewd guess or an imaginative penetration of her mind, but because she can see that Marianne is agitated. This is why Elinor tells her to be 'composed'. As Marianne's feelings are strong, Elinor urges her not to 'betray what you feel to every person'.

The truth about human feelings is, therefore, exactly the opposite to what the Romantics imagine. It is not a case of trying to make public what is private but controlling what by its very nature is already public.

Understanding feelings

To understand the feelings of others is to understand how the mind works. Because feelings are essentially public, we already have in our reasonings about what we observe the requirements for understanding the feelings of others. This means that

there is no suggestion in *Sense and Sensibility* that Elinor's sense works by intuition or imagination.

That statement does not deny that there is no such thing as either intuition or imagination; it merely asserts that sense does not operate by them.

On the one occasion that Elinor depends upon what we might call intuition, she gets the matter in question wrong. When Marianne draws attention to the hair in Edward's ring, Elinor immediately concludes that it is her own.

6.8 Edward's feelings

'Marianne spoke inconsiderately what she really felt – but when she saw how much she had pained Edward, her own vexation at her want of thought could not be surpassed by him.' (vol. 1, ch. 18)

What Edward feels for Elinor

Even when she is suffering the immediate effects of Lucy's disclosure, Elinor is certain about Edward's feelings for her: 'His affection was all her own. She could not be deceived in that' (vol. 2, ch. 1).

An immediate response might be that Elinor is allowing the wish to be the father of the thought and thereby triumph over awkward facts. A further response might be that she is depending upon intuition to make this judgement.

But there is plenty of evidence in the text to support Elinor's very strong claim, couched in the language of philosophy, that in the matter of Edward's feelings for her she cannot be deceived.

To reach a state of assurance, all she has to do is put together what she knows.

Understanding Edward

It is clear that Edward has talked of her and Marianne. For example, the Steele sisters' knowledge of Norland is surprising. We deduce from this that Edward has talked about Elinor and Norland. If he has done this to, of all people, Lucy, his heart must be very full of Elinor. We might imagine that on the subject of Elinor he was far more voluble at Plymouth than he ever is on any subject at Barton.

Lucy's and Edward's feelings

It can also be deduced from Lucy's behaviour that she has seen that Edward's affections are for Elinor rather than herself. The narrator indicates that Lucy is rather too hasty in disclosing her secret. Is this a desperate move: she must choke off the opposition, because a man who no longer loves one is better than no man at all?

The reader hears Sir John reveal the 'F' name at the end of colume 1, chapter 21, and Lucy speaks at the beginning of chapter 22. Even when she is being gratuitously cruel, Lucy reveals too much. She would not say 'you must have seen enough of him to be sensible he is very capable of making a woman sincerely attached to him' if she were only aware of *Elinor*'s sincere attachment. If she were sure of Edward's devotion she might rather enjoy the cosy knowledge that the girl from Sussex will get nowhere, but by speaking she betrays the fact that she knows for whom Edward now feels strongly.

Lucy also marks out Edward as her man by her gift of a ring with her hair in it, symbolic of commitment. That Edward wears it instead of removing it in front of Elinor, while at the same time lying about its origins when confronted, demonstrates his split self, riven between duty and desire.

Lucy feels the need to stake her claim to Edward because her suspicions were aroused, and she found out the truth by the same method that Elinor uses – she reasoned about what she observed. Edward's behaviour towards her had changed. Lucy has a great deal of common sense, which she uses to her own ends. She only *fakes* sensibility for the same selfish purposes. Where Elinor and Marianne are tender, Lucy is hard – as hard as steel.

6.9 Narrator, sense and reader

'But so it was.' (vol. 3, ch. 14)

Following the narrator

When the narrator tells the reader, in the words quoted above, that, unlikely as it once seemed, Marianne formed a second attachment, the very brevity of the sentence is a way of marking the narrator's trust that the reader will both follow and understand the event. (Another reading would suggest that the narrator wants to move quickly over ground that she suspects the reader will have difficulty in conceding. She significantly does not have Marianne and Colonel Brandon converse together either.)

The narrator and Elinor

One of the features of *Sense and Sensibility* is that it is impossible, at least much of the time, for the reader to separate the narrator and Elinor.

One of the ways in which the reader is close to Elinor is that both use their sense to work out what is going on.

We are often invited to think as Elinor does in order to follow the intricacies of the plot:

the novel requires us to exercise as well as to approve of sense.

Colonel Brandon and Willoughby

Take the case of the relationship between Colonel Brandon and Willoughby. There is a buried narrative in *Sense and Sensibility* which concerns the lives of the two men in Marianne's life. Occasionally, events from this narrative emerge in the main plot, but for the rest the reader must exercise his or her sense and deduce from what is shown a sequence of events that forms, unusually for Jane Austen, a dramatic tale of romance.

Willoughby bursts into the novel as a Romantic hero who saves Marianne by sweeping her off her feet, literally. He retains an air of mystery; Sir John Middleton knows little of him apart from his prowess in hunting, and, later, Charlotte Palmer can tell the Dashwoods nothing apart from the fact (perhaps an important one) that, unlike Mr Palmer, 'he is in the opposition' (vol. 1, ch. 20). This probably means that he is a traditional Whig, one of those landowning gentry who ruled for most of the eighteenth century but who, with the coming of the war, found themselves on the opposition benches, opposite, we may assume, members such as Mr Palmer, who supported the Prime Minister, Pitt. A criticism of the Whigs was that they were inclined to impulsive innovation. Such a one is Willoughby who declares he would 'instantly pull Combe down, and build it up again in the exact plan' of Barton Cottage, if he had the money (vol. 1, ch. 14).

The narrator gives Willoughby little to say, though one thing that does emerge is that he has had dealings with Colonel Brandon. His tone is aggressive enough for Elinor to ask why Willoughby dislikes him. The tone of his reply is at odds with what he has to say:

> I do not dislike him. I consider him, on the contrary, as a very respectable man, who has every body's good word and nobody's notice, who has more money than he can spend, more time than he knows how to employ, and two new coats every year. (vol. 1, ch. 10)

Although it makes sense that Willoughby should begrudge Colonel Brandon his money, something is odd here. The syntax of Willoughby's sentences is neatly, even elegantly, balanced, and yet what he is saying borders on bitterness. And the reasons he actually gives in no way account for the animus with which he speaks.

Given this, we should ask whether

it is probable that, when he seduced her, Willoughby knew exactly who Eliza Williams was. Can his strong language be put down to guilt at the wrong he has done Colonel Brandon?

Or to interpret it more darkly,

was the seduction of Eliza a way of getting at Colonel Brandon?

Colonel Brandon's conduct

Is it also possible that Colonel Brandon – like Marianne, a character of strong feelings – allowed personal factors to colour his behaviour with regard to Willoughby. On a mundane level it seems likely that envy induced his criticism of the hang of Willoughby's curricle! Far more seriously, the Colonel leaves for London on the morning of the proposed visit to Whitwell. The business is clearly urgent as he goes by 'post' – a form of public transport usually avoided by the gentry.

The narrator says that Willoughby's sentimental remarks concerning the cottage were delivered 'about a week after Colonel Brandon had left the country' (vol. 1, ch. 14). Willoughby leaves the following day, so we must assume that Mrs Smith was informed about his seduction and abandonment of Eliza Williams that very morning. This is Willoughby's account:

> Mrs Smith had somehow or other been informed, I imagine by some distant relation, whose interest it was to deprive me of her favour, of an affair, a connection.' (vol. 3, ch. 8)

The language is vague – 'some distant relation' – but Willoughby goes on to add: 'with heightened colour and an enquiring eye, – "your particular intimacy – you have probably heard the whole story long ago"'. Who else but Colonel Brandon could Willoughby think might have told the sordid story to Elinor?

So if he has worked out that the Colonel might have told Elinor, the vague talk about the 'distant relation' is a smokescreen. Does Willoughby see, as the reader who exercises sense might see, that it is Colonel Brandon who has informed Mrs Smith? (We *are* speculating here, however. See the Preface to this volume.)

It is difficult to think of its being anyone else. We know that Eliza confessed the name of her seducer to Colonel Brandon. We also know (vol. 2, ch. 4) that a journey to London took three days (possibly quicker in the case of a post). The narrator's 'about a week' (vol. 1, ch. 14) gives time for Colonel Brandon to go to London, persuade Eliza to divulge the name of her seducer and write to Mrs Smith.

The rest of what we know of the Willoughby/Brandon narrative also fits. Willoughby arrives in London, and 'within a fortnight' of the Colonel's departure the duel is fought (vol. 2, ch. 9).

If we use our own sense to uncover it rather than have it revealed to us, the ardour of Colonel Brandon, who shows himself quite Willoughby's equal in passion and dash, is more vivid and therefore more important in the plot. In particular, the buried narrative helps the reader to see Colonel Brandon more clearly. When we consider the characters of the two men who compete for Marianne, it becomes apparent that one is eventually revealed as a mere philanderer, whereas if Marianne likes romantic men, then she has certainly acquired one in her marriage to Colonel Brandon.

7 Engagement

7.1 Sensibility once more

'I considered the past.' (vol. 3, ch. 10)

A review

There is in the writing of *Sense and Sensibility* an understanding of human behaviour in the light of particular moral principles and particular features of thinking and feeling.

For some it is the least enjoyed and the least praised f Jane Austen's novels, perhaps because of its apparent desire to lead the reader to think in a very specific way about the conduct of human life.

The reader might feel that he or she is being got at.

It is, however, full of vigour and humour, and in subtle ways subverts itself, drawing attention to the contradictory nature of human behaviour. It hints at an anger and frustration with the female lot and even (against the judgement of the narrator?) a questioning of the absolute desirability of feminine restraint. It is in its ambiguities that much of its interest and fervour lie (see 8.12).

The plot importance of sensibility

The plot belongs to Marianne. If we do what she says she has done in the wake of her illness – consider her past – a romantic tale emerges.

Marianne dramatically meets the handsome stranger, is (apparently) courted ardently by him before being mysteriously abandoned by the same charismatic hunter and left in a state that Elinor sees as dangerously uncertain. The 'sensibility' plot presents the reader, as it does Elinor, with the problem of what Willoughby is up to.

Willoughby, again myseriously, proves to be inconstant. Marianne is publicly rejected in the sense that she is shown not to have any special place in his affections. The rejection is confirmed by the cold terms of his letter. Marianne suffers. The suffering, sustained throughout the middle sections of the novel, results in an illness which threatens her life.

The quiet Elinor

By contrast, Elinor's disappointment and suffering is something reserved for the reader alone. Because only we know of it, there can be no interesting incidents other than ones that ironically reflect on her state. The public life of the novel is concerned with Marianne, not the moral heroine who meditates over her grief in privacy and silence. It is important to the plot that Elinor's lover is for the most part kept firmly out of the way.

Marianne's creed

The cult of Sensibility proves as direful for Marianne as Gothic fiction proves for Catherine Morland. The result of her overt display is that her heart is open to everybody. She might be irritated by the knowing remarks of Sir John Middleton and Mrs Jennings, but given the way she has chosen to orchestrate her feelings, she can hardly complain if they hear her.

The restraints of sense

Elinor's suffering is passive rather than active, as is the operatic case of Marianne. (Were she in a Puccini opera, Marianne would be the star role.) Elinor can meet her family at the dinner table only two hours after receiving the devastating news of Edward's prior engagement without giving anything away.

7.2 Sense and sensibility together

'I have the highest opinion in the world of his goodness and sense. I think him every thing that is worthy and amiable.' (vol. 1, ch. 4)

Judging conduct

Elinor is talking about Edward's qualities. Of course, the reader later discovers that Edward has failed in the qualities Elinor praises, but perhaps the irony is that although he has not shown goodness in his treatment of Elinor or sense in his attachment to Lucy, Edward, nevertheless, is someone who is really both good and sensible as well as worthy and capable of arousing love. Another significance in what Elinor says emerges in the manner of her expression. She links the qualities with an important word.

The important word

It is not unusual in literature that significances are found not only in the big words such as 'honour' or 'love' but in those 'scaffolding' words that hold meaning together in sentences.

In *Sense and Sensibility* a very important word is 'and'.

The novel is not called *Sense or Sensibility,* nor does it have a sub-title such as *The Passions Restrained.* The novel is about both sense *and* sensibility.

The linking of 'sense' and 'sensibility' might not have puzzled Jane Austen's readers in quite the way it does readers who have learnt to think in the vocabulary of Romanticism. Romanticism tends to polarize the rational and the imaginative, because it is chiefly concerned with essentially emotional matters such as expression. In Jane Austen's day the two words could be used so as to bring out common features.

Dictionary definitions: sense

Both terms are interestingly poised between the mental and the moral. When we encounter them we no doubt decide that the book will be asking us to consider with tact and discrimination the feelings and actions of characters who display the qualities named in the title.

If we turn to Johnson's *Dictionary* (1755), we find that the two terms are not markedly different from each other. Johnson gives ten definitions of 'sense'. A number of these are very close to the meaning the word has in Locke (see 6.4). The fifth definition sounds as if it could have Elinor in mind: 'Understanding; soundness of faculties; strength of natural reason.' However, for the purposes of understanding the closeness of 'sense' and 'sensibility', it is the fourth definition which is the most interesting: 'Sensibility; quickness or keenness of perception.'

Dictionary definitions: sensibility

Johnson gives two definitions of 'sensibility': '1. Quickness of sensation. 2. Quickness of perception.' So, 'sense' is defined by 'sensibility', and 'sensibility' is defined in terms almost identical to those in which 'sense' is defined.

Quickness

The difference between the two terms appears to lie in the word 'quickness'. Johnson offers four definitions; the first, second and fourth are: '1. Speed; velocity; celerity. 2. Activity; briskness . . . 4. Sharpness; pungency.' The picture begins to form: 'quickness', the quality that specifically defines 'sensibility', is a mental movement that works with speed. In his third definition of 'quickness' we arrive at the point of our lexical departure: 'Keen sensibility'. The definition, significantly, is drawn from the writings of John Locke.

Thought and feeling

Sensibility, then, applies to thought as well as feelings. It is thinking (and seeing) which is conducted sharply, keenly and quickly. Can it not be said that when Elinor suspects that in the case of Colonel Brandon 'the misery of disappointed love had already been known by him' (vol. 1, ch. 11) she is exercising her sensibility in that she is being quick in her perception? And it *is* perception, not intuition. Jane Austen, of course, cannot be expected to use words in exactly the same way as Johnson, but readers should not expect her to be less subtle and supple. That she sees linkages should be evident from the 'and' of the title.

Title and writing

But if we accept the force of 'and', we have to recognize that something approaching the paradoxical is encountered if the terms of the title are set against the drift of some of the writing.

The tendency of the writing to invite the reader to see contrasts between Elinor and Marianne is at odds with the title with its implicit proposal that sense and sensibility can coexist.

No argument can quite abate the force of this problem. But a reader can ponder two lines of thought.

Different purposes

The first is that Jane Austen is doing different things at different times. Sometimes she wants to polarize and at other times she wants to suggest that the two qualities can be brought into a harmonious tension.

Dialectic

The second point is that though the novel does not quite work like a Hegelian dialectic of thesis, antithesis, synthesis, there is something approaching that. Thesis, antithesis is wrong, because sensibility is not the antithesis of sense, but the idea of a movement of thought that synthesizes two different ideas to produce a third is at work in the case of Marianne.

Marianne needs another term in her life – judgement – so she can use her sense to govern her sensibility.

7.3 The problem of presentation

'The next morning brought a farther trial of it, in a visit from their brother, who came with a most serious aspect to talk over the dreadful affair.' (vol. 3, ch. 1)

Talking

The above quotation presents the problem of presentation in *Sense and Sensibility*: many of the themes of *Sense and Sensibility* emerge through talk. It is a novel of ideas, and those ideas are very frequently present in the conversations.

The problem with talk

The obverse of this emphasis upon talk is that the reader might feel that Jane Austen has failed to find incidents which embody the novel's substance.

The reader finds the novel's central ideas discussed but do we witness events in which those ideas are given a concrete form?

Sense and Sensibility, so the criticism runs, is a notional rather than an enacted or embodied work.

The reader might feel dissatisfied because he or she might feel there are too many occasions when the narrator *tells* us the important things rather than *showing* us these things emerging in the fullness of their human actuality in action and incident.

It is not the purpose of this chapter to offer a full defence of the novel. Rather, it will make two points: one minor and the other an argument that will be pursued for the rest of this chapter.

More than merely stated

The minor point is that there are moments in *Sense and Sensibility* when we do feel that the ideas are more than merely stated.

Such a moment comes when Marianne falls ill after heedlessly exposing herself to the damp grass at Cleveland. Not only is the illness the natural outcome, and therefore the enactment, of her wilful neglect, but the severe fever is contracted while she has been picturing Willoughby, the cause of her susceptibility to illness, at his home 'not thirty miles' away (vol. 3, ch. 6).

A successful embodiment of a theme?

The second defence is that the issue of whether or not Marianne and Willoughby are engaged pervades the first half of the novel. It is certainly present in the debates between Elinor and her mother and the conversation Elinor attempts to have with the distressed Marianne. Yet it is not merely confined to talk.

The issue of engagement is related to incidents such as Willoughby's cutting off a lock of Marianne's hair, his driving her to Allenham and their correspondence. Perhaps these incidents are not fully worked out enough to convince us that the theme is really embodied. What can be said is that

the issue of engagement relates to many of the ideas the novel reveals about the workings of sense or sensibility.

7.4 Misery

'Tell her of my misery.' (vol. 3, ch. 8)

Trouble and anxiety

Sense and Sensibility is in many ways a dark novel.

The tone of *Sense and Sensibility* is often subdued and troubled, and the characters are anxious, uncertain and preoccupied.

In the first volume Edward is troubled. Mrs Dashwood, Marianne and Fanny are aware of Edward's feelings for Elinor, yet Elinor is conscious that all is far from well with him:

> There was, at times, a want of spirits about him which, if it did not denote indifference, spoke a something almost as unpromising. (vol. 1, ch. 4)

Edward is enigmatic; that 'something', so potently imprecise, indicates a sympton requiring an explanatory cause.

Marianne' s misery

In the second and third volumes, it is Marianne who is afflicted by a misery, which, she makes clear, is intolerable.

The vocabulary of unhappiness is intense in the tone and the frequency of its use.

In the middle of the book – from volume 2, chapter 7 onwards – there is writing that, in its emotional weight, is more burdened than any other passages in Jane Austen.

At one point Marianne leaves the room with 'an hasty exclamation of misery' (vol. 2, ch. 8). In the same chapter, Elinor says: 'her sufferings have been very severe'. She adds that 'it is a most cruel affliction'. In the following chapter, Marianne wakes 'to the same consciousness of misery' that was hers before she slept. She turns on the well-meaning Mrs Jennings with 'tears which streamed from her eyes with passionate violence'. At this stage in the novel, as Hermione Lee has remarked, 'tears are her text' (Melvyn Bragg, *In Our Time – Sensibility.* Discussion with John Mullan, Hermione Lee, Claire Tomalin, Radio 4, 3 January 2002. We are indebted to this discussion for amplifying some of our ideas on sensibility). When Marianne reads a letter from her mother, which speaks confidently of a happy outcome: 'she wept with agony through the whole of it'. Marianne wants to return home: 'she was wildly urgent to be gone'. The first paragraph of the tenth chapter shows Marianne more in control, but, in Elinor's eyes, no 'less wretched', her mind being 'settled in a gloomy dejection'. It gives Elinor pain to see Marianne 'brooding over her sorrows in silence'.

Marianne's scream

Chapter 7 of the second volume deals with Marianne's state immediately after Willoughby's 'rejection'. Elinor, aroused by Marianne's 'agitation and sobs', watches her 'with silent anxiety'. Marianne maintains a 'sort of desperate calmness' till 'a return of the same excessive affliction'. She stops Elinor from speaking 'with all the eagerness of the most nervous irritability'.

It is not only Marianne who suffers. When Marianne receives a letter, Elinor, who sees it must come from Willoughby, 'felt immediately such a sickness at heart as made her hardly able to hold up her head'. Elinor, entering their room, sees her sister stretched on the bed, 'almost choaked by grief'. Perhaps we are too familiar with the idiom 'choked by grief'; nevertheless, we should not overlook the physical power of the image. It prepares us for what is to come. Those choked by grief cannot speak so have only the language of cries left to them. Those choked by grief cannot eat either.

Elinor sits beside her, kisses her hand 'and then gave way to a burst of tears, which at first was scarcely less violent than Marianne's'. The pain of affliction cannot be confined to the one who first feels it. For a while Marianne is unable to speak; she puts the letters into Elinor's hand 'and then covering her face with her handkerchief, almost screamed with agony'. (Note that, despite her acute sensibility, Marianne's scream *is* muffled.) Because 'she knew that such grief, shocking as it was to witness, must have its course', Elinor 'watched by her till the excess of suffering had somewhat spent itself'.

This passage shows Elinor aware of the quasi-independent life of feelings and aware, too, that they must be allowed to take their course before they abate. One critic, Tony Tanner (*Jane Austen,* Macmillan, 1986, pp. 85–8), plays on the near pun of 'scream' and 'screen', finding in Elinor's making of screens (decorated guards intended to shield faces from the heat of fires) a symbol of the way the restraint of feelings protects the self from the tumult of wild emotions. (It could also be claimed that it is a symbol of Elinor's determination to shield her sister.)

A screen also conceals feelings from the controlling pressures of society. This is not to say that feelings are private but that the one who cannot screen feelings is in danger of becoming a public spectacle. It is significant that though it is morally worthy, Marianne's outburst against Mrs. Ferrars' calculated rudeness comes in the scene in which Elinor's screens are being discussed (vol. 2, ch. 12).

Marianne's scream is the cry of a victim. She is a victim in at least two senses.

She has been abandoned by Willoughby for, apparently, no reason. Her cry is an appropriate protest against the inexplicable nature of Willoughby's conduct. Were

Marianne to reflect on her state, she might conclude that those things that cannot be explained cannot be talked about, so a scream is a fitting way of venting her feelings. It would be typical of Marianne at this point to believe that no other form of expression was valid.

The second sense in which she is a victim is that she has put herself in this position. She has lived a life in which the public restraint of feelings has had no part. Consequently, the easiest course is to howl. She has also put herself in this position in another sense. She has allowed herself to become attached to a man without the protection of a formal engagement.

Explanation

The narrative enticement of the novel works by inviting the reader to seek explanations for the way characters behave. The reader has to remember that Marianne's behaviour does need explaining.

Because it is not known on what basis the attachment between Marianne and Willoughby rests, Elinor has no way of coming to terms with the distress of her sister.

The need for explanation again points to the issue of engagement. Are Willoughby's actions those of a man who is renouncing an engagement or, as it turns out, a man who is careless of whom he hurts?

Much the same can be said of Edward. Both Edward's low spirits and Marianne's distress invite the reader to seek explanations.

After varying degrees of narrative expectation, explanations are supplied. The production of explanations is a confirmation of the need for reasoning.

The fact that puzzles can be solved is an indication of the kind of world the novel creates:

the movement of the plot shows that the world of the novel is a rational one in which all puzzles can be satisfactorily explained through the exercise of sense.

The desire for an explanation is felt by both the characters and the reader. In particular it is felt by Elinor, who wants to understand the nature of Marianne's terrible distress and the low spirits of Edward.

7.5 The private and the public

'"Engagement!" cried Marianne, "there has been no engagement."' (vol. 2, ch. 7)

Secrecy

It is important to see that the world of *Sense and Sensibility* is one in which causality operates. This leads to the insight that the pervasive misery of the first half of the book has its origin in the nature of the understandings Marianne and Edward have come to with those to whom they are (or were) attached.

The misery both Marianne and Edward experience is caused by, in the first case, an unformulated and in the second an incompletely formulated romantic association.

To put it simply, both

Marianne and Edward lack the protection of a regularized engagement. The social institution of the engagement embodies, and in embodying corrects, what is wrong with sensibility's wilful assertion of the self.

The plot works to show that

the explanation of Marianne and Edward's misery is to be understood in terms of their respective failures to sanction their attachments in the public ritual of engagement.

Their misery stems from their inability to understand that a public engagement protects all those mutual and private feelings that make an overt understanding desirable. This point requires further exploration.

7.6 Engagement and romantic individualism

'I felt myself,' she added, 'to be as solemnly engaged to him, as if the strictest legal covenant had bound us to each other.' (vol. 2, ch. 7)

Sense and Sensibility is about learning the difference between *feeling* oneself engaged and having, if not a strict legal covenant, a publicly sanctioned *recognition* that the state of engagement exists.

Irregular engagements

The secret engagement of Edward and Lucy and the enigmatic nature of the attachment between Marianne and Willoughby raises the issue of what is public and what private. The novel suggests that it is not enough for people to feel they are engaged. Such feelings require the expression and the protection of a formal, open understanding. The narrator's cognisance of the public and the private entails a critique of Romantic individualism.

Rules of engagement

Elinor has to recognize that as Edward and Lucy correspond, they must be engaged: 'a correspondence between them by letter, could subsist only under a positive engagement' (vol. 1, ch. 22).

Her thinking is in accordance with contemporary social etiquette, which decreed that unmarried young women and men could only write to each other if they were formally engaged. R. W. Chapman states this stipulation with force and finality: 'An inflexible law forbade correspondence between marriageable persons not engaged to be married' ('The Manners of the Age', in the Oxford edition of *Emma,* 1923, p. 512). In *Northanger Abbey* it is a (daring) sign of her parents' liberality that Catherine Morland's correspondence between their daughter and Henry Tilney is discreetly overlooked, because they know that, though permission has been withheld by General Tilney, Henry has proposed to and been accepted by Catherine.

The rule about correspondence might seem quaint, unnecessary and irksome but it had this advantage:

it created and preserved a distinction between the public and the private.

One of the most irritating, and even distressing, aspects of Sir John and Mrs Jennings's banter is that they fail to observe the public/private distinction. Hence, the tiresome joke of 'F' being 'the wittiest letter in the alphabet' (vol. 1, ch. 21). Implicit in Jane Austen's presentation of their boorish manners is the vital point that if either of the Dashwood girls were known to be engaged, they would have been spared embarrassment.

The public declaration of an engagement creates for the contracting couple a private space that it would be improper for others to transgress.

In this there lies the critique of Romantic individualism.

Those who want to create a space for the free expression of emotion should recognize that this is best done by the enactment of a publicly confirmed institution.

Those who do without this institution lay themselves open to curiosity and impertinence.

The ambiguities of secrecy

An engagement is public, so a private agreement does not provide a sufficiently protecting framework.

Edward suffers, because although there is no doubt that he and Lucy have entered into an engagement, the attachment is purely private, so he is forced to live a double life of pretending he is not engaged.

As a consequence, he behaves in a regrettably ambiguous way to Elinor. She knows that he loves her, and others can also see this, but he cannot make a declaration or even play the coded game of hints. And because the engagement is secret, he can be honest with neither Lucy nor Elinor. This accounts for his misery.

The perils of no engagement

Marianne and Willoughby are vulnerable in a different way. They are not engaged but behave as if they are. Their neglect of social conventions, a characteristic of the cult of sensibility, proves to be damaging. Because no one knows how things stand between them, they become the subject of gossip, particularly in the gossip-hungry streets and assembly rooms of London. Colonel Brandon reports that Marianne's 'engagement to Mr. Willoughby is very generally known' (vol. 2, ch. 5). This can do Marianne no good; a woman's reputation can easily be harmed if she is thought to behave as if she is engaged when she is not.

Marianne is also vulnerable in relation to Willoughby. She defends him by saying that he has 'broken no faith with me' but has to admit that she can say this because he 'never absolutely' said that he loved her: 'It was every day implied, but never professedly declared' (vol. 2, ch. 7). Marianne is not fully aware that the words she utters mean that she can assume nothing about Willoughby's feelings.

'Declared' is a particularly sensitive word; a proposal of marriage is often spoken of as a declaration, and a declaration, if accepted, is necessary for an engagement. If Willoughby's love was never 'professedly declared', Marianne should have concluded that it did not exist.

In danger of seduction

To pay attention to a woman with loving words and actions (the lock of hair, the offer of the horse) but stop short of a declaration can be the action of a seducer.

The parallel between Eliza Williams and Marianne consists in their both being preyed upon by a seducer. Both girls are robbed: Willoughby takes Eliza's virginity, and Marianne yields to him her independent spirit.

His language of explanation contains a horrible irony. He openly admits to Elinor that he 'was trying to engage her regard, without a thought of returning it' (vol. 3, ch. 8). He has no intention of engaging her as a future marriage partner.

The effect is that

Marianne does not know how she is placed; she has all the comforts and stimulations of a lover's talk but nothing of the locating security of an engagement.

The narrator plays with the word 'engagement' with relish where both Edward and Willoughby are concerned. When Mrs Dashwood invites Willoughby to stay at Barton in the future:

> 'My engagements at present,' replied Willoughby, confusedly, 'are of such a nature – that – I dare not flatter myself –' (vol. 1, ch. 15)

Since Willoughby has to cope with problems arising from the woman he *should* now engage himself to – Eliza – and leave the woman that he has appeared to be and now *wants* to be engaged to – Marianne – in order to engage himself to another – Sophia – so he might extricate himself from his financial and emotional mess, it is small wonder he is confused!

Incomprehensible behaviour

Where Marianne and Willoughby's secrecy is concerned, Elinor, the reasoner, has good grounds for doubt, because their behaviour does not make sense. No more do Edward's moods.

The neglect of the social institution of engagement subjects behaviour to the threat of incoherence.

7.7 The life of the self

'a natural ardour of mind' (vol. 1, ch. 10)

The case for engagement

The case that is built up through the writing about engagement is that

those things which we value in human life are secured more firmly if we adhere to the traditional institutions of our society.

The case works by offering to travel a long way with the Romantic individualist.

The Romantic encourages sensitivity, appreciates art, delights in nature, respects the happily not always predictable swelling and subsiding of human feeling, knows that it is good to feel strongly about what matters and seeks to nourish the inner life of the sensibility. It is a list many would wish to sign up to.

The one who speaks for sense (another word might be order) also wants to affirm those things. The difference between the Romantic individualist and the one who speaks for sense is not one of values but what might be called tactics.

The Romantic believes that expression and a disregard of convention will release us into the possession of those qualities, whereas sense insists that these things are only really attainable through restraint and adherence to convention.

Paradoxically, the glamorous qualities – imagination, spontaneity, rapture – depend for their existence upon the mundane ones such as discipline, attention and practice.

Getting feelings wrong

The consistent view of the novel is that

those who follow the cult of sensibility actually have a crude and simple view of the very things they value.

When feelings are paraded they are coarsened, because in making them overtly public, subtlety and nuance is lost. An unrestrained sensibility actually narrows the range of feelings, because it only counts as legitimate those that can be given a *dramatic* expression. There is more to art than 'that rapturous delight' (vol.1, ch. 4), which is aroused in Marianne. Some art has an 'Impenetrable calmness'. (vol. 1, ch. 3)

7.8 Inwardness

'serious reflection' (vol. 2, ch. 1)

Reflecting

Sense and Sensibility affirms something that sometimes it appears to be denying.

In spite of its explicit, even trenchant, criticism, of the excesses of the expressive, Romantic sensibility, *Sense and Sensibility* is a very 'inward' novel; it values reflection and the efforts we make both to understand our own feelings and imaginatively share those of others.

The first chapter of the second volume shows the emotionally devastated Elinor striving to come to terms with the news of Edward's clandestine engagement to Lucy. The writing is characteristic of Jane Austen in that it is formally written in the third person but reads with the directness of a first-person narration. The pithy summary is that 'if her case were pitiable, his was hopeless'. 'Hopeless' must be given its full weight; Elinor feels for Edward, who cannot expect that his unhappy state will ever change.

Narrator and reader

What Elinor, and, of course, the reader, imaginatively feels is the weight of the emotional burden Edward has been carrying. Through Elinor's insight into his misery, the reader may look back to all those passages, particularly his visit to Barton after seeing Lucy, and sympathetically share the strain and distress of his divided state. We might do something similar in the case of Colonel Brandon when we learn of his anguish over Eliza and the parallel between her and Marianne that is so uncomfortably clear to him (vol. 2, ch. 9).

The narrator does not, with the exception of Mrs Jennings in volume 3, chapter 3, choose to give us direct access to the undisclosed thoughts and feelings of any character other than Elinor. Her feelings, and, through her, the feelings of others, are brought strikingly home to the reader.

Therefore the considerable weight of the novel's inwardness is mediated through a character whose chief function in the plot is to temper undisciplined subjectivity.

Concealing feelings

Inwardness then is not a contradiction of the public nature of feelings.

The fact that the reader can understand what Elinor is feeling shows that the language of feeling – for instance, resentment and indignation – is public.

Elinor knows that the expression of feeling comes all too easily to those who are distressed; hence the 'necessity of concealment' is spoken of in the language of military discipline – she has to 'command herself' and 'guard every suspicion of the truth' from her family (vol. 2, ch. 1).

Undetected feelings

When tested, Elinor can control her feelings in public. The passage in which she first appears before her family after the devastation of Lucy's disclosure is very important in the novel's presentation of the life of feelings:

> And so well was she able to answer her own expectations, that when she joined them at dinner only two hours after she had first suffered the extinction of all her dearest hopes, no one would have supposed from the appearance of the sisters, that Elinor was mourning in secret over obstacles which must divide her for ever from the object of her love, and that Marianne was internally dwelling on the perfections of a man, of whose whole heart she felt thoroughly possessed and who she expected to see in every carriage which drove near their house. (vol. 2, ch. 1)

This is a very surprising passage; no one would have discerned either the desolation of Elinor or Marianne's expectations. The narrator is intimating that it is very difficult for anyone to know what is going on in another human heart.

Surprising as it seems, given its emphasis on the public, what emerges in *Sense and Sensibility* is a sense of the particularity and the inscrutability of personal experience.

Italics

In *Sense and Sensibility* the formal signifier of the particularity of personal experience is italics. In volume 3, chapter 9 Elinor, the last character Willoughby 'seduces', can think of him only as 'poor Willoughby' and for an unrestrained moment 'wished Willoughby a widower'. Then she remembers Colonel Brandon:

> Then, remembering Colonel Brandon, reproved herself, felt that to *his* sufferings and *his* constancy far more than to his rival's, the reward of her sister's love was due, and wished anything rather than Mrs Willoughby's death. (vol. 3, ch. 9)

The italicized *his* does more than distinguish the Colonel from Willoughby, the character with whom he is so often paralleled. It invites the reader to do what Elinor does – think of the *particular* nature of the suffering he has undergone and the quality of his constant devotion to Marianne.

The reader must perceive sensitively. Remembering the anguish of Colonel Brandon's narration to Elinor (vol. 2, ch. 9), we have to picture for ourselves the way his knowledge of Eliza's fate must have made him fear for Marianne. This picturing is similar to the way we have to use our sense to deduce chains of events not dealt with explicitly in the novel. In both cases, it is Elinor who is the model for how this should be done. She is the model of sense and sensibility. Working out links is what sense does and feeling our way into a character's experience requires the keenness of perception which is called sensibility.

The mystery of experience

One of the deepest preoccupations in *Sense and Sensibility* is with the unique mystery of individual experience.

The novel prompts the question whether we can ever appreciate the grain, the texture of another's inner life.

After Edward's proposal, the narrator writes of the feelings of the two sisters:

> Marianne could speak *her* happiness only by tears. Comparisons would occur – regrets would arise – and her joy, though sincere as her love for her sister, was of a kind to give her neither spirits nor language. But Elinor – How are *her* feelings to be described? – From the moment of learning that Lucy was married to another, that Edward was free, to the moment of his justifying the hopes which had so instantly followed, she was everything by turns but tranquil. (vol. 3, ch. 13)

The indescribable character of Marianne's feelings is evident in her expressing herself not in words but tears. Tears are no doubt more accurate, since nothing in the experience allows her an appropriate language. The rhetorical question about how Elinor's feelings are to be described remains unanswered; the closest the writing gets is the negative 'anything but tranquil', but that cannot function as an exact description. The inner experience of both sisters is not something that can be conveyed with any precision.

The remarkable achievement of *Sense and Sensibility* is that it preserves the mystery of the inner world from the dual dangers of conventional expression and rigid formula. Sensibility understood as the keen, inner edge of experience rather than effusive self-declaration is safeguarded in *Sense and Sensibility.*

8 Geography

8.1 Inner space

'She was stronger alone.' (vol. 2, ch. 1)

Space, sense and sensibility

The restraint and reserve practised by Elinor may be said to preserve inner space – that region in which experiences can be reflected on and feelings understood, judged and enjoyed.

Those who wish to obliterate the distinction between private and public endanger the very things they want to celebrate – the pleasurable variety and individuality of human feelings.

To re-work the words of the title:

sense preserves sensibility.

Inner and outer space

At some important moments in the novel

the exploration of inner space is made possible by an outer space that allows for quiet reflection.

When Elinor reflects that she is 'stronger alone', she is specifically thinking about secrecy, yet in order to come to this resolution she needs to be on her own. The private space of the cottage, though confined, allows her to be '*at liberty* to think and be wretched' (vol. 1, ch. 22; our italics).

8.2 Space and feeling

'but requiring at once solitude and continual change of place' (vol. 2, ch. 7)

The location of feelings

In *Sense and Sensibility*

the characters' relationship with space is expressive of their emotions.

Strong feelings are often evoked by the positioning of characters within domestic spaces. When in London Marianne is expecting Willoughby to call, she walks 'backwards and forwards across the room' (vol. 2, ch.4). The confinement of feelings that cry out for expression is enacted in her restless walking, and through the poignancy of her crouching by the drawing-room fireside the reader sees how much she needs a greater consolation than ever a fire can provide.

After Willoughby publicly snubs Marianne, she kneels 'against one of the window-seats' to write and, upon receiving his reply, is found by Elinor 'stretched on the bed, almost choaked by grief' (vol. 2, ch.7). Her postures on both occasions are significant: the position she takes up for writing is a kind of supplication, and her prostration is an emblem of abandonment.

In spite of these postures being essentially conventional, they are given the uncomfortable acuteness of emotional vulnerability by being located in a room where, normally, the sisters enjoy the hospitality but not the security of a home.

Spaces and plot

There is also a link between the use of space and plot. Marianne's wilful reclusiveness – '[she] had never left the house since the blow first fell' (vol. 2, ch. 10) – anticipates a later location of the plot – the confines of the sick chamber at Cleveland. Her self-neglect entails a neglect of the social world, so the deterioration in her health is accompanied by a withdrawal from society that is complete in the isolation of the Cleveland bedroom.

8.3 London spaces

'The house was handsome and handsomely fitted up.' (vol. 2, ch. 4)

Houses

Sense and Sensibility locates events in a number of houses: Norland, Barton cottage, Berkeley Street and Cleveland. In addition, there are important scenes in Barton Park, Gray's, the jewellers in Sackville Street and Harley Street, where Mr and Mrs John Dashwood 'had taken a very good house for three months' (vol. 2, ch. 12). We also hear of Allenham and Delaford, and Marianne yearningly travels in her imagination to Combe Magna.

Much of the narrative is located in London.

Berkeley Street

Over a third of the novel takes place during the Dashwood sisters' residence in London at Berkeley Street, the home of Mrs Jennings. Moreover, this substantial episode lies at the heart of the novel: Berkeley Street is the location in which the effects of rejection are played out; important plot concealments and dislosures occur there; in its rooms emotional gulfs between characters are opened up; and the shouldering by Elinor of painful responsibilities, such as telling Edward of Colonel Brandon's offer of the Delaford living, is acted out within its walls.

It is more than sequentially related to the Cleveland episode: both houses are Jennings/Palmer residences, and the illness which breaks upon Marianne in Cleveland has its origin in London. Furthermore, both Berkeley Street and Cleveland are the locations of those unexpected entries that are such a feature of *Sense and Sensibility.*

Formally speaking, the Berkeley Street/Cleveland sections are enclosed by the

Dashwoods' residence at Barton. If we add to that an opening section at Norland and, beyond the last page, residence at Delaford for both the sisters, there is in the novel a residential/locational pattern, which, if not exactly symmetrical, is almost classical in shape (see 1. 2). It is the kind of literary architecture we would expect from a novel that ponders deeply on the government of feeling. Sense requires the orderliness of classical architecture (see 3.11).

The unfamiliar, perhaps even alien, environment of London makes this the darkest part of the novel for the sensitive Dashwood sisters. The anguish is more sustained than in any other Jane Austen novel. When Marianne, out of her mind at Cleveland, begs that her mother should not go round by London, she demonstrates the black nightmare that the place has become for her, emblematic of death of hope, death of love and a despair that could lead to her own (self-induced) death.

Sense and Sensibility anticipates the severe criticism of London life that is made in *Mansfield Park*. London is associated with triviality. John Dashwood's decline into unfeeling snobbishness should be read as a comment upon the superficial materialism of the city.

London and privacy

Berkeley Street is free from many of London's faults but it does show that

London life is in danger of blurring the vital distinction between the private and the public.

Berkeley Street is so like a busy thoroughfare that privacy becomes difficult. There is more privacy in the narrow confines of Barton cottage than in the handsome home in Berkeley Street.

Private psychic space is invaded within the house. Mrs Jennings means well, but Marianne finds her 'indulgent fondness' oppressive and leaves the room with 'an hasty exclamation of Misery' (vol. 2, ch. 8).

Visitors

A regular caller is Colonel Brandon. His love provokes a public solicitude which does not accord with the tumult of Marianne's state. The reader feels sorry for Colonel Brandon but can understand the frustration of Marianne's exasperated remark – 'We are never safe from *him*' (vol. 2, ch. 9). In a house where characters are wanting to accommodate themselves to loss, any intruders are a violation, as the Henry Dashwoods were at Norland.

8.4 Country residences

'It is but a cottage.' (vol. 1, ch. 5)

Barton Cottage

Barton Cottage in no way matches the splendours of Norland: 'In comparison . . . it was small and poor indeed!' (vol. 1, ch. 6). The words 'small and poor' are carefully chosen.

Like many physical descriptions in Jane Austen, the words resonate beyond the point of their immediate application.

The language used of Barton Cottage becomes an expression of the status and situation of the Dashwood women.

Dispossession

We are directed to the comparison with Norland in order to bring out a feature that is a blend of event, location and theme:

the novel is concerned with the insecurity brought about by dispossession. For an author who values stability and tradition, being dispossessed and turned away is fearful and troubling.

The particular discomfort of the Dashwood women is that the very institution which should protect them from insecurity – the family – is the cause of their homelessness. (We should remember that dispossession is not always a grave matter; the account of the discovery of the engagement between Lucy and Edmund has John Dashwood on his knees, pleading with the hysterical Fanny not to eject the Steele sisters immediately. Compare this burlesque account with the ejection of Catherine Morland from Northanger Abbey.)

Preserving family esteem

Mrs Dashwood's initial reaction to Barton Cottage is to talk of extensions. This shows her need to brace her own and her family's esteem.

8.5 Dream homes

'I advise every body who is going to build, to build a cottage.' (vol. 2, ch. 14)

Picturesque cottages

The spatial confinement of Barton Cottage should be recalled when Robert Ferrars airily discourses on the pleasures of cottage life (vol. 2, ch. 14)

Robert Ferrars is fashionable. A feature of contemporary taste was the cult of rusticity that had as its architectural expression the picturesque cottage. Such cottages were designed by architects such as T.F. Dearne and Robert Lugar, and landscape artists such Robert Hill, Samuel Prout and John Varley painted them. John Nash, one of the leading architects of the day, built a little village of highly fanciful cottages round a green at Blaise Castle. Robert Ferrars's pleasure in cottages was no doubt also due to the considerable body of writing about them: a representative writer being James Malton, whose *An Essay on British Cottage Architecture* was published in 1798. Writers valued small windows, overhanging eaves and rustic colonnades.

A real cottage

Robert Ferrars talks easily about an ideal rural retreat. But Barton Cottage is neither a retreat nor a whim; the Dashwoods have to live there. Nor is Barton Cottage picturesque:

> as a cottage it was defective, for the building was regular, the roof was tiled, the window shutters were not painted green, nor were the walls covered with honeysuckle. (vol. 1, ch. 6)

Jane Austen is directing her readers to recognize that Barton is not in the manner of the dream cottage.

It might not accord with Romantic taste but it is a place in which romance blossoms. It is where Willoughby and Marianne sing their songs and discuss books. Significantly, it is Willoughby who does not live there who is eloquent about its delights. He plays the part of the man of sensibility on learning of Mrs Dashwood's plans for improvement. A feature of sensibility is that subjective responses determine judgement. Subjectivity (selfishness?) is evident when he says: 'Not a stone must be added to its walls, not an inch to its size, *if my feelings are regarded*' (italics added).

Robert Ferrars and Willoughby have this in common:

their presuppositions and subjective responses prevent them from seeing houses as spaces in which other people have to live.

Emotion and Barton

The Dashwoods, in particular Elinor, adapt to the cottage. Within its confined spaces she manages to conduct both a public and a private life.

After Tom's account of meeting Lucy, the Dashwood women believe that Edward is now married. On Edward's surprise arrival, embarrassing misunderstandings continue, until Edward clearly informs them that Lucy is now Mrs Robert Ferrars. Elinor's reaction shows her awareness that the inner space of strong feeling should be matched by outer spatial privacy:

> Elinor could sit it no longer. She almost ran out of the room, and as soon as the door was closed, burst into tears of joy, which at first she thought would never cease. (vol. 3, ch. 12)

Her precipitant departure reminds us of Marianne's – its impetus is acute sensibility. Yet Elinor is so schooled in public constraint that she does not give way to a torrent of joyful tears until 'the door was closed'. She shows the proper adjustment of overwhelming feeling to private space. For all its charms, Emma Thompson's film gets this scene entirely wrong; Elinor would never weep in public.

8.6 Cleveland

'Marianne entered the house with an heart swelling with emotion from the consciousness of being only eighty miles from Barton, and not thirty miles from Combe Magna.' (vol. 3, ch. 6)

The geography of feeling

Marianne's arrival at Cleveland shows how in *Sense and Sensibility* physical space is the site for emotional response.

Cleveland in itself is not an evocative building. What matters to Marianne is its contours in her emotional geography. Those places that are closest to her heart are, relatively speaking, short distances away.

Marianne's longing for Willoughby is associated with the collapse of her health. Perhaps the severe discomforts of being ill in alien places show that emotionally, as well as spatially, Marianne has yet to find her true home. For Marianne, Cleveland is a place of hopeless longing.

Sickness at Cleveland

The writing about Marianne's illness concentrates on two features: the care of those nursing her – Marianne is at last prepared to acknowledge : 'the unceasing kindness of Mrs Jennings' (vol. 3, ch. 10) – and the wandering of her mind.

It is difficult not to understand the latter as a judgement: those who, in the voicing of feelings, want to transgress the customary boundaries of expression are likely to suffer the consequences of such dangerous exploration. Furthermore, the desire to give full vent to feelings ends in the pathos of garbled cries rather than a clear sense of what one is undergoing. Jane Austen avoids the operatic thrills of a 'mad scene' by making Marianne's derangement occur within the private space of a Cleveland bedroom.

The lessons of the sickroom

The sickroom becomes a place of learning. The full effect of this is seen later in Marianne's 'confession'. The sickroom is the scene of moral awakening:

> 'My illness has made me think – It has given me leisure and calmness for serious reflection. Long before I was enough recovered to talk, I was perfectly able to reflect. I considered the past; I saw in my own behaviour since the beginning of our acquaintance with him last autumn, nothing but a series of imprudence towards myself, and want of kindness to others.' (vol. 3, ch. 10)

The gusto with which she speaks is pleasingly characteristic of the 'old' Marianne, but the vocabulary indicates change in judgement. Thinking is now central. Her tone is composed. Marianne sees clearly the nature of her own behaviour. *Sense and Sensibility* provides a specific space for Marianne's realization of her misguided past conduct. She who has misjudged the relationship between the public and the private is forcefully confined by her illness in a place where she can come to terms with the significance of what has happened to her.

8.7 Norland

'Dear, dear Norland!' (vol. 1, ch. 5)

Nor land

Sense and Sensibility opens with two contrary pictures of life in a large country house:

we hear of the secure traditions of a long-established estate and the instability of the family, who, in addition to the disorientation of bereavement, are in danger of losing their home.

The threat to their way of life is enacted in a grim pun:

the Dashwood women will have neither house nor land.

An English estate

The opening paragraph of the novel gives a strong sense of its significance. Norland has an enduring Englishness: 'The family of Dashwood had been long settled in Sussex. Their estate was large, and their residence was at Norland Park, in the centre of their property'.

The family's long settlement and the size of the estate signal peace, security and England's placid greatness. Being 'in the centre' is a traditional image of value; the welfare of the Norland estate depends upon the probity, responsibility and integrity of the Dashwoods. The above passage goes on to tell us that 'for many generations, they had lived in so respectable a manner, as to engage the good opinion of their surrounding acquaintance'.

Already the novel is advertising its themes; the word 'engage' anticipates the importance of emotional attachments being given a formal and public sanction (see 7.6). The 'lesson' of *Sense and Sensibility* is given at the very start: we need the protection of public institutions (in this case, the law) if the sensibilities of our tender, inner world are to thrive.

Settled

Yet one word – 'settled' – indicates that the family is endangered. There is irony here: the Dashwood women are not settled at all.

The word 'settled' also has as one of its meanings the legal and financial arrangements made by a man for his widow. Henry Dashwood's uncle's will, drawn up under the influence of excessive sensibility induced by a nauseating child, is such as to make it impossible for Henry to make a proper settlement for his widow.

8.8 The management of the estate

'Other great and inevitable expenses too we have had on first coming to Norland.' (vol. 2, ch. 11)

Enclosure

The family name of Dashwood may continue but under the new régime the neighbourhood and the estate suffer.

In volume 2, chapter 11 John Dashwood reveals to Elinor why his income is not as large as is commonly supposed:

> The enclosure of Norland Common, now carrying on, is a most serious drain. And then I have made a little purchase within this half year; East Kingham Farm, you must remember the place, where old Gibson used to live. The land was so very desirable for me in every respect, so immediately adjoining my own property, that I felt it my duty to buy it.

Enclosure was a means whereby land that was once unfenced and open could be subdivided into individual fields with hedges, dividing off each parcel of land. The enclosure of common land required a parliamentary Act. Thousands of such Acts were passed in the latter half of the eighteenth and the first decades of the ninteenth centuries. Whole tracts of land that were once held in common – the common lands of England – were acquired by the rich.

We can imagine that this is what happened in the case of Norland Common: a single individual, John Dashwood, buys land that was once the common possession of all. The narrator gives enough detail for us to imagine how the loss of Norland Common affected the rural poor.

East Kingham Farm

The fate of East Kingham Farm might parallel the main plot of the novel. We do not know what has happened to 'old Gibson' except that he is no longer the 'King' of his 'ham' (an Anglo-Saxon word meaning settlement). Perhaps, like the Dashwood women, he has been reduced to being a tenant. As with the main plot, the story of 'old Gibson' is one of dispossession.

Changes at Norland

John Dashwood has no sensibility and thus little regard for those features of the landscape that have gradually emerged over the years. In order that Fanny should have her greenhouse, gone are 'the old walnut trees' and 'the old thorns' (vol. 2, ch. 11) and with them, we may assume, all the pleasures of tangle and picturesque untidiness.

8.9 Allenham

'they had gone to Allenham' (vol. 1, ch. 13)

A compensation for Norland?

Having lost Norland, we can imagine that Marianne, who had plangently bidden farewell to its subtle beauties, might see the prospect of Allenham as a compensation for her deprivation.

Allenham – the dream house

Allenham has something of the dream house about it – a desirable residence that, at the time of her visit, she has some hope of occupying. The prospect is surely that of her own hoped-for marriage as well as 'a view of the church and village, and, beyond them, of those fine bold hills' (vol. 1, ch. 13).

Furniture

Yet Marianne's attitude to the furniture shows how dangerously near she can come to the mental world of John and Fanny Dashwood. She describes the furniture as 'forlorn' and thoughtlessly says that it could be 'newly fitted up – [for] a couple of hundred pounds'. That sum is a tenth of what she, in a later conversation (vol. 1, ch. 17), regards as her 'competence'. It demonstrates the untrustworthy nature of sensibility that Marianne, who wants nothing if she can have love, plans on spending a lot on just one room, whereas Willoughby, who waives love for money, says he would settle for living in a cottage.

8.10 Delaford

'Delaford is a nice place.' (vol. 2, ch. 8)

Patterns in the plot

Sense and Sensibility opens at Norland and closes with Elinor and Marianne living on another estate – Delaford.

Those who like patterns in plots might discern an almost religious shape in the loss of Norland and the eventual happy ending of settlement in a new Eden – paradise lost and paradise regained.

A picture of Delaford

Mrs Jennings evokes the charms of Delaford at the point when Marianne is devastated by Willoughby's rejection.

> Delaford is a nice place; exactly what I call a nice old-fashioned place, full of comforts and conveniences; quite shut in with great garden walls that are covered with the best fruit trees: and such a mulberry tree in one corner. Lord! How Charlotte and I did stuff the only time we were there! Then, there is a dove-cote, some delightful stew ponds, and a very pretty canal' (vol. 2, ch. 8)

It is easy to imagine Marianne liking this enclosed, fruitful and old-fashioned plot. The stewponds may go back to the middle ages. Nature and art blend well; the grounds are cultivated but, on the strength of 'old-fashioned', it seems unlikely that the gardens are laid out merely to satisfy whims or provide views.

The implicit contrast is with Norland under John and Fanny Dashwood. Nothing at Delaford suggests that work on the estate disrupts the life of the surrounding countryside or is detrimental to the feeling of history that the estate exudes. 'Old-fashioned' has a quite precise meaning when applied to country estates; it means unimproved. That is to say, it has escaped the efforts of landscape gardeners to impose a smoothness upon the grounds (see 12.9 and 13.4).

8.11 Responsibility

'He could hardly suppose I should neglect them.' (vol. 1, ch. 2)

Norland and Delaford

Marianne expresses her loss of Norland, and though she does not rhapsodize over Delaford, we must suppose that it is the kind of place in which she will be happy. But, of course, she would not be happy with the kind of place Norland has become under John Dashwood.

The contrast between Norland and Delaford is important for the moral and political vision of the book, because Jane Austen favours continuity, stability and tradition.

Her narrator, by inviting our sympathy for those who have lost their home, also prompts us to think well of a society whose prominent members have a high sense of responsibility for those over whom they have power.

Colonel Brandon's family

Colonel Brandon is contrasted with other members of his family. Delaford under Colonel Brandon is a successful estate, but in his father's day it was 'much encumbered'. His father's failure to nurture the estate is paralleled by Colonel Brandon's brother's lack of responsibility in marriage. His neglect of his wife (does the absence of an heir and 'his pleasures were not what they ought to have been' – vol. 2, ch. 9 – hint at homosexuality?) leads to the tragedy of Eliza – the scandal of her adultery, an illegitimate child and her premature death.

The state of the nation

In many passages in the book there is the uneasy feeling that

England is a nation in which the wrong people are in charge.

This moral and political diagnosis sees snobbery and materialism as the corrosive forces. Eliza is forced to marry Colonel Brandon's brother, so that the struggling Delaford estate can acquire her large fortune (see 14.13).

The Ferrars family

The people who are most sharply criticized for their misuse of power are the Ferrars family. The economically and socially powerful Mrs Ferrars is cold, rude and spiteful, yet although she has the capacity to ruin characters' lives, she is held in check by the narrator. It is significant that one of her defenders is the morally obtuse John Dashwood!

Social origins

The narrator also suggests that, socially speaking, the origins of the Ferrars family are not elevated. Why are they so keen for Edward to enter politics or at least drive a barouche? Why are they so opposed to Elinor's marrying Edward and why does Mrs Ferrars speak glowingly of Miss Morton being Lord Morton's daughter (vol. 2, ch. 12) if they were not a family of newly established wealth bent on securing their place in society? Significantly, there is silence on the matter of where their wealth comes from, and Mr Ferrars is never mentioned.

Miss Grey

The implication is clear: the Ferrars family are hypocritical as well as grasping and snobbish. In the world of *Sense and Sensibility*, the Ferrars family are not alone in their inconsistency.

It is possible that the woman whom Willoughby marries for financial gain (fifty thousand pounds) has social origins in keeping with her name – Miss Grey. We are never told the source of her wealth, and her parents are never mentioned.

8.12 A hole in the canvas

'The wind roared around the house, and the rain beat against the windows.' (vol. 3, ch. 7)

We have mentioned that the construction of the novel is ordered, in keeping with eighteenth-century rationalism. This appears to underline the novel's advocacy of sense and reason.

But, perhaps, as hinted in 5.1, the novel gets out of hand. Or perhaps Jane Austen *wanted* to open up a breach between one character – Marianne – and the narrator. Or perhaps the reader acknowledges that there is a problem nowadays in reading Elinor as an unambiguously praiseworthy character and deliberately looks for debate within the text, one offering alternative ways in which females might behave. Whatever the reason, holes in the canvas do at times afford glimpses of other possible readings. A case can be made for looking at the novel in terms different from those so far adopted.

The breaching of space

Decidedly unsettling is the breaching of space within the classical symmetry of the novel. Space is breached once by Marianne and Willoughby when they trespass upon Mrs Smith's property without her knowledge, and twice by Willoughby alone. The first occasion is when he carries Marianne into Barton Cottage without ceremony, the second when his carriage, torches flaring, impacts upon Cleveland. Both incidents occur in a storm. Their atmosphere is distinctly Gothic and are emblematic of the force of passion and of deep sensibility. They rock the equilibrium of both establishments, just as Willoughby by his seduction of Eliza rocks Colonel Brandon's ordered life. Jane Austen does not deny the power of unbridled passion or argue it away. It remains, red and raw, in scenes that remain with the reader when details of the novel's thesis have long died away.

Willoughby even usurps the geography of the novel's measured and moderate language with his talk of thunderbolts, daggers, blackguards, scoundrels, devils, angels and souls.

An animal lover

Willoughby is associated with animals throughout the novel. Sir John praises his black pointer bitch (his evil genius?). He lives to hunt – both beasts and women. Sir John had intended to give Willoughby one of Folly's puppies. Willoughby proves himself *to be* one of Folly's puppies!

He wants to give Marianne a horse – Queen Mab. The very name suggests the fanciful nature of the gift. She is truly the fairies' midwife! Neither Willoughby nor Marianne consider how she will be afforded or stabled. The dreams she affords are all that matters. Marianne and Willoughby will be able to gallop full-pelt across the downs, bridles loose, devouring space!

Soul mates

Yet for all their voracious appetite for wandering, driving forth unchecked and filling space with their dancing, it cannot be denied that for a while Marianne and Willoughby share a meeting of two minds that amounts to an enjoyment almost of spiritual space.

They share a passion for opera and poetry. (An irony is that Willoughby does not care for Pope, though he rapes a lock.) Willoughby is talented at music as well as Marianne. Through love of the arts, together they grope towards the sublime.

Elinor's laconic fear that they will have exhausted every topic on a second encounter brings forth a spirited if exaggerated defence on the part of Marianne:

> I have been too much at my ease, too happy, too frank. I have erred against every common place notion of decorum; I have been open and sincere where I ought to have been reserved, spiritless, dull and deceitful. (vol. 1, ch. 10)

Here the case for sensibility flares into real debate. It is a debate amounting to the political about the truth and transmogrifying power of the emotions. Marianne, after all, has been true to herself. As Claire Tomalin says:

> Marianne goes through the fire of betrayal and humiliation by the man she trusts and loves, and expresses remorse for 'a series of imprudence towards myself'; but the reader is likely to feel that she has acted innocently and purely, and with a consistency that justifies what she has done. The justification is endorsed by Willoughby's continued love for her after he has jilted her and made his prudent, mercenary marriage. (*Jane Austen: A Life*, 2nd edn, Penguin Books, 2000, p. 157)

There seems to be an anger and frustration that drives the novel at times. Women's lot is proven from the beginning to be outrageous, as the Dashwoods become outcasts, for all their caring sense and sensibility, at the whim of, and in favour of, the male. Rather than preserving themselves by a sensible acceptance of their lot, women in the future might use the passion that they repress or squander on grieving to get the law on inheritance changed.

For, perhaps in spite of the narrator, Marianne is the pioneer, not Elinor. She is the one who anticipates how society and sexual politics will alter. Did Jane Austen invest in her the passionate intensity that she herself feels at the ridiculous position of women? For they might as well be gagged and bound! She has mocked their psychic imprisonment already in *Northanger Abbey* when she laconically hopes that Catherine does not dream of Henry before he has dreamt of her!

What Marianne pleads for is freedom of expression and honesty between the sexes such as might exist between mother and daughter. Elinor is quick to urge her mother to find out whether Marianne and Willoughby are really engaged. But she who advocates direct questioning will not ask Edward directly what is wrong with *him*. She has a right to an explanation – Edward's behaviour towards her has been ambiguous. But *she* thinks she has no such right. They are not, after all, engaged! So she stifles her irritation and treats him with the courtesy that a member of the family should command.

Meanwhile, she has to sit around, fettered, waiting for fate – or Edward himself – to sort Edward out.

Marianne has no such intentions. She deserves an explanation, so she demands one by writing first although she too is not engaged. Unwise in the contemporary climate, but the way of the future, not of the past.

This is why some readers feel a sense of loss in Marianne's volte-face and her acceptance of marriage to Colonel Brandon. We feel that this remarkable woman has been banked down. Eventually she promises, 'I shall now live solely for my family . . . and if I do mix in other society it will only be to show that my spirits are humbled, my heart amended, and that I can practise the civilities, the lesser duties of life, with gentleness and forbearance' (vol. 3, ch. 10). She goes on to say that her memory of Willoughby 'shall be regulated, it shall be checked by religion, by reason, by constant employment'. Marianne's chastened acceptance of her lot completes the pattern of a *conventional* contrast-novel, but it belies *this* novel's passion that, in the memory of the reader, refuses to be banked.

Elinor besieged

Is it significant that Elinor, even for one moment, even in the face of Willoughby's seduction of Eliza, could wish Willoughby a widower? It shows how acutely she feels for her sister, how aware she is of the depth of Marianne's feeling for Willoughby and how understanding she is of how exquisite that love had seemed to be. For one moment sensibility rules, as spoilt youth is forgiven. It is a revolutionary moment in Jane Austen's work. (The fate of those who are charismatic but flawed will be returned to in Mansfield Park.)

But this is not the first time that Elinor is subject to unreasoning sensibility. So reassured is she that Edward appears to wear a lock of hair in his ring that she does not feel outrage that he should have taken her (so to speak) by stealth. Willoughby, after all, does ask!

Taken by storm!

Finally there is both humour and tragedy in the capacity of Marianne, wandering at large in a landscape, to be surprised by bad weather. She is careless whenever she ventures abroad and is never properly equipped. Jane Austen must have smiled at the thought of marrying such a one to a man who has foresight enough on 'a very cold damp day' (vol. 1, ch. 8) to consider a flannel waistcoat!

8.13 A Comedy

'She was full of jokes and laughter.' (vol. 1, ch. 7)

For *Sense and Sensibility,* we must remember, is a comedy. We are required to believe that Elinor will be happy with Edward and that Marianne is saved from a life of misery with Willoughby (see Elinor's frank remarks in volume 3, chapter 11). It is one of the novel's many neat reversals that Marianne, who once imprudently scorned wealth, ends up married to a man restored to riches by his own prudence.

We are also required to believe that Elinor's relative lack of wealth will not blight her happiness. It is true that the narrator prepares us for this in the modesty of the sum that would constitute her 'wealth' (see vol. 1, ch. 17). There must also be a thematic appropriateness in the fact that she who has never sought money as a means to happiness but has nevertheless been realistic about it shows that she can be happy with little. *She* is the one who bears out Marianne's romantic notion that where there is love, one can live modestly. The space of the Delaford parsonage must have an important place in the geography of emotions.

Part III

Pride and Prejudice

ELIZABETH, as they drove along, watched for the first appearance of Pemberley Woods with some perturbation; and when at length they turned in at the lodge, her spirits were in a high flutter.

The park was very large, and contained great variety of ground. They entered it in one of its lowest points, and drove for some time through a beautiful wood, stretching over a wide extent.

Elizabeth was delighted. She had never seen a place for which nature had done more, or where natural beauty had been so little counteracted by an awkward taste ... and at that moment she felt, that to be mistress of Pemberley might be something! Pride and Prejudice

9 Narrative and themes

9.1 Sisters

'It shows an affection for her sister that is very pleasing.' (vol. 1, ch. 8)

The two sisters in *Sense and Sensibility*

In terms of plot design and movement, *Pride and Prejudice* has much in common with *Sense and Sensibility*:

both novels are about two sisters who undergo the trials of love before finding happiness.

In *Sense and Sensibility* the central consciousness is Elinor's. She has to exercise the virtue of patience until it is possible for Edward to declare his love for her. Because we are not given direct access to the workings of her mind, Marianne is not the novel's central character although she is the one who has all the learning to do.

The two sisters in *Pride and Prejudice*

In *Pride and Prejudice* the roles are reversed.

The central consciousness is Elizabeth – charming, witty and devoted to her sister yet, like Marianne, a character who stands in need of the education that comes through experience and self-knowledge.

In formal terms, Jane is a secondary heroine; we do not see into her mind. To her is given the Elinor role of patient suffering.

9.2 Hinderers

'She often tried to provoke Darcy into disliking her guest.' (vol. 1, ch. 10)

Sisters who hinder

As in the plot of *Sense and Sensibility*, there are sisters who impede the happiness of the central figures. In this respect, Jane Austen's novels resemble those folk tales in which the central characters, often travellers, encounter those who help or hinder their progress. Formal patterning often enforces this motif – two helpers might be balanced by two hinderers.

In *Sense and Sensibility* Anne and Lucy Steele hinder Elinor and Marianne, while in *Pride and Prejudice* this role is performed by Mr Bingley's sisters.

In *Pride and Prejudice* the responsibility for the hindrance is, as in *Sense and*

Sensibility, chiefly the work of one sister. Poor Miss Steele does not have the guile (nor the motive) of her scheming younger sister, Lucy, and though the Bingley sisters are sometimes presented as jointly responsible for Jane's misery, it is Caroline Bingley rather than Mrs Hurst who is increasingly seen as the (rather desperate) hinderer. A successful ploy of the plot is that Elizabeth is unaware that she and Caroline are in competition.

Helpers

In *Sense and Sensibility* Marianne comes to recognize the goodness of Mrs Jennings and to see Colonel Brandon as both a helper and the one who will fulfil her romantically. Help in *Pride and Prejudice* is provided by the parents Elizabeth should have had – the Gardiners.

9.3 Dialogue

'It is *your* turn to say something now, Mr Darcy.' (vol. 1, ch. 18)

Yet the two novels *feel* quite different.

The prominence of dialogue

One reason for this is the kind of writing that dominates *Pride and Prejudice* – dialogue.

There is no dialogue in *Sense and Sensibility* till the second chapter, whereas *Pride and Prejudice*, after its opening two sentences of witty narratorial comment, entertains the reader with a lively dialogue. Many of the dialogues work like drama.

Dialogue and character

One of the reasons that the dialogue has dramatic force is because it is vividly characterized:

the characters have their own distinctive styles.

For example, Mrs Bennet is eager, agitated yet imperceptive. She is prey to lurid imaginings. Her style is flamboyant and unfocused. In contrast, Charlotte Lucas has the authoritative manner of a narrator: 'Happiness in marriage is entirely a matter of chance' (vol. 1, ch. 6).

Dialogue and theme

The issues of the novel emerge in the dialogue.

In the first chapter, for instance, we read of the influence of parents, the prospects of marriage and the importance of money. Play is made of the word 'design'. Later, Darcy gives the word a sinister nuance when he writes of Wickham who, bent on the seduction of Georgiana, goes to Ramsgate 'undoubtedly by design' (vol. 2, ch. 12). Used of Wickham, the word takes on all Jane Austen's disapproval for those who use ruses in pursuit of romance.

Dialogue and ideas

Sense and Sensibility contains passages of diverting dialogue, but it perhaps lacks not only the wit of *Pride and Prejudice* but the ability of the dialogue to give full expression to the substance of the novel. Too often in *Sense and Sensibility* dialogue is illustrative; characters speak (even exist?) in order to exemplify certain preestablished moral positions. Events function too like medieval exempla – they illustrate the moral themes of the book. Whereas in *Pride and Prejudice*

Elizabeth and Darcy exist beyond the ideas concerning pride and prejudice played out through and around them.

9.4 Variety of characters

'I never met with so many pleasant girls in my life.' (vol. 1, ch. 3)

A big cast

The human drama of *Pride and Prejudice* is further seen in a greater range of characterization. Even some of the 'walk-on' parts are important in the movement of the plot; for instance, Mrs Reynolds' unsolicited testimonial helps Elizabeth to see Darcy's virtues.

Oliver MacDonagh observes that there are many girls in this big cast *Jane Austen: Real and Imagined Worlds*, Yale University Press, 1991, p. 89). Because there are ten unmarried young women, we can appreciate the anxiety of Mrs Bennet. We can also relish the nervy rumour spread abroad that Mr Bingley is bringing down a further *twelve* women from London!

The central characters are created fully and, though the term must be used carefully, with some degree of realism. And the men are given lives of their own apart from the romantic hopes of young women and scheming mothers. Jane Austen has also devoted care to fashioning her closed or flat characters. Lady Catherine's insolent haughtiness encroaches on the preserve of the gods: 'The party then gathered round the fire to hear Lady Catherine determine what weather they were to have on the morrow' (vol. 2, ch. 6).

Parallels

The large cast allows the emergence of a number of thematically significant parallels between the characters. Elizabeth is similar to Jane in that she is horrified by Lydia's moral failings, yet in their liveliness Elizabeth is not essentially different from Lydia. Mary is reflective like Jane; and the issue of Kitty is whether she will turn out to be a Lydia or an Elizabeth. Lydia, of course, is linked with Georgiana Darcy in that both are objects of the predatory Wickham. Caroline Bingley may despise the vulgarity of Mrs Bennet, yet in her pursuit of Darcy she is as unsubtle as the woman she despises. Lady Catherine and Mrs Bennet both try to arrange marriages for their offspring, and Darcy hoped at one time that Bingley would marry Georgiana. Mr Collins is a clergyman and Wickham claims that he wanted to be one; both try to recommend themselves through the smoothness of their manners.

9.5 Community and war

'the recent arrival of a militia regiment in the neighbourhood' (vol. 1, ch. 7)

The neighbourhood

In *Pride and Prejudice* the characters are given a social context. In *Sense and Sensibility* there is little sense of a community beyond family. By contrast, the Bennet girls are seen in a family, amongst relations, in the local town, at assemblies and travelling. The word 'neighbourhood' (first used in the second sentence) marks the difference between the two novels.

The militia and the war

A further dimension of the novel's public aspect is its interest in the impact of the militia. This gives a specific context to the Bennet family's lives – the war with France (often called the Napoleonic Wars). Great Britain was at war with France for most of the years from 1793 to 1815. The militia regiments were established to prevent an invasion. They had no barracks but moved round the country as deemed necessary by the commanders. The '–shire militia' (it was a literary convention not to give a name) are in Hertfordshire for about eight months and then move to the south coast (the most vulnerable area) at Brighton.

War and gaiety

Perhaps the dances and assemblies of Meryton should be understood as deriving their rather desperate gaiety from the real though unstated threat of invasion, battle and death. Dressing up Chamberlayne as a woman is the kind of jape that occurs when women fear losing the company of a regiment, and the soldiers fear losing their lives.

Might such a complex of hopes, fears and longings figure in the elopement of Lydia and Wickham? Wickham's motives are not easy to discern, but the war might in part account for why he recklessly abandoned his calculated mercenary pursuits for the ephemeral pleasures of sexual indulgence.

War and Mr Wickham

There is no talk in the novel about the war. But even in a novel that sparkles as effortlessly as *Pride and Prejudice* there may be an anxious concern for the life of the nation similar to the troubled preoccupations of *Mansfield Park* and *Persuasion*.

If there is such a concern, its focus is Wickham. We might ask: what is he doing in the army? He appears to have two interests: gambling and finding a rich wife. He is a soldier of fortune in the sense that he is in the war in order to make himself rich. Perhaps Wickham is to be censured partly for the way he holds lightly a military discipline that his nation requires of him. How does Wickham know that France will not invade while he is absconding from the camp with Lydia?

The plot and the militia

The chief plot function of the militia is to provide plot possibilities.

The militia – and the Netherfield party – fulfil the familiar comic function of the arrival of strangers. Frequently, strangers are welcome because they provide the possible resolution of an impasse.

Here the impasse is that

both Meryton and Longbourn seem curiously short of men.

In addition to the heads of families and one man who works – Mr Jones the apothecary – the only other man we hear of is Mr Robinson, who talks to Bingley about Meryton assemblies (vol. 1, ch. 5). It is not said whether he is unmarried. Wickham in his regimentals represents a sexual charisma lacking in the locality. (Have the other young men joined the army?)

Elizabeth and the militia

The presence of the militia in Meryton becomes a touchstone for Elizabeth's growth towards sound judgement and self-knowledge. She is not as giddy as her two youngest sisters, but nothing suggests that she is averse to the company of so many young men. When she does see through the plausible charms of George Wickham she still feels regret for the departure of the militia.

With the entail hanging over the family, a young woman has to be alert to all the situations which might supply a suitable husband, even if she keeps this to herself and does not appear concerned.

9.6 How the narrative works

'she related to her the next morning the chief of the scene between Mr Darcy and herself' (vol. 2, ch. 17)

The drama of *Pride and Prejudice*

It is appropriate to talk of *Pride and Prejudice* in dramatic terms.

***Pride and Prejudice* is narrative in more than a formal sense. The themes of the novel are given a distinctly narrative shape, so that the reader responds to them in a way which is quintessentially literary.**

It is strange to talk about a novel this way: is not the point of a novel to work out its ideas in terms of the story it tells? Such a statement, however, is more of a prescription or evaluation than a description of how many novels work.

Film and television

One difference between *Sense and Sensibility* and *Pride and Prejudice* is the relative extent of their popularity in film and television versions. Whilst *Sense and Sensibility* formed the basis of a successful film in 1996 it has never enjoyed the filmic and televisual success of *Pride and Prejudice.* Some aspects of this success are tangential to the novel. Darcy, for example, is not the main character, though some versions are memorable for his representation by Laurence Olivier, Alan Badel and Colin Firth.

This may tell us something about the strong narrative nature of *Pride and Prejudice*; by comparison, no actor has made his name or considerably enhanced his reputation by playing Edward Ferrars, and, good as she was as Marianne, it was *Titanic* that established Kate Winslet as a star.

Narrative and the establishment of meaning

***Pride and Prejudice* consistently works by making the narrative itself establish the novel's thematic interest.**

There *are* passages of intellectual and moral debate but they arise naturally out of the narrative. For example, when Elizabeth and Jane discuss what Wickham has said about Darcy, a number of central issues are aired: can an unworthy man have a worthy friend? Is there a limit to the extent to which someone can be deceived?

The embodiment of themes

Embodiment of the novel's meanings works in two closely related ways:

the themes of the novel emerge in and through its events; the passage of time is the means by which important ideas are established.

Pride and Prejudice is about pride and prejudice because specific events reveal those qualities in characters' behaviour, and the novel is about learning to know oneself because this is what happens to Elizabeth.

9.7 The unfolding of the plot

'She could not bear such suspense.' (vol. 3, ch. 10)

The opening

The novel opens in a mood of expectation: Netherfield has been taken by an unmarried man with a considerable fortune. Even the figurative language has a narrative tendency: 'To be fond of dancing was a certain step towards falling in love' (vol.1, ch. 3). Steps are taken in dances and into the future.

Irony

What is usually called dramatic irony works through time. In the light of an event, a retrospective glance allows an earlier one to be read ironically. Elizabeth, piqued by Darcy's denigrating remarks, says to her mother, 'I may safely promise you never to dance with him.' (vol. 1, ch. 5). However, when Darcy approaches her at the Netherfield ball she complies. Her earlier resolution is ironically exposed; the surprise of the request makes her do what she believed was unthinkable. The ironic reversal of her acceptance prepares us for further ironies. Later she will refuse to 'dance' matrimonial steps with Darcy, but this will be because, not knowing him, she does not know what she is doing. But at the end of the novel, in full knowledge of his worth and her heart, she does consent to 'his application for her hand'.

Mrs Bennet's expectations

Mrs Bennet is not a subtle imaginer, but what she does anticipate is dramatically clear.

Mrs Bennet looks at the future as if she were a confident author, who knows exactly how the plot of her novel is going to work out:

What she wants are outcomes similar to Romantic novels: 'The business of her life was to get her daughters married' (vol.1, ch. 1). For Mrs Bennet the plot is simple.

Such a character allows the narrator to make a knowing contrast between Mrs Bennet's simple expectations and the actual winding path of the narrative. One of the ironies of the writing is that none of the marriages is directly due to her inept scheming.

Plot devices

Plot devices have the function of making the reader anticipate the movement of the story.

The mutual attraction of Bingley and Jane so near the beginning of the book advertises itself as the source of plot business. The reader is also likely to be alerted to Elizabeth's hostility to Darcy. Promising material!

Plot impediments

Plots progress by overcoming impediments. Love plots need directions; equally, they need forces that will deflect their trajectories

***Pride and Prejudice* is inventive in the number and variety of its impediments.**

The Bennets have the respectable status of a gentry family, but they enjoy no security because the Longbourn estate is entailed on a male heir. They are further inhibited by socially less than glamorous relations on their mother's side. Mr Gardiner is in trade. The chances of the girls' getting rich husbands are thereby diminished.

As with most impediments in a love plot, the Bennet girls' lack of fortune is introduced early on. What is more subtle is the way that it is only at the mid-point of the plot that Elizabeth becomes aware of how comprehensively the behaviour of her family creates an impediment to a successful marriage.

It is a characteristic of the novel's narrative mode that thematic significances often emerge in retrospect.

The passage of time is required for Elizabeth to become fully aware of what a disincentive to respectable alliance the behaviour of her mother, father and younger sisters is. An important aspect of her growing up is her acknowledgement that Darcy's criticism of them was sound: 'The justice of the charge struck her too forcibly for denial' (vol. 2, ch. 13)

The overcoming of impediments

In *Pride and Prejudice*

events that look like impediments turn out to be factors that assist the happy resolution of the plot.

Jane Austen sometimes regards plot development in a providential light (see 16.12). At its simplest, good emerges from what looks like an evil. (This pattern emerges in *Northanger Abbey* where the narrator draws attention to the fact that General Tilney's interference actually aids the lovers.) When Elizabeth visits Pemberley with her maternal aunt and uncle she expects Darcy will recoil from such low acquaintances. However, it turns out, as the novel's last sentence puts it, that the Gardiners were 'the means of uniting them'. Lydia's elopement works similarly, as does Lady Catherine's interference.

Lies

Another way in which the plot is designed to have future significance is the matter of Wickham's lies. Once a lie is uttered and characters are deceived, there must be an occasion later in the narrative when the working of the lie is seen for what it is and the liar exposed.

Readers are tested alongside Elizabeth. Many readers will admit that they too believed Wickham's tale. His lie has important consequences: Jane is puzzled and troubled by Wickham's revelation, Elizabeth rejects Darcy and, when the truth is recognized, there is the problem of what to do with such knowledge.

Retrospection plays an important part. Once Elizabeth is awakened to Wickham's lies, she can re-assess the scene in which she is 'seduced' by his plausible fictions. Experience and the passage of time have sharpened her perceptions. In spite of her claim that 'Her heart had been but slightly touched' (vol. 2, ch. 3), her attachment to Wickham has remained vividly with her: 'She perfectly remembered every thing that had passed in conversation between Wickham and herself.' But retrospection changes the significance of the past:

> She was *now* struck with the impropriety of such communications to a stranger, and wondered it had escaped her before.

Plot possibilities

Plot turning points encourage characters and readers to look to the future. The event that most disturbs the lives of the Bennet family is Lydia's elopement. The future direction of the narrative is very open at this point. Mrs Bennet has graphic fears: 'I know he [Mr Bennet] will fight Wickham, wherever he meets him,and then he will be killed, and what will become of us all?' (vol. 3, ch. 5). This is typical of an outlook shaped by the improbabilities of popular fiction.

Elizabeth sees the consequences of Lydia's folly in terms of her own future. What will happen to those possibilities that were beginning to emerge at Pemberley?

Sometimes future possibilities are opened up without the character realizing it. In the crisis of the news of Lydia's elopement, Elizabeth confides in Darcy. His gloomy, silent pacing makes her feel that 'her power was sinking' (vol. 3, ch. 4). Darcy's silent inwardness, in fact, forms one of the novel's most important proleptic moments; it is only when Elizabeth has accepted him at the close of the novel that he reveals what was the actual subject of his meditation:

> she soon learnt that his resolution of following her from Derbyshire in quest of her sister, had been formed before he quitted the inn, and that his gravity and thoughtfulness there, had arisen from no other struggles than what such a purpose must comprehend. (vol. 3, ch. 16)

His silence at the inn was, therefore, a moment of testing. Testing requires a narrative form. In his struggle to realize ('comprehend') what would be involved, Darcy must have faced the emotional dificulties of assisting Wickham and resolved that his action, though taken exclusively out of love for Elizabeth, must be kept hidden from her. It is up to the reader to see more than Darcy. He has rescued Lydia and the Bennet family. Unlike Mr Collins, who counselled Mr Bennet 'to throw off your unworthy child from your affection for ever' (vol. 3, ch. 6), Darcy, who looks after the dependants on his own estate, has performed a deed of Christian charity. Unlike Mr Collins the preacher, he understands the parable of the lost sheep.

Retrospection

'Retrospection' is a word it is difficult to avoid in a discussion of the plot movement of *Pride and Prejudice*. When, in the crisis of Lydia's elopement, Elizabeth throws

> a retrospective glance over the whole of their acquaintance, so full of contradictions and varieties, [she] sighed at the perverseness of those feelings which would now have promoted its continuance. (vol. 3, ch. 4)

Retrospection allows insight into the self, and that insight leads Elizabeth to recognize the nature of her feelings. The language indicates that Elizabeth realizes that feelings have an almost independent existence. They are like other people; they can be sighed over but not controlled.

Retrospection has moral consequences. In volume 3, chapter 16 Mr Darcy and Elizabeth look back with embarrassment and shame upon the winding path that has led them to the brink of marriage. Jane Austen knows that this is what lovers do. There is nothing quite so pleasurable in lovers' talk as reviewing those moments which were formative in the establishment of a loving attachment.

Elizabeth, perhaps fearing Darcy is becoming too earnestly oppressive in his conscience-stricken recollections, urges him to 'think only of the past as its remembrance gives you pleasure'.

For Darcy, however, recollection is painful and unavoidable. It is for Darcy a moral duty. The knowledge of one's shortcomings 'ought not to be repelled'.

The narrative form allows the reader to see that characters win moral awareness from their dwelling upon the passage of time.

9.8 The debate about marriage

'You know it is not sound, and that you would never act in this way yourself.' (vol. 1, ch. 5)

Charlotte and the prudential marriage

The issue of how love should be expressed and what kind of marriage is most desirable is conducted in narrative terms.

The debate about marriage starts with a conversation in which Elizabeth and Charlotte Lucas exchange with frank good humour their very different ideas about how Jane should act with regard to Bingley and what can be expected from the married state. Yet although the form is what might be called intellectual dialogue, it is prompted by events that have just taken place. At the Meryton assembly Bingley has danced with Jane twice. It is, therefore, a natural development of the plot that Charlotte and Elizabeth, the two wittiest women in the novel, should discuss the issues arising from this burgeoning attachment (vol. 1, ch. 6). Elizabeth, perhaps rather smugly, reflects that no one else is likely to perceive how deeply Jane's feelings have been engaged.

Given that this issue has an almost philosophical character– how can we judge what others are feeling? – it is understandable that Charlotte should respond in language that has a 'general' or a 'representative' quality. She may sound more like a journalist or (were there such a thing) a worldly-wise and even cynical book on the etiquette of courtship. Yet in spite of the general nature of the debate, the issue she addresses is one that the plot has already made very real – Jane's future happiness.

Charlotte's aim is certainly to warn Jane via Elizabeth and may, in part, also be a criticism of Elizabeth for gaining such unthinking satisfaction from Jane's feelings being concealed from others. What is the point of such concealment, argues Charlotte, if even the object of it is unaware of its existence? Her terms are boldly general: 'If a woman conceals her affection with the same skill from the object of it, she may lose the opportunity of fixing him.'

The word 'fix' had a number of meanings. Johnson lists six, of which the first comes closest to Charlotte's use: 'To make fast, firm or stable.' A woman must make sure that she has her man where she wants him. The language of the last sentence brings out what is not evident in Johnson's definition: the extent to which the word had acquired a distasteful nuance when associated with courtship. 'Fix' strongly implied a calculating and perhaps even a scheming attitude (it is so used by John Dashwood in *Sense and Sensibility* vol. 2, ch. 11). As K.C. Phillipps says, the word 'seems already to be too blunt for the more acceptable characters' (*Jane Austen's English,* André Deutsch, 1970, p. 76).

Charlotte states the consequences of her view with a colloquial gusto: 'In nine cases out of ten, a woman had better show *more* affection than she feels.' This is a central issue in Jane Austen – the politics of wooing.

Jane Austen's consistent view is that scheming of any kind ought to play no part in matters of the heart.

Charlotte is representatively prudential: 'Happiness in marriage is entirely a matter of chance.' Elizabeth detects a rhetorical indulgence here: 'You make me laugh, Charlotte; but it is not sound. You know it is not sound, and that you would never act in this way yourself.'

Again this is promising material. Our narrative senses are alerted!

Fixing in action

The events that follow Mr Collins's proposal are carefully designed to show the resolute consistency of Charlotte's philosophy and the severe tests that those who refuse to demonstrate all or more than they feel have to undergo. The themes are embodied in the narrative.

Elizabeth demonstrates consistency in her refusal of Mr Collins. She cannot marry a man whom she could not make happy and who is incapable of making her so.

Charlotte visits Longbourn soon after Elizabeth's refusal. By 'walking to the window and pretending not to hear' (vol. 1, ch. 20), Charlotte learns that Mr Collins's quest for Elizabeth has ceased. The rest of the day she spends listening to him. Charlotte has said nothing, but, in retrospect, we realize that she must have come to momentous decisions as she stood by the window, pretending not to hear.

Jane tested

On the same morning, Jane receives a letter from Caroline Bingley announcing that the whole Netherfield party has left for London, where, she hopes, a romance will develop between her brother and Darcy's sister.

The careful placing in the narrative of the departure of the Netherfield party prompts the reader to reflect that Charlotte might have had a point.

Had Jane shown more affection than she actually felt she might by now have 'fixed' Bingley, and no such exodus would have occurred. Jane Austen has no doubt that Jane has behaved properly, yet she recognizes how dangerous such composure and control can be in a world which demands the cheap tokens of unambiguous signs.

Showing more than one feels

Mr Collins is not short of unambiguous signs from Charlotte:

> Charlotte's kindness [in listening to Mr Collins] extended farther than Elizabeth had any conception of; – its object was nothing less, than to secure her from any return of Mr Collins's addresses, by engaging them towards herself. (vol. 1, ch. 22)

The narrator call this a 'scheme'. What follows is an entertaining burlesque upon the strategies of romantic love; Charlotte sees Mr Collins approaching so meets him 'accidentally in the lane', where she no doubt receives several of those pre-prepared 'little elegant compliments' which Mr Collins pays to Charlotte with 'as unstudied an air as possible' (vol. 1, ch. 14).

Charlotte's justification

Charlotte knows that her behaviour will be inexplicable to Elizabeth, but she has little difficulty, though momentary embarrassment, in showing Elizabeth that there is a rationale for what she has done:

> 'I am not romantic you know. I never was. I ask only a comfortable home; and considering Mr Collins's character, and situation in life, I am convinced that my chance of happiness with him is as fair, as most people can boast on entering the marriage state.' (vol. 1, ch. 22)

We might exclaim that there is insufficient hope and imagination here: surely Charlotte can picture to herself something better than marriage to Mr Collins? What we cannot criticize is the soundness of her thinking: if all one wants from marriage is 'a comfortable home', it hardly matters with whom it is shared.

For Charlotte it is a truth universally acknowledged that a single woman without a good fortune must acquire a husband, come what may!

Paired histories

It is not necessary to follow the narratives of Jane and Charlotte to the end of the novel.

Charlotte has shown more than she feels, and Elizabeth and the reader wonder whether she will find happiness in such a marriage.

Jane Austen refuses to sacrifice human complexity for the neatness of a moral scheme; Elizabeth is surprised, though pleased, that Charlotte has been able to accommodate herself so readily to her lot.

When Elizabeth leaves Hunsford there is a kind of obituary on Charlotte's chosen life, delivered with some of the unflinching common sense that Charlotte herself evinces:

> Poor Charlotte! – It was melancholy to leave her to such society! – But she had chosen it with her eyes open; and though evidently regretting that her visitors were to go, she did not seem to ask for compassion. (vol. 2, ch. 15)

If she really did believe that 'happiness in marriage is entirely a matter of chance', Charlotte can have no logical grounds for complaint, for all states of happiness or misery are compatible with such a statement. This is not to say that the reader cannot find anything to criticize,

for Charlotte's choice of Mr Collins shows her willingness to work with an idea of human life that makes disappointment impossible.

Jane, however, has expectations, and, therefore, is open to disappointment. Though the novel is not mediated through her consciousness, her misery is evident. Jane's disappointment, her failure to secure her man, are dealt with in the chapters before Elizabeth's visit to Hunsford, and therefore prepare us for those scenes in which Charlotte manages her 'comfortable house' with its colony of chickens.

The issues of marriage – the motives for entering the state and the hopes one entertains of it – are enacted in the juxtaposing of the two young women.

9.9 Morality and narrative

'And for *this* we are to be thankful.' (vol. 3, ch. 7)

The passing of time

One of the interesting moral dilemmas of *Pride and Prejudice* emerges through the narrative:

certain moral issues becomes seriously problematic when viewed in retrospect.

The passage of time has brought about a state of affairs that might have been prevented had a particular action been taken earlier.

As there is often a time element in moral decisions, the narrative form of fiction is a fitting way of representing to ourselves what it is to act morally.

The time element in *Pride and Prejudice* gives expression to a very interesting moral perspective. The difficulty of anticipation and the sobering experience of retrospection form a criticism (perhaps even a refutation) of that species of moral reasoning commonly known as utilitarianism (see 15.8)

Utilitarianism

Utilitarianism proposes that the worth of any action should be judged by its effects. If an action increases pleasure, it is good, but if it results in more misery then it is bad. The two terms most commonly associated with utilitarian thinking are 'pleasure' and 'pain'. Good actions increase pleasure; bad ones increase pain. Utilitarianism is the theory or practice of whatever is useful, profitable or convenient, and those requirements are to be measured according to the scale of pleasure.

The theory was first formulated by Jeremy Bentham (1748–1832). He was interested in legal and social policy and formulated the principle of utility as an alternative to the, as he regarded them, unhelpfully vague notions of rights or social contract. A right had somehow to be intuited, whereas utility could be measured.

Difficulties with utilitarianism

The criticism Jane Austen implicitly offers for this theory is one that is dependent on narrative form in that it involves the passing of time.

Lydia's elopement

In her distress, Elizabeth tells Darcy the news she has received from Jane about Lydia's disappearance. She also trusts him (as he trusted her about Wickham's attempted seduction of his sister) with her regret:

> 'When I consider,' she added, in a yet more agitated voice, 'that *I* might have prevented it! – *I* who knew what he was. Had I but explained some part of it only – some part of what I learnt, to my own family! Had his character been known, this could not have happened.' (vol. 3, ch. 4)

The result of Elizabeth's news and her repining is that it makes Darcy ponder deeply about what he ought to do now and what he ought to have done in the past. He too feels morally responsible for his public silence about Wickham's shortcomings: 'He called it, therefore, his duty to step forward, and endeavour to remedy an evil which had been brought on by himself' (vol. 3, ch. 10). Darcy's language is strong. 'Duty' makes the issue an explicitly moral one, and the causality is very firm.

On not making a disclosure

Elizabeth also sees the issue of disclosure in moral terms. When she returns from Hunsford, she divulges the contents of the letter, in so far as it relates to Wickham, to Jane. What she wants is advice on whether anyone else should be told: 'I want to be told whether I ought, or ought not to make our acquaintance in general understand Wickham's character' (vol. 2, ch. 17).

She asks Jane what she 'ought' to do. The use of 'ought' shows that she looks on this as a moral question. 'Ought' is also used when she gives her conclusion: 'it ought not to be attempted'. Both sisters, in fact, give moral reasons for remaining silent.

It should be noted that, in both cases, the future implications of actions have a bearing on the matter: Elizabeth decides that disclosures made in private are not intended for broadcasting, and Jane believes that moral exposure may render future reformation impossible for Wickham.

The failure of utilitarianism

After Elizabeth hears of Lydia's elopement, there are passages of dialogue in which characters discuss whether they might have foreseen this outcome. It is not just a matter of not foreseeing what Lydia might do; it is actually a case of knowledge of the future being impossible in this case. Nothing could have indicated that Wickham would so tempt Lydia. And even if Elizabeth had feared that Lydia might abscond with Wickham, there is no guarantee that disclosure of his past would have prevented her.

Pride and Prejudice, therefore, shows that a utilitarian view of morals fails in its very foundations. A morality which judges the worth of an action upon its consequences must have some degree of certainty about what will happen in the future. Once it is admitted that this is impossible, the theory fails. This is more clearly seen in the narrative form of prose fiction that in philosophical prose. Elizabeth looks back and is convinced (and so, too, must the reader be) that as the elopement was unforeseeable, she could not have acted to prevent it and thereby, to give utilitarianism its last fling, avoid future misery.

It is unlikely that Jane Austen read Bentham's work, though not impossible that she became aware of its assumptions through conversation. A glance at the index of any book on Jane Austen's social context shows that critics do not think that Bentham is an important figure in the understanding of her work. But no one would deny that the nature of morality is one of her major preoccupations, or that her thought is enacted in her books. In the case of *Pride and Prejudice* the least that can be said is that through her presentation of characters who cannot know the future consequences of withholding a piece of information, an implicit criticism of the kind of thinking usually called utilitarian is advanced.

10 Elizabeth and her men

10.1 A couple approved

'Nothing could give either Bingley or myself more delight.' (vol. 3, ch. 17)

Women in the plots

The plots of Jane Austen novels are driven by female wants and needs. (See 20.1.)

The women are therefore the central figures. The men are never primary.

In terms of plot, the men merely serve the females.

This they do in one of two ways.

In broad plot terms, the men either fulfil female desire or they test female tenacity. They may do both, of course.

Elizabeth's destiny

The novel makes it clear that

Elizabeth Bennet has an appropriate destiny.

As she was probably Jane Austen's favourite heroine, we can imagine there is full authorial approval of Elizabeth as the mistress of Pemberley. Jane Austen said of Elizabeth: 'I must confess that I think her as delightful a creature as ever appeared in print, and how I shall be able to tolerate those who do not like *her* at least I do not know.'

The title explicitly determines that this is Elizabeth and Darcy's novel; speaking simplistically, Elizabeth represents 'Prejudice' and Mr Darcy represents 'Pride'. Interesting and important as she is in the plot, the title makes no room for Jane.

The novel comes closest to popular romantic fiction and indeed is almost a kind of Cinderella story. A man who is 'as good as a Lord' (vol. 3, ch. 17), according to his prospective mother-in-law, is enchanted against his will and better judgement by the second daughter of an eccentric gentleman whose estate is entailed on the male side.

Turning point

The moment in the narrative that fully confirms the appropriateness of the attachment is when Darcy comes round the corner from the stables at Pemberley, a changed man. A deep blush suffuses the features of both hero and heroine. Tony Tanner in his Introduction to the Penguin English Library edition of the novel equates blushing with a kind of erection of the head! Things hot up in Derbyshire!

It has been hinted almost from the beginning of the novel that

the deep and intricate Darcy, with his profound intelligence, dazzling wit and penchant for debate is the kind of man with whom Elizabeth will find intellectual, emotional and erotic fulfilment.

And that is the priority in the plot: first, Elizabeth's needs, followed by Darcy who tests and fulfils.

10.2 Mr Collins

'"Really, Mr Collins," cried Elizabeth with some warmth, "you puzzle me exceedingly."' (vol. 1, ch. 19)

But before the chance meeting at Pemberley, Elizabeth has to come to terms with a number of other men. The important question in every case is: what function does each of Elizabeth's men play in her life?

Mr Collins comes to woo

Mr Collins moves Elizabeth to laughter and vexation. He is a prig: solemn, obtuse, self-centred and smug, with no sense of humour. He is under the influence of Lady Catherine de Bourgh, to whom he is excruciatingly servile.

He comes to Longbourn, virtually on the instructions of Lady Catherine, to woo. Darcy says apropos of Miss Bingley, 'whatever bears affinity to cunning is despicable' (vol. 1, ch. 8). Mr Collins is the epitome of cunning, albeit of a touchingly innocent kind.

Mr Collins upon his arrival proves to be tactlessly inept. Pleased with his dinner, he enquires which of his cousins is the cook. (One feels this might have influenced his choice!)

Mrs Bennet (one of the two Longbourn women who take to him – the other is the learned Mary) looks very favourably on Mr Collins's decision to seek a wife among her daughters. Having been warned off Jane, Mr Collins transfers his affections to Elizabeth in the time that it takes Mrs Bennet to poke the fire.

The art of proposing

Mr Collins's proposal is one of the novel's high points of comedy, yet in and through Mr Collins's absurd protestations, several important points about the nature of love and marriage emerge.

Mr Collins essentially views women in an old-fashioned light.

He sees women basically as objets d'art – charming, elegant females. He has no respect for women as rational beings. It is ironic, therefore, that he should choose Charlotte.

By contrast, what emerges is Elizabeth's twofold need:

to have another take an interest in her for her own sake and to experience the delights of eros.

Mr Collins's proposal to Elizabeth is a mockery of what a proposal should be, not least in its haste. Even if Elizabeth had found him agreeable, she would never have agreed to marry him so soon, merely to achieve a stable future.

That Mr Collins is not swept away by passion is obvious from the fact that 'he set about it [the proposal] in a very orderly manner' (vol. 1, ch. 19). Mr Collins's excessively long declaration works as a burlesque of what marriage, in Elizabeth's, the narrator's and the reader's eyes, ought to promise. His first reason for marrying Elizabeth has everything to do with vaunting his 'easy circumstances'. It is as if matrimony is a kind of carrying card that demonstrates that he has 'arrived'. It seems strange that his second reason, that it will make him happy, does not come first. He mentions nothing about making Elizabeth happy. His third reason, which he believes *ought* to have come first, is that his marriage is advised by Lady Catherine. The most sinister part of the proposal is that

Mr Collins wants to quell Elizabeth's spirits and sense of humour to ensure that she is acceptable to his patron.

Mr Collins comes at last to speak of 'the violence of his affections' but moves straight on to money, declaring that he takes no interest in it. Yet he knows in full detail Elizabeth's entitlements. He ends on a deplorable note, assuring her that 'no ungenerous reproach shall ever pass my lips' (on the subject of her lack of fortune) when they are married.

Mistress of Longbourn

In plot terms his proposal is a crucial moment. In rejecting Mr Collins, Elizabeth is effectively rejecting, for herself and the rest of her family, the Longbourn estate. Charlotte Lucas is often said to have opted for a prudential marriage but

Elizabeth has far stronger motives than Charlotte to opt for Mr Collins; she is poor and, as things stand, her family will be homeless. Her refusal of Collins shows Elizabeth's trust in the workings of a romantic providence.

Mr Collins shows Elizabeth what she does *not* want. His proposal is a test of the principles she outlined to Charlotte and demonstrates her refusal to sacrifice herself even to the future security of her family.

10.3 Mr Wickham

'A young man too, like *you,* whose very countenance may vouch for your being amiable.' (vol. 1, ch. 16)

No sooner has Mr Collins singled out Elizabeth as his future mate than she meets someone who genuinely holds out considerable interest for her.

George Wickham turns out to be one of the most smooth-talking, persuasive and perfidious of Jane Austen's anti-heroes.

He is handsome, charming, attractive, deceitful, manipulative, cunning and shameless. He appears upon the scene when Elizabeth still carries in her head Mr Darcy's snub. From the start he, in contrast, appears to find her very attractive, singling her out at Mr and Mrs Phillips's evening party above Jane. (Jane Austen knows the power of erotic interest:Henry Crawford pays this persuasive compliment to Fanny Price long before her beloved Edmund.) Because he is so plausible and good-looking, Elizabeth seems to abandon all her critical faculties.

Wickham is the test: he confirms prejudice. He is a kind of black testimonial against Darcy.

He meets Elizabeth's wayward inclination to stigmatize.

When men meet

Wickham produces a change in Mr Darcy's demeanour on encountering him. This Elizabeth witnesses with a great deal of curiosity but has too much sensitivity to enquire further. She should have been alerted perhaps by the fact that Wickham has no such discretion. He has been acquainted with Darcy's family since infancy. This is of such interest to Elizabeth that she is unaware of questions that seem innocuous but are in fact probing her. Wickham clearly wants to know whether he has carte blanche to denigrate Darcy.

A test of Elizabeth's discretion

When Elizabeth states emphatically how disagreeable she finds Mr Darcy, doubtless Wickham cannot believe his luck. One wonders at her indiscretion in trusting a complete stranger with her views. It also proves that her response to Darcy is irrational. Even Wickham seems surprised. On Elizabeth's declaring: 'Everybody is disgusted with his pride.' (vol. 1, ch. 16), Wickham feels secure enough to progress.

When Mr Wickham compares Mr Darcy's father with the current Mr Darcy, he speaks loosely in heightened language. Although Elizabeth would like to press him further, her finer feelings prevent her from prying.

Elizabeth is in sharp contrast with Wickham for whom no subjects seem barred. In any case Wickham cannot leave the subject alone and soon reverts to it unprompted. Elizabeth does not notice that she and Wickham have not a great deal to say to one another unless the subject is Mr Darcy.

A snare to thought

Elizabeth does not question Wickham's allegations or consider that it is Mr Darcy's entire honour that is being impeached. Surprisingly, her sceptical mind does not read the danger signs. She does not notice Wickham's being guilty several times of what Darcy perceptively describes as 'an indirect boast' (vol. 1, ch. 10). Had Elizabeth been less prejudiced and infatuated, she might have seen warning signs in the fact that Wickham mourns his deprivation of the rôle of clergyman in terms of the loss of 'a most valuable living'. There are no regrets for a spiritual and pastoral vocation denied.

A rational account?

There is irony in Elizabeth's response: 'Elizabeth allowed that he had given a very rational account of it' (vol. 1, ch. 16). Reason is absent in both account and response. Elizabeth acquaints Jane with her discoveries and should, as a result of her sister's reaction, have experienced a resurgence of those commonsensical queries that had arisen in her head in the course of Wickham's narrative. Jane's *is* the voice of reason: 'It is impossible . . . Can his most intimate friends be so excessively deceived in him? Oh! no' (vol. 1, ch. 17)

Wickham's popularity

Wickham's familiarity with the Bennet family is achieved almost as speedily as Mr Collins's. Elizabeth's Aunt Gardiner is concerned that a match between Elizabeth and Wickham would be most imprudent. But providence is at work; Elizabeth regrets potential blighted but is soon able to reassure her aunt that Wickham has taken up with someone else, who has suddenly acquired £10,000. Elizabeth sees that she is not in love with Wickham, though he is far and away the most agreeable man she has met. She forgives her favourite in a way that she could not forgive Charlotte for pursuing the prudential motive.

Wickham is useful to Elizabeth because he proves to her that strong physical attraction is not the same as love.

The testing of testimony

When Elizabeth visits Rosings, she at first acknowledges the truth of what Wickham has told her about Darcy's aunt, Lady Catherine de Bourgh. His delineation of *her* proves accurate. Darcy's letter, however, causes Elizabeth to rethink her judgement of Wickham.

Elizabeth is obliged to ponder Wickham and Darcy's irreconcilable testimonies.

Elizabeth now sees what, had she not been so taken with his fine figure and handsome face, she should have considered questionable about Wickham's conversation. In the light of such considerations, his pursuit of Miss King *was* mercenary, and his interest in herself either due to an erroneous belief about the extent of her fortune or due to the attention which she had all too prematurely lavished upon him.

The regiment is to leave Meryton soon after Elizabeth returns home. Now her eyes are open. She has learnt to be more discerning: 'She had even learnt to detect, in the very gentleness that once delighted her, an affectation and a sameness to disgust and weary' (vol. 2, ch. 18).

The snarer snared

Wickham attempts to resume his attentions, and Elizabeth feels annoyed at his complacency. She is mischievous enough to bring up the subject of Darcy. Wickham is clearly worried and craves reassurance. All Elizabeth's remarks are chosen to disconcert.

Elizabeth amuses herself at Wickham's expense. Getting to know him has proved an important staging post on her journey to self-knowledge. Wickham's function is first, knowingly, to seduce Elizabeth away from reason and then, unwittingly, to force her into it through disgust at him and at herself.

10.4 Mr Darcy

'It is settled between us already, that we are to be the happiest couple in the world.' (vol. 3, ch. 17)

A man bewitched

Early in the novel Elizabeth claims that 'intricate characters are the *most* amusing' (vol. 1, ch. 9). And certainly her hero *is* intricate. However,

Darcy's multifaceted plot relationship with Elizabeth exceeds in complexity that of his character.

What chiefly matters is what he does to her.

If we were to take the opening sentence of *Pride and Prejudice* at face value, this is to be a novel about catching your (rich) man. So Darcy is immediately significant.

This unredeemed and conventional subject is soon undermined, though, by a heroine who appears uninterested in catching men at all. She seems to reject completely her mother's agenda. It is the *hero* who becomes intent, against his will, in securing *her*. She is so at variance with any woman he has met before that he is 'bewitched' (vol. 1, ch. 10).

Balance

In *Women in Love* D.H. Lawrence speaks of the balance that must be achieved between a man and a woman. Tony Tanner also discusses the fact that, in various ways, such a balance exists between Elizabeth and Darcy. (Introduction to the Penguin English Library edition of *Pride and Prejudice*, 1972, pp. 40–1). In doing so, he goes a long way to explaining why the novel is so satisfactory on a cerebral level as well as being high romance and comedy.

As he points out, Elizabeth is said at one stage to show an 'indifference to decorum' (vol. 1, ch. 8), and her liveliness hovers for ever on the edge of something beyond constraint. It is apt that Darcy slyly asks if she would like to fling herself into a reel when Miss Bingley plays a spirited Scottish air. Darcy finds such energy attractive.

Regulation, horizon and energy

Darcy, in contrast, upholds a proper sense of pride. As Tony Tanner says: 'throughout his behaviour is a model of regulation' (p. 41). But regulation leads to stiffness and aloofness, of which Darcy is guilty. Tanner points out that Jane Austen wrote *Pride and Prejudice* at a time when major shifts in thought were taking place and that Elizabeth and Darcy are able to unite these two opposing modes (pp. 44–5). He sees Jane Austen as basically approving of the eighteenth-century cast of thought. So the maintaining of boundaries must always be respected. Tony Tanner contrasts eighteenth-century thinking with the Romantic poet and artist Blake, who 'took the word 'horizon', transformed it into 'Urizen' and made that figure the evil symbol of all that restricted and restrained man' (p.45). Elizabeth, at the same time as being determined to play her social and familial roles responsibly, is energy personified. Tony Tanner quotes from Blake's poem *The Marriage of Heaven and Hell*:

> Energy is the only life, and is from the Body; and Reason is the bound or outward circumstance of Energy. Energy is eternal Delight. (p. 46)

Tony Tanner concludes that Jane Austen in *Pride and Prejudice* 'shows us energy and reason coming together, not so much as a reconciliation of opposites, but as a marriage of complementaries' (p. 46). So there is no loss, only gain, both to selves and society, as

Georgiana Darcy, in amazement, sees in Elizabeth's and Darcy's combining respect with playfulness and ease.

Darcy as challenge

In volume 1, Darcy, though Elizabeth's proper counterbalance, is increasingly an object of Elizabeth's dislike. In volume 2 he causes her real pain on Jane's account. She has become increasingly irrational about him. From the time when he writes to her after his proposal, though, she begins to reassess him.

Like Wickham, Darcy challenges Elizabeth to exercise her reason.

He has been challenging her in this way, unwittingly, ever since he began to admire her.

Elizabeth is convinced that she has Darcy's measure. But the truth is she hardly knows him.

Before his proposal, Darcy keeps visiting Hunsford Parsonage. Charlotte declares that he must be in love with Elizabeth. Elizabeth discredits this and is amazed at his often sitting in silence when he calls. What Elizabeth cannot take on board is how different Darcy is from her. This exposes her limitations. She never thinks that his silences could be the result of deep feeling.

Darcy is a romantic figure, but instead of his love being tempestuous and overflowing, it is silent and controlled.

Something that Elizabeth learns from a chance remark from Colonel Fitzwilliam, also staying at Rosings, makes Darcy the last companion that she wants. She realizes that it is Darcy, not Miss Bingley, who has been the cause of Bingley's separation from Jane.

So at the point in the novel where Elizabeth attracts Darcy irresistibly and he repels her utterly, the moment has come for the very indiscreet announcement of his feelings for her.

Elizabeth's prejudice is at its height to match Darcy's pride. The title of the novel has reached its apotheosis.

Darcy's four proposals

Darcy can be thought of as making four proposals before his final one is accepted. Increasingly they provide Elizabeth with what she wants and needs. They can be summed up as the inept proposal, the letter, Pemberley and Lydia.

The inept proposal

In contrast with Mr Collins's proposal which nearly drives Elizabeth to laughter, Mr Darcy's (vol. 2, ch. 11) reduces her to tears. Elizabeth recoils from Darcy's proposal, but his staccato delivery as he paces the room is in accordance with her own instinct for spontaneous feelings. Darcy's words come out in a kind of burst, the simplest of sentences to convey the most urgent of emotions:

> In vain have I struggled. It will not do. My feelings will not be repressed. You must allow me to tell you how ardently I admire and love you.

Contrast this with the control of Mr Collins – his subordinate clauses – and his complacency:

> Believe me, my dear Miss Elizabeth, that your modesty, so far from doing you any disservice, rather adds to your other perfections. (vol. 1, ch. 19)

What is striking about Darcy is how much he imposes his physical presence on the room. We have no idea what Mr Collins is doing as he addresses Elizabeth.

Darcy's language is a curious combination of the ardent and the insulting.

Darcy's proposal affords Elizabeth release.

She lays her objections on the line. He has insulted her and ruined the happiness of her sister. He has reduced Mr Wickham to poverty. At this stage, Elizabeth's anger reaches such a pitch that she is nearly shouting at him. Perhaps this is a sign that she had been more involved with Wickham than she had thought.

Her vitriol sends Darcy strutting in distress across the room. He clearly has taken the last accusation to heart. The candour that Darcy displays doubtless makes Elizabeth determined not to spare hers, and she spells out for him how she has long believed in 'your arrogance, your conceit and your selfish disdain of the feelings of others' (vol. 2, ch. 11).

The letter

Darcy's letter is perhaps under the circumstances the 'real' proposal although it contains no repeat of his offer. It shows him happier as a man of argument, happier still when he can formulate his case on paper. The clarity of this 'proposal' comes by way of a history and retrospection.

Darcy's first proposal confirms everything that Elizabeth thinks she knows about him. Darcy's letter makes Elizabeth realize that she will have to think again.

At first she wants to believe it is all lies. But at last she brings her reason to bear. She sees her mistakes when she interprets past events through present intelligence.

The proposal and the letter begin a process of re-education for both Darcy and Elizabeth.

Elizabeth has not been entirely unjust to Darcy nor has she totally lacked discernment where he is concerned. Through her honesty she prepares the way for their happy endings. She gives him insights that nobody else could, and in time he acts on them. Similarly, Darcy's criticism of the way her family had behaved on the night of the Netherfield ball is acknowledged as just.

The persuasions of Pemberley

The Pemberley visit supplements the revised impression that Elizabeth was beginning to form of Darcy on receipt of his letter. She is curious to see his home, which suggests she now wants to learn more about him. The place plays on her in the opposite way from which places usually work in love affairs. Normally, one falls in love, and the places associated with the beloved become loved in their turn.

Darcy's place is his advocate – another sort of proposal. His grounds woo Elizabeth silently, as the man has often done himself.

Darcy's portrait recommends him. Elizabeth suddenly acknowledges 'a more gentle sensation towards the original' (vol. 3, ch. 1).

The shock of Elizabeth's and Darcy's meeting one another is profound. Now that Elizabeth's mind is running on him, it is as if some deeply held wish is father to the fact. She turns to look again at his *house*, and *he* appears. Afterwards, Elizabeth cannot believe the transformation. Now her mind is completely fixed on him. He fills her imagination. What is running through *his* mind?

He continues to woo her. He even introduces his sister as an inducement! Perhaps he feels that her gentleness will impress Elizabeth as a possible family trait and make her think again!

When Elizabeth and the Gardiners return Miss Darcy's call, the collection of cold food and magnificent fruit that is gathered round the table appears emblematic of the great fruition that may yet be. Fruit is often a symbol of the promise of love, and there is enough here to be worthy of a wedding feast.

The Lydia effect

The very next day Elizabeth has just read the two letters concerning Lydia when Mr Darcy appears. It is as if her need summons him (vol. 3, ch. 4). Though, when the wedding is accomplished, Elizabeth, who sees how well-suited she and Darcy are, regrets what she told him about Wickham. It is fortunate that she does so. When she sees what he has done to save Lydia, Elizabeth recognizes that:

Mr Darcy is worthy to be her hero as he has assumed the Christian duty of seeking the lost.

Potential fulfilled

Elizabeth's respect for Darcy is now profound. The rich need not be proud and thoughtless hedonists, preoccupied only with preserving rank and wealth within families. Through scrupulous regulation Darcy, who guards and guides a whole neighbourhood, has continued the tradition of his highly regarded father in assuming responsibility for the Bennet family (see 9.9). Treatment of the fallen Lydia is a telling yardstick; Mrs Bennet indulges, Mr Wickham seduces, Mr Bennet pursues (but is relieved to have the burden of paying for her recklessness removed), Mr Collins condemns, the Gardiners provide sanctuary, but Mr Darcy redeems.

In redeeming Lydia, Darcy redeems himself.

Elizabeth's criticisms, taken so much to heart, allow him to go the second mile. The Darcy whom the housekeeper, Mrs Reynolds, knows shows himself to be as responsible and generous as she claims.

Gratitude

Gratitude is the basis for Elizabeth's falling in love with Darcy, gratitude that he should still love her in spite of her faults. Elizabeth sees Darcy as crucial to her maturing. Through him, she is able to grow beyond the jealous preservation of her own ego to an awareness of an objective world, which requires careful, detached and ever vigilant reading.

Darcy is there to provoke, intrigue, disgust and astound her, and to be the butt of her disapproval. Then his function is to enlighten, disarm and delight her. In the end he will fulfil her in a way that no man of lesser brain, looks, taste or moral fibre possibly could.

The successful proposal

When Darcy and Elizabeth meet again at Netherfield, Elizabeth feels all the discomfort of the situation acutely. Darcy looks at the ground and says nothing. This is *not* what Elizabeth wants or needs, so she forms 'a desperate resolution' (vol. 3 chap 16). Recognizing that Darcy cannot know how she feels, she expresses her gratitude on behalf of the whole family. This leads to a declaration and the proposal that confirms Elizabeth's deepest hope.

The amount of withheld joy, implicit in the letter (vol. 3, ch. 18) from Elizabeth to Mrs Gardiner announcing her engagement, bursts forth at the end, as Elizabeth announces: 'I am happier even than Jane; she only smiles, I laugh.' Elizabeth's letter is full of confidence, love, presumption, delight and a kind of girlish glee: 'Mr Darcy sends you all the love in the world that he can spare from me. You are all to come to Pemberley for Christmas.'

One can imagine the joy that will reign at Pemberley. No other house in the novel is said to contain joy except the home in the aptly named Gracechurch Street.

10.5 Colonel Fitzwilliam

'in person and address most truly the gentleman' (vol. 2, ch. 7)

When she meets Colonel Fitzwilliam, Elizabeth has been pestered by Mr Collins, regrets what might have been with Wickham, is disappointed, on Jane's behalf, in Bingley and has a horror of Mr Darcy.

Colonel Fitzwilliam, about thirty, not handsome, but very much the gentleman in 'person and address', restores Elizabeth's confidence in herself and the male sex.

He is an easy conversationalist, demonstrating in everything his good-breeding. Jane Austen expects the reader (and maybe Elizabeth) to see him as worthy of being a possible suitor.

On their first evening at Rosings, Elizabeth cannot but be aware that he singles her out for special attention immediately and throughout the evening. Needless to say, he can far more truly appreciate Elizabeth's worth than a superficial charmer and moral degenerate such as Mr Wickham or the crassly insensitive moral buffoon, Mr Collins. He sits by her and they talk with great animation. Elizabeth senses that she is appreciated by a discerning man. He makes Rosings entertaining in a way that it has never been before. After coffee he reminds her that she had promised to play for him and he presses his physical proximity for a second time. He must delight her since, if only in jest, he is disparaging of Darcy.

Colonel Fitzwilliam continues to seek out Elizabeth at the parsonage. She thoroughly enjoys his company. This, together with the fact that he very plainly admires her, reminds her of 'her former favourite George Wickham' (vol. 2, ch. 8). She cannot help comparing the two and though she finds 'less captivating softness' in Colonel Fitzwilliam's manners, she believes 'he might have the best informed mind'.

It is Colonel Fitzwilliam who lets slip inadvertently that Darcy was to blame for the separation of Bingley and Jane.

Part of Colonel Fitzwilliam's function is to fuel Elizabeth's prejudice against Darcy at a crucial time.

But although Colonel Fitzwilliam and Elizabeth have so much in common, he eschews the opportunity to consider an engagement as a future possibility through taking too worldly a view of her financial situation.

Colonel Fitzwilliam thus proves to Elizabeth how influential prudential motives are.

He recognizes Elizabeth's worth, yet, for all his ease of manner and affability, he takes more notice of money (and status?) than Mr Darcy. He is more like his aunt and Mr Wickham: 'Colonel Fitzwilliam had made it clear that he had no intentions at all, and agreeable as he was, she did not mean to be unhappy about him' (vol. 2, ch. 11). His plot function is to draw attention to the greater suitability of Mr Darcy.

10.6 Mr Bennet

'I could not have parted with you, my Lizzy, to any one less worthy.' (vol. 3, ch. 17)

The owner of Longbourn

Mr Bennet, as owner of a property entailed in favour of the main line, seems to take a frivolous approach to the arrival of a young, wealthy, single male to the area. But Mr Bennet's apparent detachment conceals his realism: he knows about the necessity of getting his daughters well married.

Contrasting marriages

Mr Bennet and Mrs Bennet provide an object lesson in how a marriage should not be.

The novel opens with a marriage in which the wife does not understand the husband and the husband glories in being misunderstood. It closes looking forward to a marriage in which happiness, empathy, teasing and laughter will feed a family, friends and an entire community. *Partly* this has been prepared for at Longbourn. The quickness of Mr Bennet's repartee is appealing when it does not border on the cruel. To be born a Bennet is clearly stimulating.

What Elizabeth gains from her father

The vigorous wit of Mr Bennet permeates the first chapter. Elizabeth has inherited this wit. She is, in this regard, absolutely her father's daughter: 'Lizzy has something more of quickness than her sisters' (vol. 1, ch. 1).

Mr Bennet is in the novel to demonstrate why Elizabeth is as she is.

He enjoys what is outrageous, and Elizabeth's unconventionality is probably learnt behaviour.

Elizabeth does not seem to have missed out on an education, despite having no governess. One suspects that Elizabeth, at least, made use of the run of Mr Bennet's study. Doubtless, Mr Bennet taught her much, perhaps through suggested reading and informed conversation.

Mr Bennet seeks consolation for an unsatisfactory marriage by withdrawing to his study, where he alternates reading with issuing broadsides at the folly of the world in satirical aphorisms. From him Elizabeth has learnt to deal with the minor blows life deals her by adopting a bright, brittle, witty tone while smarting a good deal at a deeper level than she, with all her intuition, is aware of.

In Elizabeth's conversation with her sister over Mr Bingley we see her father's influence on her verbal style. They both tend towards the laconic. When Jane is enthusing over Mr Bingley's qualities, Elizabeth adds to the list: 'He is also handsome . . . which a young man ought likewise to be, if he possibly can. His character is thereby complete' (vol. 1, ch. 4).

Elizabeth wonders at Jane. She does not realize how few are like herself and her father; they are receptive of meanings that escape others and highly sensitized to people's foibles and weaknesses, including their own.

Elizabeth's need to get away

Elizabeth is the only member of the family who has any real understanding of her father. She is painfully aware that the mismatch between her parents has led to a less than cohesive family. She knows that her father has not treated his wife with decorum or brought his younger daughters up to be sensible, aware of others or even reputable.

Mr Bennet finds his wife's conversation too predictable, so he needs a sparring partner. This he finds in Lizzy. In this respect he is Darcy's forerunner, and in intellect, wit and love of reading, he is not unlike him. Indeed, he prepares Elizabeth for him, not least in being complex.

Intellectually Lizzy is the substitute for the wife he should have chosen. He is too dependent on her, though, missing her greatly when she is away and hastening her return.

The poignancy of *Pride and Prejudice* is that although Elizabeth loves her father – he is after all *the* man in her life – she has to distance herself from him.

She needs to escape the place that she has come to occupy in his life and she needs to escape his viewpoint. Unlike Elizabeth, Mr Bennet has detached himself to such a degree that he can view with composure the sight of his family making fools of themselves. Similarly, he sees his neighbours as a butt for his ridicule and not a cause for his compassion. His attitude, though pithily and wittily expressed, seems shallow and heartless compared with the empathy and kindness with which Elizabeth and Jane try to engage with people. There is more to life than wit.

Elizabeth is endangered by cynicism; her Aunt Gardiner recognizes the disappointment that is fuelling her as she reviews her position on men.

> Thank Heaven! I am going tomorrow where I shall find a man who has not one agreeable quality, who has neither manner nor sense to recommend him. Stupid men are the only ones worth knowing, after all. (vol. 2, ch. 4)

Mutual advisers

Both father and daughter feel the need to speak out when each thinks the other is in danger of grave misjudgement.

Elizabeth feels impelled to warn Mr Bennet of the imprudence of Lydia's going to Brighton and advise him not to let her go. Although Mr Bennet is flippant in his response, he later concedes wryly that Elizabeth was right.

The real test of Mr Bennet – his learning of the prospective engagement of Elizabeth to Darcy – shows him behaving like a truly caring parent. He is highly disturbed by it and advises his daughter to reconsider what she is doing. Here he proves himself as heroic as Darcy. Without being insensitively direct about it, he confides in her, giving her the benefit of his wisdom gained through bitter experience. He has never explicitly expressed *his* disappointment in marriage; now he does so only because *Elizabeth* might benefit.

> 'I know your disposition, Lizzy. I know that you could be neither happy nor respectable, unless you truly esteemed your husband . . . My child, let me not have the grief of seeing *you* unable to respect your partner in life. You know not what you are about.' (vol. 3, ch. 17)

His plea is particularly poignant in view of the fact that the intimacy of their shared family life is coming to an end. However, it is likely that Mr Bennet finds intense satisfaction in Elizabeth's marriage to Darcy. There he can see that 'marriage of true minds' that might have been his had he not been 'captivated by youth and beauty' (vol. 2, ch. 19) but waited to meet someone as individual as he.

11 Different kinds of pride and prejudice

11.1 Title words

'With a strong prejudice against every thing he might say . . . It was all pride and insolence.' (vol. 2, ch. 13)

Pride and Prejudice, like *Sense and Sensibility,* features two abstract nouns. The titles, therefore, proffer moral and philosophical challenges.

Both 'pride' and 'prejudice' have moral force in Johnson. His first two definitions of 'pride' are '1. Inordinate and unreasonable self esteem. 2. Insolence; rude treatment of others.' ('It was all pride and insolence.') Prejudice is also defined with a moral edge. '1. Prepossession; judgement formed beforehand without examination. 2. Mischief; detriment; hurt; injury.'

'Pride' is rich in religious associations. It is the most grievous of the seven deadly sins because it is the one from which all others stem. To place oneself above God and other people leads to envy, gluttony, wrath and so on. Milton's Satan (a figure that exercised an interestingly ambiguous attraction for the Romantic age) is marked by pride. Indeed, Johnson's first definition is drawn from Milton. Jane Austen would know from scripture and the Prayer Book that God 'scatters the proud in the imagination of their hearts'.

11.2 Mistaken judgements

'We will not quarrel for the greater share of blame.' (vol. 3, ch. 16)

'Pride' and 'prejudice' are terms of observation and judgement as well as moral discrimination. Pride often leads to distorted vision. Elizabeth's pride in her capacity to read character makes her prejudiced against Darcy.

Both Darcy and Elizabeth have deep understanding, yet they fail to be as perceptive as they pride themselves on being.

Darcy expected Elizabeth to be delighted by his proposal. Likewise, Elizabeth had no inkling, until she thought more objectively on receiving Darcy's letter, that she could possibly be wrong about Wickham.

What we see and how we judge are central preoccupations in Jane Austen's work (see 18.6). If it is not improper to call her outlook philosophical, it might be said that she combines the empirical tradition's emphasis on everyday knowledge (can I really be sure that I see this table?) with an interest in the more penetrative aspects of thought. Thomas Reid insisted that all perceptions involve judgement, and Coleridge found a place for the integrating work of the imagination. Both stressed that understanding is a complex business. Jane Austen, while cautious about the imagination, saw that perception is a subtle and sometimes a difficult matter. Perhaps such an understanding made her show Elizabeth's wisely deciding not to dispute with Darcy 'the greater share of blame' in their mutually mistaken judgements. Seeing and judging others is a very difficult phenomenon.

Yet everyone in the novel does it. Elizabeth and Darcy are not the only ones to harbour pride and prejudice. Most of the characters make prejudiced judgements out of pride. Indeed, *Pride and Prejudice* might be said to advance a phenomenology of the two abstract nouns that constitute its title. The variety of 'prides' and 'prejudices' warrants us seeing the author as painting, as Butler does in his sermons, a broad and a sharply characterized canvas of human failings.

11.3 Pride in one's own discernment

'I, who have valued myself on my abilities!' (vol. 2, ch. 13)

Elizabeth Bennet

Elizabeth has good reason to pride herself on her reading of character. She is acutely perceptive. As A.H. Wright points out *Jane Austen's Novels – A Study in Structure*, Penguin, 1962, pp. 11–12) she can read her family, read the merits and faults of the Bingleys after very few meetings, see through Mr Collins from his first letter and take the measure of Lady Catherine de Bourgh. She has those qualities of perception that Catherine Morland in *Northanger Abbey* painfully has to acquire.

Elizabeth's learning is perhaps the more challenging because in seeing through her own prejudices she has to acknowledge the distorting lens of her pride. She believes initially that she has every reason to trust her judgements – and what she takes to be the evidence – where Darcy and Wickham are concerned. However, once she reads Darcy's letter she is (typically?) hard on herself:

> 'I have courted prepossession and ignorance, and driven reason away . . . Till this moment, I never knew myself.' (vol. 2, ch. 13)

'Prepossession' is Johnson's language ('Prepossession; judgement formed beforehand without examination'). Elizabeth dramatizes herself as the forward woman who 'courted' ignorance and, in the manner of rejecting a suitor, drove away reason. Pride has fed her prejudice:

> Of neither Darcy nor Wickham could she think, without feeling that she had been blind, partial, prejudiced, absurd.
>
> 'How despicably have I acted!' she cried. – 'I, who have prided myself on my discernment!'

The strength of 'absurd' shows that false readings arising from pride make a nonsense of morality and meaning. Elizabeth has made mistakes that her sister Jane, even with her capacity for giving people the benefit of the doubt, would never make.

Mary Bennet

One of the entertainments of the text is that it is the earnest but very inexperienced Mary who pontificates on the most serious of the seven deadly sins.

Mary, 'who piqued herself upon the solidity of her reflections' (vol. 1, ch. 5) gives a little diatribe on the subject of pride. This ends up with a nice distinction between pride and vanity – 'Pride relates more to our opinion of ourselves, vanity to what we would have others think of us.' (vol. 1, ch. 5). Mary is complacent. She suffers from both.

Mary has no self-knowledge and no sense of fun. Unlike Elizabeth, she is given no moment of awakening. Essentially a closed character, Mary likes to read 'great books, and make extracts' (vol. 1, ch. 2) and trots out her ideas, however ill-digested and ill-timed, such as her 'useful lesson' on Lydia's fall: that 'loss of virtue in a female is irretrievable . . . one false step involves her in endless ruin' (vol. 3, ch. 5).

Elizabeth rolls her eyes. In the event, Mary gets Lydia's fate wrong, for ruined she is not! Lydia's fall only matters to Mary because in her pride she has the opportunity to display the somewhat hackneyed moral sentences she has culled. Morality for Mary is a pretext for 'performance', a demonstration of her capacity for supposed profundity of thought.

11.4 Pride in self and social standing

'The distinction had perhaps been felt too strongly.' (vol. 1, ch. 5)

Sir William Lucas

Pride has social and political associations. Jane Austen confines Sir William Lucas virtually to one characteristic – he is comically preoccupied with his having been presented at St James's. His business and his home in a small market town no longer satisfy him, so he has moved to a house proudly designated Lucas Lodge.

The Lucases like to keep their distinction – 'in general . . . they visit no new comers' (vol. 1, ch. 1). But they are pleased to make an exception where prospective matrimony is concerned, as with the arrival of Mr Bingley.

Because Sir William wishes to be considered on a par with people of rank and wealth, he ineptly and patronizingly commends Mr Darcy's dancing: 'It is evident that you belong to the first circles' (vol. 1, ch. 18).

Sir William is eager to ape people with rank. He loves to flaunt his knowledge of the manners of the great acquired through his 'situation in life' (vol. 2, ch. 6). His overall position on rank is uncertain, as it is with Mr Collins. He cannot help paying it great deference, and yet it is as if he is never really looking at the object, except as it reflects upon himself. In short, he suffers from the prejudice of distorted vision arising from pride itself. Deep down, he feels as superior as anybody. When Mr Collins owns the Longbourn estate, he declares, both he *and* his wife will make their appearance at St James's!

Miss Bingley and Mrs Hurst

Both Miss Bingley and Mrs Hurst have a place in Jane Austen's thorough taxonomy of pride and prejudice. They are both 'proud and conceited' (vol. 1, ch. 4), considering themselves to be socially far superior to the Bennets. This is ironic, for 'their brother's fortune and their own had been acquired by trade' (see 12.3). They are glorified Gardiners, though without the latters' moral sense.

All their characteristics stem from their pride in their looks, their fashionable education, their fortune of £20,000 and their incapacity to stay within it! They are social climbers: Miss Bingley has Georgiana Darcy earmarked for her brother and Mr Darcy for herself. Their disagreeable traits also stem from pride. They find Mrs Bennet socially 'intolerable' (vol. 1, ch. 6); they put down their 'friends', criticizing Elizabeth behind her back and being extremely scathing about the Bennet sisters having relatives in Cheapside. The comedy lies in their overweening pride's having no basis in their talents; in the evenings Mrs Hurst has to resort to playing with her bracelets and rings.

Mr and Mrs Collins

Mr Collins is very proud. He sees society as a rigid hierarchy, and considers 'the clerical office as equal in point of dignity with the highest rank in the kingdom'. (vol. 1, ch. 18) (How does he square this with the Bible?)

In spite of his convictions, he is intent on abasing himself before people of rank. His unrelenting onslaught on those with patronage is beautifully summed up in the line 'And with a low bow he left her to *attack* Mr Darcy' (vol. 1, ch. 18 our italics). Lady Catherine de Bourgh is served up as a mighty titbit to potential brides, and for houseguests she becomes, before the days of the National Trust, a tourist attraction.

It is one of Jane Austen's entertaining subtleties that Charlotte proves the ideal wife for him. He boasts that he and Charlotte are always of one mind. This sounds ridiculous; yet they agree on their central mission: social climbing and material advancement. Not by instinct deferential like her father and her husband, Charlotte is prepared to ingratiate herself with Lady Catherine to further the marital cause. Given that Mr Collins's obsequiousness in the face of rank is a form of self-advancement, it is easy to imagine him, as a result of Mr Bennet's letter 'advising' him that Mr Darcy has more to offer (vol. 3, ch. 18), transferring his fussy attentions to the Derbyshire magnate.

11.5 Mr Darcy's pride

'I could easily forgive his pride, if he had not mortified *mine*.' (vol. 1, ch. 5)

Johnson, in recognition of common usage, does not only define 'pride' negatively. His third and fourth definitions could be descriptions of Darcy: '3. Dignity of manner; loftiness of air. 4. Generous elevation of heart.' The first encapsulates Darcy's demeanour; the second his rescue of Lydia. Pride can be a virtue as well as a sin. The novel turns on the nature of Darcy's pride. Mrs Reynolds, Darcy's housekeeper, denies that her master has any pride. Charlotte Lucas's view is that Darcy has a *right* to his pride. He has the wealth and antecedents. Elizabeth comes to see (and surely the reader is invited eventually to agree) that 'he has no improper pride' (vol. 3, ch. 17).

Pride in one's lineage

Elizabeth's path to enlightenment is one that Darcy also travels. He must disentangle proper from improper pride. Is he right in seeing pride as justified 'where there is a real superiority of mind' (vol. 1, ch. 11 – see 10.4)? Is he right to take pride in his lineage? How should he have responded when he realized the hold that Elizabeth Bennet was beginning to have over him? What should we make of his efforts to conceal signs of admiration, so that 'nothing . . . could *elevate* her with the hope of influencing his felicity' (vol. 1, ch. 12; our italics)?

Pride when proposing

In terms of pride, Mr Darcy's proposal is hardly distinguishable from that of Mr Collins. It is Darcy's pride that makes him believe that Elizabeth is bound to accept him. His is a case of pride feeding prejudice; Elizabeth has given him no indication that she admires him.

So preoccupied is he with the issue of status that he is unaware of her rising contempt. Her rebuke turns out to be pivotal to the plot; his insensitive manner has saved her the 'concern' that she would have felt if he had 'behaved in a more gentle-man-like manner' (vol. 2, ch. 11). In retrospect, Darcy painfully encounters his own pride. Darcy has considered himself by birth and manners a gentleman.

The letter that Elizabeth receives the day after the proposal begins by sounding defensive and petulant. But the reader sees that the tone changes.

Darcy's reform begins in the very act of writing.

11.6 Pride in family

'He is a gentleman; I am a gentleman's daughter; so far we are equal.' (vol. 3, ch. 14)

Darcy is actually right when he surmises that Elizabeth's pride is hurt by the aspersions he casts on her family. However, he prepares Elizabeth for her confrontation with Lady Catherine.

Elizabeth the upstart

Lady Catherine, determined to stop Elizabeth's marrying Darcy, adopts a similar line of put-down to her nephew. Clearly, Lady Catherine believes that Elizabeth is on the make, that she is, in fact, a Charlotte Collins. She never considers that Elizabeth is deeply in love with Darcy and he with her.

Elizabeth's response to Lady Catherine is magnificent. Not for her to be cowed that Darcy and Anne De Bourgh 'are descended on the maternal side, from the same noble line'. Mr Darcy 'is a gentleman; I am a gentleman's daughter; so far we are equal'. And for all his riches, Mr Darcy *is* only a gentleman. He has no title. It is up to the reader to see that Mr Darcy's haughtiness has unintentionally helped Elizabeth to cope with his aunt.

Lady Catherine knows the 'conditions' of Elizabeth's mother's relatives, but irony works against her.

Elizabeth knows that her Aunt and Uncle Gardiner behave more truly like gentlefolk than ever does Lady Catherine.

Elizabeth, keenly attuned to absurdities, must relish this; she would never have argued *her* claim to 'the gentry' if Lady Catherine had not forced it upon her.

11.7 Prejudice in favour of one's offspring

'If I wished to think slightingly of any body's children, it should not be my own however.' (vol. 1, ch. 7)

Prejudice

Because the novel is mediated through the consciousness of Elizabeth, and because Elizabeth, although proud, is chiefly marked by her wilful forming of prejudices,

***Pride and Prejudice* is more about prejudice than pride.**

The substance of the latter part of the novel is Elizabeth's gradual and painful shedding of her prejudices. Certainly, the reader must believe that Mr Darcy has struggled to overcome his pride, but it is only the *results* of the struggle, not the struggle itself, that the reader encounters. In turning, therefore, to prejudice we meet the chief matter of the book.

Mr and Mrs Bennet

Prejudice makes an appearance in the first chapter; the arrival at Netherfield of a young man of fortune prompts Mr Bennet to show prejudice in favour of his daughter Lizzy, and Mrs Bennet puts forward the claims of *her* two favourites. What Mary and Kitty make of all this can only be imagined!

Mrs Bennet, famous in her youth for her looks and still a handsome woman, is bursting with pride in Jane. She is thrilled with Jane's success with Mr Bingley at the Meryton Assembly compared with Charlotte Lucas's. She shamelessly praises Jane in front of Mr Bingley. When Jane is ill at Netherfield, Mrs Bennet boasts about how uncomplainingly she copes with suffering, 'for she has, without exception, the sweetest temper I ever met with. I often tell my other girls they are nothing to *her*' (vol. 1, ch. 9). (Patience under suffering was a conventional female virtue.)

Perhaps Mrs Bennet's most extraordinary prejudice is the one in favour of whichever daughter marries youngest. She is delighted to have Lydia married at only fifteen. It does not seem to trouble her, once the marriage is accomplished, how it came about.

Lady Anne De Bourgh

Lady Catherine's prejudice in favour of her daughter would be poignant if it were not so ridiculous. Because she has to make the excuse of illhealth for potential unfulfilled, every claim she makes is unprovable. She is certain that Anne, like herself, would have 'been a great proficient' (vol. 2, ch. 8) at the pianoforte, if she had learnt! Is there a hint that Lady Anne's ill health is the result of interbreeding? Not the least unsavoury fact about Elizabeth Bennet is that she is health personified and undoubtedly capable of producing an heir. Could Anne?

11.8 Prejudice in favour of class distinction

'She likes to have the distinction of rank preserved.' (vol.1, ch. 6)

An admiration for rank can turn an insult into a compliment. When Mr Collins exclaims at the size and furniture of Mrs Phillips's drawing room and declares that he 'might almost have supposed himself in the smaller summer breakfast parlour at Rosings' (vol. 1, ch. 16), she bristles. But when she hears what Rosings is and who owns it, she 'would hardly have resented a comparison with the housekeeper's room'.

Mrs Bennet's response to the typically insulting behaviour of Lady Catherine is similar. Although Lady Catherine ignores her, Mrs Bennet complements her civility: 'She is a very fine-looking woman! and her calling here was prodigiously civil' (vol. 3, ch. 14).

Lady Catherine and Miss De Bourgh

Lady Catherine is prejudiced as well as proud. Lady Catherine's rudeness (one of the delights of the novel) is a function of her unquestioned prejudices about her social position and the privileges attached to it.

Lady Catherine builds her awesome reputation on what Elizabeth terms 'the mere stateliness of money and rank' (vol. 2, ch. 6). Every remark she makes appears to be a special favour to her company. In fact, through inviting the Collinses and their guests to Rosings, she satisfies her own curiosity and relieves her boredom.

Miss De Bourgh makes all the same assumptions about the entitlements of rank as Lady Catherine does. She keeps Charlotte standing chatting in the cold. She takes it for granted that Mrs Jenkinson should do everything for her. Like her mother, Miss De Bourgh holds forth the entire time, though in a low voice and only to Mrs Jenkinson. She makes no effort to communicate with Elizabeth.

That Lady Catherine believes herself incontrovertible is demonstrated by the way that after dinner at Rosings she speaks without stopping till coffee time. She has no prejudices in favour of the rational engagement of dialogue!

Lady Catherine on Elizabeth's marriage

Lady Catherine's prejudice is fully present in the way she tries to find out whether Elizabeth is engaged to her nephew. That she wants such a report 'universally contradicted' (vol. 3, ch. 14) balances out the famous opening sentence of the novel, 'It is a truth *universally acknowledged* ...' (our italics).

Lady Catherine cannot credit the savoir-faire with which Elizabeth parries her most outrageous statements. Her whole argument is founded on the assumption of rank – that Darcy will accord with her and her late sister's arrangements, and that Elizabeth is indeed a nobody who would mind being a pariah in the Darcy family. In her anger she makes Elizabeth sound like a woman of easy virtue, as she speaks of her 'arts and allurements'. But it is Lady Catherine who is using art, the art of appealing to rank: 'Miss Bennet, do you know who I am?' (vol. 3, ch. 14).

Mr Collins warns his cousin and 'her noble admirer' not to run 'hastily into a marriage which has not been properly sanctioned' (vol. 3, ch. 15). Mr Collins, a clerk in holy orders, thinks that the sanction given to marriage by Holy Church still requires the validation of Lady Catherine.

11.9 Prejudice in favour of Wickham

'Elizabeth went away with her head full of him.' (vol. 1, ch. 16)

The relationship of Elizabeth with Mr Wickham is a tale of rampant prejudice in his favour.

A way with words

The prejudice in favour of Mr Wickham is the common one of being attracted to charm of person and of manner. Mr Wickham follows up his introduction to Elizabeth with easy conversation. Noone could be in starker contrast with Mr Darcy (see 10.3).

Wickham works on Elizabeth through his way with words.

He is quite a rhetorician. Notice the repetition of 'same' and the careful paralleling of two touchingly unequal destinies:

> 'We were born in the same parish, within the same park ...inmates of the same house, objects of the same parental care.' (vol. 1, ch. 16)

His emotive language achieves its end. He deals in superlatives. He praises Meryton as providing 'excellent acquaintance'. He presents himself in the sentimental role of 'a disappointed man'.

Although Wickham uses such words to reinforce his plight with the full weight of their meaning, he is quick to skirt over others as if they carry no meaning at all.

He says that Darcy made claims of 'extravagance' and 'imprudence' against Wickham – 'in short anything or nothing'. It is surprising that Elizabeth lets this pass.

The prejudice of others

The novel is like a detective story, with evidence building up now against Darcy and later against Wickham. The latter even receives a back-handed commendation from Mr Bennet: 'Let Wickham be *your* man. He is a pleasant fellow and would jilt you creditably' (vol. 2, ch. 1).

Mrs Gardiner, too, because Wickham has a Derbyshire connection and is so personable, thinks she recollects having heard Darcy spoken of as 'a very proud, ill-natured boy' (vol. 2, ch. 2).

Prejudice in favour of Wickham also exists in a character whom we never see – Mrs Younge. She has presided over an establishment formed for Georgiana Darcy in London and is in league with Wickham. They are two of a kind and incapable therefore of loyalty, but it is interesting to conjecture how, for mutual self-interest, they may hunt together.

Elizabeth's stubbornness

No matter what warnings Elizabeth receives about not trusting Mr Wickham – from Bingley via Jane, from Miss Bingley, eventually from Mrs Gardiner and, indirectly, from Darcy himself – she continues naïvely to believe 'there was truth in Wickham's looks' (vol. 1, ch. 16). Her Aunt Gardiner tries to suggest there is perfidy in Wickham's unheralded change of affections from Elizabeth to Miss King, but Elizabeth will have none of it.

Lydia

Lydia's prejudice in favour of Wickham proves stronger than her virtue. Part of Lydia's obsession with Wickham arises from her prejudice in favour of officers. This she shares with Kitty and even her mother. Wickham is seen as a shimmering young man who 'wanted only regimentals to make him completely charming' (vol. 1, ch. 15).

Lydia's prejudice in Wickham's favour and her blindness to his true nature are apparent in the ironic note that she leaves for Harriet Forster.

Lydia has not a thought that Wickham would only marry for money and that he has none himself. Money and morality do not enter into the equation. This is pure infatuation, lust and idiocy: 'there is but one man in the world I love, and he is an angel. I should never be happy without him, so think it no harm to be off' (vol. 3, ch. 5).

Darcy tries unsuccessfully to persuade her to leave her disgraceful situation. Lydia has no use for her friends and does not even care when Wickham and she marry as she knows it will happen 'sometime or other' (vol. 3, ch. 10).

In Lydia Mrs Bennet speaks: it is the same blend of prejudice and ignorance of the self.

The uses of prejudice

In his *Reflections upon the Revolution in France* (1790), Edmund Burke argues the usefulness of prejudice. None of us, he argues, can work out difficult matters for ourselves. We need the judgements the past has already made to be our guide. In other words, we need that which has been pre-judged – prejudice. He points out that those who think about the big questions often end up endorsing prejudgements:

> If they find what they seek, and they seldom fail, they think it more wise to continue the prejudice, with the reason involved, than to cast away the coat of prejudice, and to leave nothing but the naked reason. (Penguin edition, 1968, p. 183)

Prejudice is not opposed to reason. It uses the reasons of the past that have proved themselves worthy of adherence.

There is in *Pride and Prejudice* an understanding of judgement that endorses Burke's interpretation of prejudice. But we might easily overlook it. Because the novel is concerned with many cases in which judgement is distorted by prejudice, readers may overlook the moments when prejudices are shown to be right.

Darcy has seen enough of Wickham to judge him as untrustworthy. In Burke's sense he has formed a prejudice. The narrative endorses Darcy's judgement.

11.10 Prejudice against Darcy

'He was the proudest, most disagreeable man in the world.' (vol. 1, ch. 3)

General prejudice

Darcy's insightful prejudice against Wickham is in contrast with the general prejudice against the squire of Pemberley. Although Darcy draws every eye to him at the Meryton assembly, he is almost immediately persona non grata. It is interesting to note how the prejudice arises. Darcy is a serious-minded young man and very shy, 'reserved, and fastidious' (vol. 1, ch. 4). The judgement passed upon him is partly the result of his not dancing with the local girls. This is taken as a direct snub. A defence would be that Darcy needs to be 'particularly acquainted with his partner' or it *would* seem like 'a punishment' to stand up with her (vol. 1, ch. 3).

The truth is that any young man is considered as marriage fodder. When he is splendidly rich, the interest is all the greater. When Darcy will not comply with the schemes of the neighbouring mothers, there is complaint.

This is probably another reason why Darcy prefers to keep to his own set. He must have met with fortune-hunters all his adult life and is wisely, in Burke's sense, prejudiced against them.

Mrs Bennet is extremely put out that Darcy spurns Elizabeth. His walking up and down, something else that Mrs Bennet holds against him, speaks of someone who is bored, too shy to do anything about it and in need of diverting conversation, but the company puts it down to superciliousness.

Elizabeth

Although Darcy is dismissive of Elizabeth on their first meeting, he soon has to think again. The art of the novel is that Elizabeth does not know this. He is still merely 'the man who made himself agreeable nowhere' (vol. 1, ch. 6).

That Elizabeth should expect mockery from Darcy is not surprising. Her supersensitivity means that she is defensive; she indirectly suggests on one occasion that Darcy may be guilty of 'vanity and pride' (vol. 1, ch. 11). He acknowledges vanity to be a 'weakness' but upholds the case for pride.

This makes Elizabeth feel she has scored a point. When she mischievously declares that 'Mr Darcy has no defect', he plays into her hands by listing what he sees his defects to be. This is both honest and trusting of Darcy. (One can never imagine Wickham doing the same.) This fuels Elizabeth's prejudice and will come in useful later. Darcy's 'implacable resentment' makes Elizabeth more convinced that Darcy is an ill-tempered man.

Later Elizabeth deliberately whips up her feelings against Darcy, by re-reading Jane's letters. It is on this evening that Darcy calls to propose. When he acknowledges that he did separate Bingley from Jane, Elizabeth imputes this to the worst kind of pride. His letter, though, makes her change her mind about him.

Elizabeth realizes, to her shame, that she has been conventionally duped. She has fallen for the flattery of one gentleman and been angered by the lack of it in the other.

11.11 Prejudice undone

'You must write again very soon, and praise him a great deal more than you did in your last.' (vol. 3, ch. 18)

Recognition and overcoming

The main business of the second half of the plot is Elizabeth's overcoming her prejudice. Darcy's letter appeals to her reason. It takes time for Elizabeth to come to terms with it, though, because she has to learn to live with a new vision of life and of herself. However, Elizabeth *is* rational, so she determines now to *act* upon what she sees.

Pemberley

When Elizabeth sees the landscape of Pemberley her reading of it is a re-reading of its owner.

She also meets Mrs Reynolds, who is certainly not prejudiced against Darcy. Her account of him makes a deep impression on Elizabeth: 'What praise is more valuable than the praise of an intelligent servant?' (vol. 3, ch. 1). Elizabeth, who still has it in her head that Darcy is a bad-tempered man, is surprised by his housekeeper's testimony that he has been sweet-tempered from childhood.

Desire

When she imagines the portrait of Darcy to be looking straight at her

Elizabeth begins to trust Eros.

For Darcy, this has long been a potent force. Some of the earlier exchanges between Elizabeth and Darcy seem to have a covert sexual charge. The scene in which Darcy dives into the lake in his shirt in the television adaptation of the novel is essentially appropriate.

Both Darcy and Elizabeth need to come to terms with erotic turmoil.

Elizabeth uses her cleansed perceptions to reevaluate Darcy when she meets him again.

The perception of friends

Elizabeth perhaps now remembers how Charlotte had encouraged her to take note of Darcy's attentions. The Gardiners, who find Darcy far superior to what they expected, provide Elizabeth with another perspective.

Intuition and reflection

Slowly Elizabeth allows events, Darcy himself and the opinion of others to assist her in reasoning away her prejudices. There is no single dramatic moment when the novelist presents Elizabeth as experiencing a breakthrough.

An increase in tender feelings towards Darcy is part of that process. Much reflection combined with intuition convinces her that Darcy is indeed the man she loves. When he saves Lydia's reputation: 'Her heart did whisper, that he had done it for her' (vol. 3, ch. 10). Unfortunately, she dares not trust this intuition. Her reason *now* prompts her to believe that 'all love must be in vain' (vol. 3, ch. 4).

The increasing urgency of Elizabeth's love for Darcy against what she believes to be reasonable is the culmination of all that has gone before. To her joy, Darcy's love proves stronger than his earlier prejudices.

The overcoming of *Elizabeth's* prejudices and her falling in love are viewed by Elizabeth with her characteristically wry self-mockery.

When Jane asks how long she has loved Darcy, Elizabeth sums up the process thus (vol. 3, ch. 17):

'It has been coming on so gradually, that I hardly know when it began. But I believe I must date it from my first seeing his beautiful grounds at Pemberley.'

12 From Longbourn to Pemberley

12.1 Marriage and the entail

'I do think it is the hardest thing in the world, that your estate should be entailed away from your own children.' (vol. 1, ch. 13)

Mrs Bennet's ambition

For almost seven years Mrs Bennet's chief pursuit in life is the marriage of her daughters. This makes the opening of the novel oppressive despite its wit. The oppression is that of a predictable, single-minded absorption. Mr Bennet's assumed obtuseness about Bingley is his way of coping with his wife's monomania.

The entail

Yet Jane Austen makes us see that Mrs Bennet has a point. The future of the Bennet estate is entailed. An entail was a legal arrangement, the effect of which was that the owner of a property was not free to pass his estate on to whomsoever he wished. In Mr Bennet's case, there is a clause stipulating that a male must inherit, so, in the absence of sons, Longbourn passes to the man most closely related to Mr Bennet.

What, then, is Mrs Bennet to do but pursue her plans with characteristically unintelligent vigour?

Pride and Prejudice **starts at a stage before the opening of** ***Sense and Sensibility*****: because Mr Bennet is alive, the family has not yet been cast out of its home.**

12.2 Longbourn

'Longbourn, the village where they lived, and of which they were the principal inhabitants.' (vol. 1, ch. 3)

Names

There is irony in the name 'Longbourn'. 'Bourn' has as one of its meanings a destination or goal. 'Longbourn,' therefore, means either the goal that has long been sought, or, perhaps more probably, the destination which once arrived at will be a place of rest for a long time. But there can be no long residence, no long bourn at Longbourn. The entail means that the Bennet girls cannot look for a destination in the house of their upbringing.

12.3 Elizabeth and Longbourn

'she had a lively, playful disposition, which delighted in anything ridiculous' (vol. 1, ch. 3)

The thinking Elizabeth does not do

At this point we should ask two questions:

where does the Bennet family's insecurity place Elizabeth?

and, more specifically,

even if Longbourn were to be her settled destination, would she be happy in it? The reader hopes that she will find a true home. The implication is that that home is not Longbourn.

The refusal of Mr Collins is the refusal of Longbourn (see 10.2). Furthermore, as the plot unfolds, one of the things Elizabeth learns is that her family does not provide her with an appropriate environment (see 10.5).

There are sections of the novel, particularly in the first half, in which *Pride and Prejudice* requires the reader to do some thinking on Elizabeth's behalf. Consider what she has to put with. She has to reason with her irrational mother about Mr Bingley, listen to her father riling her mother, suffer Lydia's juvenile non sequitur 'for though I *am* the youngest, I'm the tallest', all this to Kitty's coughing!

This atmosphere affects Elizabeth. Her declaration 'I may safely promise you *never* to dance with him', spoken of Mr Darcy, is hardly more sensible than her mother's prejudice. The easy adoption of excessive attitudes cheapens the discourse of one witty enough knowingly to mix the categories of morality and beauty – a young man 'ought' to be handsome 'if he possibly can' (vol. 1, ch. 4).

Elizabeth's needs

It is not just a question of who Elizabeth will marry. If she is to avoid being the victim of those very qualities that make her engaging,

Elizabeth needs her *own* family, friends, company and conversation. Otherwise, she is in danger of ending up like her father – being witty by being negative. (See 10.5.)

12.4 Houses and Societies

'Sir William stayed only a week at Hunsford; but his visit was long enough to comfort him of his daughter being most comfortably settled, and of her possessing such a husband and such a neighbour as were not often met with.' (vol. 2, ch. 7)

Being settled

Sir William, we must suppose, is a man who is easily pleased. If that is his voice – 'such a husband and such a neighbour' – then it is a voice without irony. He is a male version of Mrs Bennet. His daughter has made a respectable marriage and has secured an entry into the kind of society that will pay attention to a man who has been presented at St James's.

It is not so for Elizabeth. The reader might ask: will Elizabeth find a home that is equal to her abilities?

Homes

If Elizabeth could not be long happy at Longbourn, the other homes in her immediate social world are no better. She could never settle in Meryton. The town offers nothing but, as Johnson defined 'merry', opportunities 'to junket'.

A single woman of distinctive gifts but no future security must be in want of a home and society that will appreciate her.

Netherfield: stability and permanence?

The kind of life lived at Netherfield is also impermanent. Mr Bingley 'was tempted by an accidental recommendation to look at Netherfield House' (vol. 1, ch. 4). There is no certainty regarding his long-term residence. Netherfield means a lower field. Is the point that it also represents a lower sphere of life?

Certainly, there was a traditional prejudice that wealth acquired from trade was inferior to that from land. It is ironic, given the name of their house, that the Bingley sisters, daughters of 'trade', want to forget that they occupy a lower field. They are, in fact, far lower in moral sensibility than the Gardiners, people of trade whom they despise (see 11.2).

Significantly, Elizabeth goes to Netherfield in the same chapter that the reader learns about the entail. The reader might ask whether the kind of life we see in Netherfield would suit Elizabeth. In some respects the answer is, yes: in Netherfield there is civilized talk (see 12.5). But in another sense it would not suit. The book values permanence of residence. If Bingley *settled,* Netherfield would be the kind of place in which a cultured and responsible life could flourish. The reader should welcome Bingley's purchase, mentioned in the last chapter, of 'an estate in a neighbouring county to Derbyshire'. There Bingley and Jane can emulate and complement the life of the great house in the neighbouring county.

The militia

Even more shifting and uncertain is the life of the militia. When Elizabeth warms to Wickham, it is up to the reader to ask whether someone whose life is already touched by uncertainty of residence could be happy married to a man, who, because of the war with France, was likely to be very frequently on the move. In retrospect,

the life of the militia becomes an emblem of Wickham himself – rootless, shifting, unstable.

12.5 Talk of Pemberley

'the care of the Pemberley property' (vol. 1, ch. 16)

The Pemberley library

It is at Netherfield that we first hear the name of Pemberley. Miss Bingley (vol. 1, ch. 8) first mentions Pemberley in toadying praise of its library: Darcy's reply introduces the note that is lacking in Elizabeth's (and Miss Bingley's) world – stability: 'It ought to be good,' he replied, 'it has been the work of many generations.' 'Work' is significant: the Darcys are rich but this does not mean that they do not work.

It is 'work' to maintain the inheritance, to uphold its traditions and enrich and renew its communal life.

Darcy's reply is consolingly impersonal and plural; Miss Bingley persists in making the matter personal: 'And then you have added so much to it yourself, you are always buying books.' His reply is perhaps the most telling statement he has made so far:

> I cannot comprehend the neglect of a family library in days such as these.

The last phrase –'in days such as these' – is so casual that readers might fail to hear in it the distinctive timbre of a man who is aware of the threats of social flux but is quietly confident that the best thing he can do is maintain tradition. It is, in political terms, the inflections of toryism, the resisting of those whose political creed is either economic self-interest or, the path taken in France, violent destruction of the past.

'Days such as these'

What dangerous books, for instance, might this discriminating man exclude from his library?

R.W. Chapman has shown that if we want to date the events of *Pride and Prejudice* we must imagine them as happening in the autumn of 1811 and the spring and summer of 1812. It is hard to see Mr Darcy finding a place on his shelves for one of Shelley's 1811 publications – *The Necessity of Atheism.*

Nor could Darcy be unaware of contemporary events. Lord Liverpool, minister for war in a hard-pressed government, was struggling to maintain support for Wellington, who, in Portugal and Spain, was playing a brilliant yet dangerous game of skirmishes and retreats against, in terms of numbers, a vastly superior French force. Conditions at home were difficult. We catch a glimpse of urban squalor in the fact that in 1800 the houses built in Bethnal Green were without sewers. It is not surprising that some commentators feared that in industrial towns there was unbelief, drunkenness and the abandonment of the institution of marriage.

Such knowledge might prompt the reader to see that in such times Pemberley is the kind of place Elizabeth Bennet needs: secure, stable and cultured.

Passing the time

At Netherfield we see how time is spent; in particular, how the evenings are passed. Were she married, Elizabeth would play cards, make music, read, write and converse. Not everyone is accomplished in these arts and pastimes. Mr Hurst is a limited man – 'Do you prefer reading to cards . . . that is rather singular' (vol. 1, ch.8).

And Miss Bingley also has shortcomings. As soon as conversation becomes abstract, she falls silent. The discussion about styles of writing takes on a contentious air when Darcy ventures a general statement about 'the appearance of humility' (vol. 1, ch. 10).

This he follows up by a critique of the cult of 'rapidity of thought and carelessness of execution', seizing on Bingley's words about quitting Netherfield in five minutes if he had resolved to leave. Darcy speculates that if a friend advised Bingley to stay another week, he 'would probably not go'. The example of the friend is exactly the kind of hypothetical situation philosphers use to drive home a point.

It is at this point that Elizabeth joins the debate. She responds in an equally philosophical manner, making the point that Darcy's argument has established less than he thought: 'You have only proved by this . . . that Mr Bingley did not do justice to his own disposition.'

When Bingley says that Darcy would think the better of him if he were to 'to give a flat denial and ride off as fast' as he could, Elizabeth draws out the foolish consequences of such a view: 'Would Mr Darcy then consider the rashness of your original intention as atoned for by your obstinacy in adhering to it?'

When Darcy next speaks, it is in the formal language of philosophical reasoning: 'Allowing the case to stand according to your representation . . . '. Elizabeth is not abashed; she asks a question that turns on a notion that is central to Jane Austen's novels: 'To yield readily – easily – to the *persuasion* of a friend is no merit with you.'

Two things are evident in this dialogue. The first is

the inability of Miss Bingley to argue at this level.

And the second is that

Elizabeth and Darcy enjoy an equality of intellectual outlook and competence.

The reader can see what Elizabeth herself is unaware of:

she and Darcy are suited to each other because they can enjoyably pass the time in the manner that people of their social standing are accustomed to.

When to that conclusion is added the embarrassment Elizabeth feels when her mother and sisters visit, we can see that her stay at Netherfield further shows the unsuitability of the kind of home she has at Longbourn and the desirability of the way of life that we may assume is enjoyed at Pemberley.

The importance of ends

The philosopher Gilbert Ryle argued that Jane Austen's morality was essentially Aristotelian. Without endorsing his entire thesis (he finds no place for the religious quality of her moral discriminations), there is one very important point that emerges from such a comparison. Aristotle taught that all actions, including moral ones, have an end or goal. The plot of *Pride and Prejudice* is strongly end-directed. Elizabeth, like all moral agents, has an end. Her goal, the reader sees before she does, is Pemberley.

12.6 The road to Pemberley

'To Pemberley, therefore, they were to go.' (vol. 2, ch. 19)

Derbyshire and Darcy

Elizabeth and the Gardiners travel from Lambton to see Pemberley. They have already enjoyed 'the celebrated beauties of Matlock, Chatsworth, Dovedale, or the Peak' and they look forward to, in Mrs Gardiner's words, the 'delightful' grounds and 'some of the finest woods in the country' (vol. 2, ch. 19).

Although Elizabeth goes in the assurance that she will not see Mr Darcy, in her thinking she cannot separate him from his county:

> With the mention of Derbyshire, there were many ideas connected. It was impossible for her to see the word without thinking of Pemberley and its owner. (vol. 2, ch. 19)

The word 'connected' has intellectual force. It is stronger than the word made popular by the influential thinker about the working of the mind, David Hartley – 'association'. Hartley (1705–57) taught that the mind associates one sense impression with another. In this way, he argued, we build up a picture of the world. The crucial point is that *we* make the associations; there is no necessary or objective link between the items we associate. But 'connection' is stronger; a connection suggests that the linked items have something in common.

If it is right to think of 'connection' in strong terms, then what emerges in the passage is the bond between a place and the person who has been nurtured or has chosen to settle there.

Pemberley means Darcy. The reader might ask the question that Elizabeth does not ask until she sees it: does Pemberley mean Elizabeth too?

12.7 Elizabeth's bourn

'in every remarkable spot' (vol. 3, ch. 1)

Elizabeth's thinking is reliable but blinkered; the challenge that faces the reader is to see better than her impeded vision allows her. Of the things that we are encouraged to see, one of the most important concerns Elizabeth's destiny or bourn. There are two things we are required to see.

Elizabeth's sense of place

The first is that on several occasions Elizabeth shows an acute sense of the connections between people and places.

For example, she goes to Rosings after she has rejected Mr Darcy's proposal. In her imagination the visit is inseparable from what the house and its occupant – Lady Catherine – would have been like had she accepted the proposal.

Elizabeth's sense of place is also present in the prominence given to the word 'spot' when Elizabeth visits Pemberley.

The word occurs three times in Elizabeth's perceptions:

> she saw and admired every remarkable spot and point of view.
>
> Her thoughts were all fixed on that one spot of Pemberley House, whichever it might be, where Mr Darcy then was.
>
> in spots where the opening of the trees gave the eye power to wander. (vol. 3, ch.1)

In the first, a spot is linked with a point of view, a place from which to enjoy a view.

Given the gentle pressure of meaning that is so often found in a Jane Austen landscape, it can also be a place in which Elizabeth can acquire understanding. In the second quotation, the exactitude of 'spot' works to establish that sense of a place glowing with value because a particular person is occupying it. In the third, it might not only be the eye which is enabled to wander; Pemberley is a place in which one can enjoy the freedom of imagining possible futures.

Getting there

The second thing the reader is required to see is that

a retrospective glance over the terrain of the novel from the viewpoint of Pemberley shows that the road of Elizabeth's life has led her there. It is straight and clear, though the travelling is hard.

12.8 Proposal, letter and ball

'She could think only of her letter.' (vol. 2, ch. 13)

Looking back

Mr Darcy's proposal and his subsequent letter justifying his actions oblige the reader and Elizabeth to re-think the Netherfield ball (vol. 1, ch. 18) and her family's way of life.

The formal and distant third-person mention in the proposal scene of 'the family obstacles which judgement had always opposed to inclination' (vol. 2, ch.11) is uncomfortably amplified in the words of Darcy's letter:

> 'The situation of your mother's family, though objectionable, was nothing in comparison of that total want of propriety so frequently, so almost uniformally betrayed by herself, by your three younger sisters, and occasionally even by your father.' (vol. 2, ch. 12)

In recalling the ball, we might feel we are being judged: should we have enjoyed so much those incidents which revealed what Mr Darcy calls 'that total want of propriety'? In particular, Mr Bennet's deflating reproof: 'That will do extremely well, child. You have delighted us long enough' (vol. 1, ch. 18).

Retrospectively, we are likely to see it as an uncomfortable instance of her father being 'contented with laughing at' his youngest daughters (vol. 2, ch. 14). To this incident there must be added the pompous Mr Collins's addressing Mr Darcy on his favourite subject – Lady Catherine – 'so loud as to be heard by half the room', Mrs Bennet's noisy discourse on the very probable outcome of Mr Bingley's interest in Jane and her ploy to be the last family to leave.

Overhearing her mother, 'Elizabeth blushed and blushed again with shame and vexation' and, significantly, it is the proximity of Mr Darcy that causes pain. Her concluding judgement falls on the whole family bar Jane:

> To Elizabeth it appeared, that had her family made an agreement to expose themselves as much as they could during the evening, it would have been impossible for them to play their parts with more spirit, or finer success.

This is severe. The theatrical metaphor is used elsewhere in Jane Austen's work to mean vulgar and corrupt behaviour (see the theatricals in *Mansfield Park*) and 'expose' has the force here of the fourth meaning Johnson gives it in his *Dictionary*: 'to lay open to censure or ridicule'.

Making sense of embarrassment

Elizabeth was pained at the time. What emerges in retrospect is the *significance* of that pain.

Her family does not provide her with the human environment she needs in order to grow beyond her pride and prejudice.

When she rereads Darcy's letter (is re-reading a metaphor for the forming of sound judgement?), she concurs, without the struggle that attended the passages on Wickham, with his view of her family.

Returning to the family

It is not surprising that the return to her family is a troubling experience. Lydia's immoderate laughter, the squabbles about going to Brighton, the dejection at the departure of the militia, Lydia's 'restless ecstacy' (a very curious echo of *Macbeth*) when she is invited to accompany Colonel Forster's wife, Kitty's resentment at not being invited to Brighton, her father's supine indifference to its perils and the 'real gloom' of her mother and sister's 'constant repinings at the dulness of everything' (vol. 2, ch. 19) make Elizabeth feel anew the justice of Mr Darcy's objections' (vol. 2, ch. 18).

Wherever Elizabeth is known

In the scene in which Elizabeth tries to reason with her father about the folly of allowing Lydia to go to Brighton, he reassures her that her three very silly sisters will not finally damage her marriage prospects. The terms in which he says this are thematically important:

> 'Wherever you and Jane are known, you must be respected and valued.' (vol. 2, ch. 18)

The word 'wherever' raises the issue of where such a place might be. For Elizabeth the novel is on the road to Pemberley.

12.9 Pemberley

'she asked the chambermaid whether Pemberley were not a very fine place' (vol. 2, ch. 19)

Seeing Pemberley

Elizabeth is aware, almost painfully so, of Pemberley as a place of delicate significance. Like many Jane Austen landscapes, Pemberley is not just a setting for action. There are significances in the place itself.

The house

Pemberley House stands, of course, for Mr Darcy. It has his qualities – it is large, handsome, robust and stands 'well on rising ground'. The contents, particularly the gallery, speak of the solidity of its established traditions. Elizabeth may only be interested in the portrait of Fitzwilliam Darcy but she sees it as it should be seen among the 'many family portraits'. The portrait suggests that art can reveal qualities in the subject. When she looked at the portrait

> she beheld a striking resemblance of Mr Darcy, with such a smile over his face, as she remembered to have sometimes seen, when he looked at her.

This is a teasing passage. In the *writing* of the novel there has not been a prominent stress on Darcy's smile; it is only at this point that Elizabeth remembers that Darcy has smiled like that at her. Is this a family smile, one reserved for those closest to him and those to whom he wishes to be close? Alternatively, is there the uncanny hint that the girl he was to meet is already in his thoughts? Is it, to put it in Donne's terms, a case of 'Twice or thrice had I lov'd thee / Before I knew thy face or name' ('Air and Angels')?

What is clear from the passage is that art can effect a meeting and a change in outlook. An interesting word here is 'gratitude'. Gratitude, according to John Gregory's popular conduct book *A Father's Legacy to his Daughters* (1774), marks the beginning of a loving attachment, because the woman is grateful for being singled out. Is this an echo of the, perhaps rather strange, response Elizabeth made to Darcy's unwelcome proposal at Hunsford, that 'she could not be insensible to the compliment of such a man's affection' (vol. 2, ch. 11)? (See the Penguin edition, 1996, p. 332.)

The grounds

The grounds of Pemberley have been carefully tended. The significance of that tending needs to be seen in the context of the contemporary debate about landscape gardening.

This was the art of shaping the grounds of an estate. This form of horticultural planning was popular throughout the eighteenth century, and the landscape architects created a number of distinctive fashions. The most famous of these was Lancelot Brown, commonly known as 'Capability' Brown, because his practice was to realize the possibilities or capabilities latent in the visual scene. He liked to create a sharp transition between the sweeping line of a wood and the smooth, dazzling green of a lawn. Another prominent aspect of his work was the damming of streams near to houses, so that they swelled into shimmering stretches of water.

By the time Jane Austen wrote *Pride and Prejudice*, Brown's designs were criticized for lacking variety and for looking artificial. A political element was present in this debate. Brown was associated with the Whig landowners, who saw landscape gardening as an expression of their power and wealth. The significant word that was used of Brown's kind of landscaping was 'improvement'. Nature in itself might be wild, untidy and rough. The improver's aim was to introduce reason and formality.

This training of nature to follow smooth, cultivated contours was not to the taste of those writers and planners of landscape that might be called tory. They favoured landscapes which expressed in their abundant variety all the forces – biological, geological, human – that had, over several generations, made them what they were. Their ideal was the picturesque – that quality in a landscape that most resembles a picture. What, however, they insisted on was that the picturesque was achieved by allowing nature to be herself. Uvedale Price (1747–1829) criticized modern improvers, because of their 'exclusive attention to high polish and flowing lines', an attention that made them neglect the two qualities which are the essence of the picturesque – 'variety' and 'intricacy'.

Picturesque Pemberley

Pemberley is picturesque. The language used recalls Uvedale Price; Pemberley park, for instance, 'contained great variety of ground'. Elizabeth sees the house 'standing well on rising ground' with its backdrop of 'high woody hills',

> and in front, a stream of some natural importance was swelled into greater, but without any artificial appearance. Its banks were neither formal, nor falsely adorned. (vol. 3, ch. 1)

The stream has been dammed at some point to make it swell, but the work has been unobtrusive so it appears natural. The reader might see that the landscape does not express pride; it does not draw attention to what the Darcys have done. (The same is true of the furnishings of Pemberley House, which are 'neither gaudy nor uselessly fine'.)

Elizabeth might not see that the landscape is other than the character she has mistakenly attributed to Darcy but she is warmly responsive to what she sees.

Perhaps her awed response that 'to be mistress of Pemberley might be something!' is too charmingly juvenile, but it does show an appreciation that could well be the springing point of a lifetime of responsible nurturing of a place that is at ease with nature.

The name

Speculation about topographical etymology might be inappropriate, apart from obvious names such as Longbourn. The justification for being etymological here is that it underlines the significance that Pemberley acquires in the text.

'Pemberley' is Jane Austen's own invention yet it sounds convincingly English. 'Pember' could mean hill from the Anglo-Saxon word 'pen'. 'Ley' means enclosure or pasture. The name therefore, might mean the hill by the enclosure or pasture. As such it is an accurate description of what is found at Pemberley. The party turns in at the lodge – the limit of the enclosure – and the road ascends 'for half a mile' to a 'considerable eminence', from where they see, across the valley, rising ground upon which the house stands. The enclosure of 'the whole Park' was 'ten miles round'.

Pemberley is still the hill within in an enclosure it must have been, when, centuries before, it received this name.

Points of view

A feature of contemporary writing about landscape was the singling out of places – 'prospects' – from which good views of the surrounding area could be enjoyed.

When Elizabeth reached the top of an eminence, 'the eye was instantly caught by Pemberley House' (vol. 3, ch. 1). The formal and definite article – 'the' – indicates that Elizabeth is a representative of the sensitive and responsive traveller.

Viewing is still a preoccupation of the visitors when they arrive at the house. In the dining-parlour Elizabeth went to a window to enjoy its prospect. The hill, crowned with wood, from which they had descended, receiving increased abruptness from the distance, was a beautiful object. (vol. 3, ch. 1)

The word 'prospect' is interesting. In the language of picturesque landscape it means the view, usually a good one, of the countryside. It also means hopes for the future.

We must be careful not to push such a point too far. The landscape is not quite allegorical, yet, coming when it does, the passage about Pemberley is in keeping with Elizabeth's gradual adjustment of vision.

12.10 The Gardiners

'Mrs Gardiner was standing a little behind; and on her pausing, he asked her, if she would do him the honour of introducing him to her friends.' (vol. 3, ch. 1)

Names

The pun is, of course, unavoidable. So, too, is the Gardiners' address. Miss Bingley and Mrs Hurst might mock relatives living 'somewhere near Cheapside' (vol. 1, ch. 8), but the natures of the Gardiners are fully reflected in their place of residence – Gracechurch street. Their contribution is a kind of ministry best described as spiritual – the healing and reconciliation of Elizabeth and Darcy. Theirs is a work of grace.

A want of propriety?

We must remember what we know and Mr Darcy does not – neither of the Gardiners display that 'total want of propriety' (vol. 2, ch. 12) that Mr Darcy found so distasteful.

The Gardiners and marriage

The Gardiners have two representative functions.

Their marriage is a model one.

The chapter in which Elizabeth leaves Longbourn for her Derbyshire holiday opened with the darkest reflections in the book about the emptiness of the Bennets' marriage. In Derbyshire she is with a couple whose lives are an example of what marriage can be. As such,

the Gardiners are the parents Jane and Elizabeth should have had.

It is significant that a changed Elizabeth is with them when she meets a changed Mr Darcy.

The social test

The Gardiners' second function is to be seen as people of whom Darcy can approve. Dramatic irony works quickly in the visit to Pemberley. What Elizabeth fears intensely is very soon shown to be quite unwarranted.

Nevertheless, Elizabeth is still 'amazed' that, on meeting him, he is so changed, a change observed in his enquiry after the very people about whom he had such reservations – her family.

The meaning of the meeting

This is where Elizabeth's road to Pemberley has brought her.

She has come to the place which the narrative has prepared the reader to see as her true home but she has come in the company of her relatives.

She cannot accept Pemberley, even if it were offered again, without the deep regret of losing the Gardiners. For Mr Darcy the dilemma is similar: here is the young woman whom he loves, yet here also are her relatives from the cheap side of society. Mr Darcy is in his proper context – his house and grounds – when he sees Elizabeth, and Elizabeth is in hers – with favourite relatives.

The themes of a character's need for a 'place', of the impediment of an unsuitable family and the need to outgrow pride and prejudice (the central issues of the novel) are all vividly present as Elizabeth's expectations of Mr Darcy's reaction – shock?, recoil? – to the association are confounded.

> That he was *surprised* by the connection was evident; he sustained it however with fortitude, and so far from going away, turned back with them, and entered into conversation with Mr Gardiner. (vol. 3, ch. 1)

Elizabeth and Mr Darcy are surprised because both have their prejudices tested and found wanting.

What looked intractable turns out to be, as the last sentence of the novel says, 'the means of uniting them' (vol. 3, ch. 19). Mr Darcy, instead of going away, turns back (the meaning of the word 'repentance') and enters into a conversation with Mr Gardiner. Perhaps the rapprochement is more than a matter of overcoming prejudices.

The picture of Fitzwilliam Darcy, hereditary owner of a large gentleman's estate, entering into a conversation with Edward Gardiner, a man 'in a respectable line of trade' (vol. 1, ch. 7), is an emblem of a pervasive theme in Jane Austen's novels – the relationship between the landed gentry and the rising classes, whose livelihood comes from the professions or trade.

Visiting Pemberley completes the moral design of the book:

Elizabeth comes to the place to which she can belong, and Mr Darcy meets those in her family with whom he can associate.

12.11 The renewing of society

'She listened most attentively to all that passed between them.' (vol. 3, ch. 1)

Architecture

What did Mr Darcy and Mr Gardiner talk about as they walked together? We may speculate on the basis of Mr Gardiner's interests.

When the three of them leave the house, and Elizabeth turns to 'look again' (she does a lot of that in the second half of the novel) 'her uncle and aunt stopped also . . . while the former was conjecturing as to the date of the building' (vol. 3, ch. 1). Architecture is a fitting conversation topic: it is a practical art, and it is not inconceivable, given the English tradition of gentleman architects, that Mr Darcy will be able to tell Mr Gardiner which parts of the building were designed by former heads of the Darcy family.

Conversation

It is in small ways such as this – polite, intelligent conversation – that society is renewed. Bonds are being established between the traditional landed gentry and the commercial classes without whom the gentry will find survival hard. But here the bond is not an economic one: the two gentlemen are brought together by the conventions of manners and, we may presume, topics of common intellectual interest. As the four of them descend to the bank of the river for the 'inspection of some curious water-plant', we may assume than another of these interests was botany.

Fishing

The topic we are told that they discuss is fishing. This seems a solitary pursuit, but, if we are to believe those who fish, it is a fraternity, almost a model community:

> Well met, brother Peter! I heard you and a friend would lodge here to-night; and that hath made me bring my friend to lodge here too.

That is the opening of 'The Third Day' from Izaak Walton's *The Compleat Angler*. Mr Gardiner had resolved not to take Mr Darcy 'at his word' (vol. 3, ch. 1), but at the end of volume 3, chapter 2 we are told that 'the fishing scheme had been renewed the day before'. The renewal, we might venture, is not just a particular scheme to go fishing.

The Izaak Walton link might be adventitious but it is appropriate. Walton's fishing was largely done in Derbyshire. Moreover, Mr Darcy might have approved of the book's quiet politics. *The Compleat Angler* was first published in 1653, during the protectorate of Oliver Cromwell. Walton, a Royalist and Anglican, might have seen in fishing a consolation for the bleakness of an age ('in days such as these') when so much that was familiar was denied the people. Perhaps in that symbol of cultural continuity and resistance– Mr Darcy's library – there was an eighteenth century edition of the work.

Such a master

Jane Austen's understanding of society is a hierarchical one. She can be amused by the inconsistencies of masters and critical of their moral shortcomings (increasingly, her theme was that England is an estate with the wrong people in charge), but she never questions a society in which certain individuals exercise power because, in many cases, they have inherited a position of influence.

Jane Austen knows that the exercise of the virtues is inseparable from social roles and as a Christian she also knows that those in power have responsibilities. She views these responsibilities in a realistic but almost fiercely exacting manner.

In the words of the Catechism of the Church of England, each person is required

> to do my duty in that state of life, unto which it shall please God to call me.

Mr Darcy does exhibit quite heroic virtue in rescuing poor Lydia, but he does not do so because of his role as the owner of Pemberley – the state of life in which God has called him – and he does not wish his deeds to become public knowledge. What is required of him at Pemberley is that he is a good landlord and master. He is more than that: 'He is the best landlord and the best master'.

This praise is confirmed by the people of Lambton, who acknowledged 'that he was a liberal man, and did much good among the poor' (vol. 3, ch. 2). Those who knew about landscape might deduce this from the way Pemberley is maintained. An argument against comprehensive improvement was that newly planted woods, as opposed to ancient ones, afforded little firewood for the poor. We imagine that Pemberley was not the kind of estate that prevented the owner from discharging his Christian duty regarding kindling.

Meeting the sister

Elizabeth's stay at Netherfield suggested to us that Elizabeth could belong to Pemberley. What the novel needs to show is that our judgement was correct. Mrs Gardiner and Elizabeth visit Miss Darcy as a reciprocal 'exertion of politeness' (vol. 3, ch. 2).

The occasion turns out to be a test. When Mr Darcy enters, Miss Bingley is aware that he tries to promote conversation between his sister and Elizabeth and 'in the imprudence of anger', takes the first opportunity of saying, with sneering civility, 'Pray, Miss Eliza, are not the –shire militia removed from Meryton. They must be a great loss to *your* family' (vol. 3, ch. 3).

The remark was aimed at lowering Elizabeth in Mr Darcy's eyes. The reader sees that Mr Darcy, Elizabeth and Miss Darcy feel pain, because of Wickham. Elizabeth summons her energies, 'exerting herself vigorously to repel the ill-natured attack', which she does by treating the question as if it were of no consequence.

She has passed the test by being quiet, low-key and composed. The conclusion is that a remark 'which had been designed to turn his [Darcy's] thoughts from Elizabeth, seemed to have fixed them on her more, and more cheerfully'.

Pemberley society

The point that emerges from a consideration of topography in *Pride and Prejudice* is that

Elizabeth's destination – her bourn – is Pemberley.

Yet it would be a mistake to read the novel in individualistic terms. *Pride and Prejudice* is not boy meets girl any more than *Romeo and Juliet* is. The novel is about moving from the society of Longbourn to the society of Pemberley. Pemberley is a house, a library, extensive grounds, tenants, dependants, employees and, as seen in the portraits, a long-established family. Elizabeth joins this society. Future visitors will see her portrait in the gallery. There is more than narrative significance in the last sentence of the second volume – 'To Pemberley, therefore, they were to go' (vol. 2, ch. 19). They go to Pemberley as a *society*.

Elizabeth at Pemberley

Elizabeth at Pemberley is not exactly the subject of the narrative, although it is important that the novel ends (unlike the BBC adaptation) with a picture of her life there. The final chapter has that slightly distant quality of a summing up. A lot is told the reader, directly and briefly. What is related, however, creates an image of the renewed society of Pemberley.

Pemberley is now lighter. At first Georgiana is astonished at Elizabeth's 'lively, sportive, manner of talking to her brother' (see 10.4), but she learns that in marriage 'a woman may take liberties with her husband' that a younger sister could not with her brother.

Pemberley educates. Kitty, we might assume, also discovers that this is the kind of society she should have grown up in: 'In society so superior to what she had generally known, her improvement was great.'

Pemberley is welcoming: Mr Bennet, the Bingleys and the Gardiners, whose welcome visits conclude the novel, are frequent visitors.

Pemberley is a source of charity. Elizabeth saves something from 'her own private expenses' to help Lydia. Lydia visits, but the narrator is silent about the effect it has on her.

Pemberley excludes. A society cannot contain everyone; there are some who by their lives have shown that they can have no share in its values. Of Wickham it is tersely said that 'Darcy could never receive *him* at Pemberley'.

The importance of Pemberley is best seen in the penultimate chapter. The last paragraph begins with the comedy of embarrassing company – that of Elizabeth's parents. This company takes from 'courtship much of its pleasure'. But the concluding part of that sentence is in a very different key. It is the most precise formulation of the theme of the novel – the search for a fitting society, which is (vol. 3, ch. 18):

> the hope of the future; and she looked forward with delight to the time when they should be removed from society so little pleasing to either, to all the comfort and elegance of their family party at Pemberley.

Part IV

Mansfield Park

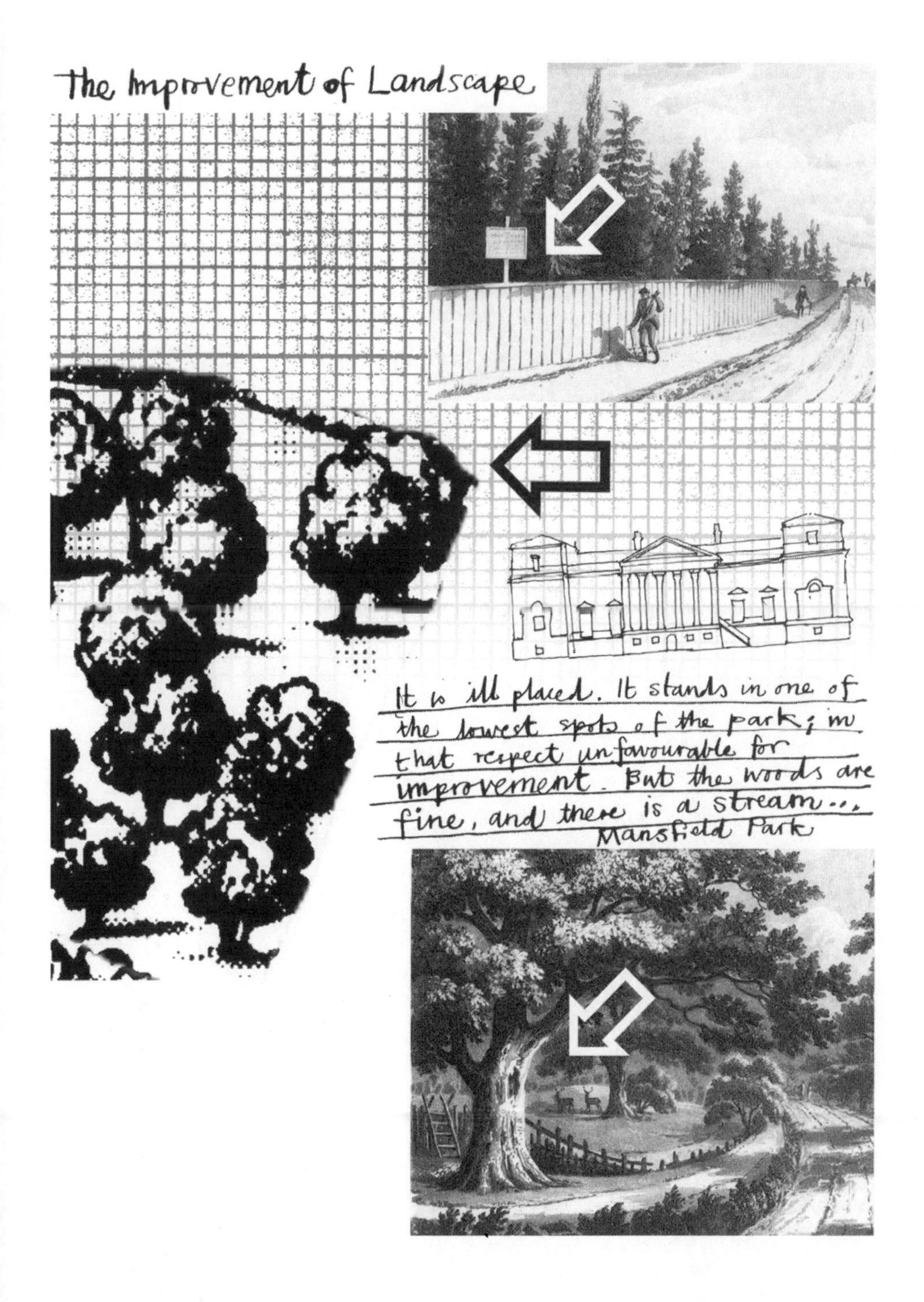

13 Art

13.1 Mr Yates: a disappointed man

'He came on the wings of disappointment, and with his head full of acting.' (vol. 1, ch. 13)

Mansfield Park values rationality and conscience and is suspicious of emotional impulse. Because (a fringe figure) Mr Yates is driven by desire – he is wild to act – we are not invited to approve of him; and yet, in a sense, Jane Austen the novelist also has a 'head full of acting'. Consideration of Mr Yates's infectious enthusiasm, therefore, raises a central issue: is art, as Plato thought, dangerous? Given that Jane Austen has chosen to write a novel and not a moral tract, we may assume that she does not reject art; but a further question remains. What kind of art does she approve of?

Two kinds of art will be considered in this chapter: the art *in* the novel and the art *of* the novel.

Disappointment at Ecclesford

The art of the theatre enters the novel with the arrival of Mr Yates. While Sir Thomas is in Antigua, Tom casually invites a recent acquaintance to stay, and Yates arrives, still driven by a yen for theatricals. His talk is of 'Ecclesford and its theatre, with its arrangements and dresses, rehearsals and jokes' (vol. 1, ch. 13).

Performance before play

The language used of Mr Yates's enthusiasms is telling:

what matters is the business of acting rather than the text that is to be performed.

And so it is with all the would-be players: 'Oh! For the Ecclesford theatre and scenery to try something with' (vol. 1, ch. 13). It is not surprising that they have a stage before they have a play to perform!

13.2 Art misunderstood

'a love of the theatre is so general' (vol. 1, ch. 13)

Content

The would-be players have misunderstood art: they have overlooked content. Literature has (is?) a text: it is *about* something. The intelligent Mary Crawford realises this: 'There, look at *that* speech, and *that*, and *that*' (vol. 1, ch. 18). This is evidence that the players should not have chosen *Lovers' Vows*. What they ignored were the words of the play.

Audience

Art is misunderstood in another way: the performance of a play requires an audience. The issue of the audience is always secondary at Mansfield; in many rehearsals, Fanny is the sole member. What drives the group is 'the inclination to act'. Each sister expresses the wish to perform 'and Henry Crawford, to whom, in all the riot of his gratifications, it was yet an untasted pleasure, was quite alive at the idea' (vol. 1, ch. 13).

Context matters as well as text.

Art is not mere self-expression and acting is more than the gratification of the impulse to perform.

13.3 Lovers' vows

'The play had been Lovers' Vows.' (vol. 1, ch. 13)

Mrs Inchbald and Kotzebue

Lovers' Vows was popular and not a little notorious. Mrs Inchbald's play of 1798 is based on August von Kotzebue's *Natural Son* or, as it was also known, *Child of Love*. By modern standards it is a short play with a big cast; the pace is swift, even hectic, and the climax satisfying in its triumph of feeling over class prejudice.

The plot

The play opens with Agatha turned out of her lodging. She reflects on the shame of her seduction and the cruelty of her abandonment but takes comfort in the thought of her son. A young soldier, Frederick, enters and goes to help, only to discover that she is his mother. Their conversation reveals her unhappy past. She went to the castle at fourteen and was educated. The son of the house courted her but when he went to the wars, she was abandoned with her child – Frederick, the child of love. Her seducer was Baron Wildenhaim. She maintained herself and her son by teaching, until sickness made her incapable of work.

Two cottagers take her in. Frederick goes (we learn later to beg) and Agatha learns that the Baron, upon the death of his wife, has returned to his castle. At the castle the Baron is entertaining Count Cassel, a prospective husband to his daughter, Amelia. She is equivocal about the Count, so the Baron asks Anhalt, a clergyman and Amelia's tutor, to speak to her about the duties of a wife and mother. The Baron and the Count go hunting.

The Baron meets Frederick, who begs. The Baron gives, but when Frederick demands more, there is violence. Frederick is taken to the castle but not before he persuades the Baron to offer his mother relief.

Back at the castle, Anhalt speaks to Amelia about marriage, but she coaxes him into talking about his love for her. (Although neither Fanny nor Mary liked the scene, it is easily the best in the play.) The Butler then gives a diverting account in verse of the incident between Frederick and the Baron.

Amelia visits Frederick in prison, where he is awaiting his execution. Another visitor is Anhalt, who advises Frederick to appeal directly to the Baron. The Butler, again in verse, tells the Baron about the Count's abandonment of a girl he has wronged. The

Count, when asked by the Baron, does not deny the accusation. The upshot is that the Baron is touched anew by remorse for *his* wronging of a girl. Amelia explains to the Baron her wish to marry Anhalt, but the Baron is unhappy at such a socially unequal match. Frederick is allowed to see the Baron. When the Baron learns that Frederick is his son he asks Anhalt to advise him. Anhalt, however, first goes to the cottage, where Agatha has eventually resolved to go to the castle to see the Baron.

Frederick tells the Baron that he should marry Agatha. Anhalt also urges him to marry her. The Baron agrees, and the play concludes with Anhalt's being permitted to marry Amelia, and Agatha's being reunited with her penitent former deceiver.

13.4 Art and life

'Henry Crawford acted well.' (vol. 1, ch. 18)

Linking lives and theatrical parts

One of the themes of the latter part of volume 1 is the relationship between art and life, and there are distinct parallels between the movement of the plot and the individual lives of the performers.

The final casting is:

Baron Wildenhaim	Mr Yates
Count Cassel	Mr Rushworth
Anhalt	Mr Edmund Bertram
Frederick	Mr Henry Crawford
Verdun the Butler	Mr Tom Bertram
Cottager	Mr Tom Bertram
Agatha Miss	Maria Bertram
Amelia Miss	Mary Crawford
Cottager's Wife	Mrs Grant

13.5 Who plays whom

'she was certain of the proper Frederick' (vol. 1, ch. 14)

Grounds for choice

None of the actors has much idea about acting, so each argues about who is most suited for a particular part not on the grounds of *acting* ability but because the part seems fitted to a personal (secret) agenda, traits and social standing. In Maria's eyes, there is a 'proper Frederick'.

Henry argues that Julia should not play Agatha because 'There is nothing of tragedy about her'. He adds that Julia would be suited to Amelia on social grounds: 'It requires a gentlewoman – a Julia Bertram' (vol. 1, ch. 14).

Tom and the butler

Some of the players are typecast. Tom is a feckless young man – a dandy, an irresponsible heir bent only on pleasure – so the jolly rhyming Butler would suit him. The Butler's entries disrupt life at the castle, just as Tom, a kind of lord of misrule, disturbs the ordered life of Mansfield.

Mary and Amelia

Amelia is a bold young woman who, on the subject of love, says to her tutor, Anhalt: 'Come, then, teach it me' (act 3, scene 2). Mary Crawford is not quite so forward, but she does ask whom she will have the pleasure of making love to.

Rushworth and Cassel

Rushworth is close enough to Count Cassel in personality and situation to make his casting a sensitive matter. The Baron's first reference to Cassel is a despairing 'am I after all to have an ape for a son-in-law?' (act 2 scene 2).

Rushworth's place in the plot also makes him embarrassingly like the Count. Rushworth bores Maria; the Count's lack of finesse does not recommend him to the sprightly Amelia. Hence, it is fitting that Maria curtails his speeches. This is unusually symbolic, even for *Mansfield Park*; before their marriage, Maria is cutting down Rushworth's role!

Moreover, passages in the text might, if Rushworth heard them, be painful to him. In the much-rehearsed first act, largely between Agatha and Frederick, a stage direction indicates that Agatha *presses him to her*, Frederick says: 'We don't want him.'

Yates and the Baron

The Baron is a seducer: Mr Yates elopes with Julia. He might also be said to have seduced the Mansfield party into performing the play.

Edmund and Anhalt

Edmund plays a clergyman and tutor: he has already effectively been Fanny's tutor and he becomes a clergyman. Like Anhalt, Edmund's manner is serious, but unlike Anhalt he eventually resists the advances of his Amelia.

Henry and Federick

It is interesting that Henry has little in common with the part he plays. (The clearest parallel is that both are bad correspondents.) Henry is not unfortunate in his birth, and though his later actions might be said to be reckless they do not lead either to revelations or reconciliations.

Henry's interest in playing Frederick is that it allows him, under the sanctions of art, to enjoy physical contact with Maria. She might have taken Frederick's line, 'These arms can now afford you support', as a coded promise of a proposal.

Maria and Agatha

Agatha is a fallen woman: Maria also falls (see 15.3). To fall is the fate of the tragic protagonist. We should remember that, when the choice of the play is being discussed, both Maria and Julia are 'On the tragic side' (vol. 1, ch. 14). Maria might be said to fulfil her dramatic aspirations in her life.

Fanny and Agatha

Fanny is not in the play, but there are parallels between her and Agatha. Both Agatha and Fanny were dependants in a big house and both of them were courted by rich and powerful men. The play opens with Agatha's ejection, and Fanny is excluded from Mansfield Park.

Because Agatha presents the fate of Maria and the situation of Fanny, the part alerts us to the importance of the parallel that runs throughout the novel between the fallen and rejected daughter and the daughter the head of the household had always wanted.

13.6 Acting?

'the inclination to act was awakened' (vol. 1, ch. 13)

Do the actors really act?

Marilyn Butler argues that:

> The impropriety lies in the fact that they are *not* acting, but are finding an indirect means to gratify desires which are illicit, and should have been contained. (*Jane Austen and the War of Ideas*, Clarendon Press, 1975, p. 232)

A different view is stated by Claudia Johnson. She wants to abolish altogether the difference between the stage and life by insisting that all the major characters act throughout the novel (*Jane Austen: Women, Politics, and the Novel*, University of Chicago Press, 1988, pp. 100–1). This will not do: if there is no distinction between what happens off and on stage, there can be no such thing as acting. Some might blur their social roles with their theatrical ones, but blurring is only possible if the two roles are distinct.

Distinctions blurred

The novel, then, maintains that there is a specific activity called acting while also showing that the distinctions between life and the stage are sometimes blurred. This is apparent in the text. Edmund is imperceptive because he is caught between the concerns of his stage role and his feelings for Mary Crawford:

> Edmund, between his theatrical part and his real part, between Miss Crawford's claims and his own conduct, between love and consistency, was equally unobservant. (vol. 1, ch. 17)

If there were no distinction in the novel between life and acting, it would be impossible to talk of Edmund's 'theatrical part and his real part'.

Other sorts of acting

Marilyn Butler is right. There is a distinction between acting and not acting and that distinction is not always observed. But Claudia Johnson's idea is useful if it is rephrased. There is acting which is not confined to the stage. In fact

some of the best performances in the theatricals episode do not happen on stage.

The distinction is between those occasions in life when we are just ourselves and those when we deliberately take up a particular role. Not surprisingly, it is the Crawfords who are adept at this non-theatrical playing.

Henry and the language of the theatre

Theatrical language is employed in the scene in which Henry negotiates Maria into playing Agatha. Julia, who also wanted the part, thinks that that Henry 'was, perhaps, at treacherous play with her' (vol. 1, ch. 14).

Mary as performer

Although Fanny does not state it explicitly she sees that the success of Mary Crawford in drawing Edmund into the company depends upon her ability to present herself as someone who needs the consolation of his presence (vol. 1, ch. 15).

Mary Crawford has to adopt a number of different 'styles' to induce Edmund to play Anhalt. The first is that of the temptress. It has no effect on Edmund, who does not respond. Her next move is to work by hints. She 'archly' points out that since Edmund is to be a clergyman, Anhalt would be the only part in the play that 'could tempt' him to act. Edmund again resists by drawing attention to the difference between the stage and life. One who chooses 'the profession itself, is, perhaps, one of the last who would wish to represent it on stage'.

If she is to be successful Mary has to be more subtle. Her next 'performance' is quite different; she offers Fanny friendship. She is no doubt genuinely shocked at the gross insensitivity of Mrs Norris, but we might see that her moving close to Fanny is intended to recommend Mary to the sensitive and upright Edmund. When the proposal to invite Charles Maddox to play Anhalt is made, Mary is apparently compliant until her last sentence: 'let *him* be applied to, if you please, for it will be less unpleasant to me than to have a perfect stranger'. But what she says to Fanny is far more forceful: 'It will be very disagreeable, and by no means what I expected.' This is heard by the one for whom it was intended. Moreover, it is not heard as an instance of manipulation but as a cry for help.

Fanny sees what Mary has been up to: 'Alas! It was all Miss Crawford's doing' (vol. 1, ch. 16).

13.7 Fanny and the theatricals

'for she had never even seen half a play' (vol. 1, ch. 14)

Fanny and plays

Fanny looks on in a number of ways. She is not a member of the group who wants to act so can witness the squabbles over the choice of the play. The language in which her observation is couched establishes a parallel between Fanny as observer of Mansfield life and as a member of an audience viewing a play. To her, the selfishness of the participants is 'more or less disguised' (vol. 1, ch. 14).

Listening

Fanny hears 'the complaints and distresses' (vol. 1, ch. 18) of the company. She is also a listener in the sense that she forms an audience for their rehearsing. When she tries to help Mr Rushworth learn his part she becomes an active listener. 'Fanny, in her pity and kind-heartedness, was at great pains to teach him how to learn, giving him all the helps and directions in her power' (vol. 1, ch. 18). 'Directions' has theatrical associations.

Fanny and the pleasures of art

The phrase 'For her own gratification' (vol. 1, ch. 14) shows that Fanny, like Edmund, is not against the pleasure of watching a performance. In Fanny's case, there is the addition of novelty; she has never seen a play. As she is able to enjoy watching Maria and Henry rehearse the first act, we may conclude that her pleasure is in *performance*. She can distinguish between Henry the man – 'She did not like him as a man' – and Henry the actor – 'she must admit him to be the best actor' vol. 1, ch. 18). She knows that art is not the same as life.

13.8 Art and morality

'so totally improper for home representation' (vol. 1, ch. 14)

Higher consequence

Yet Fanny knows that 'every thing of higher consequence ' is against the presentation of *Lovers' Vows.*

Fanny's doubts are inseparable from those of the narrator.

There are four problematic areas: the text of the play, the delicate position of Maria, the certain knowledge that Sir Thomas would disapprove and, shown, but not articulated by Fanny, the physical disturbance of the house.

The text

When Fanny first takes up *Lovers' Vows,* she is amazed 'that it could be chosen in the present instance'. The difficulty lies in the text: 'the situation of one [Agatha] and the language of the other [Amelia], 'so unfit to be expressed by any woman of modesty' (vol. 1, ch. 14).

Fanny is shocked; but the novel does not show upon what grounds. We can only surmise that it is because Agatha is the mother of an illegitimate child and Amelia is the initiator in her love dialogue with Anhalt.

Maria and the play

When Fanny reads the play she has her cousins in mind: 'she could hardly suppose her cousins could be aware of what they were engaging in' (vol. 1, ch. 14). *Mansfield Park* does not depend very much upon irony, but here it works against Fanny. Each Bertram sister hopes that the play will lead to an engagement.

Both the Bertram sisters are all too aware of what the first act requires the players to do – two embraces, two cases of the head cradled on the other's breast and one of Agatha's hand pressed against Frederick's heart. This is why they are eager to be 'engaging in' acting, only, as said above, 'acting' is not the best description of what Maria is doing. Little does she know that Henry *is* acting, in that he does not have warm feelings for her. The word 'engaging' is a reminder of Maria's status as well as her aspirations. She *is* engaged to Mr Rushworth, and this requires modesty in the presence of other men. Edmund is aware that Maria's 'situation is a very delicate one' (vol. 1, ch. 13) He makes this judgement before *Lovers' Vows* has been chosen, so his remarks apply to *any* kind of acting.

Maria, like Lucy Steele in *Sense and Sensibility,* does not allow her engagement to restrain her. Her desire to play Agatha can only be understood as an attempt to provoke Henry into a declaration. This is not adultery but it is a breach of fidelity, and of fidelity on both sides. Maria is effectively casting off Mr Rushworth, and Henry, who presses her hand to his heart, rouses hopes he has no intention of fulfilling. Maria is 'in a good deal of agitation' that, her father having returned, 'Crawford should now lose no time in declaring himself' (vol. 2, ch. 2). Henry, however, has no such intention; he is content, on and off the stage, to engage with her only playfully.

Sir Thomas and theatricals

Ecclesford was not the only country house in which the leisured classes delighted in amateur performances. Edmund, however, knows that his father would disapprove. In moral terms, Sir Thomas would probably follow Edmund. There is something about any acting that promotes, to use one of Edmund's words, 'familiarity' (vol. 1, ch. 17).

Edmund first raises the issue of his father when the idea of acting is first discussed. Edmund feels it would be unseemly to indulge when Sir Thomas is endangered. Tom's defence of acting on the grounds that Sir Thomas encouraged the boys to recite is confuted by Edmund's pointing out that recitation 'was a very different thing'. Edmund then puts forward two further points: Sir Thomas would never allow his grown up daughters to act, because his 'sense of decorum is strict' and the building of a theatre 'would be taking liberties with my father's house'.

Sir Thomas's return confirms Edmund's view. Sir Thomas values 'domestic tranquility' and he is purposeful in 'the destruction of every unbound copy of "Lover's Vows" in the house, for he was burning all that met his eye' (vol. 2, ch. 2). Burning books is not something that we can read innocently. It is a moment when the situation of the reader makes it difficult to cope with what is probably the intention of the writer. We might also feel uneasy at the way the novel apparently resorts to domestic power as the safeguard against disorder.

Disturbing the house

It might be easier for the reader to sympathize with what Sir Thomas finds has happened to 'his own dear room' (vol. 2, ch. 1). The scene in which he enters 'the Theatre' is perhaps the funniest in the novel. Mr Yates is better acting the role of the gentleman than cavorting upon the stage; indeed, 'The house would close with the greatest eclat.'

The encroachment has been more than physical. The name and therefore the meaning of the room begins to change. It is called 'the Theatre' (vol. 1, ch. 14). Sir Thomas returns to a home which is beginning to be understood in alien terms.

13.9 A community divided

'Every body began to have their vexation.' (vol. 1, ch. 18)

Henry's judgement

Henry Crawford is not good at estimating how Fanny will respond. When they meet at the Grants', he looks back 'with exquisite pleasure', because the theatricals provided 'such an interest, such an animation, such a spirit diffused! Every body felt it' (vol. 2, ch. 5).

Henry assumes that the pleasure he took in 'employment' and 'bustle' was universal. The reader knows this was not so.

Sufferers

In the busy house there are 'two solitary sufferers' (vol. 1, ch. 17). Fanny suffers at the prospect of Edmund acting out his role of would-be lover of Mary Crawford, and Julia feels rejected by Henry. 'Fanny saw and pitied' Julia, but her brothers and Aunt Norris are inattentive.

A house divided

The theatricals divide the house. Fanny is treated as a sort of servant: 'we want your service' (vol. 1, ch. 15). The service is taking the part of the Cottager's wife, a role which Mr Yates has already said was to be played at Ecclesford by 'the governess' (vol. 1, ch. 14). Fanny's refusal provokes the embarrassing insult from Mrs Norris about 'who and what she is' (vol. 1, ch. 15), and the business of making costumes allows the aunt to criticize Fanny's idleness.

But the performers are also divided amongst themselves. The reason for this is that

the theatricals nourish a spirit in each of selfish individualism.

A group bent on satisfying its own whims is not one that can share reasoning because they have no agreed principles about which to argue. Edmund discovers this when he tries to persuade Maria to withdraw from the role of Agatha. Her reply is that 'I really cannot undertake to harangue all the rest upon a subject of this kind' (vol. 1, ch. 15).

Working together

The theatricals episode establishes a political point:

the creation of a community with shared values is not easily achieved.

Yet perhaps there are hints that even this diverse body of individuals was coming together. Fanny is drawn into the preparations and finds herself 'useful to all' (vol. 1, ch. 18).

But Julia remains unreconciled; her only consolation is the self-righteous pathos of "*I* need not be afraid of appearing before him [her father]." (vol. 2, ch. 1)

13.10 Literature and painting

'three transparencies' (vol. 1, ch. 16)

Shakespeare

Isobel Armstrong argues (*Mansfield Park*, Penguin Critical Studies, 1988) that *Lovers' Vows* is enclosed by two Shakespeare plays: the Sotherton episode suggests *As You Like It,* and in volume 3, chapter 3 Henry reads from *Henry VIII.*

The Sotherton garden scenes enact the kind of escapes into a rural world that are central to *As You Like It.* The play depends upon characters who overlook each other, and so reminds us of the times Fanny overlooks the capers of her cousin Maria in the wilderness.

Henry VIII is explicitly mentioned. Isobel Armstrong regards the play as a commentary on issues in the novel – change in the life of the nation, the legitimacy of authority, the delegation of power and the influence of women. In both the resolutions are ambiguous.

Does, for instance, *Henry VIII* endorse Elizabeth as the monarch-to-be or is it more concerned to show the moral shortcomings of Henry? Similar questions may be asked of *Mansfield Park*: is it a critique of Sir Thomas's government or a celebration of a new England embodied by Fanny, Edmund and William?

Isobel Armstrong's thesis raises the question of how far it is legitimate to use a reference as a major interpretative tool. Equally, it is uncertain how far the reader should take two other instances of art in the novel: Fanny's pictures and her books.

Pictures

The passage about Fanny's pictures comes in the quiet opening of volume 1, chapter 16 when we see Fanny in the contemplative seclusion of the East room –there are transparencies in 'the three lower panes of one window, where Tintern Abbey held its station between a cave in Italy, and a moonlight lake in Cumberland'. What is to be made of these images?

Jane Austen would expect her readers to see in them the artistic tradition of the picturesque. Were there more references, a reader might be tempted to speculate on links with the novel. As it is, it would be wise to restrict discussion to what the transparencies reveal about Fanny's taste. Two points emerge; the first is that

a liking for ruins, caves and moonlit lakes indicates that Fanny's imagination is one which we now call Romantic. (See 5.10)

Jane Austen is often thought of as anti-Romantic, yet she gives Fanny Romantic inclinations. But, second,

Fanny is the means by which Jane Austen engages in a critical debate with those Romantic responses which are subjective and individualistic.

One of the shifts that took place in the Romantic period was weighting perception more on the side of the subject than the object. This led to the understanding that the self is, in part, the architect of its own vision. (see 5.10 and 18.14)

Once this role is admitted, it is possible to slide into the view that the self is the arbiter not only of what the mighty world is like but also of what constitutes the moral world. A manifestation of this is the kind of individualism that prompts Mary Crawford to say of religious devotion:

> it is safer to leave people to their own devices on such subjects. Every body likes to go their own way – to choose their own time and manner. (vol. 1, ch. 9)

Mansfield Park can be read as asking a question: is it possible to give due weight to the subjective element in the responsive appreciation of nature and yet resist the individualism that is a consequence of making the self the judge in matters of perception and morality? The novel wants to affirm that this can be done. It bravely tackles art – the most individualistic of activities – as the area in which the case for a Romanticism that does not reduce morality to personal whim is made.

Books

Fanny reads. She 'had been a collector [of books], from the first hour of her commanding a shilling' (vol. 1, ch. 16). Moreover, it looks as if she is up to date in her reading. Among her books is 'Crabbe's Tales', which was published in 1812, the year when Jane Austen was writing *Mansfield Park.*

There is one quite clear parallel between Crabbe and *Mansfield Park.* In *The Parish Register,* published in 1807, Crabbe tells the tale of Fanny Price, a poor girl who is wooed by a baronet. She resists. Jane Austen must have taken the name from Crabbe. However, as the plot is a familiar one – the poor village beauty preyed on by the powerful gentleman – it does not illuminate Jane Austen's novel, though it clearly is not far from the plot of *Lovers' Vows* and parallels *might* be drawn between Fanny and Henry. (For a further discussion see D.W. Harding, *Regulated Hatred and Other Essays on Jane Austen,* Athlone, 1998, pp. 107–9.)

Another way of thinking about the significance of Crabbe is the picture of human life that emerges in his tales. It is often observed that he shares with Jane Austen a sense of the inscrutable elements in human behaviour.

The actions of Crabbe's characters are sometimes inexplicable. In his most famous tale of 1812– *Peter Grimes* – Peter's father is pious and kind but, unaccountably, his son is a morose, violent outcast. Jane Austen is aware of the inexplicable in human behaviour: what, for instance, is to be made of Mrs Norris? At one point the inscrutability of her behaviour is expressed in a single word: 'she disliked Fanny, because she had neglected her' (vol. 3, ch. 2). Why 'because'? What can be the causal link between neglect and dislike? The word order matters: Mrs Norris does not neglect Fanny because she dislikes her but dislikes her *because* of her neglect. Jane Austen makes sure we know how to judge Mrs Norris's conduct, even though we do not know how to account for her actions. Moral clarity and psychological impenetrability constitute Jane Austen's characterization (see 15.10).

13.11 The heroine questioned

'And Fanny . . .' (vol. 1, ch. 5)

Readers divided

The art of *Mansfield Park* has divided readers, largely because of the character of Fanny.

Jane Austen collected the opinions of her family: one of her brothers, Edward, 'admired Fanny', but her mother thought Fanny 'insipid'. 'Insipid', a favourite Jane Austen word, meant lacking in life or spirit. Reginald Farrer, writer and botanist, was very hostile: 'fiction holds no heroine more repulsive in her cast-iron self-righteousness and steely rigidity of prejudice' (B.C. Southam, *Jane Austen: The Critical Heritage*, Vol. 1, Routledge & Kegan Paul, 1968).

In the twentieth century D.W. Harding spoke for many when he said that because Fanny endorses conventional virtues 'she is the least interesting of all the heroines'. (*Regulated Hatred and Other Essays on Jane Austen*, Athlone, 1998, p. 18).

What is the case against Fanny?

Silence

There is a piece of literary criticism that has become quite famous in the discussion of Jane Austen's work . In *Computation and Criticism: A Study of Jane Austen's Novels and an Experiment in Method*, (Oxford University Press, 1987), J.F. Burrows did some sums: Fanny, he counted, utters 6,117 words and thinks 15,418. Those figures give a mathematical exactitude to the impression that Fanny is withdrawn and uncommunicative. On the drive to Sotherton we learn that she 'did not desire' others' conversation – 'Her own thoughts and reflections were habitually her best companions;' (vol. 1, ch. 8). Little wonder that some readers, frustrated by a novel that polarizes characters for didactic purposes, have preferred the witty liveliness of Mary to the silence of a lamb. Mary is a literary cousin of Elizabeth Bennet; is Fanny too like Mary Bennet?

Yet Fanny uses her silence. As she says to Mary Crawford about Henry's conduct : 'I was quiet, but I was not blind' (vol. 3, ch. 5). As Burrows's statistics show, Fanny thinks, and unlike Mary Bennet she thinks to some purpose. An acute perception of others and the self is the fruit of her contemplative silence. Self-knowledge is what she hopes for in others. When she reads of the rumour of Henry and Maria's elopement, 'she hoped it might give him a knowledge of his own disposition' (vol. 3, ch. 15).

Conversation

And Fanny does talk. She is eloquent on the sublimity of nature (see 16.10) and she has much to say on female choice. Her silence and her speech work together:

Fanny's silence can be resistance and her speech criticism.

Passivity

Closely related to silence is passivity. Fanny does very little and what she does fatigues her: 'Fanny fatigued and fatigued again' (vol. 3, ch. 7). When she started riding she trembled. She shrinks and she often weeps. In Portsmouth Fanny sits 'in bewildered, broken, sorrowful contemplation' (vol. 3, ch. 7). Her heart is at Mansfield, and when the crisis of Tom's illness breaks, she can only be a passive recipient of news. Sometimes it appears that

Jane Austen thinks there is an equation that unites emotional sensitivity and moral insight with passivity and even physical weakness.

Fanny is more alert than any one else in Mansfield to good and evil. Sir Thomas cannot understand Fanny: 'She was so gentle and retiring, that her emotions were beyond his discrimination' (vol. 3, ch. 6). Yet it is Fanny who has the most acute sense of his goodness.

Tractability

Fanny gives in. She is used to being summoned (see 13.9) and she does all that her two aunts require of her without question or complaint. She is forbearing. Sir Thomas in his 'advice of absolute power' to go to bed on the night of the ball hopes that 'he might mean to recommend her as a wife [to Henry Crawford] by shewing her persuadableness' (vol. 2, ch. 10). Just how persuadable she might be is shown in the narrator's declaration that if Henry had persevered with his suit 'Fanny must have been his reward' (vol. 3, ch. 17).

The difficulty with her tractability is seen in the wording of a passage in which Fanny compares herself to the more active Susan:

> Susan was only acting on the same truths, and pursuing the same system, which her own judgement acknowledged, but which her more supine and yielding temper would have shrunk from asserting. (vol. 3, ch. 9)

We must remember that this is Fanny thinking, so the remark about her 'supine and yielding temper' is one she makes about herself. Yet it is a devastating judgement. Fanny's 'habits of ready submission' (vol. 3, ch. 5) look like a function of a weakness of personality, an unwillingness to assert herself.

Yet the chief emotional and moral drama of the novel is Fanny's refusal to accept Henry. The power and authority of Mansfield Park is against her: Sir Thomas is overbearing, Edmund is obtuse in his failure to understand her reluctance, and Henry, with the encouragement and sanction of Sir Thomas, persists with an inconsiderate zeal. Yet Fanny remains firm, showing no sign of being either supine or yielding. Again, refusal comes through silence and criticism. Silence can be a sign of strength, and speech from one who usually says little has force. In a world of male power, a woman has some freedom in her refusal to speak. When she does speak, the thoughtful Fanny deploys her carefully pondered moral language.

Priggishness?

Some critics accuse Fanny of being a prig. D.W. Harding, usually so balanced, writes: 'And Fanny is a dreary, debilitated, priggish goody-goody' (*Regulated Hatred and Other Essays on Jane Austen*, pp. 121–2).

Harding is wrong. Fanny is morally discriminating. She takes lapses like Henry's improper and unfeeling behaviour during rehearsals very seriously, as she tells Edward. But even if there is something of the 'holy huddle' about Fanny and Edmund's confidential exchanges, there is still no justification for calling Fanny a prig. A prig is offensively confident in judgement, but when Fanny speaks in criticism, she 'trembled and blushed at her own daring' (vol. 2, ch. 5).

Fanny is hesitant, tentative and uncertain.

She is often right, but she does not always *feel* she is. It is understandable that she is felt to be frustratingly timid, but that is quite different from accusing her of priggishness.

13.12 Christians and feminists

'you mean to refuse Mr Crawford?'
'Yes, Sir.' (vol. 3, ch.1)

Fanny's refusal can be applauded by Christians and feminists. Mrs Norris criticizes her by saying she 'takes her own independent walk' (vol. 3, ch. 1). That independence, that refusal to conform to the wishes of others, makes her a distinctly original heroine.

Meekness

An element of that originality is her meekness. Humility, forbearance and self-abandonment to divine providence are not virtues that always appeal. (Is hostility to Fanny merely hostility to Christianity?) If we understand Fanny's religion, there are pleasurable ironies. We may be angry that Mrs Norris tells her that at the Grants', Fanny 'must be the lowest and the last' (vol. 2, ch. 5). Yet in a religious sense (though not one intended by the widow of a clergyman) Fanny *is* one of the lowest and the last, because, in the teaching of Jesus, it is precisely those who enter the Kingdom of God. The meek will inherit the earth.

Feminist defences

Recent defences of Fanny have come from some of the feminist critics. Claudia Johnson claims that Fanny is independent enough to resist the male hierarchy, though she also thinks that Fanny is not fully aware of exactly what is wrong with the government of Mansfield. In *Jane Austen, Feminism and Fiction* (Athlone, 1997 p. 101), Margaret Kirkham argues that Fanny 'is drawn in such a way as to make comparisons and contrasts between her character and that of a number of more sentimental models...and the exemplary young woman of the more sentimental kind of conduct book'. Though some of Fanny's characteristics are superficially similar to those set out for emulation in the conduct books – a submissive attitude and weakness that encourage men to be protective – Margaret Kirkham emphasizes how Fanny departs from such a model by not being an entirely naturalistic character. When the narrator calls her, in the second paragraph of the final chapter, 'My Fanny', her literary status as a created character existing in a fictional world is made clear. Her proper mode of existence is the novel rather than the assembly room.

This is an insight at least as old as the superb criticism of Richard Simpson, a Roman Catholic Shakespeare scholar. In 1870 he wrote a lengthy piece on Jane Austen, which included the following speculation about *Mansfield Park*: 'what would have followed if Henry Crawford had not run wild, and if the hero had consequently married the anti-heroine, and the heroine the anti-hero' (B.C. Southam, *Jane Austen: The Critical Heritage*, Routledge & Kegan Paul, 1968, p. 245). In calling Fanny and Edmund the anti-heroine and anti-hero, Simpson recognizes their literary status and in so doing also recognizes that the Crawfords have many of the characteristics that fit them to be the hero and heroine of the book.

Fictional pleasures

Regarding Fanny as a literary creation helps to focus the problem some readers have with Fanny:

Fanny troubles some readers because she does not provide the kind of pleasures so often associated with the more conventional heroines of fiction.

A character who is silent, passive, tractable and morally vigilant is not going to delight the reader with her wit, excite us by her actions, stir us with admiration at her defiance or engage our sympathy and interest as we watch her negotiating the perilous path to moral enlightenment. The general point must be conceded: Fanny as a character does not satisfy conventional – romantic, sentimental – taste. And this surely is deliberate.

***Mansfield Park* does not satisfy the expectations of the reader schooled in the conventions of popular fiction.**

Mansfield Park is distinctive because it renounces so much that art usually gives us. If it is dark, serious, earnest and even brooding, it is because Jane Austen is showing the reader something important through her denial of the more customarily pleasurable elements of fiction.

The answer to the reader who complains that there is insufficient interest – action, liveliness, wit, zest – in Fanny is that this is precisely what Jane Austen intends. *Mansfield Park* is a work of fiction that deliberately denies the reader some of the common pleasures of fiction.

Romance and the narrator

Two examples will bring this out. The first is the book's neglect of romance. Unlike *Pride and Prejudice* there is no interest in how Edmund changes his mind about Fanny. Furthermore, the narrator boldly asserts that sibling love is the strongest emotion. When William visits Mansfield, he and Fanny can share the memories of their past. 'An advantage this, a strengthener of love, in which even the conjugal tie is beneath the fraternal' (vol. 2, ch. 6). If the narrator explicitly locates the heart of the novel in a brother/sister bond, then the conventional pleasures of romance are going to be, emotionally speaking, secondary.

The directing force of the narration also denies the reader some of the pleasures of autonomy. *Mansfield Park* is not an 'over-to-you' novel. It is far more like a medieval work in which the interpretative space allowed to the reader is diminished. At certain points, as above, the reader is simply required to assent. This, in part, explains the last chapter. The tone is unflinchingly fierce. Judgement, firm and final, has been passed.

Purposes additional to art

Why should Jane Austen write in this way? The answer must be that she has purposes in addition to artistic ones. As the chapter headings indicate, this is a novel about morality, politics and God. If art is all too easily associated with habits that are inimical to the proper ordering of life, the maintenance of society and the recognition of the supremacy of God, then art in some of its manifestations – the indulgence of the emotions and the freeing of the imagination – must be subdued. As far as Fanny is concerned, the novel challenges the reader to prefer quiet virtue to liveliness and wit. It is an honest challenge, because the narrative shows us the diverting and entertaining nature of the life which we are called upon to refuse. By leading the reader to recognize but refuse the enterprise of Maria in crossing the ha-ha, the novel becomes more than didactic. The didactic work seeks to make virtue attractive and vice repellent.

Jane Austen recognizes that in literary terms there is far more scope in representing vice and that virtue does not supply the novelist with the kind of material that often interests the reader.

The difficulties of reading

The reader indeed is central to discussions of *Mansfield Park*, because it is a novel written to provoke. No character in Jane Austen is the object of such fierce criticism as Fanny. D.W. Harding, who may go down as one of the most intelligent readers of literature in the twentieth century, is close to rant in his condemnation of her. Is it, one might ask, because he sees all too clearly the moral and religious foundation of the novel and because that is not to his taste he turns his fury on Fanny? Certainly, the strength of his language suggests that it is something other than a novel that has stirred him.

Those who find the morality and religion of the novel displeasing have a problem. In its medieval way it concentrates the reader's mind on tradition, suffering, duty, contemplation, quiet and the practice of religious devotion. In a small field, with no ample space for the resourceful mind to wander in, the only option is to accept the novel in the terms in which it presents itself or to reject it, virtually in its entirety.

Appealing art?

Although *Mansfield Park* admittedly makes severe (and austere) demands on the reader it remains a remarkably popular novel. Many seasoned readers declare themselves, sometimes with a tinge of surprise, to be Mansfield Parkers. And nor is it unknown for the novel to make an immediate impact. An intelligent general reader decided to try Jane Austen and reported that her favourite was the one about the little girl in the big house.

Two conclusions might be drawn from its popularity. The first is its similarity to the Cinderella story and, despite its differences, its links with *Jane Eyre* also should not be overlooked. The second is that although it eschews so much that makes art interesting, its features do make an appeal to the reader. Can it be ruled out that part of its appeal is the way it deliberately refuses to gratify our craving for certain kinds of art?

14 Politics

14.1 Political interpretations

'so much of politics . . .' (vol. 2, ch. 5)

Jane Austen's attitudes?

The political interpretation of Jane Austen's novels is relatively new. Many readers have assumed that the dinner conversation at the Mansfield parsonage is representative of Jane Austen's attitude to political issues. Fanny only listens to 'so much of politics between Mr Crawford and Dr Grant'.

New readings

The publication of Marilyn Butler's *Jane Austen and the War of Ideas* in 1975 marks the start of the debate as to the nature and importance of politics in Jane Austen's work. Marilyn Butler showed that, since contemporary fiction was politically aware, the same might be true of Jane Austen herself.

Political readings

It is necessary to say something about what it might mean to give a political reading to Jane Austen. There is virtually no argument about political principles or policies in the novels. Nor are there many references to public events.

A more fruitful approach to the issue of politics may be made by widening the scope of the term:

In Jane Austen politics is about the conduct of life.

This will include how power is exercised, how trade is conducted and even how households engage with their neighbours.

14.2 Contemporary politics

'in the same county, and the same interest' (vol. 1, ch. 4)

Understanding the past

Thinking about politics raises the issue of understanding a past age. In Jane Austen's day, politics was a very different business in at least three ways.

The franchise

The first is that Jane Austen lived in an era when few people were allowed to vote. Sir Thomas, an MP, would have a very small electorate. It was not until 1832 that the franchise (those entitled to vote) began to widen.

Political parties

The second point is that the political parties or groupings were not as well defined as they are now. Most MPs were men of independent means who had no financial need to sit in the House of Commons. There was certainly political rivalry between the groupings but, unlike today, it was not conducted in terms of two distinct parties with separate agendas.

Political principles

The third difference is probably the most important one. The two major groupings were the Tories and the Whigs. The Tories emerged in Jane Austen's lifetime as the forerunners of the Conservative Party, while the Whigs eventually became the Liberal Party.

The biggest change has taken place in the Tories. Nowadays, the Conservative Party stands for economic free enterprise, but in Jane Austen's day this was the preserve of the Whigs. The Tories preferred to trust in traditional institutions, such as the family, the Church and the country estate, because these depended upon the cooperation of a community rather than the enterprise of an individual. Traditional Toryism was suspicious of individualism; modern Conservatism endorses it as the very basis of society.

Sir Thomas initially favours Maria's engagement to Mr Rushworth because the young man was in 'the same interest' (vol. 1, ch. 4). This probably means that Mr Rushworth, like Sir Thomas, supported the landed (Tory) as opposed to the merchant classes (Whig).

Whigs and Tories on change

Perhaps the most significant difference between the Whigs and Tories lay in the issue of change. The Whigs tended to think that as the years passed some improvement in the life of the nation would occur.

The Tory view was that change was not impossible but that it could only happen within inherited institutions. These should be conserved through change.

Burke and Godwin

The most eloquent spokesman for the conservative view was Edmund Burke. Burke had started his parliamentary life as a supporter of the Whigs, but he saw in the French Revolution the destruction of all the institutions that defined the nation of France. He did not believe that such destruction was necessary. His most succinct statement of the Tory position came in 1790:

> A state without the means of some change is without the means of its conservation. (*Reflections on the Revolution in France*, Penguin Edition, p. 105)

Burke's thinking is very different from that of William Godwin. Godwin was on the radical wing of politics, so cannot be described as an ordinary Whig. In a chapter from his *Enquiry Concerning Political Justice* (1793) entitled 'Human Inventions Susceptible to Perpetual Improvement' he concluded with this unbounded hope for the future:

> Is it possible for us to contemplate what he [mankind] has already done without being impressed with a strong presentiment of the improvements he has yet to accomplish? (Penguin Edition, p. 163)

The French Revolution

The French Revolution divided the Tories and the Whigs. Burke did not doubt that change in France was necessary but what he saw was the destruction of those institutions which might have guided change. Some Whigs, on the other hand, hoped that France would be improved. In the wars with France that followed the Revolution, the Tories secured power (they had been in opposition for much of the eighteenth century). Under Pitt they pursued policies based on the preservation of national life.

The Revolution and the wars form the political backdrop against which Jane Austen's characters acted out their lives. Perhaps the most important function of that backdrop was to sharpen the issue of change: should the nation look forward to a different and better world or should it trust to its institutions to save it from disorder?

14.3 Ideas

'I see your judgement is not with me.' (vol. 1, ch. 16)

Mansfield Park is a novel of ideas: education, dependency, gratitude and family relationships are some of its issues. Many of these ideas are concerned with public matters; education is one, the status of the clergy another. These interests have led to its being called 'a condition of England novel'.

A condition of England novel

Condition of England novels hold up a mirror to English life. They seek to present, in the title of Trollope's later novel, the way we live now. Their purpose is often to give an evaluation of contemporary life. In the case of *Mansfield Park*, we may imagine that the novel is implicitly asking: given there is a war with France, how does the nation face up to its responsibilities and trials? The answer, if that is quite the word, will be discerned in the attitudes and actions of the various characters.

14.4 Improvement

'The subject of improving grounds.' (vol. 1, ch. 6)

A wide-ranging word

The contemporary issue of improvement is capable of a political interpretation. The word 'improvement' is used frequently in *Mansfield Park*. Henry Crawford claims that he alone has noticed 'the wonderful improvement that has taken place in her [Fanny's] looks' (vol. 2, ch. 6). 'Improved' is an elusive word; in those passages that suggest improvement in people, differences in the motives of perception make the word richly nuanced.

Landscape gardening: Capability Brown

The word had a quite specific use in landscape gardening (see 12.9). An Improver would examine a landscape for its capabilities.

Brown (1715–83) was a significant figure because he showed just how radical landscape improvement could be. He was chiefly concerned with the *form* of a landscape, so even removed whole woods to show the underlying shape of the ground. His sweeping lines and grand, open vistas celebrated the wealth and splendour of the (often Whig) owners. That the eye could range across vast terrains might have been a factor in reading Brown's landscapes as expressive of liberty (see 12.9).

Humphrey Repton

In his belief that the importance of the owner should be expressed in the landscape, Humphrey Repton (1752–1818) was Brown's aesthetic heir. So taken was he with the 'united and uninterrupted property' of ancient families that he was prepared to remove cottages, for example, if they impeded the view of the mansion and its park.

Payne and Price

Some dissented: most notably, two Herefordshire writers and landscape architects. Richard Payne Knight (1750–1824) and Uvedale Price (1747–1829) argued that the grounds of large estates should look natural. Payne's regret that Brown's 'innovating hand' destroyed the interest of secret places of tangle, shade and moss is expressed in *The Landscape: A Didactic Poem* (1794). Brown's 'innovating hand . . . dealt . . . curses o'er this fertile land' and he 'Banish'd the thickets of high bow'ring woods' (*The Genius of the Place*, eds John Dixon Hunt and Peter Willis, Elek, 1975, p. 345).

Price lamented the loss in an improved landscape of those qualities that make it picturesque. What improvers destroyed, Price argued, was an appreciation that the beauties of a natural landscape are the work of time.

Landscape politicized

With their stress on the value of natural growth, Knight and Price are likely to appeal to a Tory imagination. In their hesitations about the capacity of people to improve the landscape, we may see what might be called a politics of landscape.

14.5 The debate about Sotherton

'It wants improvement, ma'am.' (vol. 1, ch. 6)

Seeing Compton

Improvement enters *Mansfield Park* as a topic of conversation when Mr Rushworth has been to see Compton, where his friend, Smith, has 'had his grounds laid out by an improver' (vol. 1, ch. 6). The frequent recurrence of the word 'improvement' (and its cognates) makes the issue thematically prominent. Sotherton, by contrast with Compton, looks 'like a prison – quite a dismal old prison'. In spite of a protest, obsequious for all its stridency, from Mrs Norris that it is 'the noblest old place in the world', Rushworth repeats his point with colloquial imprecision: 'It wants improvement, ma'am, beyond any thing. I never saw a place that wanted so much improvement in my life; and it is so forlorn'.

'Forlorn' is an enticing word. Rushworth thinks that Sotherton has an abandoned look. He may be unintentionally right. The house with its largely unregarded family portraits and effectively disused chapel has a hollow feel. Is this because the owner is also 'forlorn'? Does his restless desire for superficial change and novelty suggest a man who in himself is directionless and lost?

Contemplating change

The apparent completeness of change has impressed Rushworth: 'I never saw a place so altered in my life.' His confidence in the happy prospect of almost instant change is shared by others. Mrs Norris encourages him: 'I would have everything done in the best style, and made as nice as possible.' Just like that.

Behind Mr Rushworth's empty enthusiasm is the suspect assumption that change is easy.

Of course, to a discerning eye the alteration cannot be as complete as Rushworth imagines. The improver, if he is in the Brown tradition, might have grubbed out established copses and planted uniform belts of trees, but the contours of the ground will have remained. In addition to shallow confidence, the discussion betrays three more attitudes that the narrator invites us to question.

'Polite' landscapes

The first is what might be called the 'polite' attitude to landscape gardening. Maria calls some cottages in Sotherton 'a disgrace' and reflects contentedly that, for reasons of noise, she is glad that the church 'is not so close to the Great House as often happens in old places' (vol. 1, ch. 8).

The tolling of bells is a reminder of the passing of time as well as a summons to raise the heart and mind in public worship. Churchyards are a memento mori. One of the purposes of the novel is to oblige the reader to engage with those features of the mortal condition that many of us would rather not contemplate.

Calculation

The second attitude is the ready resort to calculation. This is in keeping with the novel's suspicion of the kind of thinking represented by utilitarianism (see 15.8). Mr Rushworth's logic is very curious. Observing that his friend Smith 'has not got much above a hundred acres altogether', he confidently declares:

> Now at Sotherton, we have a good seven hundred, without reckoning the water meadows; so that I think, if so much could be done at Compton, we need not despair.

Rushworth's assumption that there must be a ratio between the size of a park and the 'capabilities' of its landscape strongly suggests that Sotherton is valued for its established and potential prestige. Is nature to be so regarded? (It is one of the oddities of the novel that Fanny, the representative of value, should be called Price.)

Taste

To assume that the mere size of the park is a significant factor is to betray a distinct lack of taste. Mr Rushworth's tasteless zeal is evident in his assurance that 'Repton, or anybody of that sort, would certainly have the avenue at Sotherton down.'

What emerges here is an ignorance of Repton's current thinking. Perhaps the irony of the passage is that Rushworth thinks of himself as advanced when he is only repeating views that have become slightly dated. Repton did not always cut down old avenues. It is possible that Jane Austen would have expected her readers to see the eager improver as both tasteless and out of touch.

14.6 Cowper

'Does it not make you think of Cowper?' (vol. 1, ch. 6)

Fanny's contribution

Fanny's response to the possible loss of an avenue of trees she has never seen might be said to display sensibility. In the first indication that she is a reader, she refers to Cowper's *The Task* (1785):

> Cut down an avenue! What a pity! Does it not make you think of Cowper? 'Ye fallen avenues, once more I mourn your fate unmerited. (vol. 1. ch. 6)

'The Task'

It is difficult not to read this passage as an invitation to look at Cowper's lines. Cowper is glad that a lord – John Courteney Throckmorton – allows him to wander in his park grounds (Weston Underwood), and it is there that the lines Fanny recalled are uttered:

> Ye fallen avenues! Once more I mourn
> Your fate unmerited, once more rejoice
> That yet a remnant of your race survives.
> How airy and how light the graceful arch,
> Yet awful as the consecrated roof
> Re-echoing pious anthems!
> (lines 338–43)

The fate of the avenue at Sotherton would be 'unmerited', and if the improver does a Brownian job, not even a remnant of old woodland would survive.

Yet a remnant does survive, not only in Cowper but she who quotes him. 'Remnant' is Biblical. It often refers to the remaining faithful people. In Micah 5 the faithful remnant return to their land. It is not hard to see the parallels with *Mansfield Park*: it is the story of one who strives to be faithful to an inheritance she values. Fanny returns to Mansfield when the family is in crisis.

Cowper's lines are religious in another sense. The long avenue recalls a church. Though 'airy' and 'light', it is as awe-inspiring ('awful') as a nave or sanctuary, whose 'consecrated roof' echoes with psalms.

Uvedale Price on avenues

As well as these lines from Cowper, did Jane Austen know the passage in Uvedale Price?

> The avenue has a most striking effect, from the very circumstance of its being straight; no other figure can give that image of a grand gothic aisle with its natural columns and vaulted roof . . . particular parts insensibly steal from it in a long gradation of perspective . . . above all other places, most suited to meditation. (*Essays on the Picturesque*, part II, ch. 1)

Cowper writes of 'the consecrated roof', Price of 'the grand gothic aisle'. Trees matter. Yet as with so much else in this metonymic first volume of *Mansfield Park*, the trees stand for an inner growth. The loss of the avenue is the loss of a sense of awe that helps meditation. It is a place in which to achieve what in their elopement Maria and Henry show they lack – 'a long gradation of perspective'. These qualities, fostered by a religion which is more than theoretical, are the quiet virtues without which there is neither stability nor peace of mind. Fanny, in speaking up for the avenue, associates herself with the then rather fashionable thinker with whom she shared her name.

14.7 The politics of the estate

'to see the place as it is now, in its old state' (vol. 1, ch. 6)

A sceptical approach

What emerges from the debate about 'improvement' is the narrator's scepticism at a presumption in favour of change and at an assumption of achieving this with ease. This view is not unequivocally voiced by any of the participants, but Fanny's preference for the work of time and an interest, were the landscape improved, in seeing the process and not merely the finished product, is sounder than that of the zealots.

Improvement and criticism

Since 1971 the place of 'improvement' in Jane Austen has been strongly influenced by Alistair Duckworth's *The Improvement of the Estate* (Johns Hopkins University Press, 1971). He contended that Jane Austen was not essentially an ironist with a romantic moral code of self-realization but a writer whose chief preoccupation was with the fabric of society and whose morality was distinctly public. In such a reading, *Mansfield Park* becomes her central work.

Burke on 'improvement' and 'innovation'

Duckworth reads Jane Austen in terms of the Burkean principle that: 'People will not look forward to the future who do not look backward to their ancestors' (*Reflections on the Revolution in France* Penguin, p. 119). This is not a contradiction. Burke distinguished between 'improvement' – necessary adjustments in accordance with the times – and what he called 'innovation' – the sweeping away of inherited features in favour of changes which were alien to the nature of the institution.

The preservation of estates

Duckworth finds it significant that one of Burke's images for the preservation of the state is the property a family inherits:

> But one of the most leading principles on which the commonwealth and the laws are consecrated, is lest the temporary possessors and life-renters . . . should act as if they were the entire masters . . . hazarding to leave to those who come after them, a ruin instead of an habitation. (*Reflections on the Revolution in France*, Penguin Edition, 1968, p. 192)

Estate and state

In terms of Sotherton, Mr Rushworth is the one charged with the responsibility of leaving to posterity a 'habitation' and not a 'ruin'. At Mansfield Park the profligate Tom might be the one who destroys the whole original fabric of his society. We may conclude:

the country estate should be interpreted as meaning the nation at large.

Sotherton and Mansfield are England; estate means state.

The problem of terminology

It is tempting to describe extensive parks and fine houses as symbols or emblems of the nation. Tempting because 'symbol' and 'emblem' are standard ways of talking about things within literary works that have further meanings. Some readers might hesitate to use such terms of Jane Austen's novels. Does it sound right to call her a symbolist?

But even if we resist the term, we have to recognize there is something about *Mansfield Park* that provokes language of this kind. Are the scenes at Sotherton an allegory of England's spiritual condition? There certainly is something representative about the house, its landscape and its uncertain future, but if we are to use allegory, how far can the term be pushed (see 15.3)?

Perhaps the best thing is to admit that none of these terms quite succeed in encapsulating what Jane Austen is doing, while at the same time insist that in the case of these estates we are dealing with issues of national importance.

14.8 The meaning of 'estate'

'the Antiguan estate' (vol. 1, ch. 3)

Several meanings

The word 'estate' has and had several meanings. Johnson gave six. The fourth – 'Fortune; possession in land' – is clearly the relevant one for a discussion of *Mansfield Park*. Johnson links wealth with land. What both have in common is a usage in terms of inheritance: one's estate is what is passed on to one by parents.

William Law

Earlier than Johnson the word was given a distinctive moral colouring by an author Jane Austen may well have known – William Law (1686–1761). He moved permanently to Kings Cliffe, Northamptonshire (Mansfield Park's county) in 1740, where he established a religious community, ran charitable institutions and wrote copiously.

His most famous book, *A Serious Call to a Devout and Holy Life* (1728), is a work of devotion and guidance. It is high-minded, earnest and 'inward' – it points to meditation, purity of soul and 'a heart always ready to praise God'. The book was widely read. Whole chapters are devoted to fictional characters who represent, by example, wise or foolish ways of living. Three such chapters are entitled:

VI The religious use of our estates and fortunes.
VII The imprudent use of estate; Flavia.
VIII The wise use of an estate leads to greater Christian perfection; Miranda.

Some passages read like a severe criticism of characters such as Rushworth and the Crawfords, who are rich and, in the case of Crawford, gifted, but who in wasting their estate do moral and spiritual damage to themselves.

Flavia and Miranda are exemplary figures. The former gets life fundamentally wrong because she is one of those whose 'religion lives only in their head' (chap. VII). This is not dissimilar to Sir Thomas's reflections on his daughters that they have been 'instructed theoretically in their religion, but never required to bring it into daily practice' (vol. 3, ch.17).

The life of Miranda is one marked by charity. She is an idealized figure, but we might remember Fanny's room (vol. 1, ch. 16) with 'her writing desk, and her works of charity'.

In her Introduction to the *Oxford World's Classics* edition of *Mansfield Park*, Marilyn Butler draws attention to the polarized figures presented by the profligate Maria and the virtuous Fanny. – 'the scapegoat as well as the angel'. A model for such polarized figures might have come from Law's juxtaposition of Flavia and Miranda.

It is not necessary to show that Jane Austen is referring to William Law to appreciate that the moral climate of his kind of writing (works of private devotion, many deliberately written for women) pervades the presentation of estates in *Mansfield Park*. Goods and property are entrusted to us; we have a solemn responsibility to use them well to hand on to our successors.

14.9 Neglect

'Prayers were always read in it by the domestic chaplain, within the memory of many. But the late Mr Rushworth left it off.' (vol. 1, ch. 9)

An estate neglected

Neglect of the inheritance – what makes it culturally and spiritually valuable – is painfully evident at Sotherton. This neglect makes Rushworth's fantasies of improvement all the more frivolous and reprehensible. If the estate of Sotherton in some way stands for the state of England, then the judgement on the nation is a severe one. What Sotherton lacks is an appreciation of what has been inherited. The life of the house is empty like the chapel and as rootless as Mr Rushworth's plans for the Avenue.

No sense of history

Sotherton has lost its sense of its own history:

> Of pictures there were an abundance, and some few good, but the larger part were family portraits, no longer any thing to any body but Mrs Rushworth. (vol. 1, ch. 9)

Mrs Rushworth has learnt Compton's history from the housekeeper who, a reader might feel, deserves better than anonymity. Given the neglect of the chapel, we may surmise that Mrs Rushworth's ignorance stems from her late husband's lack of interest. Compton is very different from Pemberley, where Mrs Reynolds both knows the history and admires the family. Moreover, at Pemberley there is a portrait of the current owner. When was the last Rushworth portrait painted? No reader should be surprised that when Mrs Rushworth leaves the house to take up residence in Bath, she enjoys 'the wonders of Sotherton . . . as thoroughly perhaps in the animation of a card-table as she had ever done on the spot' (vol. 2, ch. 3).

Inheritance and liberties

The political aspect of neglect is brought out by Burke, who appeals to his readers to consider 'our liberties in the light of an inheritance'.

> It has a pedigree and illustrating ancestors. It has its bearings and ensigns armorial. It has its gallery of portraits; its monumental inscriptions; its records, evidences, and titles. (*Reflections on the Revolution in France* Penguin Edition, 1968, p. 121)

Burke's passage is like a tour of Sotherton (vol. 1, ch. 9) with an emphasis on what is no longer present. There are, as Fanny says, 'no inscriptions, no banners' (vol. 1, ch. 9). It is difficult to believe that the portraits provide a tradition of 'illustrating ancestors' to the heedless buffoon who is the inheritor. It is hard to avoid the deep and searchingly critical conservatism of the writing.

Unworthy inheritors

Also very hard to overlook is the demanding judgement that finds the inheritors entirely wanting. Things are different at Mansfield, if far from well. Sir Thomas has preserved his estate; indeed, the serpentining contours of the plot trace the threats, near disasters and chastened survival of the way of life he values and strenuously seeks to protect.

But if Mansfield does survive it does so only because Sir Thomas comes to see that he has preserved the form but endangered the inner life of the estate.

It is not quite a matter of preservation without change, because he admits Fanny into the family circle. The closest he gets to recognizing his failure is in the harsh final chapter when, darkly reflecting upon the public failures of his daughters to live up to the standards he has sought to maintain, he contemplates the perfidious influence of Mrs Norris before recognizing that 'something had been wanting *within*'. The very inarticulate nature of the formulation indicates how elusive that 'something' is. Perhaps the novel enables us to see that it is embodied in Fanny, who, in spite of her shortcomings and lack of charisma, is not merely 'the daughter he had always wanted' but the daughter Mansfield needed.

14.10 Slavery

'the heat was enough to kill any body' (vol. 1, ch. 7)

Slavery debated

The issue of how the novel treats slavery has recently been vigorously though inconclusively debated. (See the notes in Kathryn Sutherland's Penguin Edition, 1996, pp. 403–4.) The post-colonial dimension of literary thinking, exemplified above all in the criticism of Edward Said, has given prominence to Sir Thomas Bertram's land in Antigua and the conversation on the slave trade that Fanny attempts to have with him shortly after his return from the West Indies (vol. 2, ch. 3).

The references may be few and no one would claim that the novel foregrounds the issue, nevertheless, for a political understanding of *Mansfield Park* (and of a passage in *Emma*: see 16.5 and 19.6), the significance of the West Indies is enticing if, perhaps, in the end elusive.

The Antiguan estate

It is well to start with a point about vocabulary: the word 'estate' is never applied to Mansfield Park. Alistair Duckworth may have built his argument about the political and moral significance of *Mansfield Park* on the virtual linguistic coincidence of estate/state, but though Sotherton is called such, Mansfield never is.

The property that is most consistently referred to as an estate is the one in Antigua. Alistair Duckworth must be right about this – Sir Thomas goes to the West Indies to improve it. It was one of the older British colonies and by the first decade of the nineteenth century its sugar exports were beginning to decline. Most of the estates were worked by slaves. Now even though John Sutherland reasonably points out (*Is Heathcliff a Murderer?* Oxford World Classics, 1996, pp. 1–9) that there is no evidence that the Antiguan estate grows sugar, we might assume that when contemporary references are vague we should interpret them in terms of prevailing rather than exceptional practices. So we may assume that the Antiguan estate grew sugar, was worked by slaves and may have been in financial difficulties.

But Sutherland is surely right in claiming that it does not follow, as Edward Said maintained, that the Antiguan estate is the chief source of Mansfield's wealth. During the French wars many landowners made considerable profits out of their English estates, and since we hear about the harvest (vol. 1, ch. 6), it is not unreasonable to assume that much of Sir Thomas's wealth comes from Mansfield Park itself.

Estates in England and the West Indies

Is it significant that the design of slave–run estates in the West Indies resembled those of large English country houses? In both there would be a mansion dominating the grounds, which supplied the wealth of the estate. In England estate labourers would work on the land; in the West Indies such work would largely be done by slaves, put to work by taskmasters. May we not assume that one of the reasons Sir Thomas had for taking his eldest heir with him was so the young man could learn something about estate management, a discipline he is unlikely to learn in England because he spends much of his time in gambling houses or at the races?

Fanny and slavery

The resemblance between the two estates might provoke the question of Fanny's status and treatment. It would clearly be a misreading to say she is reduced to the status of a slave. Yet during Sir Thomas's absence, Fanny, far from strong, has been working in the hot sun cutting roses and has walked twice to Mrs Norris's house. The reader would not wish to be clumsy here, but in the hot sun, the journeys and a hard taskmistress is there not the shadow of a suggestion that we might think of the conditions endured by those bringing in the sugar crop? And if we do, perhaps our sympathies are not only given to the one who suffers the beating of the Northamptonshire sun.

Lord Mansfield

The possibility that we might be right in paralleling the two estates is given, by implication, some support by Margaret Kirkham's point about the book's title. (*Jane Austen, Feminism and Fiction*, Athlone, 1983 and 1996, pp. 116–19). The crucial legal judgement about slavery in England was delivered in 1772 by Lord Chief Justice Mansfield.

Mansfield presided over a case concerning James Somerset, an African who, although in irons, had managed to escape from a ship anchoring in the Thames. There was no doubt that Somerset had been bought as a slave in Virginia; the issue was whether that status had any legal standing in England. The law was not clear on the matter. Mansfield's judgment in the case of Somerset appeals directly to moral sentiments. He argued that as slavery was in itself 'so odious' the only thing that could permit the keeping of slaves was a law positively allowing it. Since no such law existed, James Somerset was a free man. Jane Austen, as Margaret Kirkham points out, had met Mansfield's niece several times in the house of her brother, Edward Knight.

The coincidence of names

The problem, of course, is what to make of this coincidence of names in a novel that touches, albeit glancingly, on the issue of slavery. Perhaps the association with the judge who freed James Somerset works in favour of the life of Mansfield. This is the place that, under the right stewardship, might liberate. If we judge Sir Thomas, for all his shortcomings, as eventually capable of making Mansfield a place in which freedom is possible, we might think of him as possessing the potential to treat those on his Antiguan estate humanely. This, though, is highly speculative. Against it we must balance the fact that Sir Thomas is a man who oppressed his children, singled out

Edmund to take to task over the theatricals, used cruelty and blackmail to try to force Fanny to marry Henry Crawford and left the family in the hands of Mrs Norris.

Fanny's question

If we read the name as conveying an encouraging view of Mansfield, though, what is to be made of Fanny's question on the slave trade? We do not know what the question is. A bill outlawing trade in slaves (but not the ownership of them) became law in 1808. But even if we take note of Fanny reading *Crabbe's Tales* (published in 1812), the issue would still be alive, so there would be point in Fanny's raising it.

Can we say anything about Fanny's question and Sir Thomas's silence? It is hard to imagine Fanny as anything other than a supporter of abolition. She reads Dr. Johnson and Cowper, both of whom favoured it.

Sir Thomas's answer

Assuming that Edmund knows both Fanny's and his father's views, would he have said about her question 'It would have pleased your uncle to be inquired of farther' (vol. 2, ch. 3) if he knew that Sir Thomas was against abolition? And if we require a reason for Sir Thomas's silence, might he have been surprised that anyone in his family circle other than Edmund had asked an intelligent question that he was unable to answer?

14.11 Stability or mobility

'Henry Crawford was gone.' (vol. 2, ch. 2)

Though the references to the West Indies (and the navy) give the novel a more than national dimension, the stance of the writing is that the real political business is met with in the family and social life in England. Two features which can be read in political terms work as polarities: stillness rather than activity and presence as opposed to absence.

Stillness

Fanny is one of those Jane Austen heroines who provoke the reader by inactivity. The provocation is deliberate. Jane Austen refuses the reader the indulgence of fictional busyness.

Henry Crawford sees Fanny's 'steadiness and regularity'. What he cannot do is recognize her qualities 'by their proper name'; it is the narrator who says she is 'well principled and religious' (vol. 2, ch. 12). It is those qualities that give her immobility stillness. Edmund, often far less perceptive than Henry, speaks more profoundly than he intends when, fagged with the civilities of the ball, he says 'But with *you*, Fanny, there may be peace' (vol. 2, ch. 10).

Activity

Fanny alone achieves a positive stillness. Of those who are busy, Mr Rushworth is her comical anti-type; he stands in the English tradition of a character with a name that is indicative of his character. He rushes about.

Henry is mobile: 'To anything like a permanence of abode . . . Henry Crawford . . . had a great dislike' (vol. 1, ch. 4). No wonder he is a good actor; he knows exactly when to exit! Like Tom he roams the country: 'Bath, Norfolk, London, York' (vol. 2, ch. 2).

Presence

We might think that there is nothing remarkable in such mobility, though the novel requires us to set Rushworth's activity against Fanny, 'whose rides had never been extensive' and who, on the road to Sotherton, 'was soon beyond her knowledge' (vol. 1, ch. 8). Fanny, apart from her exile in Portsmouth, is always present in Mansfield.

Absence

Tom Bertram will one day become, like Mr Rushworth, the head of the family estate, but whereas Rushworth shows the wrong sort of interest in his property, Tom virtually ignores it. He is very rarely there. As the heir to Mansfield he interests Mary but Tom is not reciprocally interested though he is prepared to be gallant. It is hard to say whether the implication here is that his inclinations are not heterosexual. What is clear is that his mobility renders him incapable of fulfilling his duties. As the heir, it is his duty to think of the future, and that involves marriage.

Spiritual stillness versus physical agitation

We should set the restless movements of Rushworth, Tom Bertram and Henry Crawford against the stillness of Fanny. She is centred in a life of common duties, while the others, in several senses, push beyond the margins.

Restlessness has political connotations and consequences:

to be constantly on the move is to satisfy the desire for novelty, and such a desire is likely to make people impatient with the traditions of a long-established social order.

14.12 London and the provinces

'Fanny was disposed to think the influence of London very much at war with all respectable attachments.' (vol. 3, ch. 14)

Urban consumers

It is important in the political landscape of the novel that Mansfield is provincial and that the Crawfords have been raised in London. Even country habits such as riding are practised with the zest of urban consumption. Mary Crawford monopolizes Fanny's mare. Riding does not tire her, because, as she says with the engaging openness of London talk: 'Nothing ever fatigues me, but doing what I do not like.' (vol. 1, ch. 7). When something occasionally puzzles Edmund about her behaviour, he puts it down to the influence of the Admiral, but her light dismissal of the clergy as moral exemplars is met by his remark: '*You* are speaking of London' (vol. 1, ch. 9). He is not always so acute. The climax of the novel is his insight into what Mary is like – 'Spoilt, spoilt!' (vol. 3, ch. 16) – but the tone of her letters – light, mercenary, frivolous, insincere –

make it clear that the culture of a fashionable urban environment has made Mary what she is.

The harp

The most vivid polarization of the ancient literary theme of country and town comes in the conversation about Mary's harp. She clearly enjoys her discovery about how to find things out in the country and affectionately patronizes with an uncritical irony a system that has its own way of working: 'our inquiries were too direct; we sent a servant, we went ourselves: this will not do seventy miles from London – but this morning we heard of it in the right way' (vol. 1, ch. 6). The 'right way' involves a little community of observers and communicators. She is slightly shocked, though enjoyably so, by her discovery that the hiring of a cart in the countryside should prove so difficult. She is taken aback when even Dr Grant 'looked rather black' when he learnt she had been trying to borrow a cart from the bailiff.

What Mary does not understand is the priority of the harvest in the countryside. Dr. Grant was the parson of the parish and as such his chief source of income was from the farming of his glebe or church lands. Edmund supplies an explanation of the country economy: 'our farmers are not in the habit of letting them [carts] out; but in harvest, it must be quite out of their power to spare a horse'.

Mary's response indicates the difference in economies, and hence in whole ways of life, between town and the country: 'I shall understand all your ways in time; but coming down with the true London maxim, that everything is to be got with money, I was a little embarrassed at first by the sturdy independence of your country customs.'

Individualism and cooperation

The politics of this little debate rests upon two very different conceptions of human society:

London represents economic individualism, whereas the countryside stands for the recognition that we are dependent upon the earth. In the country society has a single purpose and works by cooperation.

Again the presumption of the novel favours a kind of conservatism – the importance of communally held values and purposes and a recognition of our bonds with an order beyond ourselves. The country way of life, celebrated in countless poems and sanctioned by the cadences of the Book of Common Prayer, enables people to conceive of a world, at once limiting and stabilizing, beyond the insatiable demands of the will.

14.13 Stewardship

'His eldest son was careless and extravagant.' (vol. 1, ch. 2)

Sir Thomas's absence raises the issue of stewardship. The absent householder is a familiar figure in literature. In the parables of Jesus, for instance, there are merchants who go abroad, leaving their goods in the hands of their servants. A feature of these parables is the return of the master, who demands an account of the servants' stewardship of his goods (see 16.8).

Regents

Roger Sales has drawn attention to the parallel with contemporary history. In February 1811, because George III was recognised as being incapable of governing, his son became Regent (*Jane Austen and the Representation of Regency England,* Routledge, 1994, pp. 56–83). Mansfield has two 'regents' – Edmund and Tom. Edmund presides briefly. Tom returns but spends much of his time away from Mansfield. While he is absent the engagement of Maria to Mr Rushworth takes place. Nor is he present for the visit to Sotherton, an episode that leads to moral licence, although only the vigilant Fanny is aware of this. The theatricals are planned under Tom. The reader is prompted to conclude that Tom has been irresponsible. The legacy of his stewardship is not reassuring.

Duties

If we respond to events by adopting a critical attitude, should we stop with the theatricals? This chapter has largely accepted the political reading of the novel that sees it as a broadly 'conservative' work that stigmatizes personal expression and the elevation of impulse over duty. Stewardship is a duty. One of the ironies that works against Henry is that he is keen that his agent, Maddison, will not trick him (vol. 3 ch. 11) but he is in part to blame because he neglects his duties through his absences from Everingham. No such criticism applies to Sir Thomas; he was absent from Mansfield only because he had to sort out his other estate.

Failings

Yet might the narrator be inviting us to find Sir Thomas wanting? Consider Maria's marriage, which Sir Thomas sees as 'an alliance so unquestionably advantageous' (vol. 1, ch. 4). We might add: advantageous to the estate. When he meets Rushworth he sees that, in his son's words, Rushworth is 'a very stupid fellow' (vol. 1, ch. 4). So 'With solemn kindness' Sir Thomas offers to intervene to release Maria. When she refuses, he was 'too glad to be satisfied', because the marriage was 'an alliance which he could not have relinquished without pain' (vol. 2, ch. 3).

What is missing

Jane Austen supplies an appropriate vocabulary. Sir Thomas is concerned for Maria, but that word 'solemn' lays bare why things go wrong. His 'failure', if that is the right word, is one of sensitivity, tact and warmth. He means well, but his texture – his heavy, suffocating rectitude – make those under his authority feel uncomfortable. Though there is another factor – Maria's disappointment that Henry has not acted – there is enough in this passage to show that her father's manner pressures her into self-destructive behaviour. Maria and Julia were wrong to throw off 'restraint' but it is clear why they should choose to do so.

Learning

Sir Thomas learns:

Sir Thomas, poor Sir Thomas, a parent, and conscious of errors in his own conduct

> as a parent, was the longest to suffer. He felt that he ought not to have allowed the marriage . . . [He had] been governed by motives of selfishness and worldly wisdom. (vol. 3, ch. 17)

The vocabulary is moral, with religious overtones, but since the subject is a marriage sanctioned largely for reasons of estate, a political understanding of it is not inappropriate. Sir Thomas should not have authorized the marriage nor been governed by selfishness. He had failed to exercise the authority his position had granted him.

Wrong government

What emerges from *Mansfield Park* is the feeling, a particularly distressing one for those who favour a conservative reading of politics, that

society is governed by the wrong people.

It is relatively easy to say this of Mr Rushworth and Henry Crawford, but the pressure of the narrative is to affirm this judgement of Mansfield itself, that emblem of England, which, like the nation, undergoes severe trials and in whose survival we are invited to rejoice. If Mansfield is the nation, we must look elsewhere for hope (see 8.11).

Mansfield Park intimates that the future of England depends not upon alliances between the rising professional classes and the landed interest. That occurs in *Pride and Prejudice*, when Jane, the daughter of a gentleman, marries Bingley, the son of trade.

In *Mansfield Park* the future is to be found in Edmund, a baronet's son who becomes a clergyman, in Fanny, essentially an orphan, and in her brother, a young naval officer. William will continue to guard the seas against invaders, and Edmund and Fanny will watch over an England that will have to live by values other than 'worldly wisdom'.

15 Morality

15.1 The seven deadly sins

'I depend on being treated better than I deserve.' (vol. 3, ch. 14)

Mansfield Park is severe; each of the seven deadly sins is represented. Maria exhibits pride in showing off Sotherton, Mrs Frazer covets Miss Bertram's house in Wimpole Street, Sir Thomas is wrathful towards Fanny over Henry, Doctor Grant is a glutton, Henry Crawford is lustful, Miss Crawford envies the Miss Owens their share of Edmund's attention and Lady Bertram is slothful.

This is fitting for a novel that has a distinctly medieval feel. The breaching of the ha-ha cries out to be interpreted allegorically. Edmund, who in the main is a power for good, resembles the 'verray, perfit, gentil knyght' from Chaucer's *Canterbury Tales*, and Fanny attributes medieval virtues to his name: 'It is the name of heroism and renown . . . and seems to breathe the spirit of chivalry and warm affections' (vol. 2, ch. 4).

15.2 Morality and language

'She is the very impossibility he would describe – if indeed he now has delicacy of language enough to embody his own ideas.' (vol. 2, ch. 12)

In Jane Austen's novels, a character's language is a moral indicator.

Fanny Price

Fanny Price has a deep moral sensibility. This is her problem. For a woman of such refined scruples, the world moves too quickly and presses too weightily upon her. Indeed, her best qualities – sensitivity, empathy, scrupulousness – are actually a disadvantage in a Crawford-dominated world.

Self-knowledge, the moral keystone to the novel, is a quality which Fanny possesses. Her super-refined sense of morality requires a delicate awareness of language and thought. The degree to which the other characters are articulate and understand the meaning of others, what they choose to talk or not to talk about and the kind of language that they select is indicative of the place they occupy in the moral scheme of things.

Edmund and language

The gap between what is formulated in the head and what is actually said is something that worries Edmund, where Mary Crawford is concerned. Edmund trusts that what Mary says as a tease does not reflect her real opinion: 'She does not *think* evil, but she speaks it . . . and though I know it to be playfulness, it grieves me to the soul' (vol. 2, ch. 9).

At first Edmund criticizes the way Mary speaks of her uncle as being 'very wrong, very indecorous' (vol. 1, ch. 7). But he soon seems to lose this discerning capacity.

For much of the novel Edmund demonstrates that, no matter how acute the understanding, it can be blunted by love.

Fanny is afraid that Edmund will marry Mary, recognize what he has hitherto failed to see and 'be poor and miserable' (vol. 3, ch. 13). She prays that Mary Crawford may not cause him to lose respectability as well. That Fanny is being overdramatic is likely because she is envious of Mary Crawford. But, where Mary is concerned, there *is* in Edmund a self-justification and an exaggeration of language. Fanny refrains from saying what she feels, trusting that Edmund will come to his own epiphany.

Edmund can also be careless in his use of language. Fanny tries to warn him about her worries regarding Mr Crawford and her cousins. Edmund dismisses her anxiety lightly. Later, when Fanny again mentions Mr Crawford's behaviour, Edmund once more brushes this off, referring to the *Lovers' Vows* days as a time of 'general *folly*' (vol. 3, ch. 4; our italics). Ironically he anticipates the word that Mary Crawford will eventually use to describe Henry's adultery. Though he and Fanny cannot recognize this, Fanny has more sense of the way that wrong can escalate.

Edmund's epiphany

Edmund's eyes are finally opened by Mary's completely inadequate choice of word to describe the 'dreadful crime' (vol. 3, ch. 16) of Henry and Maria's adultery. She broaches the subject willingly; she has 'no modest loathings'. At last Edmund comes to recognize that: 'Her's are faults of principle, Fanny, of a blunted delicacy and a corrupted, vitiated mind.' (vol. 3, ch. 16).

Contrast the paucity of Miss Crawford's response – 'What can equal the folly of our relations?' with that of Fanny:

> it was too horrible a confusion of guilt, too gross a complication of evil, for human nature, not in a state of utter barbarism, to be capable of! (vol. 3, ch. 15)

The truth about Mary entails a distinction between morality – doing what is right for the right reasons – and respectable behaviour. It is the fact that Henry and Maria were not discreet enough to get away with adultery which is the greater 'folly' in Mary's opinion.

Lecture

Mary Crawford takes a child's line where the language of morality is concerned. She always uses the same word for moral criticism – 'lecture'. It is even the word she chooses to express the way that Edmund speaks to her on the subject of his grief over her response to the behaviour of Henry and Maria: 'A pretty good lecture, upon my word.' (vol. 3, ch. 16)

Not naming

Mary, in common with Henry, suffers from an incapacity to name the qualities that she finds in the one she loves.

She is unaccustomed to finding such qualities among the society manners of her London acquaintance. As her response lacks coherence, so does her thought process.

It is as if both Henry and Mary *feel* the pleasure and benefit of being around Fanny and Edmund but can neither *verbalize* it nor, at a deep level, appreciate what is before them:

> There was a charm, perhaps, in his sincerity, his steadiness, his integrity, which Mary Crawford might be equal to feel, *though not equal to discuss with herself.* She did not *think* very much about it, however. (vol. 1, ch. 7; our italics)

Similarly Henry is a man of sense, so he appreciates that Fanny is a woman of good principles 'though he was too little accustomed to serious reflection *to know them by their proper names*' (our italics).

The plain style

It is surprising that Mary, with her elegant spoken and written style, finds Edmund so attractive, because he is, in his own words, 'a very matter-of-fact, plain-spoken being'. (vol. 1, ch. 9). He goes in for none of the extravagant rhetoric of the practised beau. Edmund is not the only character whose sterling qualities are reflected in directness of language. William Price expresses himself in 'clear, simple, spirited details' (vol. 2, ch. 6) in which Sir Thomas discerns 'everything that could deserve and promise well'. Jane Austen is anticipating the judgements about language that emerge in *Emma*: Mr Knightley's direct style is to be preferred to Mr Elton's florid compliments and Frank Churchill's long letters.

Silence

Language is not the only moral indicator in the novel. Silence can be.

Mary Crawford advocates silence in the face of Henry and Maria's moral disgrace. She presumably does not want Henry frightened off marriage by too heavy a hand, so her advice is that Sir Thomas should 'be quiet. Do not let him injure his own cause by interference' (vol. 3, ch. 16). That way he may secure a patched-up job.

15.3 The ha-ha

'you will be in danger of slipping into the Ha-Ha' (vol. 1, ch. 10)

The wilderness at Sotherton is the most thematically rich passage in the whole of Jane Austen's work. The moral issues that the book so seriously (earnestly?) engages with are embodied in the dialogue, actions and settings of the wilderness into which the young people pass.

It is Miss Crawford who draws Edmund and Fanny into the 'wilderness' and questions Edmund's decision to become a clergyman. She has no idea of the enormity of her hubris when she declares: 'A clergyman is nothing' (vol. 1, ch. 9). In an episode when the bad manners of Mr Crawford and Miss Bertram are going to lead to worse, Edmund stoutly rebuffs Miss Crawford's view, declaring that a clergyman's 'situation

. . . which has . . . the guardianship of religion and morals, and consequently of the *manners* which result from their influence' cannot be called nothing. (our italics)

On Fanny's saying she is feeling tired, Edmund takes her arm and offers the other to Miss Crawford. In feeling Mary's touch for the first time, Edmund's accepted gallantry becomes 'gratification'. He clearly wishes for closer contact, for he says Mary's touch is only that of 'a fly'. With her 'arch smile', Mary Crawford is a temptation by her very presence, a contemporary Eve who comments on their 'serpentine course'.

The allegory

The scenes in the wilderness, and particularly the episode in which Maria crosses the ha-ha, embody the nature of the moral life. Morality must make distinctions: there are some things that are forbidden. The Garden of Eden, the biblical image behind the whole wilderness episode, had its prohibitions. Eden, though a paradise, was a world where moral rules applied.

The transgression of crossing the ha-ha has something in common with the Eden story. What makes the book's 'garden' significant is the existence of social regulations that forbid those who use it to stray. Therefore Maria's decision to cross the ha-ha stands for her decision to do that which is forbidden.

Once we see the allegorical functioning of the ditch and the gate, other emblematic codings, often moral in nature, can be entertained. The locked gate is a symbol of Mr Rushworth's authority as lord of the manor. The lock is also, traditionally, emblematic of the female sex organs. Only the one who has the authority should enter. With the reference to tearing (as in Marvell's 'To His Coy Mistress'), the taking of virginity, the prerogative of the husband, might also be alluded to. The danger that Maria is in not only echoes the primal error – the fall of mankind – but anticipates Maria's own fall, when she commits adultery.

Transgression

From the moment that Miss Bertram, Mr Crawford and Mr Rushworth arrive at Fanny's bench, almost everything that the two former say and do is capable of wider interpretation. Very soon Miss Bertram desires to pass through the iron gate. Has Maria guessed that Mr Rushworth will be required to fetch the key?

Flattery and seduction

Mr Crawford takes the opportunity to hint at a reluctance to see Miss Bertram married. She is well aware that he is playing word games with her. She supposes that he alludes literally to the sunny park when he talks of 'a very smiling scene before you' (vol. 1, ch. 10). Miss Bertram herself chooses to reply in metaphorical terms: 'unluckily that iron gate, that ha-ha, give me a feeling of restraint and hardship. I cannot get out, as the starling said.' (A ha-ha is a trench which forms a boundary without impeding the view. The surprise it generates gives rise to its name.)

Maria thus prompts Crawford's initiative. She vocalizes dissatisfaction. By confiding, if only obliquely, in a man who has been making advances to her, she issues a challenge to him to act upon his word.

Adultery

With words loaded with sexual innuendo, Crawford suggests that 'with my assistance' Miss Bertram might slip the gate and temporarily skirt her engagement – she will, he implies, have 'little difficulty' in defying moral authority if she really wishes to be 'more at large'. At such a tempting suggestion, Miss Bertram appears to have reverted to the literal and fails to see that anything more is at stake than annoying Mr Rushworth. This she can quickly justify: 'Prohibited! nonsense! I certainly can get out that way and I will. Mr Rushworth will be here in a moment you know – we shall not be out of sight.'

But Mr Crawford has no scruple about evading Mr Rushworth or implicating Fanny. They are heading for 'the grove of oak on the knoll', a suitably pagan-sounding destination for this hedonistic pair!

Fanny knows they are doing something very wrong and that she must prevent it by warning her cousin:

> 'You will hurt yourself, Miss Bertram,' she cried, 'you will certainly hurt yourself against those spikes – you will tear your gown – you will be in danger of slipping into the Ha-Ha. You had better not go.'

Fanny speaks absolutely literally, but there is an urgency in her words that give them prophetic authority. Her perhaps somewhat naïve words contain implications that reach far beyond their everyday meanings. Miss Bertram could be irreparably damaged. Something is going to be rent. She is in danger of falling. She must think again.

Our sister's keeper?

When Julia turns up, she loosely uses the language of religion to express the time she has spent with Mr Rushworth's 'horrible mother' – 'Such a penance as I have been enduring'. In her thoughtless use of language, she also seems to foreguess Maria's fate. When Fanny pities Mr Rushworth for exerting so much effort for nothing, Julia replies: '*That* is Miss Maria's concern. I am not obliged to punish myself for *her* sins.'

15.4 Morality and education

'Give a girl an education, and introduce her properly into the world, and ten to one she has the means of settling well without further expense to anyone.' (vol. 1, ch. 1)

Fanny's influence

Sir Thomas's experiment in 'improving' an adopted niece is initially viewed as carrying some risks for his own family. This would be upsetting if his daughters were younger, but as it is: 'I hope there can be nothing to fear for them, and everything to hope for her, from the association.' Likewise Mrs Norris believes that Fanny will learn to be good from her cousins as well as gather other aspects of her education.

Irony is one of the means by which Jane Austen highlights false moral assumptions, such as Sir Thomas's and Mrs Norris's. In the event, of course, the Bertram girls could have learnt much about the moral life from *Fanny*, had they the inclination to observe her.

Female education

Jane Austen is sharply critical of the inadequacies of female education. Maria Bertram had an expensive education at the hands of Miss Lee, conducted under the anxious supervision of Sir Thomas. Yet she makes a disastrous marriage. The kind of education she receives, therefore, cannot be good *enough*.

Learning by heart was the main method of learning, and Maria takes a simplistic view of what it means. She appears to consider that the amount of knowledge that is required of her is finite and that cramming in facts is an end in itself.

Fanny and Maria

Maria has no recognition that one needs to reflect on what one learns. Nor does she read widely. Fanny's reading list gives food for the imagination and fosters the moral life. Fanny wants to widen her horizons and understand other people and other lands. While her uncle travels, she does the same in her imagination by taking 'a trip into China', courtesy of Lord Macartney. (vol. 1, ch. 16). She is concerned about the abolition of slavery, in which Maria and Julia take no interest (see 14.10 and 16.5).

In their education, as in other areas of the novel (such as sexual morality), Maria and Fanny are contrasted.

Mrs Norris courts and reports favourable accounts of Julia's and Maria's reputation in the neighbourhood, and the sisters grow up thinking they are without faults. In fact, they are entirely without the uncommon acquirements of 'self-knowledge, generosity and humility' (vol. 1, ch. 2). Their father, too late, comes to *his* epiphany: 'He feared that principle, active principle, had been wanting' (vol. 3, ch. 17).

Fanny's broad perspective

Fanny studies under the same régime as her cousins but she has already learnt a lot, as her uncle comes to recognize, under 'the advantages of early hardship and discipline, and the consciousness of being born to struggle and endure' (vol. 3, ch. 17).

Fanny's dual upbringing seems to have given her a capacity for taking an interest in everything: the state of the countryside, the soil, the children, the villagers are what she observes on the way to Sotherton (vol. 1, ch. 8). With Fanny's capacity to reach out to all, one can imagine what interest and concern she will show as a clergyman's wife.

15.5 Morality and social context

'the most valuable knowledge we could any of us acquire – the knowledge of ourselves' (vol. 3, ch. 16)

Morality must address the society of those who espouse it.

The attraction of glamour

Henry and Mary Crawford, young Londoners of money and fashion, burst upon the parsonage. They are worldly and sophisticated.

Where the Bertram family are by upbringing morally restrained, Mary and Henry Crawford are at liberty and at large.

They move freely in a glittering world of friends, parties and 'improvements' (vol. 1, ch. 6). They communicate through puns and bons mots. This way of life they bring to Mansfield.

Stuck in the past

Initially, Edmund is struck by what is wrong with Mary Crawford, alluring as he finds her. It is Fanny who suggests that her impropriety is a reflection on her upbringing. Edmund seizes on this and increasingly gives Mary the benefit of the doubt.

Like Fanny, Mary has been brought up by an aunt and an uncle. Her uncle, the Admiral, is a vicious man. Her aunt is dead. She dismisses her formative years with laughter, descending to the crass.

However, for all that Mary now wishes to put the past behind her, she seems stuck there. This impedes her potential for moral development.

Marriage to a clergyman

Edmund soon falls for Mary and she becomes attracted to him. It is apparent, though, that Miss Crawford has no sympathy with Edmund's vocation.

Mary believes riches and distinction to be the end to which one should direct an adult life, whereas Edmund argues for honesty.

Mary takes a very simplistic view of the clergy. She sees them only as deliverers of sermons.

Mary selects from life what coincides with her wishes and, like a child, pretends the rest does not exist. So she takes a keen interest in Thornton Lacy, the living that will be Edmund's. It is the butt of her fantasies, as she imagines herself married to Edmund. In her vision there is no church and no parsonage, only a gentleman of independent means who can afford to keep the house, greatly improved according to her brother's plans, as a part-time residence, spending half the year only in the country.

Too fixed to change

Fanny thinks that the only thing that Edmund and Mary have in common is their mutual fascination. Mary does admire and feels comforted by Edmund's qualities but cannot grasp that it is exactly those qualities that have led to his vocation. That Edmund will not abandon his vocation for her calls forth her wrath. She was angry 'with Edmund for adhering to his own notions and acting on them in defiance of her' (vol. 2, ch. 11).

Mary would deny Edmund free will if she could.

She is somebody who cannot adjust her thinking.

Mary does not have the flexibility to work out her priorities, make adult choices and lead the moral life.

She reads marriage as 'a manoeuvring business' (vol. 1, ch. 5), not a moral business.

She is a hedonist in a novel that speaks for rational restraint. Mary's approach to life at last forces Edmund to recognize that she is too damaged for him to love her. It is telling – and ironic – that Mary Crawford remembers with such nostalgia the week when Edmund *had acted the part of a clergyman* and had recommended matrimony to her. Mary is left in the end in a kind of limbo. She finds Edmund's qualities irreplaceable when at last she begins to look.

15.6 A yen for change

'his own habits of selfish indulgence appear in shameful contrast' (vol. 2, ch. 6)

Henry the rake

Henry's apparent desire to change makes him the most morally ambiguous figure in the novel.

He is the person who *actively* appreciates and marvels at Fanny. Edmund tends to take her excellence for granted though he is knows that it is rare.

Life is a game of speculation to Henry. He builds up Maria Bertram's expectations to the point where she believes that he will ask her to call off her engagement in order to marry him, then leaves the county. On his return he speaks lightly of Maria in public and smiles knowingly, in a way that 'made Fanny quite hate him' (vol. 2, ch. 5).

He then decides that he cannot be content without making 'a small hole' in the heart of a woman whom he can now see has grown sexually attractive.

Henry is heartless to the point where right and wrong have no meaning for him.

Henry the committed

Henry had meant to spend a fortnight on Fanny Price and move on. But he finds himself falling in love.

He has had no limits imposed upon him by his much-loved uncle. Fanny's boundaries are securely drawn. Perhaps Henry finds it comforting to know where he stands for once.

If Henry had no moral sense, he would have tried to breach Fanny's goodness. Instead, he wants to honour it and make her Mrs Crawford.

Henry Crawford recognizes in Fanny a depth of character and understanding that can help him go beyond his own past triviality. She considers others. In her you can trust and with her you can share: 'I could so wholly and utterly confide in her,' said he, 'and that is what I want' (vol. 2, ch. 12).

Unlike Mary, Henry does not want to change the person he loves. He is prepared to change himself. Henry has the flexibility to move towards the moral life.

Constant or not?

However, Henry is not, as Fanny is, an ever-fixèd mark. Unlike Mary, though, he can see the hollowness of society life. He has a romantic streak that makes him want to emulate those in public life. But whereas serving country and community is a vocation for William and Edmund, Henry is prepared to do it only by proxy. He secures the promotion of William. Fanny is overwhelmed.

Nevertheless, nothing can change Fanny's view that Mr Crawford can do nothing as a 'constancy'.

Under Fanny's influence, Henry does begin to shoulder the responsibilities of a land owner, but this does not last.

Losing track

Halfway through the novel Henry Crawford literally loses his way 'after passing that old farm house, with the yew trees' (vol. 2, ch. 7). This sounds suitably Gothic, home of dark spirits and of the cold. The reason that Henry gives is that 'I can never bear to ask'. It is not for Henry to seek out counsel.

By the end of the novel Henry will have lost his way entirely, and with it the irreplaceable Fanny Price.

Brothers and sisters

The moral life has its origins in our earliest society. Here Jane Austen is marvellously un-Freudian: it is in the company of our brothers and sisters that we learn to see how we should conduct ourselves (see 13.12).

Sadly, in the case of the Crawfords, other influences have made them unsound. However, they do display the gentler virtues in the warmth of their brother–sister relationship. They are far closer than the Bertrams.

The Crawfords seem to have a capacity for unfettered happiness and equal exchange. Perhaps this is why Henry Crawford has 'moral taste enough' (vol. 2, ch. 6) to be much taken by the other brother and sister. The quality of their fondness is something that he shares with Mary. Had Mary and Henry not been influenced by London, their love for one another would have been their most distinctive moral feature.

15.7 The exacting nature of the moral life

'she had begun to feel undecided about what she *ought to do*' (vol. 1, ch. 16)

The difficulties of guidance

We all need moral guidance. The Crawfords were not soundly guided by the Admiral. The part played in the moral life by education, advice, persuasion and influence is one of Jane Austen's major themes. In *Mansfield Park* Fanny is initially guided by Edmund, but for most of the narrative it is she who should be *his* guide.

One of the difficulties of Fanny's love for Edmund is that she does not allow herself to be as clear in her advice as, perhaps, she should. Fanny is, however, an astute listener.

Edmund seeks succour from Fanny more than she does from him.

Fanny has the integrity to perceive where Edmund might be over-stepping the mark, so, much as she wants to help, she requests him not to seek advice about Miss Crawford. Here Fanny takes on Edmund's scruples for him.

Edmund does not consult his conscience as opposed to his self-interest nearly as much as Fanny does.

Fanny is unwavering in what she knows to be right, no matter how unpleasant the consequences. She does her duty by her Aunt Bertram, her Aunt Norris and her uncle, until the will of the latter is at variance with her duty to herself.

An enigmatic equation

It is Fanny's fate to be misunderstood. She is accused of obstinacy and ingratitude by her Aunt Norris over her refusal to comply with her cousins' request to act in the play. In fact, Fanny undergoes a real moral crisis, recognizing the complexity of her motives. She analyses them with an intensity that leaves her doubting. We watch her experiencing intractable moral dilemmas.

Shrinking from taking part, she wonders whether the major reason why she will not concur is that it would be an ordeal for her to act. Conviction of the unsuitability of the play and of her uncle's disapproval form part of her opposition, but she still fears that she might be selfish and ungrateful.

Material objects cloud the issue. She is inclined to suspect the truth of her own scruples, and as she looks around her, 'the claims of her cousins . . . were strengthened by the sight of present upon present that she had received from them' (vol. 1, ch. 16).

It is poignant to see Fanny endeavouring to make her presents fit into this moral equation. The presents have been carelessly given by moneyed cousins. Indeed, a table is covered with replicated presents – 'work-boxes and netting-boxes' largely given to her by Tom.

Fanny makes her decision not to take part in the play and lives with it, until the fact that Mrs Grant is incommoded means that she has to think again. Fanny, like all those of sensitive disposition, blames herself if something occurs that is against her conscience. So when she is asked to stand in for Mrs Grant at the dress rehearsal, 'she had known it her duty to keep away. She was properly punished' (vol. 1, ch. 18).

Meanwhile, Fanny continues to prove herself all too human where Edmund is concerned. She cannot help but feel happy when Miss Crawford has made Edmund miserable during the Mansfield ball. She acknowledges that: It was barbarous to be happy when Edmund was suffering. (vol. 2, ch. 10).

But the relief of knowing that their engagement is not imminent is too much for her.

Jane Austen allows Fanny all the paradoxical feelings of a moral being facing the overwhelming claims of the heart.

15.8 Utilitarianism

'Fanny could not answer him.' (vol. 1, ch. 16)

Morality and ethics

Sometimes philosophers make a distinction between morality and ethics.

Morality is defined as the rules by which we order our lives, and ethics is the theory upon which those rules are built.

Jane Austen's novels show her characters making moral decisions; but do they also embody an ethic? The answer must be that though it is not the task of a novelist to provide a systematic moral theory, readers might see in the presentation of moral action – characters' dilemmas, their dialogues and deeds – a picture of what it is to be a moral agent.

It is not unknown for some philosophers to regard novels as more complex – and therefore more complete – presentations of the nature of moral thinking.

The search for an ethic in Jane Austen has intrigued philosophers. Gilbert Ryle saw her as closer to Aristotle and Shaftesbury (1671–1713) than the more explicitly Christian thinking of Richard Price (1723–91), because he felt that, although she was unquestionably a devout Christian, the turn of her mind in moral questions was more secular than religious.

Bentham's utilitarianism

By way of a further speculation about the nature of Jane Austen's moral outlook, we suggest that a feature of *Mansfield Park,* as of *Pride and Prejudice,* is a dissatisfaction with the kind of thinking which is now called utilitarianism. In popular language, utiliarianism is a system of moral thought that aims to achieve 'the greatest happiness for the greatest number' (see 9. 9).

The distance between Bentham and Jane Austen

Although Jane Austen might have read Bentham or heard him talked about, his 'hedonic calculus' (the belief that pleasures and pains can be counted up and used to settle the rightness of an action) seems very remote from the woman who read the sermons of Bishop Sherlock and wrote prayers. After all, there is only one Henry Crawford. If Jane Austen had wished to write a utilitarian novel in which the greatest happiness would have been possible for the greatest number, she could have done it by creating at least two Henry Crawfords!

The word 'utility' appears four times in *Mansfield Park,* and there are eight occasions when 'pleasure' and 'pain' are coupled together. These are key words in Bentham's thought system. Can it be that Jane Austen recognizes the potency of a way of thinking that she feels must be resisted before it attenuates the beliefs to which she adheres?

Utility

The uses that Jane Austen makes of the word 'utility' look as if she is trying to resist any Benthamite colouring.

The meaning in all cases is simply 'usefulness'; there is no indication that Jane Austen is imposing on the word a principle of evaluating action.

Pleasure and pain

'Pleasure and pain' – the poles of human experience, hence their long-established use in philosophy – likewise appear without the implication of a Benthamite calculus. Occasionally comparison slightly colours the usage of 'pain and pleasure'. One carries a touch of elegant humour in that it applies Johnson's remark from *The History of Rasselas, Prince of Abyssinia* that 'Marriage has many pains, but celibacy has no pleasures' to Fanny's two homes: 'Mansfield Park might have some pains, Portsmouth could have no pleasures' (vol. 3, ch. 8). But to put it in Benthamite terms, the 'balance' is easily made, so easy, in fact, that it would be wrong to think of it as being a calculation at all. The most that can be said about such feelings is that they are features of the grain of life.

The dangers of utilitarianism

Moreover, Jane Austen indicates in one episode the dangers of weighing consequences. The occasion is Edmund's decision that in order to prevent their losing 'privacy and propriety' by inviting Charles Maddox to act, he, Edmund, must take the part of Anhalt. He claims he does not like the '*appearance*' of inconsistency but makes his proposal because he can see 'no other alternative' (vol. 1, ch. 16). Fanny's response is significant: 'Fanny could not answer him.'

There is nothing to be said to one who ventures on the perilous business of calculating the pains and pleasures of outcomes.

Do Jane Austen's novels have an ethical basis?

Can anything be *positively* said about her ethical outlook?

The point that the only way to cope with, say, the theatricals is to recognize that there are some things that one must not do leads one to think that her morality might be described as a Christian version of the virtues.

Such a reading is close to that outlined by Alasdair MacIntyre in *After Virtue*, (Duckworth, 1981). He attaches importance to 'the virtue which Jane Austen calls "constancy"' (p. 181) and insists that, in vaunting that, 'she is concerned with social roles'. These he sees as the basis for virtues such as duty, responsibility and fidelity (p. 185).

What guides us to an ethical life?

We may ask a further question: what guides us in our pursuit of the virtues? Here part of a dialogue in Portsmouth between Fanny and Henry is significant. Henry is seeking to make Fanny interest herself in the management of his estate. He asks for her advice:

> 'I advise! – you know very well what is right.'
> 'Yes. When you give me your opinion, I always know what is right. Your judgement is my rule of right.'
> 'Oh, no! – do not say so. We have all a better guide in ourselves, if we would attend to it, than any other person can be.' (vol. 3, ch. 11)

Jane Austen here is following Bishop Butler, who held that conscience was 'the guide assigned to us by the Author of our nature' (Sermon III: 'On the Natural Supremacy of Conscience'). Conscience is 'the rule of right within', and it is assuredly to conscience that Fanny is directing Henry when she says 'we all have a better guide in ourselves'.

15.9 The limits of morality

'Bitterly did he deplore a deficiency which now he could scarcely comprehend to have been possible.' (vol. 3, ch. 17)

Mansfield Park is a morally demanding work: both characters and the reader are subject to exacting judgements.

One of the demands that the novel makes is the requirement to see that a moral sense needs to work together with other human qualities.

Sir Thomas

Sir Thomas is a paradox. He is arguably the most complex male character in the novel. He is a man of principle, a man with a conventional sense of, and an insistence upon, correct behaviour. He is obviously a charitable man who wants to do his best for the Prices. But he has his major failings. He is proud and interested in reinforcing the standing and monetary position of the Bertram family. A more important aspect of his failure is that he can be cold, ruthless, unjust and repellent.

Growth through suffering

Sir Thomas wants to love his children but the severity with which he follows up their formal education and the rigidity with which he enforces his principles cause three of his children to rebel.

The character of Sir Thomas indicates that a stern moral code alone is not adequate to lead his children to the moral life. For what Sir Thomas lacks are the softer virtues.

Sir Thomas lacks the tenderness, sympathy and sense of play that help children to reciprocate and grow. He lacks Fanny's empathy and imagination.

Sir Thomas has to suffer the near death of his heir, witness the ruination of his elder daughter and experience the perfidy of Mr Crawford, proving Fanny right and he wrong, before he can rejoice in the son whose integrity will not fail him and find in Fanny the daughter he has always longed for.

15.10 The mystery of evil

'In this world the penalty is less equal than could be wished.' (vol. 3, ch. 17)

Mrs Norris represents something against which morality struggles; she lacks insight and is often wrong. She favours, indulges and praises Maria, so that she appears 'an angel' (vol. 1, ch. 4). Her life's coup is the alliance between Mr Rushworth and Maria, her favourite niece. It is the grandness of the match, of course, that leads to her self-congratulation. She cannot see that Mr Rushworth is a fool.

Mrs Norris had not a thought that acting in a play could bring Maria into moral danger. She is disconcerted when Sir Thomas takes issue with her for lack of guidance – she had not even seen the impropriety! She had been too preoccupied with economy.

Mrs Norris's obsession verges on the pathological. J. Wiltshire attributes it to: 'a neurotic compensation for her inferior family position whose other manifestation is the remorseless bullying of her even poorer niece, Fanny Price' (*The Cambridge Companion to Jane Austen,* Cambridge University Press, 1997, p. 59).

But there seems more to it than that.

There is something inexplicable about Mrs Norris's idea of adopting one of the Price children, only to reject her with incalculable cruelty at every turn.

On Mrs Norris's berating Fanny for not obliging her cousins considering 'who and what she is' (vol. 1, ch. 15), Miss Crawford moves away from her, declaring: 'this *place* is too hot for me'. Certainly there is an intense burning energy that emanates from Mrs Norris.

Fanny is all gentleness, Mrs Norris all vitriol. Fanny's 'little white attic' (vol. 1, ch. 1), an outward statement of her inner self, could not be in stricter contrast with the White House, where Mrs Norris dwells, with a spare room for a 'friend' who, chillingly, never puts in an appearance.

When Fanny returns from Portsmouth, Mrs Norris was:

> but the more irritated by the sight of the person whom, in the blindness of her anger, she could have charged as the daemon of the piece. (vol. 3., ch. 16)

But it is Mrs Norris who is 'the daemon of the piece'. Her temper made her 'every where tormenting' (vol. 3, ch. 17) ever since Maria's elopement. Sir Thomas had thought of her for a long time as 'an hourly evil . . . she seemed a part of himself, that must be borne for ever'.

Maria who does not love Mrs Norris gains her. No one else, not even Fanny, regrets her loss.

Evil distorts and stains. The distortions lead to immoral acts. Mrs Norris's behaviour is immoral. But, furthermore, it is inexplicable. Why is she so vehement that Fanny should be denied the pleasures – even the necessities – of life?

At this point it becomes clear that more than morality is at stake. Morality cannot explain why life is distorted. It is, as the title of this section suggests, a mystery. A mystery beyond morality, a mystery that requires another context in order to be, if not understood, then at least coped with. The key to coping lies in the character of Fanny Price.

16 God

16.1 Welcoming the stranger

'Edmund was uniformally kind.' (vol. 1, ch. 2)

Clergymen

Jane Austen's father was a priest, so the presence of clergymen in her novels is hardly surprising. In *Mansfield Park*, the hero's decision to enter the ministry is central.

Edmund's seriousness is one of the ways in which the novel takes religion seriously.

The Bertram children

Fanny's reception by the Bertram children is telling. Edmund is 'uniformally kind'. Tom treats and teases her. The two Bertram daughters despise her for her lack of knowledge.

From the start Edmund's choice of profession seems appropriate. He has the requisite qualities for pastoral care. We might say he has a vocation or calling.

A profession

Such terms are not used in the novel. Edmund is happy to talk of the sacred ministry as a 'profession'. Nor does Edmund hesitate to admit that the hope of a living had some influence with him.

16.2 Seeking ordination

'But why are you to be a clergyman?' (vol. 1, ch. 9)

A lofty conception

Yet Edmund sincerely holds a lofty conception of the priesthood. Mary regards it as a last resort; Edmund's response is a question: 'Do you think the church itself never chosen then?' (vol. 1, ch. 9). That 'itself' values the thing it refers to. It is also a moral and perhaps even a religious gesture. The priesthood is not a means to anything higher. It has intrinsic merit.

A certain thing

Edmund never has doubts about his decision. Before the Mansfield ball, he ponders 'two important events now at hand . . . ordination and matrimony'. *Mansfield Park* does not ask: should the hero choose love or duty? Ordination is certain, whereas marriage to Mary Crawford is not.

Receiving ordination

On ordination, Edmund realizes 'His duties would be established' (vol. 2, ch. 8). The verb is passive. Passives are often used in religious discourse to indicate an implied divine action. Here there is an understanding of the implications of the rite, which will confer the particular grace that is proper to the ritual in question.

16.3 The priesthood

'No one can call the *office* nothing.' (vol. 1, ch. 9)

The ministry justified

Mary's attitude implies that no justification can be advanced for taking orders, whereas 'The profession, either army or navy, is its own justification' (vol. 1, ch. 11).

Edmund has, in fact, advanced a full justification for taking orders while he, Fanny and Mary walked in the wilderness at Sotherton. (The setting itself provides justification emblematically: those in the wilderness need guides.)

To Mary's 'A clergyman is nothing', Edmund replies:

> I cannot call that situation nothing, which has the charge of all that is of the first importance to mankind, individually or collectively – which has the guardianship of religion and morals, and consequently of the manners which result from their influence. (vol. 1, ch. 9)

It is a big claim. The clergyman has social as well as individual responsibility. He exercises 'guardianship' (compare Burke: 14.2) over 'religion and morals' – the two factors that give society values and direction.

Conduct and manners

Mary believes that people should 'choose their own time and manner of devotion'. Left to oneself, one is unlikely to form any clear doctrines so she speaks of religion in terms of behaviour. How can two sermons a week 'govern the conduct and fashion the manners of a large congregation'?

Edmund admits that in London it is unlikely people will be able to observe a clergyman closely. Yet he wants to make a distinction between the two terms Mary has used – 'conduct'and 'manners': 'The *manners* I speak of, might rather be called *conduct,* perhaps, the result of good principles'.

The empirical temper of the English mind makes it easier to talk about observable aspects of behaviour than those doctrines of the creed that attempt to give voice to the inexpressible. Yet Edmund's language, while concerning itself with the ethical, points to the *source* of all moral values. 'Good principles' is a term that he then defines in a more explicitly religious way as 'doctrines'.

Edmund approaches the mysteries of religion by way of the observable transactions of moral behaviour.

16.4 The life of the clergy

'Sir Thomas,' said Edmund, 'undoubtedly understands the duty of a parish priest.' (vol. 2, ch. 7)

The issue of clergy residence

Edmund returns to the point about influence: 'as the clergy are, or are not what they ought to be, so are the rest of the nation'. The corollary of this view is that a parson should live in his parish. This precept is firmly held by Edmund and his father. The notion is new to the Crawfords. Discussing improving Thornton Lacey (vol. 2, ch. 7), Henry would like to rent the parsonage. Sir Thomas expresses his belief that Edmund 'will occupy his own house at Thornton Lacey'. Edmund replies that he 'has no idea but of residence.' Sir Thomas explains that he would 'have been deeply mortified, if any son of mine could not reconcile himself to doing less'. His view is that:

> 'a parish has wants and claims which can be known only by a clergyman constantly resident, and which no proxy can be capable of filling to the same extent'.

Sir Thomas is a private man. That he should speak so feelingly about the issue of residency suggests his deep commitment to the Church's ministry.

Pluralism

The issue of residency is inseparable from that of pluralism. Pluralism was the practice whereby one clergyman would be vicar of several benefices. When Sir Thomas says that 'no proxy' could be as satisfactory as a resident parson, he is referring to the practice of employing curates to look after some of the parishes (often the smaller ones) a pluralist holds.

From his tone, we may judge that Sir Thomas saw pluralism in a moral light. As with the estate, residency is necessary for the proper stewardship of the Church's inheritance.

Is Edmund a pluralist?

Dr Grant is a pluralist. He takes a Canon's stall in Westminster Abbey, but remains the incumbent of Mansfield, until his death allows Edmund to fill the living.

Some readers have suggested that Edmund is also a pluralist because on his move to Mansfield the text does not explicitly say that he relinquished Thornton Lacey (see Avrom Fleishman, *A Reading of Mansfield Park,* University of Minnesota Press, 1970, p. 19). The argument that he is not rests upon the unyielding nature of his father's principles.

16.5 The life of the Church

'They had been instructed theoretically in their religion, but never required to bring it into daily practice.' (vol. 3, ch. 17)

Taking religion seriously

Edmund is presented as a devout and fervent Christian. Mary Crawford, in their last meeting, enquires sneeringly whether his eloquence formed 'part of your last sermon?' She continues:

> when I hear of you next, it may be as a celebrated preacher in some great society of Methodists, or as a missionary into foreign parts (vol. 3, ch. 16)

Methodists espoused a religion of the heart that carried out their faith practically. Following their father-in-God, John Wesley, they had, by 1812, formally separated from the Church of England, but were still known as a 'society'. Mary's verbal smirk sees Edmund finding the established Church too stuffy and adhering to a more enthusiastic and active sect. Methodists also contributed to missionary work overseas.

Conduct

Mary is right, surely, in seeing that Edmund's seriousness is consistent with Methodist enthusiasm and missionary zeal. He is also concerned about right conduct as we see in his talks with Fanny. Some feel that Fanny's and Edmund's disquiet at Mary's thoughtless remarks about her uncle smacks of preciousness, but it is their uncle's kindness in taking care of the Crawfords that Fanny defends.

The Clapham Sect

Critics have pointed to the similarity between Edmund and Fanny and the group of evangelicals known as the 'Clapham Sect'. 'Evangelical' comes from the Greek word for gospel. The Clapham Sect consisted of influential people who lived in the south London village of Clapham and whose deeply held religious beliefs were expressed in charitable works. Their most notable member, William Wilberforce, campaigned for the abolition of the slave trade. They were also active in the establishment of missionary and benevolent societies. They set a new tone of seriousness, which contrasted with the prevailing London carelessness over morals and religion. Evangelicals were suspicious of private theatricals, because, they claimed, such activities led to a loosening of sexual morals. Their stance was basically conservative; wishing to avoid the tumult of the French Revolution, they aimed at public reforms to prevent social unrest.

Fanny, Edmund and the Clapham Sect

The similarities between the attitudes of Edmund and Fanny and the activities of the Clapham Sect are obvious. The two are suspicious of the theatricals and resist the London carelessness of Mary's attitude to religious practice. Their inner lives are marked by a devout earnestness. This earnestness in Fanny is something that Henry recognizes; she will not be won by 'gallantry and wit' but with 'seriousness upon serious subjects' (vol. 3, ch. 4). Those words echo Edmund's judgement on Mary. In the

Sotherton chapel he gently advances the view that 'Your lively mind can hardly be serious even on serious subjects' (vol. 1, ch. 9).

16.6 Evangelicals?

'the influence of fervent prayers' (vol. 2, ch. 9)

Faith, feeling and contemporary culture

Yet we must not be too hasty. Fanny herself derives much pleasure from the play. Her opposition stems in part from her sense, entirely correct as it turns out, that Sir Thomas would not approve. It does not follow that she would be against private theatricals on principle.

The Clapham Sect's religious seriousness must be set in context. *Mansfield Park* was published in the same year as Wordsworth's massive meditative poem *The Excursion,* and while Jane Austen was writing about the responsive and at times lyrical Fanny Price, Beethoven was composing his exuberant seventh symphony. Strength of feeling mattered; exploring the inner life characterized the age.

Is 'Mansfield Park' evangelical?

Jane Austen appears, at the time of writing *Mansfield Park,* to share a concern with inwardness, earnestness and moral scrupulousness with the evangelicals, though these characteristics were not the preserve of that group. *Mansfield Park* can be said to be religiously aware without being explicitly evangelical.

Ordination?

The novel cannot be said to be 'about' Edmund's ordination though it is of great importance. Rather, it deals with what is ordained or 'given'. The moral law is fixed, the universal frame of nature is there for the sensitive to stand in awe of and the Church is a presence that sanctions and sanctifies human life.

16.7 A religious novel

'A whole family assembling regularly for the purpose of prayer, is fine.' (vol. 1, ch. 9)

Religion and novels

The issue of ordination and the way the pressures of the age are felt in the novel places *Mansfield Park* among those novels that deal with religion. There is, however, a difference between religion as a human practice and religion as an engagement with the One from whom all blessings flow. To call a chapter on *Mansfield Park* 'God' is to suggest that it is not just a novel that deals with religion but one which is, in a particular sense, religious.

Religion and English literature

This is not a case that can be easily established. English writers, with a few dramatic exceptions such as Bunyan and Christopher Smart, are usually restrained in religious matters. Hence, many readers do not know how to cope with medieval literature, in which the interpretative scope is limited, and we are obliged to see that the overtly religious issues are what they appear to be. The English long ago got round this by deciding to write the kind of literature that stems from Chaucer rather than Langland's *Piers Plowman*: that is, we have opted for character and distancing irony rather than shared beliefs that make sense of humanity as a whole – the fair field full of folk.

'Mansfield Park' and medieval literature

Is there something distinctly medieval, something approaching Langland's sublimely unambiguous vision, about *Mansfield Park*? Certainly its last chapter, so alien in tone to liberal minds, has something of the consummating power of a medieval last judgement. Everyone is judged; there are rewards and punishments. Maria sharing a house with Mrs Norris is even worthy of Dante's hell. And one of the effects of mediating most of the action through Fanny's consciousness is that the reader is likely to feel reproved if his or her judgement strays from the demanding perceptions of the protagonist (see 13.12).

16.8 Parables

'My father is come.' (vol. 1, ch. 10)

Echoes of the parables?

A religious understanding of *Mansfield Park* might start from the echoes in the plot of the parables of Jesus. This is not a question of direct influence or allusion but rather that many of the situations in the novel present unspectacular everyday life. The parables of Jesus are concerned with losing coins, inviting people to dinner and making bread. *Mansfield Park*, as ever with Jane Austen, consists of the occurrences of everyday life. Of these the act of coming home is given particular prominence. Might we see in the surprise return of Sir Thomas something of the force of, for example, the return of the lord of the household in Luke 13: 35–8? Those performing the play are not like the servants who 'wait for their lord'. And might Sir Thomas's journey to Antigua be understood as a variant upon the Prodigal Son (Luke 15: 11–32) with those *who stay behind* indulging in riotous living?

Symbols?

Parables are not essentially symbolic because their meanings emerge through narrative. Yet parables occasionally create symbols; for instance, the lost sheep, who needs to be rescued. It would be wrong to call *Mansfield Park* a symbolic novel in the same way in which Kafka's *The Trial* is.

Yet the narrative gives significance to objects and events in a way that makes it not misleading to call them **symbolic or emblematic**. (See 15.3.)

Symbolism occurs in references to the east – in Christian iconography, the direction from which Christ will return to judge the world. Ironically, if it is that, Fanny notes that Sotherton, a house empty of religion, faces east. A further irony is that in his proposals for the improvement of Thornton Lacey, Henry wants to turn the front of the house to the east (vol. 2, ch. 7). When he attempts to recommend himself to Fanny, he himself might be said to be turning to the east.

The East room

Fanny is associated with the east. At Mansfield Park she has the use of the East room. (See ref. to works of charity – vol. 1, ch. 18). Its physical orientation suggests the fundamentally right ordering of Fanny's values.

16.9 Wonder and memory

'How wonderful, how very wonderful the operations of time, and the changes of the human mind.' (vol. 2, ch. 4)

Inner depths

It is in Fanny herself that the religious understanding of life is most clearly presented. One of the effects of making hers the mediating consciousness of the novel is that we see the depths of her inner life. She is a heroine who in wanting to defend Edmund 'knelt in spirit to her uncle' (vol. 2, ch. 1) and who, when convinced that her beloved Edmund will marry Mary Crawford, can only relieve her agitations by 'the influence of fervent prayers for his happiness' (vol. 2, ch. 9).

The gift of wonder

Fanny wonders. Her wondering is not the kind that poses a question that requires an answer but rather an amazement at the way the world is.

One of the things that makes Fanny different from the other young women is her capacity to find some aspects of the world astonishing.

Memory

After Maria and Julia's departure, Fanny finds herself more in the company of Mary Crawford. There is no real meeting of minds, as Fanny derives only 'occasional amusement' from Mary's light conversation about topics Fanny 'wished to be respected'. Yet Jane Austen, alert to the unaccountable aspects of human behaviour, says that Fanny continued to see her (vol. 2, ch. 4).

It is also unexplained, though not implausible, that in Mary's presence Fanny is able to vent her feelings of wonder. Seated in the shrubbery, conventionally in literature a place of repose and meditation, Fanny reflects on its growth and how this will alter the memory of it over the years: 'How wonderful, how very wonderful the operations of time, and the changes of the human mind!'

The objects of wonder are inextricably woven together. Fanny's mind senses the wonder of nature and the wonder of its own mysterious operations.

Then Fanny refines her wonder at the human mind:

> If any one faculty of our nature may be called *more* wonderful than the rest, I do think it is memory. We are to be sure a miracle every way – but our powers of recollecting and of forgetting, do seem peculiarly past finding out.'

The emotional pressure of her words might be imagined as deriving from incidents in the novel of momentous remembering and forgetting. Fanny, when Mary monopolizes her horse, vows that 'if she were forgotten, the poor mare would be remembered' (vol. 1, ch. 7). And in the heady events of Sotherton and the theatricals the memory of some of the characters as to their situation was 'so bewildered and so weak'.

Thinking about memory

Fanny's amazement has links with some of those philosophers who puzzled over the nature of memory. John Locke wrote that sometimes 'ideas . . . fade and vanish quite out of the understanding, leaving no more footsteps . . . than shadows do flying over fields of corn' (quoted in *Memory* by Mary Warnock, Faber & Faber, 1987, p. 17). The image of shadows over fields captures something of the elusive nature of memory that so intrigues Fanny. In his *An Essay Concerning Human Understanding* (1690, book 2, ch, 10), Locke remarks that in some, memory 'is very tenacious, even to a miracle'. Fanny also uses the word 'miracle' but more generally: we are a 'miracle every way'. Her apprehension is close to the Bible: 'I will praise thee; for I am fearfully and wonderfully made' (Psalm 139:13).

The reader might smile at the irony of Fanny's preoccupation with memory in view of her poisonous aunt's conclusion that she 'has probably none [no memory] at all' (vol. 1, ch. 2). Had Mrs Norris's favourite, Maria, activated hers, she would not have trusted Henry Crawford twice!

16.10 Nature

'The evergreen!' (vol. 2, ch. 4)

Trees

Having failed fully to engage Mary in conversation about Mrs Grant's landscaping, Fanny turns to variety in trees (vol. 2, ch. 4). If *people* can be talked about in images drawn from the natural world, then what Fanny emblematically muses on here is the puzzling difference between herself and the Bertram sisters, who have enjoyed 'the same soil and the same sun'.

The word that Fanny's informed expressions of delight turns on is 'variety'. Behind her words is a long tradition of Christian and classical thought that values the diversity of creation. Fanny is not quite finding in the arrangement of the world evidence of the hand of the creator. Her wonder is one that is touched off by the unstated intuition that the splendour of the world points beyond itself to the one who nourishes the variety of creation.

16.11 Stars and the sublime

'the sublimity of Nature' (vol. 1, ch. 11)

The great globe

Between the confusions of the visit to Sotherton and disturbances of the theatricals, there is a moment of calm when Edmund joins Fanny by the window.

In language very similar to the lyrical outburst Fanny is about to make, the narrator says the scene outside 'was solemn and soothing, and lovely' and that 'the brilliancy of an unclouded night' contrasted with 'the deep shade of the woods' (vol. 1, ch. 11). In the face of this beauty and stillness

> Fanny spoke her feelings. 'Here's harmony!' said she, 'Here's repose!' Here's what may leave all painting and music behind, and what poetry only can attempt to describe.'

Fanny again responds in wonder rather than arguing from a feature of the world to the maker of all things. And yet the *feel* is decidedly religious. Meditating on nature, Fanny says, has ethical consequences, because there would be less 'wickedness and sorrow' if 'people were carried more out of themselves by contemplating such a scene'.

Responding to the stars

This comment seems critical of Edmund although that can hardly have been Fanny's intention. When Edmund and Julia return from an evening at the parsonage:

> For a few minutes, the brother and sister were too eager in their praise of the night and their remarks on the stars, to think beyond themselves. (vol. 1, ch. 7)

The reader can sharply contrast those who could not 'think beyond themselves' with the one who felt that in contemplating stars people would be 'carried more out of themselves'.

Fanny's language

Fanny's language is more expressive in the star-gazing scene than anywhere else in the novel: 'harmony', 'repose', 'tranquillize', 'rapture', 'sublimity' and 'contemplating'. It is the elevated language of a mind seeking and responsive to what is almost ineffable. Painting and music are left behind, and poetry alone can 'attempt' a description.

Poetry of the night

What Fanny is doing – evoking the wonder of the night sky – places her in a tradition of poetry of the night. This was a popular subgenre in eighteenth-century verse. The most famous works are William Collins's 'Ode to Evening' (1747) and Thomas Gray's 'An Elegy Written in a Country Churchyard' (1751). The prevailing tone of night poems is meditative; they have a religious dimension. On occasions their language is akin to hymns but the connection cannot be taken very far. The language of hymns is Biblical and doctrinal, whereas night poems and the stargazing passage are more subjective and evocative. Several of the crucial words in the stargazing scene – 'soothing', 'harmony', 'repose', 'tranquillize', 'rapture', 'sublimity' and 'contemplating' – are not used in the Bible. An exception is the star 'Arcturus' which occurs in *Job* 9: 9, 28: 32.

Sublimity

Another word in Fanny's speech that has religious implications is 'sublimity'. With the sublime we encounter Burke again – *A Philosophical Enquiry into the Origin of our Ideas of the Sublime and Beautiful* (1757). Fanny's awe is akin to Burke's remark that 'wherever God is mentioned as appearing or speaking, every thing terrible in nature is called up to heighten the awe and solemnity of the divine presence'. (part 2, section 5). Similar is Bishop Butler who finds 'such an expanse of power, and wisdom, and goodness, in the formation and government of the world' (sermon VII).

The moral and the religious

Fanny's musing are more moral than metaphysical.

In Jane Austen it is the moral life which is the place where religious experiences are encountered.

We see this in the use of words such as 'conviction' and 'guilt'. 'Conviction' was frequently used of the moment when one's wickedness was powerfully brought home to one. 'Guilt' can be used in a legal sense but it also means the state of being sinful. In the use of both words there is also an element of the sublime:

> To the greater number it was a moment of absolute horror.
> Sir Thomas in the house! All felt the instantaneous conviction. (vol. 2, ch. 1)
> The horror of a mind like Fanny's, as it received the conviction of such guilt… (vol. 3, ch. 15)

Horror and the sublime

The word 'horror' is part of the vocabulary of the sublime. There is a moral sublime – the encounter with an overwhelming evil or good. When the language of morality and the sublime blend we are in the realm of religion. In her sensitivity to the vastness of the night sky and her recoil from evil, Fanny Price is Jane Austen's most fully developed religious character.

Because readers share the consciousness of the central figure, the experience of reading *Mansfield Park* is one of sharing Fanny's religious perceptions. In that sense it can be claimed that the novel is about God.

16.12 Providence

'not greatly in fault themselves' (vol. 3, ch. 17)

Not perfect

Fanny Price is not a perfect creature. It is true that she is one of those Austen heroines who do not need to learn very much, but she has her faults. More importantly, the narration makes it clear that if things had turned out other than they did she would have done what, for most of the novel, she regards as wrong. For instance, Fanny thinks it wrong to marry a man whom she does not love, but in the final chapter the narrator says that if Henry had 'persevered . . . Fanny must have been his reward', adding, perhaps surprisingly, that the reward would have been 'very voluntarily bestowed'.

Special providences

How then does she survive? The answer must be given in religious terms. The Christian doctrine of providence says that God governs the world in order to save sinful mankind. It is part of this doctrine that sometimes, however mysterious the workings might be, God shows particular favours to specific individuals. Doctrine calls these 'special providences'.

The narrator speaks of 'an opening undesigned and unmerited', which 'led him [Henry] into the way of happiness'. A possibility has been opened up which 'led' him. The language is of people as the objects of actions done by an other than human agent (vol. 3, ch. 17).

The workings of providence

The consequence of reading the novel as being, on occasions, about providence is that the reader sees that Fanny is protected from harm. This is a hard thing to say in a culture that discounts plot resolutions that are in accordance with a set of beliefs that exist independently of the novel. Each reader will have to decide whether the moments of 'special providence' stray too wide from the concerns of the plot.

A general defence of the legitimacy of these moments would take the form of recognizing the religious atmosphere of the book. If in a number of ways the novel *is* preoccupied with religious issues, then the providential working of the plot is congruent with the temper of the novel.

16.13 Protected

'She acknowledged it to be right.' (vol. 2, ch. 9)

Meeting Edmund

One incident which is presented in terms of a pleasant surprise but which might, from a religious perspective, indicate that a benevolent providence is at work is when Fanny, thinking 'every thing an evil belonging to the ball', goes to her own room feeling 'incapable of happiness':

> As she walked slowly up the stairs she thought of yesterday; it had been about the same hour that she had returned from the Parsonage, and found Edmund in the East room. – 'Suppose I were to find him there again to-day!' said she to herself in a fond idulgence of fancy. 'Fanny,' said a voice at that moment near her. Starting and looking up she saw across the lobby she had just reached Edmund himself. (vol. 2, ch. 9)

Edmund, without intending it, is there when she wants the comfort of his presence. In the phrase 'and looking up' there is an echo of Biblical language – 'and looking up to heaven' (Mark 7: 34) – which might nudge us to think of the incident as more than coincidence.

The need to be saved

Slightly stronger are three incidents in which Fanny is protected. The novel takes what might be called an evangelical line with Fanny when she is tempted. She has principles but, like all people, she is weak. She, like all the other characters, needs to be saved.

The return of the master

Fanny's need to be rescued is most clearly seen in the theatricals. Although she believes that to perform *any* play without Sir Thomas's permission is wrong, she is gradually drawn into the rehearsals. As the rest of the performers probably know about how she has been helping, it seems natural to ask her to fill in a minor part during a crisis. She gives in:

> as Edmund repeated his wish, and with a look of even fond dependence on her good nature, she must yield . . . she was left to the tremors of a most palpitating heart, while the others prepared to begin. They *did* begin – and being too much engaged in their own noise, to be struck by an unusual noise in the other part of the house . . . (vol. 1, ch. 18)

No longer is Fanny one apart; the 'they' includes her. We do not know that she has had to say anything in rôle, but she agrees to do something that she knows is wrong, and perhaps she, also, is too preoccupied to hear a noise which is unusual. Fanny cannot now save herself. With the unexpected suddenness of a householder in one of Jesus's parables, Sir Thomas returns to rescue one whose own capacity for resistance was exhausted.

Saved from Henry

Another moment of 'rescue' comes when Henry is beginning to succeed in recommending himself to Fanny. The narrator here is blunt: Fanny would not have escaped 'heart-whole . . . had not her affection been engaged elsewhere' (vol. 2, ch. 6).

In discovering her strong attachment to her brother, Henry thinks he has found a 'method of pleasing her'. Henry consults his Admiral uncle's naval journal and goes to Fanny with the glad news of William's arrival home.

But the providential force of brotherly love is there to protect Fanny. William has already written to her, so Henry's scheme is defeated: 'He proved, however to be too late. All those fine first feelings, of which he had hoped to be the excitor, were already given' (vol. 2, ch. 6).

It may be we are not supposed to overlook the erotic undertones of the passage: Henry as an 'excitor' wishes to have for himself her 'fine first feelings', much in the same way in which we must suppose he enjoyed arousing similar feelings in Maria. What protects Fanny is a stronger (indeed, the narrator says the strongest) love. Her love for William preserves her from Henry as does her love for Edmund.

The necklace

The most emblematic moment of providence concerns the necklace and the cross. It is as if the world accommodates itself to Fanny's wishes (something that other Jane Austen heroines have to learn that the world *does not do*) so that she can, with a free conscience, do that which she most wants.

William has given her a cross, which she wishes to wear at the ball. But she has no chain. She is uneasy about accepting a necklace from Mary Crawford (her reasons are left inscrutable) so is overjoyed when Edmund gives her a plain chain. But when he hears of the one from Mary he presses Fanny to wear that. Reluctantly Fanny complies, but: 'the one given her by Miss Crawford would by no means go through the ring of the cross. . . . His therefore must be worn' (vol. 2, ch. 9).

The evils of life

There is even a hint that in the workings of providence apparently unmitigated evils will work for good. This is something that has to be thought through with the utmost tact, because the suggestion that providence subjects some people to suffering with the aim of benefiting others is religiously abhorrent. Perhaps the best way of representing the working of providence is to affirm that no matter how bad a situation is, some good can be brought out of it.

In the case of *Mansfield Park* the good that comes out of the chaos of the final chapters is Fanny's return to the house she has come to regard as home.

Comforting

Fanny cannot comfort Lady Bertram, because Maria's 'case admitted of no comfort'. All Fanny can do is listen and bear with the distraught mother with 'the voice of kindness' (vol. 3, ch. 16). But Fanny's greatest service to Mansfield lies in her being the confidante of Edmund. On the fourth day – 'a wet Sunday evening – the very time of all others when if a friend is at hand the heart must be opened' – Edmund speaks to her. (vol. 3, ch. 16) The family has heard an affecting sermon. As Dr. Grant is in Bath (vol. 3, ch. 13), we must assume that it was preached by Edmund.

The narrator says that in Fanny Edmund has 'one of whose affectionate sympathy he was quite convinced'. His tone might almost be described as intimate; at one point he says: 'Guess what I must have felt.' He holds nothing back: 'I will tell you every thing'. But he will not insist she listen if she does not wish it. Fanny's response is a silent yet eloquent compliance.

Although his subject is Mary Crawford, the very way in which he talks to Fanny (not unlike the time spent with her at the ball when he felt at peace) indicates his love for her. Sometimes readers complain that we are not shown the growing love of Edmund for Fanny but if we can pick up the nuances in Edmund's confession, we can see it exists. We must remember that neither the confession nor its sequel would have come about had there not been a crisis that threatened the very future of Mansfield Park.

16.14 Return and the future

'they removed to Mansfield' (vol. 3, ch. 17)

The close

Mansfield Park closes with its own particular version of a return to a desired dwelling. Fanny, like Catherine Morland and the Dashwood women, has been ejected from the place she had come to regard as home. In the third chapter of the novel, when her removal to the White House is projected, her response to the less than perceptive Edmund shows what Mansfield has come to mean for her: 'I love this house and every thing in it.' (vol. 1, ch. 3). Her projected relocation is an anticipation of her removal, upon Sir Thomas's orders, to Portsmouth.

As with so many episodes in *Mansfield Park* allegory suggests itself as a fitting way of describing this loss of her Eden, until we remember that Mansfield, the place where Tom learnt profligacy and Maria adultery, is, for all Portsmouth's clouds of 'moving dust' and 'milk a mixture of motes floating in thin blue' (vol. 3, ch. 15), morally inferior to her parent's bustling home. Note how the Portsmouth home scars the unconscious. The house that holds many children is redolent of our endings and our beginnings, harbouring dust and milk. And the Portsmouth people still preserve a feeling for beauty, as in the remarks about the ship sailing out of Portsmouth harbour: 'If ever there is a perfect beauty afloat, she is one' (vol. 3, ch. 7).

Back to Mansfield

Yet it *is* loss to Fanny, who realizes how the word 'home', which 'had been very dear to her', applies no longer to Portsmouth but to Mansfield: 'Portsmouth was Portsmouth; Mansfield was home' (vol. 3, ch. 14).

It is to that home that Fanny returns at the close. Not to the big house but to the parsonage. (vol. 3, ch. 17). The reader should feel the satisfaction of an arrival which completes the pattern of ejection and restoration, a pattern that gives shape to several of Jane Austen's plots. Fanny's return reminds us of some of the novel's preoccupations: Edmund's and her 'true merit and true love' is implicitly affirmed over against infatuation and passion. Their enjoyment of 'country pleasure' contrasts with the heady distractions of London. The prominence of 'home' – 'their home was the home of affection' – expresses the importance of dwelling in the novel, and the closing sentence about all within 'the view and patronage of Mansfield Park' establishes that alliance, so valued by Edmund and his father, between the gentry and the Church.

Hope

But with unobtrusive delicacy we are shown that, as in many comic plots, the end is also a beginning. The penultimate paragraph ends:

> and to complete the picture of good, the acquisition of Mansfield living by the death of Dr. Grant, occurred just after they had been married long enough to want an increase of income, and feel their distance from the paternal abode an inconvenience.

Perhaps this might be regarded as yet another case of the gentle pressure of providence, but if we only read it as that we might fail to ask what it was that made their move at that moment 'the picture of good'.

The word 'picture' initially suggest those collections of engravings of country houses that enjoyed contemporary popularity. The addition of 'good', however, points to an imaginative picture of an emblematic or moral kind. This is a picture of how life both ought to be and, in this instance, is.

The couple who have 'been married long enough to begin to need an increase of income' are expecting their first child. What is good is that Fanny and Edmund are fulfilling the first of the 'causes for which', according to the Book of Common Prayer, 'matrimony was ordained':

> It was ordained for the procreation of children, to be brought up in the fear and nurture of the Lord, and to the praise of his holy name.

No other Jane Austen novel ends with the promise of the next generation. Only this most Anglican of her novels closes with the Prayer Book duties and vocations of parenthood. It may be that Fanny's children will become the inheritors of Mansfield. What we are more certainly assured of is that Mansfield, and therefore England – the field of man like the fair field full of folk – will survive, and that Fanny's children will be brought up in 'the fear and nurture of the Lord' to praise his holy name.

Part V

Emma

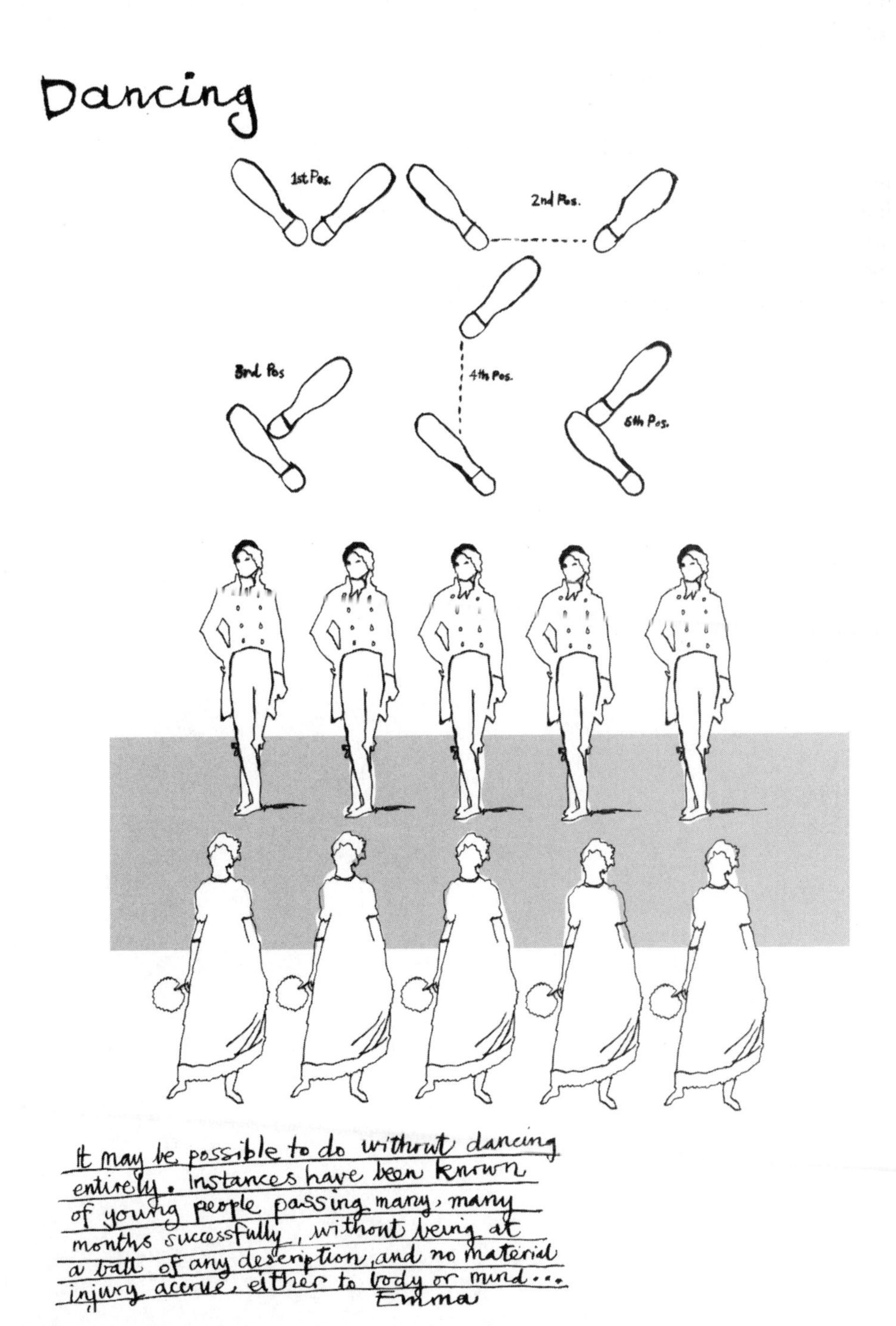

Dancing
1st Pos.
2nd Pos.
3rd Pos
4th Pos.
5th Pos.
It may be possible to do without dancing entirely. Instances have been known of young people passing many, many months successfully, without being at a ball of any description, and no material injury accrue, either to body or mind...
Emma

17 One world

17.1 Imagining a world

'Not that I imagine he can think I have been encouraging him hitherto.' (vol. 2, ch. 13)

Worlds, imaginary and real

Emma is a young woman who is sure that the world is as she sees it. She has to learn that her version of things is, in large measure, something that she has created.

In this respect Emma resembles Catherine Morland. However, in *Northanger Abbey* we see two worlds: the actual world of families and friendships, and the Gothic 'literary' world of Catherine's fantasizing.

We encounter a single, everyday world in *Emma,* located in a small town in Surrey.

17.2 Emma, the world and the reader

'immediately fixed on Highbury' (vol. 2, ch. 6)

What Emma sees

Only rarely does the narrative mediate events through any character other than Emma. Because Emma's mind works upon the world she sees before her,

the plot, characters and themes of *Emma* are derived from the physical and social world of the town the author calls Highbury.

Authorial imagining

Perhaps Jane Austen recognized a similarity between the way Emma imagined a world of romances from the people around her and the way she, as an author, drew her plot, characters and themes out of a familiar world.

Plot material

Compared with the previous four novels, what is remarkable is that

the plot material of *Emma* is found in the details and events of daily life.

In *Emma* there are only two moments that might be described as dramatically useful in a *literary* sense; both are reported rather than shown. Miss Bates tells how a 'sudden whirling round of something or other' almost swept Jane into the sea (vol. 2, ch. 1). The second is Harriet's encountering the gypsies. These events are not disruptive drama but material for gossip and speculation.

Important incidents

The important incidents arise out of what is familiar. Emma's incautious jest is spoken on a hot day during an outing to nearby Box Hill. Mr Elton's proposal occurs because of a minor hitch in travel arrangements.

17.3 The weather

'Though now the middle of December, there had yet been no weather to prevent the young ladies from tolerably regular exercise.' (vol. 1, ch. 10)

Moods and weather

Every day English weather provides material for *Emma*:

weather contributes to the plot, mood and themes.

Matching weather to mood was a preoccupation of Romantic literature. In one passage in *Emma* – the crucial one that climaxes in Mr Knightley's stumbling proposal – the mood is reflected in the weather: 'A cold stormy rain set in' one evening which affected Mr Woodhouse, and a disconsolate Emma was reminded of 'their first forlorn tête-à-tête, on the evening of Mrs Weston's wedding-day' (vol. 3, ch. 12). The appearance of the sun next day brings Mr Knightley.

Snow and sunshine

There are moments when the weather makes perhaps more subtly unexpected contributions. Two are provided by the weather we associate with winter and summer.

Mr Woodhouse's alarm about the snow in part contributes to Emma's being placed alone in a carriage with the amorous and inebriated Mr Elton, where Emma has to suffer not only an ardent declaration but also the embarrassed silence which ensues upon her resistance.

Coming late to the strawberry picking, Frank complains about the oppressive heat. In retrospect, we learn that his discontent is caused by his quarrel with Jane. Yet how appropriate for the novel's plot and themes is his distracting complaining! Given that Jane is spoken of as feeling the cold, we may eventually discern that what Frank could not cope with was its sudden and surprising opposite – the 'excessive' heat of her too long suppressed anger. Talk of heat gives painful force to one of the novel's (and Jane Austen's) chief themes: the incendiary nature and destructiveness of secrecy.

17.4 Highbury village

'Highbury, the large and populous village almost amounting to a town.' (vol. 1, ch. 1)

The geography of Highbury

In *Emma* there is a profusely detailed picture of Highbury as both a physical place and a small society.

The novel provides the reader with a vivid picture of the physical shape and location of Highbury. Several of the incidents have a specific setting: for instance, Emma dates her successful promotion of the match between Anne Taylor and Mr Weston from the day the two women 'met with him in Broadway-lane', where, because of the mizzle, 'he darted away . . . and borrowed two umbrellas for us from Farmer Mitchell's' (vol. 1, ch. 1).

The estates of Randalls and the much larger Donwell are precisely located: Randalls, 'only half a mile' from Hartfield (vol. 1, ch. 1), is in the Highbury parish, while Donwell, 'about a mile from Highbury' (vol. 1, ch. 1), is in the next one (vol. 1, ch. 3).

Highbury itself is near Cobham, seven miles from Box Hill, nine from Richmond and, a significant detail, sixteen miles from London.

Distances

Jane Austen adroitly manipulates the emotional relativities of distance.

Sixteen miles is not a great distance (Frank Churchill travels to and from London in a single day), but when feelings are fraught, someone who is sixteen miles away can feel disorientatingly remote. Mr Knightley removes himself to London just when Emma needs his reassurance most.

Places

Some scenes have a pictorial fullness reminiscent of contemporary painting. Emma anticipates that when Harriet marries Mr Elton she will 'get intimately acquainted with all the hedges, gates, pools and pollards of this part of Highbury' (vol. 1, ch. 10). The details give the scene the topographical exactitude of Constable's *Flatford Mill*, whose hedges, lock gates, canal water and remains of pollarded trees were, incidentally, first sketched out in 1814, the year of *Emma*'s composition.

A village tour

Something of Highbury's extent is gleaned from 'all three' (Emma, Frank and Mrs Weston) walking about together. They see the house of Frank's grandfather and a cottage still occupied by 'an old woman who had nursed him' (vol. 2, ch. 6). The Crown Inn detains them, where Frank's interest is caught by 'the large room visibly added . . . many years ago as a ball-room'. This room prompts a digression into the social history of Highbury (vol. 2, ch. 11).

The shop

Their walk brings them to the shop – Ford's – and afterwards they see the church and the vicarage. Later, Ford's provides the viewpoint from which Emma sees aspects of village life that, given her privileged position, she does not usually encounter. The scene feels like a contemporary painting by, say, Bonnington, Cox or Crome: 'the butcher with his tray, a tidy old woman travelling homewards from the shop with her full basket, two curs quarrelling over a dirty bone, and a string of dawdling children round the baker's eyeing the gingerbread' (vol. 2, ch. 9).

17.5 Highbury society

'pray let us go in, that I may prove myself to belong to the place, to be a true citizen of Highbury' (vol. 2, ch. 6)

A big cast

One of the distinctive features of *Emma* is the strong sense it gives of the people of Highbury. The 'cast' is larger than in any other of the novels. There are about a hundred characters, and though many of them are only referred to (and some not named), their presence in the text gives a sense of a whole community. *Emma* is a novel about what it is to belong to a society.

The characters the reader does not meet

The large cast also provides an opportunity for the pleasurable pastime of speculating about the lives of those whom readers do not directly encounter. The major characters are intimately detailed, so we have some idea as to what it would be like to have dealings with them. What, for instance, must it be like to be Mr Woodhouse's cook, Serle (vol. 2, ch. 3)?

Social ranks

The novel presents several different levels of society. Emma visits the poor family with Harriet (vol. 1, ch. 10), and Miss Bates and her widowed mother are saved from some of the constrictions of poverty by the kindness of Mr Knightley and Mr Woodhouse.

Servants

There are servants: Tom at Randalls, Patty at the Bateses', ostlers at the Crown Inn and at Hartfield the coachman, James, whose daughter, Hannah, works at Randalls. Mr Woodhouse praises Hannah's civility, remarking upon the fact that she 'always turns the lock of the door the right way and never bangs it' (vol. 1, ch. 1). Later, he is critical of Frank Churchill – 'he is not quite the thing' (vol. 2, ch. 11) – because the young man keeps doors open, thereby creating draughts. Mr Woodhouse seems comically fussy, but Frank's conduct later shows that, in the moral sense, he is indeed not quite the thing. *Emma* is not Mozart's *The Marriage of Figaro,* but Jane Austen does hint at an admiration and sympathy for some members of the servant class.

Independent characters

There are characters who, whilst they are under the authority of their masters, have the independence of belonging to what would now be called a profession. Mr

Knightley values the man we must presume to be his steward, William Larkins. The Martins of Abbey-Mill are tenants of Mr Knightley, but, as far as the conduct of their business goes, seem to enjoy a degree of independence. In or near the village there is William Coxe, the lawyer, and Mr Perry, the shrewd apothecary. Dr Hughes, who is present at the ball, is likely to be a clergyman (Doctor of Divinity) rather than a medical man.

The Estates

Mr Knightley owns a large estate which his forebears must have acquired when the monasteries were dissolved, and Mr Woodhouse one only slightly less important. Mr Weston has risen from trade to own the small Randalls estate.

Miss Bates and village life

It should be noted that one of the functions of Miss Bates is to give a sense of village life. As the daughter of a sometime vicar of the parish, she still mixes with the gentry, but it is one of Emma's grumbles that visiting Miss Bates places one 'in danger of falling in with the second and third rate of Highbury' (vol. 2, ch. 1).

Miss Bates's talk teems with names of characters, some of whom, partly because they are not gentry, we never meet. We hear of John Saunders (an optician?), Patty, Mrs Wallis and her boy (a servant, presumably), as well as many familiar names.

17.6 Getting about Highbury

'and walked home to the coolness and solitude of Donwell Abbey' (vol. 3, ch. 5)

Jane Austen puts the physical and social conditions of the village to use in two ways. The first is that the village provides a context for three activities that promote the plot: journeys, visits and walks.

Journeys and newcomers

A convention of a comic plot is that the arrival of strangers disturbs the settled, sometimes stagnant, community. Frank Churchill is the chief disturber; he disrupts the life of Highbury in a number of ways.

He plays up to Emma, who, for a short while, wonders whether she is in love with him. Mr Knightley is unreasonably (though, as it turns out, not unjustifiably) hostile to the newcomer. Frank's conduct deeply disturbs Jane, and, as Roger Sales points out, he is, like Tom Bertram in *Mansfield Park*, a disturber of space and rearranger of furniture (*Jane Austen and the Representation of Regency England*, Routledge, 1994, p. 143).

The newcomer is the subject of gossip. Frank's ride to London, apparently for a haircut, troubles Emma, is not liked by Mrs Weston and provides his father with 'a very good story' (vol. 2, ch. 7).

Only in the closing sections is it revealed that Frank brings with him a secret, the disclosure of which entirely reshapes the characters' understanding of their experiences, and the reader's experience of the plot. It is often the function of the newcomer to scheme and deceive.

Journeys and distress

A second function of journeys is to heighten distress. Emma, troubled by her conduct at Box Hill and Jane's sufferings, learns that Mr Knightley is leaving for London: it was 'an unexpected blow' (vol. 3, ch. 9). We later learn that Mr Knightley withdrew to London because he was jealous of Frank's attentions to Emma and that his return journey was prompted by 'fond solicitude' (vol. 3, ch. 8). Jane Austen exploits those ordinary occasions of departures and arrivals to explore the tensions created by uncertainty.

Visits

In presenting visiting as a central activity of the Highbury society, Jane Austen ensures that

visits alert the reader to the trajectory of the plot.

The first 'event' of *Emma* is a visit. Both Emma and her father are in low spirits after Miss Taylor's marriage. Emma wonders how she will ever find a companion equal to Miss Taylor. Mr Knightley walks in. From the perspective of the plot, this might be described as emblematic.

The etiquette of visits

Small societies depend upon visits, and etiquette requires that they are returned. Emma recognizes that the call Elizabeth Martin pays to Harriet must be reciprocated. Although Emma only allows Harriet fourteen minutes, Harriet relaxes into enjoying their company, a feature which finds its full significance in her eventual acceptance of Robert Martin.

John Knightley on visiting

John Knightley is comically eccentric in his aversion to visiting. His 'mute astonisment' that Mr Weston should 'walk half-a-mile to another man's house, for the sake of being in mixed company till bed-time' (vol. 2, ch. 17) is funny precisely because his estimation of the social visit is so at odds with the rest of society.

Visiting and concealment

Visiting is part of Frank Churchill's stategy for concealing his attachment. His father's encouragement of his visiting Emma and Emma's welcoming of a man who has 'always interested her' (vol. 1, ch. 14) mean that the reader is unlikely to see his visit as part of a scheme.

The duty of visiting

Visiting is a duty. Emma knows this in relation to Mrs and Miss Bates. Her full recognition of this comes when she tries to heal the wounds of the Box Hill episode by visiting Miss Bates the following day:

> In the warmth of true contrition, she would call upon her the very next morning, and

it should be the beginning, on her side, of a regular, equal, kindly intercourse. (vol. 3, ch. 8)

Emma's regrets are often couched in religious terms, particularly those which deal with penitence and remorse. Words such as 'forgiven', 'ungracious' (used earlier in the above extract) and 'contrition' convey the severity of her failure to act charitably.

The duties of life in Highbury are not strenuously demanding, but each member of the society is to be judged by the high and exacting standards of Christian obligation.

Jane Austen's view is quintessentially Anglican. Each of us, in the words of the Catechism, should do our 'duty in that state of life unto which it shall please God to call me' (see 12.11). Emma has been called into a rank of society in which she can do good by visiting someone who, because of her poverty, has few comforts.

There is what we would now call a political dimension to Emma's treatment of Miss Bates. Emma can sustain the community of Highbury by playing her role, for example, visiting those who are emotionally dependent upon her recognition of them.

Warren Roberts points out that because Emma is unable to understand how social relationships are conducted in a hierarchical society, she tries to marry Harriet to Mr Elton rather than the socially more appropriate Robert Martin. His summary is: 'Until Emma's humiliation and consequent reformation she did not support the social order as she should have'. (*Jane Austen and the French Revolution*, Athlone, 1995, p. 56).

Walks

Because Highbury is small, walking is a convenient form of recreation but women lay themselves open to criticism and danger if they venture forth alone (see 19.1). This should be remembered when we read that haunting scene in which Emma hears that Jane Fairfax 'had been seen wandering about the meadows, at some distance from Highbury' (vol. 3, ch. 9).

Walking and the plot

The walking incident that reveals how Emma's mind works and provides the most important material for the plot is the one in which Harriet, out with Miss Bickerton, takes fright at the gypsies, before Frank Churchill intervenes. When Harriet talks of her change from 'perfect misery to perfect happiness' (vol. 3, ch. 4), Emma immediately assumes that Harriet refers to this dramatically romantic incident. It is as if Emma does not understand how life – and the novel in which she features – works. The really significant events are those essentially ordinary incidents, such as the pleasure of securing a partner at a ball.

17.7 Class

'The Coles were very respectable people in their own way.' (vol. 2, ch. 7)

The carefully detailed presentation of various social ranks yields one of the novel's most important preoccupations:

***Emma* is about the multiple pressures of class.**

As Emma is the character who is most conscious of class differences, the narrative is permeated with an awareness of social status and the little giveaways that show that a character is in the dark. Nothing indicates that Mrs Elton has any doubts about the status of Maple Grove.

Class and power

Emma is also aware of class power. As the daughter of the family, which is 'first in consequence' (vol. 1, ch. 1) in Highbury, Emma can help the poor. The vivid detail, like a subject for a genre painting, of Emma 'overtaken by a child from the cottage, setting out, according to orders, with her pitcher, to fetch broth from Hartfield' (vol. 1, ch. 10) shows the influence inherent in Emma's social position. Presumably, it was she who ordered the child to fetch the broth.

The danger of power, particularly in the case of Emma, is that it is a temptation to snobbery.

Class and comedy

Jane Austen, however, attenuates the unpleasant effect of Emma's snobbery by treating her comically. Take the invitation from the Coles. They have been settled in Highbury for some years, are 'friendly, liberal, and unpretending' but 'of low origin, in trade, and only moderately genteel'. (vol. 2, ch. 7) Emma is aware that her presence at a dinner would confer on them the status that they seek. This she is reluctant to give.

The Coles and the Westons

The irony is that the text makes it clear that what the Coles are now, the Westons once were. Mr Weston is from 'a respectable family, which for the last two or three generations had been rising into gentility and property', but his wealth, like that of the Coles, came when he 'engaged in trade' (vol. 1, ch. 2). What makes Mr Weston different is marrying Miss Taylor. A further irony is that the Mr Weston connection is the key to Emma's eventually accepting the Coles' invitation. If she goes, she might be able to dance with Mr Weston's son. When pleasure is promised, social limits may be transgressed.

Emma and Mrs Elton

Were she to be aware of it,

the most humilating aspect of Emma's snobbery is that it is not unlike that of Mrs Elton.

With respect to social attitudes, Mrs Elton is sometimes like a parody of Emma (see 19.1). Emma thinks that the Coles are too forward in their invitations: Mrs Elton has 'quite a horror of upstarts'. Her example of 'upstarts' is the Tupmans, a family 'lately settled . . .and encumbered with many low connections' who expect 'to be on a footing with the old established families' (vol. 2, ch. 8). Mrs Elton immediately undercuts her own position by revealing that her brother-in-law is only, at the most generous reckoning, the second generation of Sucklings to own Maple Grove.

A further example of Emma's snobbery is that she is snobbish *on behalf of others.* She insists, on no secure evidence, that Harriet is the daughter of a gentleman. (This shows her inclination on occasions to interpret life as a romantic novel.) Therefore she believes that Harriet 'is superior to Robert Martin' (vol. 1, ch. 8). Emma increasingly recognizes the Martins' virtues, but can only think of them in class terms. 'She would have given a good deal...to have had the Martins in a higher rank of life' (vol. 2, ch. 5).

Endorsing rank

Thinking of this kind not only governs the plot but does so in a manner that requires our endorsement. We are asked to say whether a marriage is appropriate, and appropriateness is in part a matter of rank.

Sometimes the judgement is a difficult matter. Is Emma's recoil from Mrs Weston's suggestion that Mr Knightley is attracted to Jane just a matter of family and social circumstances?

The reader might be uncertain about Mr Knightley and Jane, but who is unable to go along with Emma's response to Harriet's hope that she might marry Mr Knightley? Although this is not just a matter of class (he is a man of 'first-rate abilities' at risk from one of 'very inferior powers' (vol. 3, ch. 11), it is hard not to refer back to Mr Knightley's remarks about prudent men avoiding such a connection. Above all to Emma such a marriage now seems wrong.

If we endorse that judgement, we have to acknowledge that we have been won over by the novel's essentially conservative politics. There are often social inequalities in Jane Austen's marriages; Emma is unusual in marrying a man who is her social equal.

The social order, metaphorically threatened by the deceptions of Frank Churchill and destabilized by Emma's own manipulations, is affirmed and strengthened by a marriage that the reader is strongly persuaded to see as deeply fitting.

Union

The last word of the novel is 'union'. Its immediate meaning is marriage, yet something of its political usage might filter into the closing statement. The marriage of Emma and Mr Knightley is a union of the two most powerful families in the neighbourhood and as such it ensures that the values and institutions of Highbury will be maintained and probably strengthened. The word unionist, meaning one who believed that the combination of groups or states created sound political systems, first occurs in 1799.

17.8 Sickness

'Oh! Good Mr Perry – how is he, sir?' (vol. 1, ch. 12)

Illness

Illness is more prominent in *Emma* than in any other Jane Austen novel.

The social nature of health

Jane Austen understands that health and illness are social as well as physiological states.

Our attitudes to being ill, the measures taken and the impact that our symptoms have upon others are all social.

Illness and manipulation

It is generally held that Mrs Churchill manipulates others. Emma, who has experience of living with a father who behaves as an invalid, has some sympathy with Frank. As for Frank himself, 'He knew her illnesses; they never occurred but for her own convenience' (vol. 2, ch. 12). Illness is not a solitary condition.

Views of Mrs Churchill

The novel works by enticing the reader to believe Frank (on this and other matters). Mrs Churchill suffers the fate, at the hands of both readers and characters, of not being taken seriously.

And then Mrs Churchill dies. The physiological problem is revealed as real, but it is always mediated through its social repercussions. Her illness controls Frank's movements, thus setting up tensions, and its conclusion is the nearest this novel of the everyday get to a deus ex machina (see 20.14). Mrs Churchill's illness and death radically reorder lives.

17.9 Diet

'After a little more discourse in praise of gruel.' (vol. 1, ch. 12)

The uses of food

Food has a number of functions in *Emma.* Eating together cements relationships. Miss Bates is also the object of another use of food – its charitable function. She receives a hindquarter of pork from Hartfield and apples from Donwell.

The medical aspect of food is associated with Mr Woodhouse's diet and his concern for his neighbours' consumption: 'What was unwholesome to him, he regarded as unfit for any body' (vol. 1, ch. 2).

Mr Perry

In matters of health and eating, Mr Woodhouse consults Mr Perry, the apothecary. At his first mention (he is one of those characters who never speaks), it is clear that his function is as much social as medical: his 'frequent visits were one of the comforts of Mr Woodhouse's life' (vol. 1, ch. 2).

He comforts by his tactful acquiescence. When Mr Woodhouse consults him about wedding cake, Mr Perry shrewdly discerns the desired answer so declares it 'might certainly disagee with many'. His children were no doubt grateful for such advice as they were to be seen later with pieces of wedding cake in their hands!

Mr Perry's status

As Roger Sales points out (*Jane Austen and Representations of Regency England*, Routledge, 1994, pp. 151–2), apothecaries were pressing for professional recognition. Originally just preparers of drugs, they had increasingly taken on the role of offering advice. The story of Perry setting up a carriage, which Frank had learned from Jane, indicates a man who is seeking the social elevation commensurate with a publicly recognized profession.

Mr Wingfield, fathers and daughters

Mr Woodhouse has his Mr Perry; Mrs John Knightley her Mr Wingfield. R.W. Chapman wondered why Jane Austen's enemies never 'fastened on to…her defiance of the probabilities of heredity' (*Jane Austen: Facts and Problems*, Oxford University Press, 1948, p. 184). But *Emma* depends upon children taking after their parents. If Isabella were not like her father, the little wrangles the two have about health and their apothecaries would not ring true. As for accounting for Emma, Mr Knightley asserts that she 'inherits her mother's talents' (vol. 1, ch. 5).

17.10 The significances of sickness

'Jane she had a distinct glimpse of, looking extremely ill.' (vol. 3, ch. 8)

Contrasting states of health

Emma gives Mrs Weston 'the complete picture of grown-up health.' (vol. 1, ch. 5), whilst Jane is ill to the point of her health 'being completely deranged' (vol. 3, ch. 9). There is, of course, a social aspect to this. Emma enjoys the security of wealth and status: Jane has no prospects other than the demeaning work of a governess.

Illness and concealment

Yet in Jane's case, other factors are at work.

It is possible to establish strong links between the history of Jane's attachment to Frank and her physical health. *Emma* endorses the desirability of the public nature of engagements. Without the safety of public recognition, engaged couples, in particular women, are vulnerable.

Jane apparently has had a cold from the seventh of November. We know that her secret engagement took place in October and that Jane has not really been well since Miss Campbell's wedding day (also in October).

Perhaps the subterfuge of her engagement had already begun to take its toll, and when Jane witnessed her best friend's legitimate, trouble-free wedding she began to sink.

As soon as the clandestine engagement becomes public, Jane's health is restored. Certainly, Frank's conduct contributed to her state, but the root cause was probably concealment (see 19.4).

Health and moral awareness

Does *Emma* suggest that there is a relationship between sickness and acute awareness?

To put the point the other way round: are those who are unaware less prone to physical illness? Emma, in her confidence, is quite unaware of the ways in which she might be wrong. Jane must be painfully aware of the deception she is practising.

17.11 News and letters

'She thought so well of the letter, that when Mr Knightley came again, she desired him to read it.' (vol. 3, ch. 15)

Spending time

Jane Austen's problem in *Emma* was how to find a significance in the minor events of everyday life. Everyday life in *Emma* takes many forms: dining, cooking, charitable acts, visiting, walking, shopping, being ill, talk, pastimes and the arts.

News

News is most useful for plot promotion. A small community lives by news. Mr Knightley tells Emma: 'I have a piece of news for you', adding, 'You like news' (vol. 2, ch. 3). Robert Martin rides round the countryside collecting walnuts for his beloved; Mr Knightley, perhaps without realizing it, woos Emma with news.

Letters

News often comes in the form of letters. One of Miss Bates's small comforts is the receiving and handing on of news from Jane's letters. This practice Emma tries to avoid. However, she falls prey to a letter with an important plot function: it announces Jane's arrival in Highbury, and prompts a speculation from Emma about the relationship between Jane and Mr Dixon.

Jane's engagement to Frank is signalled by her receiving his letters. Mrs Elton's tactless persistence that one of her men collect Jane's post increases the burden of her secret engagement.

The scrupulous Jane, running out of anything to report, is reduced to passing on confidential news. She divulges Mr Perry's secret plans for a carriage and this backfires.

Frank's letter

In a book of hints and secrets, Frank's lengthy explanation of his conduct is something the reader requires. His letter (vol. 3, ch. 14) does two things: explains much that was unclear and poses the problem of how to judge Frank.

Its explanations help us to see the proleptic nature of the plot. For example, through them the reader, and Emma, can see the true significance of Jane's piano.

It is not easy to assess Frank's self-presentation. His behaviour towards Emma is ambiguous. His rationale for it is disingenuous and morally questionable. He writes to win over Mrs Weston and, doubtless, indirectly, Emma. A judgement has to balance the apparent candour with which he owns up and the assumption that he will be forgiven. Is his prose too plausible and too presumptuous? Yet before we find him guilty we should hesitate.

Mr Knightley and Frank

The most critical view of the letter comes from Mr Knightley. But Mr Knightley has never really forgiven Frank for the interest that Emma took in him. Does this affect his judgement (vol. 3, ch. 15)?

17.12 Pastimes

'Its character as a ball-room caught him.' (vol. 2, ch. 6)

Dancing

The narrative voice declares with comic disdain that 'It may be possible to do without dancing entirely' (vol. 2, ch. 11). This is not true of Jane Austen the novelist. Dances develop character through conversation, tease the reader with the uncertain status of a relationship, suggest the frissons of desire, test moral worth and are emblematic of marriage.

The pleasures of planning

Emma shows Jane Austen alert to the truth that the pleasure of public celebrations lies, in part, in the planning. 'You consent – I hope you consent?' (vol. 2, ch. 11), Frank asks Emma in language that suggests wooing and sexual solicitation. Emma is delighted to dance because it shows the world how well they perform together and it is a display 'in which she need not blush to compare herself with Jane Fairfax'.

What Frank does to the Crown Hotel is an image of what he does to Highbury: he moves the settled furniture of people's expectations, deceiving them into thinking Emma is his object while it is Jane with whom he has been dancing.

The ball

The ball shows how generous Mr Knightley is. Only someone of his status could enact what must remain unspoken – a rebuke of Mr Elton's lack of courtesy and charity. The irony is that for Harriet his ' kind action' (vol. 3, ch. 11) could be a sign of love. Reading back, we can locate such a sign, not in Mr Knightley's chivalry, but in Emma's approving glance.

Reading

In *Emma* reading indicates three things: cultural refinement, the moral qualities of the one who reads and an image for one of the book's main subjects – the nature of perception.

Reading matter

In Mr Knightley's eyes, Emma 'will not submit to anything' that requires 'a subjection of the fancy to the understanding' (vol. 1, ch. 5). Does Emma share with Harriet a taste for Gothic romance?

Robert Martin shows real taste in his choice of Goldsmith's *The Vicar of Wakefield.* Its subject is significant – folly enlightened.

Robert Martin is comprehensive in his reading and recognizes its public role. His home contains novels, agricultural science and, probably, poetry (the usual contents of collections called *Elegant Extracts*), which he reads aloud.

Emma's novelistic tendencies

Emma is a kind of novelist. She brings her fancy to bear on those she knows. One of the doubtful things she teaches Harriet is the exercise of this faculty.

Unfortunately, Emma has an imagination severed from reason. It is lurid but impoverished. Its limits are seen in the way that she can imagine Mr Knightley married to Harriet.

There is a subdued parallel between books and friends. Rather than Emma's befriending Harriet, Mr Knightley believes she would be better off reading through her 'very good lists'. Like Mr Knightley we can see that Emma would also be better advised to befriend Jane (see 19.1) than fantasize about her.

Reading and interpreting

In this sense reading is an image for the whole book. Emma's misreading arises out of boredom and the enjoyment she has in arranging people's lives. Jane Austen's theme might be summed up here as elsewhere in the phrase from T.S. Eliot that F.R. Leavis used to define the nature of literary criticism: the common pursuit of true judgement.

Games

Apart from reading, parlour games are the commonest form of family entertainment. Mrs Goddard loves piquet, there is backgammon at Hartfield and 'merry evening games' (vol. 1, ch. 4) at Abbey-Mill-Farm.

It is in games that material drawn from familiar events proves most thematically rich. The game might be taken as the chief image of the novel.

The formal games characters play resemble the manoeuvres of their conduct, and tactics of deception are close to the games of deflection that the author plays with the reader.

Alphabets

The alphabet game (vol. 3, ch. 5) involves a troubled scene of uncertain perceptions, embarrassed reactions and puzzled reflections. Frank's motive in proposing it is twofold: to distract the company from thinking further about his blunder over Perry's carriage and to communicate with Jane. Mr Knightley senses that a game other than with alphabets is being conducted: 'It was a child's play, chosen to conceal a deeper game on Frank Churchill's part.' Language as metaphorically rich as this might be continued by saying that Mr Knightley cannot be sure of the rules or who knows them.

Games and interpretation

The plot of the novel hangs on interpretation. Mr Knightley would like to interpret the confusing manoeuvres in the darkening room. Emma (mis)interprets Mr Elton's courtship and Jane's clandestine love. Harriet (mis)interprets Mr Knightley's attentions.

***Emma* explores the necessity and dangers of interpretation.**

The importance of interpretation is manifest in the game of riddles (vol. 1, ch. 9). Emma can interpret one such riddle and assign authorship to Mr Elton. What she fails to interpret is his purpose. Her metaphors for this piece of misreading are appropriately literary: 'It is a sort of prologue to the play, a motto to the chapter; and will soon be followed by matter-of-fact prose.'

Games and the reader

Yet the feeling of 'we see, but she does not' is part of another game. Do we penetrate the riddle of Frank's behaviour? Do we see what no character sees till it passes with the speed of Cupid's arrow though Emma's heart – that she must marry Mr Knightley? Such questions show that comparison between *Emma* and detective fiction is apt.

Jane Austen tests her readers just as severely as she does her characters.

17.13 Music

'They had music.' (vol. 2, ch. 2)

Public performances

Music is a feature of domestic entertainment. From Emma's point of view, music is too close to games: public performance means unequal competition with Jane.

Music and deception

Music is also akin to games in that performance becomes the occasion for Frank's double-dealing. The scene at the Coles', in retrospect, reveals ironies. The order of Frank's vocal accompaniment – first Emma, then Jane – mimes what would seem to be the history of his attachment.

The piano and Mr Knightley

The irony that runs through the scene is the gossip about Mr Knightley's being a possible admirer of Jane and, thus, the piano's donor. Emma's failure to recognize why this causes her such distress is more personally relevant than her failure to guess the piano's true source.

The social dimension of music: pianos

Jane Austen recognizes the social dimension of musical accomplishment.

In the early nineteenth century the piano was acquiring an interestingly ambiguous status. It was a sign of respectability. The Coles' acquisition of a piano before anyone can play indicates consciousness of class pressure.

The erotic potential of the piano is present in Frank's gift. It is a reminder of Weymouth (did he and Jane sit together on the stool?) and an assurance of his continuing affection. The passage in which they sing duets is, like the gift itself, an image of their originally harmonious understanding. At a time of uncertainty, Frank could also be promising emblematically the respectability of a future domestic life.

There is another social dimension to music, less pleasant for Jane. She will have to teach it. Mrs Elton acknowledges her high marketability but adds that she would be further advantaged 'if you knew the harp' (vol. 2, ch. 17).

The text has returned to the erotics of music. The harp was an advantage to a young lady because performing threw her breasts into profile. Parents might see that a daughter would advance her marriage chances by such a display, but for Jane, the governess, it might put her in danger from a genuinely unscrupulous 'Mr Dixon'.

Songs

Jane Austen does not frequently make much of the actual music her characters play. An exception is the song 'Robin Adair'. Frank implies that the music sent with the piano is a reminder of happy, illicit times between Jane and Mr Dixon. Frank says that 'Robin Adair' was 'his favourite'.

It is clearly Frank's: why else would he send the music? The theme of the song is a long struggle of a young woman to marry the man of her choice. Should Emma know the song, there is deception in this, too: the man in question, like Mr Dixon, was Irish.

Traditional songs

Robert Martin brought 'his shepherd's son into the parlour one night on purpose to sing to her [Harriet]'. If one speculates about what sort of folk song he performed, an answer is there in the previous sentence: 'He [Mr Martin] had gone three miles round one day, in order to bring her some walnuts' (vol. 1, ch. 4).

'Gathering walnuts' sounds just like the kind of folk song which was collected from the yeoman and peasant classes thirty years later by a descendent of John Boldwood, the maker of Jane's piano. In 1843 Revd John Broadwood published *Old English Songs* as 'sung by the Peasantry of Weald of Surrey and Sussex' (see Maud Karpeles, *An Introduction to English Folk Song*, Oxford, 1987, p. 78). If we translate Broadwood into the fictive world of Highbury, we can imagine him encouraging the now mature shepherd to perform the songs he had once sung to a pretty girl in the parlour of a Surrey farmhouse.

17.14 Manners

'In one respect, perhaps, Mr Elton's manners are superior to Mr Knightley's.' (vol. 1, ch. 5)

Manners, easing the running of Highbury or any society, have this in common with music:

manners might be understood as being a combination of taste and technique, where taste means goodwill and technique means the various forms of politeness that propriety requires.

Manners and character

In *Emma*

Jane Austen uses manners to reveal character and probe moral capacity.

They also offer a way of making discriminations about gentility. Emma tells Mr Knightley that 'nothing but a gentleman in education and manner has any chance with Harriet'. His reply is forceful: 'Robert Martin's manners have sense, sincerity, and good-humour to recommend them; and his mind has more true gentility than Harriet Smith could understand' (vol. 1, ch.8).

In that debate there emerges the issue of whether manners are essentially acquired – technique – or whether they should be a reflection of a character's essential self – taste. Emma has commended Mr Elton's mannners to Harriet as a model any young man might follow.

The movement of the plot shows that his manners are all acquired surface. He turns out to be proud and on occasions rude – a man with a capacity for malice (see 20.7).

The debate about manners

Mr Elton's bad behaviour confirms Mr Knightley's position in the manners debate. Manners should disclose rather than conceal character. Ironically, Emma is accurate when describing Mr Weston and Mr Knightley, but not Mr Elton whom she is hoping to recommend to Harriet. Speaking of Mr Weston and Mr Knightley she says of the former that 'There is an openness, a quickness, almost a bluntness in Mr Weston, which every body likes in *him*' and of the latter that his 'downright, decided, commanding sort of manner . . . suits *him* very well' (vol. 1, ch. 4).

Manners and scheming

Emma is also right in considering that Mrs Elton's use of the word 'Knightley' (vol. 2, ch. 14) reveals her as a self-regarding upstart. But Mrs Elton is so gauche that she inevitably shows what she is like. To Frank Churchill, manners are a means of concealment.

By the end of the novel, it is he rather than Mr Elton who is seen as the embodiment of manners as artifice. In his very early call at Hartfield, in itself a kind of deception, Emma approves of his 'well-bred ease of manner' (vol. 2, ch. 5). An ease of manner is present in his long self-justifying letter to Mrs Weston. Can we be sure that he really feels remorse for his conduct? Emma's remark that it is 'much, much beyond impropriety!' (vol. 3, ch.10) is difficult to resist.

Emma sees quite early on that Frank's manners are not easy to understand. One of Jane Austen's themes is that judging anyone's intentions is a difficult business. The presentation of manners in *Emma* shows how much more difficult this is when the manners are assumed to conceal. The direct is better than the suave. Honesty is preferable to spin.

18 Imagination

18.1 Narration

'She was sorry, but she could not repent.' (vol. 1, ch.9)

The opening

This is the opening sentence of *Emma*:

> Emma Woodhouse, handsome, clever, and rich, with a comfortable house and happy disposition, seemed to unite some of the best blessings of existence; and had lived nearly twenty-one years in the world with very little to distress or vex her.

It is a sprightly start: a brisk trochaic rhythm in the first four words, a climax on 'the best blessings of existence' and an enticing close with the hint that what is to come *might* distress or vex.

Formally speaking, the narration is in the third person; Emma Woodhouse or 'she' is the subject of the verbs. The narration also has access to Emma's thoughts; we are told that 'Emma was aware' of the difference between a Miss Taylor at Hartfield and a Mrs Weston at Randalls.

A distinctive narrative style

The whole of the narration of *Emma* can be classified as third-person with frequent access to Emma's mind and occasional access to the minds of other characters. Yet, as critics frequently point out, there is in the novel a special form of third-person narration.

In volume 1, chapter 3 there is a long sentence that starts in the standard third-person narrative mode. Emma has invited Harriet to Hartfield:

> She was not struck by anything remarkably clever in Miss Smith's conversation, but she found her ... so artlessly impressed by the appearance of every thing in so superior a style to what she had been used to, that she must have good sense and deserve encouragement.

The question here is: whose voice is heard? The sentence opens with the narrator who tells the reader what Emma noticed about Harriet. But the close is different; when we read of Harriet deserving encouragement, is it not clear that this is Emma's voice rather than the narrator's?

It might be said that the way the first-person viewpoint appropriates the substance of the sentence is a formal concomitant of the way Emma monopolizes Harriet's life.

Emma the narrator

Moreover, there is no longer, as there was at the beginning of the sentence, a difference between the narrator's view and that of the central character.

In this narrative mode

passages that are formally written in the third person actually convey first-person viewpoints.

The narrative (sometimes called direct free style) combines the 'objective' manner of third-person narratives with the inner, 'subjective' force of first-person writing.

18.2 Reliability

'Mr Elton in love with me! – What an idea!' (vol. 1, ch. 13)

Emma's judgement

Because the novel is about a character whose judgement is not always sound

the narrative of *Emma* is often in the hands of a character, whose judgement is unreliable.

Unreliable narrators

Unreliable narrators intrigue readers. If a narrator is unreliable about one point, how can the reader place trust in all the rest? There is usually an element of play in unreliable narrations. Will we be able to discern what can and cannot be trusted?

18.3 Judgement

'Oh! No, I could not endure William Coxe – a pert young lawyer.' (vol. 1, ch. 16)

Getting things right and wrong

It looks as if Jane Austen wants the reader to get some things right and some things wrong.

She trusts us to get the morality right.

We recognize Emma's failures of judgement; for example, she dismisses people merely because of their position in society.

Why is it that we are not usually misled into making some of the moral mistakes committed by Emma?

One factor is the result of a shift in social attitudes towards class. Because the assumptions about society have changed, we find it difficult to understand, let alone sympathize with, Emma's remark about William Coxe.

But there are four other elements that help to keep our judgements alert.

The narrating voice

The first is the narrating voice.

Few readers differ from the narrator in their estimate of Emma.

Emma, we are told, has been 'doing just what she liked' for some time. We soon see – and judge – her doing 'just what she liked' with Harriet.

Debate

Debate between Mrs Weston and Mr Knightley about Emma's friendship with Harriet also gives a useful perspective (vol. 1, ch. 5). Mrs Weston sees the advantage in the situation. Mr Knightley is often right about Emma though he does not fully understand what it is like to live as she does.

If Mrs Weston helps the reader to appreciate how Emma is circumstanced, Mr Knightley's contribution is to the point regarding what she lacks in judgement. The disadvantage of Harriet is that Emma cannot 'imagine she has any thing to learn herself, while Harriet is presenting such a delightful inferiority'. It is hard to disagree that Emma needs to learn. The irony is that Mr Knightley is right in his general diagnosis but wrong in his prediction. Emma learns a great deal from her friendship with Harriet and learns it in the concrete actuality of experience rather than imbibing it notionally through a few pithy precepts of conduct.

Mr Knightley's insights

Mr Knightley helps us to get Emma right. One of the judgements Emma needs to come to is that Harriet is very fortunate in receiving a proposal from Robert Martin. This is a judgement that Emma eventually arrives at herself, but could she have done so without Mr Knightley's firm prompt about the young farmer's qualities?

Emma is made painfully aware of Mr Knightley's moral intelligence in his rebuke after Emma's insulting of Miss Bates on Box Hill: 'How could you be so unfeeling to Miss Bates?' (vol. 3, ch. 7).

Johnson gave as one of his definitions of 'feeling': 'Expressive of great sensibility.' It is that sensibility – that awareness, sympathy and tact – that has been absent from Emma's behaviour.

That Emma's remark is a gross moral transgression has come to be a staple position in the reading of Jane Austen. Mr Knightley is distinguished for the way he has concern for the feelings of people who are both trying and socially unimportant. His perceptive kindness is a moral touchstone of the novel against which Emma should be judged.

Other minds

Jane Austen is careful not to allow us access to many of the characters' minds. But she sometimes invites the reader to speculate about what might be going on in the psyche of other characters. When Emma says of the supposed author of the charade, that 'He may be sure of every woman's approbation while he writes with such gallantry' (vol. 1, ch. 9), we can understand Mr Elton's taking this as encouragement.

It is possible to speculate about what characters to whose minds we do not have access might be feeling. This bears upon the moral dimension of the reader's experience because, once attempted, it opens up difficult areas of the text that the chosen narrative mode does not explore.

18.4 Misleading the reader

'What has it been but a system of hypocrisy and deceit – espionage and treachery?' (vol. 3, ch. 10)

Questions the reader should ask

The reader often gets the details of the plot wrong.

Even when we have anticipated Emma's discovery that she and not Harriet is the object of Mr Elton's wooing, we might be inclined to follow Emma's reading of events. To how many readers is it clear that Frank is not interested in her but in Jane Fairfax?

Morality and perception

There are reasons why Jane Austen deliberately misleads her readers. In matters of morality and perception, Jane Austen tests the acuteness of her readers and her characters.

A mystery story

Another reason for Jane Austen's misleading the reader is that

Emma, upon first reading, is essentially a mystery story.

Mystery stories have a strong forward movement; the reader must want to reach the plot wind-up, when all puzzles will be made plain. If we quickly guessed what Frank Churchill was up to, we could not be intrigued by the plot's uncertainties.

Yet that is not a complete statement of the nature of doubt in *Emma.*

Doubt in *Emma* extends to the very nature of the text we are reading.

There are two kinds of doubt.

Doubt within the text about what characters are up to and doubt that it actually *is* a mystery text.

The two kinds of doubt are related. We do not know with any certainty that there is a question that needs answering about Frank Churchill's conduct. Emma's view that perhaps he was interested in her but that his interest, like hers, subsided is not implausible. We may conclude that

we are intended to follow Emma in making mistakes, because the mystery of the novel, if it is indeed that kind of work, depends upon the reader's not seeing more than Emma does.

18.5 Insight and sympathy

'The hair was curled, and the maid sent away, and Emma sat down to think and be miserable.' (vol. 1, ch. 16)

Sharing an outlook

It is a common experience of reading that our participation in a character's consciousness inclines us to that character. Emma is not generous about Jane Fairfax, but friendship with Jane would involve greater familiarity with Miss Bates. We recognize that that would be particularly trying for the quick-witted Emma.

Emma and Miss Bates

Miss Bates is a severe test for Emma. We know that Emma is uncharitably impatient with the poor spinster, but she knows that, too. It becomes a matter of self-reproach that she is not active in 'contributing what she ought to the stock of their scanty comforts' (vol. 2, ch. 1). In the word' ought' we hear Emma herself recognizing that she has fallen short of her duty. We see that Emma is wrong, and so does she.

The narrative mode allows the reader to maintain a judgement of Emma *and* view her sympathetically, because the reader's insight into Emma's mind reveals her conscience.

The language of religion

Emma deploys the diction of religion in some of its most climactic passages. Moreover, the particular aspect of religious vocabulary that Jane Austen uses is that which deals with penitence and remorse.

The act of disclosure to Harriet that Mr Elton does not love her requires religious language: 'The confession completely renewed her first shame – and the sight of Harriet's tears made her think she should never be in charity with herself again.' 'First shame' might remind us of mankind's first shame – the discovery of nakedness – and we may be prompted to think of Emma's manipulation of Harriet as exposed before the judging eye of God in her conscience. Being in charity with oneself is an echo of the *Prayer Book*, in which those who are to make their communion are asked if they are 'in love and charity with your neighbour'.

18.6 The difficulties of interpretation

'She looked back as well as she could; but it was all confusion.' (vol. 1, ch. 16)

The main theme

The narrative mode of *Emma* creates what might be called the main theme of the novel (and perhaps the main theme of Jane Austen's work):

***Emma* is about the difficulties of interpreting and judging our experience correctly.**

A philosophical predicament

What we make of what we see and the impediments we encounter in coming to a sound judgement is one of the chief preoccupations of British philosophy. The more we seem to understand what is before us, the more we realize our general ignorance.

Knowledge and the novelist

Jane Austen is aware that we do not possess a perfect knowledge of others, because our means of knowing what they are up to are liable to let us down. Because observation, interpretation and judgement are the stuff of novels, particularly one in which third-person narration becomes, effectively, first-person narration, the novelist is obliged to engage with epistemic issues (concerning the nature of knowledge).

18.7 The language of knowledge

'Mr Knightley, a sensible man.' (vol. 1, ch. 1)

The vocabulary of understanding

The ordinary and everyday business of life involves making our minds up about what is happening around us. *Emma* is built upon getting things wrong.

A concern for what it is to know and what happens when a character is mistaken is evident in the language of *Emma*.

Jane Austen deploys a complex cognitive vocabulary: that is to say, there are words for knowledge, for getting things wrong, for the state of being wrong and for the factors that impede understanding.

This vocabulary is not restricted to Emma herself: one of the novel's features is that many of the characters are in pursuit of understanding.

Sensible

Mr Knightley is 'a sensible man' (vol. 1, ch. 1). Two of Johnson's definitions are still pertinent: '5. Having moral perception. 6. Having quick intellectual feeling; being easily or strongly affected.' Mr Knightley is strongly affected in a moral sense by Frank's conduct, and, intellectually, he is perceptive.

Mr Knightley and understanding

Mr Knightley values 'understanding'. When he comments on Emma's plans to do more reading, he says that she will not submit to 'a subjection of the fancy to the understanding' (vol. 1, ch. 4). He must be using the word to cover at least both knowledge and judgement (Johnson's first definition).

Rational, reasonable and prudent behaviour

The words 'rational' and 'reasonable' are used of behaviour that is sensible and safe;

there is a touch of pragmatism, of behaviour being accommodated to social expectations. The closely associated word is 'prudence'.

Mr Knightley says to Emma that Mr Elton is 'not at all likely to make an imprudent match'. He 'may talk sentimentally, but he will act rationally' (vol. 1, ch. 8). 'Rationally' here is close to 'with self-interest'.

18.8 The language of error

'to see that Harriet's hopes had been entirely groundless, a mistake, a delusion, as complete a delusion as any of her own' (vol. 3, ch. 13)

Words for being wrong

The novel works by disclosing truths in the light of which errors can be detected. The words for getting things wrong – 'blunder', 'mistakes', 'misinterpreted' – have force because the reader sees what the truth of any situation is.

Blunders

'Blunder' is used several times. Johnson defines it with some force: 'A gross and shameful mistake.' A blunder is something that people with understanding should not make. Emma confides in Mr Knightley that her conviction that Mr Elton loved Harriet was 'a series of strange blunders' (vol. 3, ch. 2).

Blindness

Something approaching shame is present in the scene in which Harriet discloses to Emma that she believes Mr Knightley might return her love. Harriet says that she has done what Emma told her to do: 'You told me to observe him carefully'. This disclosure disorientates Emma. She wonders how she can understand 'The blunders, the blindness of her own head and heart!' (vol. 3, ch. 11).

Frank's errors

Emma is not alone in making mistakes. Frank Churchill admits to one 'blunder' when he divulges that he knows about Perry's wishing to acquire a carriage. The irony is that it is a lesser event that pressures him into admitting shame. His impropriety in suggesting a secret engagement ought to have forced shame upon him.

Mistakes and misreading

Mistakes and misinterpretations characterize Emma's misreading of Mr Elton and his misreading of her behaviour.

***Emma* is about the difficulty of understanding what others are thinking and feeling. Emma herself sees no difficulties. If the reader understands just how difficult it is to grasp what others are up to, then Emma's confidence becomes a source of irony.**

When she reads Mr Elton's charade she immediately sees the remark about Harriet's 'ready wit' as evidence of Mr Elton's blind love. In her mind she enjoys a little dialogue with Mr Knightley: 'For once in your life you would be obliged to own yourself mistaken' (vol. 1, ch. 9). These passages are the prelude to her first awakening to the fact that it is *she* who is 'grossly mistaken' (vol. 1, ch. 17).

18.9 On being deceived

'None of that upright integrity, that strict adherence to truth and principle, that disdain of trick and littleness, which a man should display in every transaction of his life.' (vol. 3, ch. 10)

The state of being mistaken is described as 'deception', 'blindness' and sometimes as 'delusion'. Being blind corresponds to all the language in the novel about observing and seeing.

Deception and perception

Emma is a comedy in which, as in Shakespeare, the plot develops because characters are deceived. In Emma's case, the deception is often self-induced.

In the latter pages of the novel, the issue of what can be perceived is crucial. After Harriet's disclosure, Emma reflects that in her relationship with Mr Knightley 'She could not flatter herself with any idea of blindness in his attachment to *her*' (vol. 3, ch. 12).

Emma must come to see that Mr Knightley's regard for her is like a philosophical conclusion: whatever can be doubted, this cannot. When he declares his love, the impossibility of Mr Knightley's loving Harriet is confirmed; it was 'a mistake, a delusion' (vol. 3, ch. 13).

The moral dimension

'Blindness' is given a moral colouring in the talk about the secret engagement between Frank and Jane:

> He never wished to attach me. It was merely a blind to conceal his real situation with another. – It was his object to blind all about him; and no one, I am sure, could be more effectively blinded than myself – except that I was *not* blinded – that it was my good fortune – that, in short, I was somehow or other safe from him. (vol. 3, ch. 13)

Emma, like the other characters, was blinded in the sense that she did not see what was going on. However, she was not blinded by love. Are we to see that not falling in love with Frank is a sign of the soundness of Emma's heart and mind?

18.10 The causes of error

'How much more must an imaginist, like herself, be on fire with speculation and foresight!' (vol. 3, ch. 3)

Imagination

In a philosophical spirit, Jane Austen explores the causes of error. Her use of words such as 'fancy', 'imagination' and 'prejudice' indicates that errors arise from the improper exercise of certain mental faculties.

Emma is indulging a whim when she encourages Harriet to picture Mr Elton showing her portrait to his family. Emma exclaims: 'how busy their imaginations all are' (vol. 1, ch. 7). It is actually Emma's imagination which is busy.

Conjecture

A similar word to 'imagine' is 'conjecture'. Emma uses it in conversation with Jane about the origin of the piano, and Frank joins in with the aim, we may decide in retrospect, of moving the talk into safer areas (vol. 2, ch. 10) and possibly of mocking Emma.

18.11 Perception

'made her quick eye sufficiently acqainted with Mr Robert Martin' (vol. 1, ch. 4)

Observation

Emma observes. When she and Harriet meet Robert Martin the narrative is suffused with her language.

> His appearance was very neat, and he looked like a sensible young man, but his person had no other advantage; and when he came to be contrasted with gentlemen, she thought he must lose all the ground he had gained in Harriet's inclination.

We distinctly hear Emma in 'very neat' and 'looked like a sensible young man', and her voice becomes stronger when she confidently decides that Mr Martin has 'no other advantage'. What is characteristic of Emma here is the speed with which she makes a judgement.

Confidence

Emma is firmly confident in her own perspicacity. This, of course, is material out of which dramatic irony boomerangs. Emma discovers that Robert Martin does have other 'advantages'. To put it bluntly: he takes the embarrassing Harriet off Emma's hands.

Prejudice

Jane Austen is showing the reader how Emma's perception works.

> **Emma's observation is shaped by what she has already decided to be the case.**

It is what in an earlier novel Jane Austen calls 'prejudice'. 'Prejudice' here means prejudgement. Once Emma has decided that Mr Elton is interested in Harriet, she interprets what she sees in terms of this preestablished notion. Harriet is close to the truth when she says 'I could not have imagined it' (vol. 1, ch. 9). But Emma can. Indeed, imagining comes easily to Emma. She sees her future self becoming closer to Frank: 'fancying interesting dialogues, and inventing elegant letters; the conclusion of every imaginary declaration on his side was that she *refused him*' (vol. 2, ch. 13).

18.12 Imagination and love

'She saw it all with a clearness that had never blessed her before.' (vol. 3, ch. 11)

If the workings of the imagination is central to romantic literature, *Emma* shows Jane Austen's reflecting that there are moral difficulties in sanctioning a practice that creates its own objects of thought.

Jane Austen is implicitly insisting that there is a difference between how things are and how we would like them to be.

The irony of clarity

One of the ironies of the book is that

Emma's language values what is clear and unambiguous.

When interpreting the Charade from Mr Elton, she says:

> I thought I could not be deceived; but now, it is clear; the state of his mind is as clear and decided, as my wishes on the subject have been ever since I knew you. (vol. 1, ch. 9)

But the narrator insists that a 'clear and decided' view is precisely what she lacks with regard to Mr Elton: 'but Emma, too eager and busy in her own previous conceptions and views to hear him impartially, or see him with clear vision' (vol. 1, ch. 13).

Clarity of vision is eventually attained by Emma when she sees that she is the one who must marry Mr Knightley: 'She saw it all with a clearness which had never blessed her before' (vol. 3, ch. 11). Clarity is a blessing when one 'sees' what one personally experiences to be true.

Jane Austen and imagination

Yet it would be a mistake to assume that Jane Austen resists the romantic reassessment of the powers of the imagination. For all her admiration of reasoning, she is not hostile to the notion that there is knowledge the certainty of which we cannot easily account for. Perception requires those powers usually spoken of in terms of sensitivity and discernment.

Penetration

A word she uses is 'penetration'. When Emma concludes that 'Harriet had no penetration' (vol. 1, ch. 4), she is thinking of more than intellectual acuity. Emma *has* that eagerness and force of enquiry to see into things and judge them rightly which define 'penetration'. She does not, however, always apply them (see Section 20.15). She recognizes this ability, though, in the Knightley brothers: 'those brothers had penetration' (vol. 1, ch. 16). John Knightley was proved right in his interpretation of Mr Elton's gallantry. He observed – deeply, thoughtfully – and with intelligent curiosity.

The symptoms of love

Romanticism might be described as what a person makes of what he or she sees. In the everyday world of *Emma*, the most interesting things to observe are what, properly interpreted, are the symptoms of love. Women, in particular, need to discern whether in the attentions a gentleman is paying there might be found such symptoms. In courtship, the social convention was that men should be active, they should be gallant (Johnson's fourth meaning is 'Inclined to courtship'), should make their feelings evident and should, at an appropriate time, make a declaration of love, usually in the form of a proposal of marriage. The man, therefore, also needs to observe; he has to discern whether his gallantries are welcome.

Is Harriet in love?

It is characteristic of Emma that she concerns herself with the signs and tokens of other people but she interprets them overconfidently. What does Harriet think of Robert Martin? 'Emma watched her through the fluctuations of this speech, and saw no alarming symptoms of love' (vol. 1, ch. 4).

With regard to whether Harriet is in love, the novel is not so much concerned to show that Emma is wrong than to bring out just how difficult such a judgement is. The crucial word is 'fluctuations'. The relevant definition of Johnson is 'Uncertainty, indetermination.' Emma decides that Harriet's 'fluctuations' are not significant. The reader probably decides that they are.

But is such a reader, like Emma, too sure about their own judgements?

Harriet's behaviour continues to be difficult to read. Emma thinks that 'The symptoms are favourable' regarding her plans for Harriet. The reader might only be more perceptive than Emma in deciding that no firm conclusions can be drawn from Harriet's behaviour. The text is inviting us to concede that we do not know.

It emerges in the text that we do not know because Harriet is not a character of strong and lasting feelings. Mr Knightley wonders whether Emma will agree that Harriet was 'not likely to be very, very determined against any young man who told her he loved her'. It turns out that Emma was right in observing that Harriet's nature can be summed up in the word 'fluctuations'. Harriet has fluctuated between Robert and Mr Elton and Mr Knightley before returning to Robert: 'Such a heart – such a Harriet!' (vol. 3, ch. 18). Emma's mistake lay not in her observation but in failing to observe what her observation really meant. Symptoms of love will differ according to the persons in whom they are manifested.

18.13 Prejudice and perception

'You are very fond of bending little minds.' (vol. 1, ch. 18)

We will now return to a topic briefly touched on in 18.11: the place of prejudice in the shaping of perception. Emma cannot come to a true understanding of what she observes because she has already made up her mind about others and herself.

The place of the mind in perception

Jane Austen is close to the contemporary concern for the nature of observation in being aware that the self can be, in part, the architect of its own vision. Wordsworth's remark in his 'Lines Written a Few Miles Above Tintern Abbey' that the 'eye and ear . . . half-create' as well as 'perceive' is fully exemplified in Emma's assessment of the behaviour of Mr Elton, Frank, Jane and Mr Knightley. Whereas this is a positive experience for Wordsworth, disclosing a liberating truth concerning the relationship between the human mind and nature, in Jane Austen it is a feature of human perception that, unless we are discriminating, will distort our understanding.

In being wrong about Mr Elton, Frank, Jane and Mr Knightley (whom she reads as an old friend) Emma is also wrong about herself.

Getting men wrong

Emma thinks that Mr Elton's seeing 'ready wit' (vol. 1, ch. 9) in Harriet is a distortion caused by love. But hers is the distortion. The charade makes sense if applied to *her*.

Does she not see that her wit and her kind of beauty are sexually attractive? She seems innocent of her own appeal, greatly admiring Jane's looks and seeing Harriet's sensuality and wide-eyed ignorance as what pleases men, even Mr Knightley.

Testing the reader's perception

Jane Austen is playing a game with the reader in making Emma's mistake in the first quarter of the novel so evident. The irony of the Mr Elton episode rests on the gap between our understanding and Emma's blindness.

Jane Austen has built up our confidence in order to subject us to a more severe test. It is generally true that readers as well as Emma fail to see through Frank Churchill. It is very difficult to interpret the actual feelings of a character, who, it is later discovered, is out to mislead.

The reader's inability to see through Frank is a function of our closeness to Emma.

The ambiguity of Frank's departing call

When Frank is called back to Enscombe, he pays Emma a visit to take leave. Both characters try to read the signs the other makes.

With hindsight we can see the significance of Frank's having called at the Bateses' when Miss Bates is absent. When he begins the sentence that is to disclose his secret, Emma thinks it the prelude to 'something absolutely serious' and returns to the civilities of visiting. He sighs and returns to gallantry. Her conclusion is that 'He was more in love with her than Emma had supposed' (vol. 2, ch. 12). Given that neither character knows what the other is really thinking, the error of Emma and the reader is to assume too readily that Frank loves her.

Speculating about Jane

Frank encourages Emma's fantasies with regard to Jane. When Emma discloses her grubby little speculations, he begins by defending Jane. But then, 'checking himself', he concedes the plausibility of Emma's suspicions. He does not *commit* himself to the views his language supplies, but he acknowledges that he does not know 'how it might all be behind the scenes' (vol. 2, ch. 6).

Prejudice exploited

But Frank does more than refrain from contradicting Emma. He exploits the opportunity her speculation gives him to indulge in a romantic but safe(ish) gesture. He rides to London, ostensibly for a hair cut, really to order a piano from Broadwood's. He can rely on Highbury to attribute donorship to Colonel Campbell, and if Emma thinks immediately of a love gesture, she will attribute it to Mr Dixon. It is true that encouraging Emma's surmises will make a future explanation more embarrassing, but when does Frank Churchill think of the future?

Self-discovery

Emma's biggest discovery is that until it was threatened by Harriet's hopes, she 'had never known how much of her happiness depended on being *first* with Mr Knightley' (vol. 3, ch. 12). The image of the arrow speeding through her heart comes straight from the mythology of Cupid (vol. 3, ch. 11). Emma can hardly be said to be wrong here, because she never said she did not love Mr Knightley. What might be said is that

Emma did not recognize the symptoms of love in herself.

18.14 A novel about knowledge

'he could not help remembering what he had seen; nor could he avoid observations' (vol. 3, ch. 5)

The status of knowledge

If *Emma* is an epistemic novel, Emma's faults may be located in her confidence in assuming that she knows what she has no warrant for knowing. It is Emma's blithe assurance about what other people are thinking that leads her astray.

Not that Emma is without powers of *self*-examination. She questions exactly what she feels for Frank. Her fault is that discriminating caution is not universally present.

Mr Knightley's syntax

In this she is contrasted with Mr Knightley. One of the ironies of the first volume is that both Emma and Mr Knightley have made up their minds about Frank *before* they have met him. Mr Knightley's Johnsonian syntax conceals a meaning quite at odds with the formality of his grammar:

> If I find him conversible, I shall be glad of his acquaintance; but if he is only a chattering coxcomb, he will not occupy much of my time or thoughts. (vol. 1, ch. 18)

The balanced clauses – 'if . . . but . . .' – suggest open-mindedness; Mr Knightley might find one or the other true. But the dismissive language of 'chattering coxcomb' shows what Mr Knightley *expects* to find.

Mr Knightley thinks

We may think Mr Knightley is prejudiced, but his suspicions about Frank show an un-Emma-like tentativeness. For example, Mr Knightley begins to suspect him of 'some inclination to trifle with Jane Fairfax'. The manner of his thinking is neither 'downright, decided' nor 'commanding' (vol. 1, ch. 4).

Romantic subjectivism

One of the reasons why Mr Knightley is uncertain (and why Emma never is) stems from his awareness of romantic subjectivism. Mr Knightley cannot be sure that, like Wordsworth in 'Tintern Abbey', his eyes are not half-creating what they see. Mr Knightley does not turn to the revolutionary Wordsworth for confirmation that he might be making it all up but to the gentler and milder Cowper, one of Jane Austen's favourite poets. When he was next in company with Frank and Jane,

> he could not help remembering what he had seen; nor could he avoid observations which, unless it were like Cowper and his fire at twilight,
>
> 'Myself creating what I saw,'
>
> brought him yet stronger suspicion of there being a something of private liking, of private understanding even, between Frank Churchill and Jane. (vol. 3, ch. 5)

Cowper's understanding of perception is not quite the kind that contemporary poets such as Coleridge and Wordworth had. Cowper insists that the subjective can be separated from the objective. He writes of how, when he is sitting in front of his fire, his mind fails to remain alert:

> I am conscious and confess,
> Fearless, a soul that does not always think.
> Me oft has Fancy, ludicrous and wild,
> Sooth'd with a waking dream of houses, tow'rs
> Trees, churches, and strange visages, express'd
> In the red cinders, while with poring eye
> I gaz'd, myself creating what I saw.
> (*The Task*, 1784, Book 4 lines 284–90)

In spite of the grating conjunction of 'I/eye', Cowper knows that the 'eye' can mislead the 'I' – the self. The Fancy, a word familiar in *Emma*, can mislead, but Cowper knows that the mind can make a distinction between appearances and actualities.

Mr Knightley is in the same position. It may be that his fancy is playing tricks on him so he imagines an understanding between Frank and Jane. But the fact that the problem is posed in Cowper's terms means that he believes there is a truth 'out there' which the mind can grasp.

Jane Austen and Cowper

Jane Austen, Mr Knightley and Cowper seem to share this point of view. But given the difficulty of coming to terms with things as they are, they believe that a thoughtful and tentative caution is the only reliable approach to the difficult business of understanding human behaviour.

18.15 The substance of the novel

'Seldom, very seldom, does complete truth belong to any human disclosure.' (vol. 3, ch. 13)

Narrators and themes

Jane Austen's narrators do not usually sum up for the reader the main theme of the novel.

The truth of perception

It is, therefore, significant that there is one passage in which the narrator openly writes of *Emma*'s substance. The topic is the truth of our perceptions, and, again significantly, it comes in the chapter in which Mr Knightley declares his love to Emma.

Mr Knightley confesses that he thought Emma's 'injunction to caution and silence' meant that he would be disappointed: 'Seldom, very seldom, does complete truth belong to any human disclosure' (vol. 3, ch. 13).

Much in this novel has been disguised (in the case of some characters completely so) and the making of mistakes is the stuff of the plot. There is no character who sees the 'complete truth' and the nature of the narrative suggests that this is true of the reader too. Jane Austen is our contemporary not least in demonstrating that truth in human affairs is almost always obfuscatory. The exception she seems to make is over the heart's truth.

Irony

What is distinctive about the ironical effects in *Emma* is that they arise out of two features of the narrative mode.

The first is that

ironic effects are made possible because of the way the third-person narrative adopts the language of Emma, thereby becoming effectively first-person.

For example, when Mr John Knightley warns Emma of Mr Elton's admiration, she amuses herself with thoughts about how easily even the most intelligent can be misled.

The language is Emma's and it rebounds on her. She is a person of 'high pretensions to judgement' who makes mistakes, and the narrative shows that she is 'blind and ignorant, and in want of counsel'.

The second feature is

the mysteries of the plot.

Emma works by forcing the reader to review the entire book in the light of its resolution. It is a book that is read very differently the second time. The reader's lack of knowledge means that much of the irony is what is called dramatic irony. A passage, be it conversation or action, is only fully seen for what it is in the light of a subsequent event. Only then can the reader look back and see the gaps between word and thought that are productive of irony. On subsequent readings, the reader may see the irony in the event itself.

Irony and being right and wrong

In the light of subsequent events, we can see that Emma is both right and wrong. Emma asks Harriet whether in the light of the Charade, she could 'have a moment's doubt as to Mr Elton's intention' (vol. 1, ch. 9). Emma discovers she is wrong about what Mr Elton's intentions are, but right in her judgement that he has very specific ones. Similarly Emma discovers that whilst she was wrong about Jane's being involved in an illicit liaison with Mr Dixon, Jane is, nevertheless, in love and, according to the etiquette of the age, behaving improperly.

Emma's misreadings of the clues in Jane's mystery blind her to its real development. Jane's imagined misconduct conceals her real indiscretion.

19 Female friendship

19.1 Cribbed and confined

'You are so much used to living alone.' (vol. 1, ch. 5)

A confined body

The men of Highbury are used to being at large. The women are confined to their reception rooms, walks in the shrubbery and brief accompanied visits to Highbury. To be at large in solitude is to lay oneself open to comment.

A confined mind

This means that female friends are of the utmost importance.

***Emma* questions what it means to be a friend.**

When Mr Knightley criticizes the growing friendship between Harriet and Emma, Mrs Weston points out that he is so used to his independence that he does not recognize the benefit of a female companion. He might concede the general point, but it is the nature of the companion that worries Mr Knightley. Harriet 'knows nothing herself, and looks upon Emma as knowing everything' (vol. 1, ch. 5).

Social confinement in *Emma* is associated with arrested development and cramped potential. It is Jane Fairfax, broader in her perspective for leaving Highbury, who is the intellectual.

Emma's matchmaking is probably in part a substitute for having a close friend of like calibre. She will not take as a friend the one woman who has been forced to make good her escape.

It is Jane Fairfax who breaches the conventional unwritten laws on the circumscription of women. She walks abroad unaccompanied to collect her (socially illegitimate) post. She steps out solo on the Donwell road. Even at her lowest, she seeks out the solitude that she needs to restore her equilibrium, eschewing temporarily the physical, social and psychological entrapment of her aunt's poky quarters, emblematically placed, like Jane herself at this juncture, just above 'trade'.

Jane's circumstances are far more claustrophobic than Emma's, but with grit she resists them: Emma seems wedded to hers, clinging to them in panic while raging against them in her heart. Emma's befriending of Harriet is emblematic of her deeply insecure state. She wants a friend who will flatteringly confirm her bid to be first in *everything* (like Mrs Weston). At the same time she is wilfully trying to bring down the entire social fabric with her suggestion that the bastard daughter of who knows who would make the ideal wife for the owner of Donwell.

Confinement and travel

Emma concerns itself with both entrapment and travel. The interloper, Mrs Elton, would like to render every dwelling that she approves the same. She is quick to seize on every feature of Hartfield that is redolent of Maple Grove, 'my brother Mr Suckling's seat' (vol. 2, ch. 14), eager to make Emma's home the simulacrum of her own impoverished heritage. She is typical of a type in Jane Austen's work who only feels secure if everything remains the same.

As Emma recognizes, Mrs Elton, in her snobbish reductionism, is the complete antithesis of everything that Emma wants and needs. What she cannot recognize, of course, is that her narrator has mischievously concocted in Mrs Elton a gross parody of Emma herself (see 17.7).

Emma's circumscribed life and outlook are replicated in the name of her village – Highbury. Emma's childlike yet deathly clinging to the status quo mirrors her stymied intellectual development. She may draw up impressive reading lists but she does not travel through books. Pathetically, she 'plays' at riddles with Harriet, buried alive in Highbury, yet privately gagging at her entombment.

The best of friends

When the novel begins, Emma has just lost her governess and surrogate mother of sixteen years, Miss Taylor. One question that the book poses is: who is going to fill the gap? Miss Taylor had been:

> a friend and companion such as few possessed, intelligent, well informed, useful, gentle, knowing all the ways of the family, interested in all its concerns, and peculiarly interested in herself. (vol. 1, ch. 1)

There *is* someone, of course. But no-one recognizes who it is.

Emma is looking for a female friend. However, Highbury affords Emma no social equals.

19.2 Manipulation and persuasion

'a loser . . . a dead weight' **'her friend'** (vol. 3, ch. 15)

Matchmaking

Mr Knightley disapproves of Emma's matchmaking; he believes that it will harm all parties.

But Emma has to manipulate and persuade to the point of emotional self- destruction before she 'hears' what Mr Knightley says.

Perhaps Emma claimed to have made Miss Taylor's match as a way of reconciling herself to it. Her motivation may have been more disinterested. Given her father's views, he must have made life difficult for the lovers.

As it happens, a friend does fall in Emma's way. Harriet Smith has long interested Emma for an apparently trivial reason – her beauty. Emma suddenly discovers that she can waive questions of intelligence and birth. This is an entirely different order of friendship from Mrs Weston's: 'For Mrs Weston there was nothing to be done; for Harriet every thing' (vol. 1, ch. 4). Moreover, Emma has already sized up Mr Elton as in need of a mate.

Emma's life has been filled with affection and she makes it her quest to help others find affection too.

The trouble is that Emma thinks she can manage others' lives more creditably than they can themselves.

What she sees as 'the greatest amusement in the world' (vol. 1, ch. 1) is actually denying people their autonomy. It demonstrates *her* essential triviality.

Hubris

Emma displays the typical arrogance of youth. She believes that she has the Midas touch. So she takes to playing God. The problem is that she treats human beings 'as flies to wanton boys' ('King Lear': Act 4, Sc. 1). Except that here what we have is a wanton girl.

Emma is not alone in desiring 'matches'. Others, mostly women, 'love a lover' and embrace potential unions, often with indecent haste. Love takes place in the imaginations of the female residents of Highbury. Passions are aroused in characters who do not agree with what others think they have seen. Emma reacts strongly against Mrs Weston's matchmaking for Jane and Mr Knightley. Jane is to Emma what Frank is to George, an object of unreason, though Mr Knightley proves to have Frank's measure far more than Emma has Jane's.

Snobbery

Emma is at her least attractive in her dealings with Harriet.

Snobbery drives the Harriet / Mr Elton match from beginning to end.

The fact that Harriet is deferential, grateful and impressed makes Emma decide she has the 'good sense' to deserve to climb socially (vol. 1, ch. 3). Emma's pleasure in Harriet's admiration of the grandeur of Hartfield is vulgar. Indeed, Emma's view of Mrs Elton – 'extremely well satisfied with herself, and thinking much of her own importance' (vol. 2, ch.. 14) applies initially to Emma herself. Emma's fine lady status makes Harriet ripe for manipulation.

Does Emma's appropriation of Harriet lower Harriet in the reader's estimation? Because we see her through Emma's eyes, do we see her as a hopeless innocent without much brain?

Emma is prepared to defend her friend to Mr Knightley as having 'better sense than you are aware of' (vol. 1, ch. 8), but she cannot see that in many ways Harriet has better sense than herself. Harriet is straightforward, like Mr Knightley. She is not a fantasist like Emma who misses the obvious at every turn. It takes Mr Knightley to appreciate by the end of the novel that Harriet has very seriously good principles (vol. 3, ch. 18), something that, initially at least, Emma lacks.

Design

Jane Austen is consistently suspicious of designing characters.

The novel forefronts her plea that human affairs should be allowed to take their natural course.

That Emma should have 'kind designs' (vol. 1, ch. 4) where other people's matrimonial prospects are concerned is a contradiction in terms.

All Emma needs to do, she believes, is detach Harriet from 'her bad acquaintance' and 'introduce her into good society' (vol. 1, ch. 3). But, as the reader recognizes, the Martins are excellent people, kindly, direct and dependable, whereas Mr Elton is mannered, over-effusive and a snob.

The enterprise of the portrait can be seen as an emblem of Emma's larger plans for her 'friend'. Emma knows what she is about. She is even prepared to manipulate the 'likeness' 'to throw in a little improvement to the figure, to give a little more height, and considerably more elegance' (vol. 1, ch. 6) (see 20.15).

Harriet, a willing sacrifice

Emma is chilling. The sharper the intelligence, the greater the capacity for mayhem. Emma appreciates companions for their contribution to her gratification. She has no sensitivity to Harriet's separate existence nor does she champion her self-determined fate. To Emma she is 'a Harriet Smith' (vol.1, ch. 4), a function not a friend.

The scene where Emma manipulates Harriet into refusing Mr Martin is terrifying. Full of confusion, Harriet stands 'by the *fire*' (vol. 1, ch. 7 our italics). Harriet's innocence of being led into a perdition of the heart is excoriating. Never is Jane Austen's use of irony more disturbing than when Emma applies emotional blackmail, forcing Harriet to choose between a husband and a 'friend'. As Emma crows, 'Now I am secure of you for ever', Harriet, we are told, 'had not surmised her own danger'. 'What an escape!' she tragically exclaims. 'Dear affectionate creature!' gushes Emma. '*You* banished to Abbey Mill Farm!' '*You* banished from Abbey Mill Farm!' the reader might echo in dread.

This is arguably more horrible than what will happen on Box Hill. 'It would have killed me never to come to Hartfield any more!' cries Harriet, the true and tender. 'it would have been a severe pang to lose you;' is Emma's cool appraisal.

We may despair at 'Careless, careless' Emma, but Jane Austen is careful. She knows that where meaning is slaughtered, so are the innocent.

Emma is the cause of Harriet's losing one young man before she secures another. Mr Knightley's warning that Mr Elton will not do has the opposite effect from what he intended. Emma knows best. She proves this by smugly disputing the authority of Shakespeare. Emma has nerve!

Wrong again

Despite her resolutions after the Mr Elton débâcle, Emma fails her friend again. Harriet slowly recovers; Emma fails dismally at repressing her imagination; she ceases to be humble though she tries to be discreet. When Fate seems to play into Emma's hands over her choice of Frank Churchill as Harriet's comforter, she gives her matchmaking a kind of literary status. She is an 'imaginist' (vol. 3, ch. 3). This justifies her!

Harriet's ascendancy

But the balance of power shifts. Emma *assumes* that Harriet is speaking of Frank Churchill, when actually it is Mr Knightley whom she has in mind. It is painful for both when they realize they have been at cross-purposes. There is no question of manipulating or persuading Harriet now. Rather, Harriet is defending her corner and hoping that Emma will not 'try to put difficulties in the way' (vol. 3, ch. 11).

Harriet is in a fair way to manipulating Emma.

Indeed, by making Emma aware of her own heart,

Harriet can be said to match-make for Emma far more successfully than the other way round.

Mrs Elton

If Emma is 'no friend to Harriet' (vol. 1 ch. 8), neither is Mrs Elton to Jane. Both take up their friendships for dubious reasons. Harriet and Jane respond for unfortunate reasons, too: Harriet because she is over-awed, Jane because she is unhappy and neglected.

Mrs Elton is constantly bullying Jane. To say that she manipulates and persuades her is too subtle.

Mrs Elton's power over Jane is not unlike Emma's over Harriet. Both consider themselves superior to their protegées. Mrs Elton believes she has Jane's best interests at heart, just as Emma believes she has Harriet's. Both only see themselves.

Mrs Elton is forcefully insistent with Jane, most dramatically over Jane's future profession. Jane has her secret reasons for playing for time. The reader knows how deeply Jane loathes the thought of being a governess, and one cannot imagine her wishing to be behoven to Mrs Elton or to one of Mrs Elton's friends.

19.3 Control of conversation

'Mr Martin is now awkward and abrupt; what will he be at Mr Weston's time of life?' (vol.1, ch. 4)

Finding out and putting down

Emma uses to devastating effect on Harriet what she has learnt from constantly shaping and guiding her father's thought and conversation.

Emma is the controller of discourse, particularly that concerning Robert Martin and Mr Elton.

Emma believes that Robert Martin is 'on the make' socially, so she starts asking questions and making remarks that will present Mr Martin in an unfavourable light.

A gentleman for Harriet

When Emma and Harriet meet Mr Martin, Emma gives her opinion brutally. Now that Harriet has met real gentlemen, Emma doubts that she could 'be in company with Mr Martin again without perceiving him to be a very inferior creature.' (vol. 1, ch. 4).

Ironically, Harriet shows unerring good taste when deciding where true gentlemanly qualities lie. She chooses Mr Knightley who shares many virtues with Mr Robert Martin.

Tellingly, Emma waives Mr Knightley as an unfair comparison and advances Mr Elton for admiration.

Take down this dictation

Emma's control of discourse extends to writing.

Emma is prepared to dictate the purport of Harriet's letter, though denying that she will do any such thing.

That Harriet is confused over Robert Martin's proposal is apparent from her tentativeness: 'It will be safer to say 'No' perhaps' (vol. 1, ch. 7). Again Emma nudges Harriet's thoughts towards Mr Elton. This prompts Harriet into being '*really almost*' determined to say that she will refuse Robert Martin (our italics).

Harriet asks Emma if she is right. Emma not only insists that she is 'perfectly right' but unscrupulously augments the strength of Harriet's wording so that there can be no possible future doubt: 'now that you are *so completely* decided I have no hesitation in approving' (our italics).

The biter bit

It is ironic, and painfully amusing, when Harriet eventually has power over Emma. She does not actually steer Emma's conversation, so there is not an exact parallel. However, Emma's questioning is now anxious, not controlling. It is both comical and sad to hear Harriet marvel at last at Emma's being 'so mistaken' (vol. 3, ch. 11) when she has been so all along.

Emma has always tried to direct Harriet's heart. But Harriet reads her own heart far better than Emma has read hers.

19.4 Woman's language

'She will give you the minute particulars, which only woman's language can make interesting.' (vol. 3, ch. 18)

When Robert Martin asks Harriet Smith to marry him for the second time, he confides in Mr Knightley. Mr Knightley informs Emma. He tells her that he can only give her a limited account: 'Your friend Harriet will make a much longer history when you see her' (vol. 3, ch. 18).

Harriet is particularly good at 'woman's language', if we are to define it in the context

of *Emma* as a propensity for detail, for talking at length, for sentiment and nostalgia. By no means all the female characters speak in this way.

Jane, for example, is sparing with words. Emma, too, is immediate in what she says, though her questioning is close, to *extract* minutiae, and she debates at length with Mr Knightley. Emma's style is rather like Frank Churchill's: ' . . . youthful, confident, presumptive, witty, dogmatic, commanding, assured' (J. Wiltshire, '*Mansfield Park, Emma, Persuasion*', *The Cambridge Companion to Jane Austen,* Cambridge University Press, 1997, p. 66).

A breathless Harriet

Harriet changes in the course of the novel, developing a will of her own and the capacity to stand up for herself. By the end she is speaking with dignity and self-respect. In this regard her painful experiences at the hands of Emma help her to grow.

Harriet's talk is one of the things that initially endears her to Emma. She speaks with 'youthful simplicity' (vol. 1, ch. 4) of the Martins. Anything to do with Robert Martin is bound to bring on a discourse as breathless, as artless and as long as Miss Bates's. Harriet is particularly fond of the word 'odd', which she applies to any spurious conjunction that appears to link herself and Mr Martin.

Miss Bates's language

When Harriet is carried away, she is engaging, but Miss Bates's speeches are one of the triumphs of the book. They are marked by lucid muddle. The impression of confusion is given by ways of speaking which actually make her meaning clear. She frequently does not finish a sentence. However, she takes it far enough for the reader to fill in the gaps. Each sentence flies off from the last but the train of thought is obvious, so that every new thought clarifies its forerunner:

> 'My dear Jane, are you sure you did not wet your feet? – It was but a drop or two, but I am so afraid: – but Mr Frank Churchill was so extremely – and there was a mat to step upon.' (vol. 3, ch. 2)

Miss Bates does not discriminate between what is important and the utmost trivia, normally of a domestic nature. She repeats herself, using marginally different phraseology.

Miss Bates's humility is part of the reason for her flow. Much of her talk voices incredulous gratitude towards her friends and is good breeding carried to excess.

As with Harriet her talk is idiosyncratic but sincere.

My caro sposo

Clichés and pretentious utterance are a mark of hypocrisy and insincerity. Mrs Elton borrows overblown and outworn poetic expressions in her reference to 'Hymen's saffron robe (vol. 2, ch. 18). She has her favourite coy phrases in reference to her husband. Although they are supposed to be endearments, they clearly take for granted that Mr Elton dotes on her. So we often hear of 'Mr E', 'my caro sposo' (vol. 2 ch. 14) and 'my lord and master' (vol. 2, ch. 16), although anyone less likely to be dictated to than Mrs Elton cannot be imagined!

Listen to me

Mrs Elton's conversation, when she is not angling for compliments, is one long parade. She is repetitive, like Miss Bates, and her two favourite allusions are to Maple Grove and the Sucklings' barouche-landau. Everything Mrs Elton utters is funny because she is a vulgar upstart.

Perhaps her funniest speech is her monologue on strawberries, that heart-shaped fruit. It demonstrates how much she is a creature of the moment and how capable she is of making a complete volte-face without recognizing it.

19.5 'Slavery'?

'There are places in town, offices, where enquiry would soon produce something – Offices for the sale – not quite of human flesh' (vol. 2, ch. 17)

Who was Mrs Elton's father?

After *Mansfield Park*, Emma is the novel with the greatest awareness of the slave trade. It is the 'friendship' of Mrs Elton and Jane that causes the issue to arise. Jane's assertion of her autonomy promotes an edgy assumption from Mrs Elton that sets the reader wondering.

How did Miss Augusta Hawkins come upon her money? Her father and mother had died some years ago, so obviously she had it from them. But how did they come by it in the first place? Emma muses:

> '*What* she was, must be uncertain; but *who* she was might be found out . . . Miss Hawkins was the youngest daughter of a Bristol . . . merchant, of course he must be called; but as the whole of his profits of his mercantile life appeared so very moderate, it was not unfair to guess the dignity of his line of trade had been very moderate also....Bristol was her home, the very heart of Bristol.' (vol. 2, ch. 4)

Contemporary readers would have followed Emma's suspicious reasoning. Bristol was central to the slave trade; her father could have called himself a 'merchant', but people would have known what that meant. Did Jane Austen expect her readers to know that the first English dealer in slaves had been a Mr John Hawkins in the sixteenth century?

A brain slave

Slavery hovers on the edge of being an emblem or an analogy and the person who articulates this is Jane. She is loath to close with one of Mrs Elton's friends to be her children's governess because she is anxious to hold on to her freedom. She is also quite prepared to look out for her own opportunities and seek: 'Offices for the sale – not quite of human flesh – but of human intellect' (vol. 2, ch. 17).

Jane is at her most sardonic here. Her remark impacts on Mrs Elton, whose thoughts go immediately to the slave trade. Mrs Elton seems oversensitive and needs to cite a respectable person close to her who will disassociate her from the very idea:

'Oh! my dear, human flesh! You quite shock me; if you mean a fling at the slave trade, I assure you Mr Suckling was always rather a friend to the abolition.' Jane hastens to reassure her that she had no such thoughts in mind. But is the implication that Miss

Hawkins's *father* was a slaver? If so Emma's uncharitable suspicions have been shown to be correct.

And Emma?

But there is a similar huge question mark about Emma herself. What is the source of the *Woodhouse* riches? Not land. Hartfield is just a 'notch' in the Donwell estate 'to which all the rest of Highbury belonged' (vol. 1, ch. 16). Wherever Woodhouse wealth comes from, it is vast, making it almost equivalent to Donwell's. It is Emma who has spare cash, not Mr Knightley. There is reason other than lack of pretention for his not often hiring carriage horses. Are the pretensions of Emma based on dirty money? Trade? What kind of trade? Is wealth on such a scale not inevitably exploitative?

19.7 Economic hardship

'She is poor; she has sunk from the comforts she was born to.' (vol. 3, ch. 7)

Poor women

Jane Austen is aware that women are often the victims of a financial system based upon inheritance.

It is the women rather than the men whom we see suffering from economic hardship.

Miss Bates is the prime example. People who are poor and bed-ridden can look, as John Abdy's son does on his behalf, for relief from the parish. Miss Bates is nowhere near that degree of poverty – she still keeps a maid and remembers days of comparative status and financial security when her father was Vicar of Highbury. But her conditions are straitened now and, as Mr Knightley points out to Emma, likely to grow more so.

No charity, please

Miss Bates must always struggle financially but never shows it because she is sensitive to the situation of others. She is so alarmed when Jane is ill that she intends to call in Mr Perry. 'The expense shall not be thought of' (vol. 2, ch. 1). Miss Bates has a proper pride and sense of what is right, and although she is sure Mr Perry would treat Jane free, she could not allow it. She considers her friend, Mrs Perry: 'He has a wife and family to maintain, and is not to be giving away his time.'

Miss Bates is very generous. Emma acknowledges that if she only had a shilling left in the world, she would give away six pence of it.

Emma does show a friendly concern, if not an intimacy, towards the Bateses. When a porker is killed at Hartfield, Mr Woodhouse thinks they should send a leg. Emma, in typically generous fashion, declares she has sent the whole hindquarter.

19.8 Precedence

'Stop, stop, let us stand back a little, Mrs Elton is going.' (vol. 3, ch. 2)

First lady supplanted

Emma belongs to the first family in Highbury. She is only too aware of the distinction that is her due. Mrs Elton bursts upon Emma with her superior claim to precedence afforded to a bride. Mrs Elton has already set herself up as some kind of rival to Emma, so gloats in her position.

Mr Woodhouse is firm on the subject: 'A bride, you know, my dear, is always the first in company, let the others be who they may' (vol. 2, ch. 14).

Mrs Elton needs no reminding of her rights. She coyly demurs when dining at Randalls but is precipitant in taking up her privilege:

> Dinner was on table. – Mrs Elton, before she could be spoken to, was ready; and . . . saying – 'Must I go first? I really am ashamed of always leading the way. (vol. 2, ch. 16)

Thwarted!

Eventually Mrs Elton should surely believe that she has had her proper entitlement to precedence. In any case, Frank Churchill probably forgets she has any due. So at Box Hill, he (unwittingly?) reinstates Emma out of gallantry: 'I am ordered by Miss Woodhouse (who, wherever she is, presides)' (vol. 3, ch. 7).

This does not suit Mrs Elton, who 'swelled at the idea of Miss Woodhouse's presiding'. She makes up for the snub, though, by insisting that the Elton carriage is the first to leave Box Hill.

My best friend

The problem is that Mrs Elton attempts to befriend Emma when first she appears in Highbury. She aspires to her, as her husband did – though neither of them would think in such terms. Mrs Elton presumably considers herself on a par with Emma. She suggests projects over which they should join forces, probably not even aware that such ventures should be voiced by Emma first.

The 'friendship' which Mrs Elton is proffering does not last long. Doubtless offended by the little encouragement she receives, Mrs Elton transfers all her attentions to Jane Fairfax. There is then no doubting where precedence lies. Mrs Elton is outrageous in the way that she considers Jane Fairfax beneath her:

> 'I am a great advocate for timidity – and I am sure one does not often meet with it. – But in those who are at all inferior, it is extremely prepossessing.' (vol. 2, ch. 15)

19.9 The duty of woman by woman

'She doubted whether she had not transgressed the duty of woman by woman.' (vol. 2, ch. 9)

Aspirations

The first time that the question of doing right by one's sex becomes an issue for Emma is on Harriet's account.

The occasion arises after Emma's quarrel with Mr Knightley over Robert Martin. The quarrel has made Emma feel more disconcerted than is pleasant. But it only takes the return of Harriet in very good spirits to 'convince her, that let Mr Knightley think or say what he would, she had done nothing which woman's friendship and woman's feelings, would not justify' (vol. 1, ch. 8).

The fact that she has wrecked Harriet's chances of security, respectability and happiness does not affect her.

Isolation

Harriet has trusted Emma from the beginning. She sees her as far more perceptive than she. Even when things go wrong over Mr Elton, she blames nobody, poignantly and ironically adding that she was unworthy of him 'and nobody but so partial and kind a friend as Miss Woodhouse would have thought it possible' (vol. 1, ch. 17).

Harriet is left peculiarly isolated by Emma. She is a woman who likes, indeed *has*, to confide in a friend. If she had trusted someone other than Emma over Robert Martin– say, a school-friend or Mrs Goddard – she would have come away more aware of the state of her heart. Emma bullies her out of love.

It is ironic that it is only when Harriet aspires to Mr Knightley, whom Emma suddenly realizes that *she* wants, that Emma thinks of Harriet as reaching above herself. Now the snobbery that Emma had felt earlier on Harriet's behalf is turned against her. Under such pressure, it is inevitable that Harriet will at least temporarily lose Emma as a friend, just at the time when she needs one most.

Mentoring

Although Miss Bates has none of Emma's acumen nor her high intelligence, Emma could learn from her straightforward dealings. She takes what is before her at face value, refusing to speculate when it comes to matches: 'In short, I do not think I am particularly quick at those sort of discoveries . . . What is before me, I see' (vol. 2, ch. 3)

Learning to be a friend

Considering the problems Emma causes for Harriet and the fact that she has never been able to come close to Jane Fairfax, one has to ask:

how capable is Emma of friendship?

Her relationship with Mrs Weston is of a different order, because Mrs Weston has largely brought Emma up. The two enjoy a special kind of intimacy and in any case, to Mrs Weston, Emma can do no wrong.

But friendship beyond her family circle seems to be something that Emma has to mature into. She does not allow the women she knows to exist sufficiently in their own right to make them into good friends.

Good examples for Emma

In *Emma*

Jane Austen presents a number of women who demonstrate the duty of woman to woman.

Jane Fairfax's friend, Miss Campbell, is one. Miss Campbell has not shown envy of Jane, though Jane is distinctly superior in accomplishments, intelligence and beauty. Neither does she mind that her intended husband, Mr Dixon, favours Jane's playing. She is secure and mature.

It has always been Mr Knightley's contention that Jane Fairfax is the accomplished young woman that Emma would *like* to be, implying that Emma is envious. Even Emma is prepared to admit that there might be something in this.

Elizabeth Martin and her sister prove far better friends to Harriet than Emma does. When Elizabeth sends Harriet a note after a chance meeting in Ford's, Harriet is left 'wishing she could do more than she dared to confess' (vol. 2, ch. 4). It is sad that Harriet dares not follow her inclination towards old friends because she is frightened of what her new 'friend' will say.

The brief visit of Harriet to the Martins, where the 'memorandum' of the girls' comparative heights, pencilled 'on the wainscot' (vol. 2, ch. 5) by Mr Martin, reminds them of their intimacy, is full of pathos. The only 'memorandum' Hartfield has of Harriet is Emma's portrait – disastrous, and an untrue likeness.

Friends

Harriet *is* well served in Mrs Goddard, as motherly as Mrs Weston, who would have encouraged her to happiness with Mr Martin (see 20.6).

The older women of Highbury seem to get on well and support one another. Presumably Mrs Cole and Mrs Perry, Mrs Otway and Mrs Hughes have muddled along together down the years. Mrs Cole passes on gossip to Miss Bates. Mrs Martin sends a goose to Mrs Goddard after Harriet has been to stay. Mrs Cole and Mrs Perry, and, of course, Mrs Elton are allowed to see Jane when she is ill. Miss Bates is 'interested in everybody's happiness' (vol. 1, ch. 3). She is the female equivalent of Mr Knightley in benevolence, and, like he, a moral anchor for the novel.

Emma pays for being the first lady in Highbury by not being a party to the close network of friends that the women of rather lower status enjoy. Not that she wants this, but part of the problem is that she has not had enough experience of adult female friendship to recognize what might be required.

A failure of loyalty

Emma's conscience does not usually come into play until she comes unstuck. However, she *is* troubled by her dealings with Jane Fairfax. The degree of her repentance, though, falls short of the severity of her misconduct.

Jane has a lot to tolerate from and, eventually, to forgive in Emma. Although Jane is her superior in accomplishments and in the use she has made of her intellectual powers, Emma has never sought her out. Jane is amiable and highly principled, yet Emma avoids contact. What does Jane feel? Is she too self-sufficient to be concerned? Does she put Emma's distance down to the gap in social standing? Might the coolness be mutual or would she have welcomed Emma's friendship?

Jane as fancy's foe

As Emma has resolved to eschew the imagination after the Harriet/Mr Elton fiasco, it is the more alarming to witness her fancy being given full rein again where Jane is concerned. As Emma listens to Miss Bates, 'an ingenious and animating suspicion' (vol. 2, ch. 1) enters Emma's brain.

Emma – we are reminded of the New Testament - has Jane's best friend's husband committing adultery with Jane in his heart.

Why does Emma conjecture thus? Does she want this paragon to fall? After all, Mr Knightley is always finding fault with Emma. He never does with Jane.

Emma and Frank in league?

When Emma meets Frank, he eventually reveals that he had met Jane often in Weymouth. Emma must glow at this because interesting information might be gleaned from Frank. Emma is equal to any of the gossips of Highbury.

Emma's loose talk with Frank, whom she scarcely knows, concerning a woman whom she has known since childhood, is a failure of duty on her part (as it is on Frank's, of course).

It seems particularly unfair that Frank has a female friend in Emma, while Jane Fairfax is as isolated as Harriet.

Because of her nature and situation, Jane would not dream of confiding Frank's and her secret to her best friend Mrs Dixon as Frank nearly does to Emma.

Repentance

The next day brings very different feelings about what Emma has divulged to Frank, though, and proves that, with hindsight, Emma can reproach herself. She clearly believes that there should be a bond of trust between woman and woman and that to break it is a serious matter:

> It was hardly right; but it had been so strong an idea, that it would escape her, and his submission to all that she told, was a compliment to her penetration which made it difficult for her to be quite certain that she ought to have held her tongue. (vol. 2, ch. 9)

Here is the rub. As Mr Knightley has said, Emma's vanity does not lie in her looks. She attributes genius to herself, never mind intelligence.

Remarkably, Jane seeks Emma out when she is in need, in spite of the fact that she must have been deeply hurt by the way that Emma and Frank behave. It is clear that Jane finds Emma the most empathic person in the strawberry-picking party. One can imagine the brouhaha if Jane had told her supposed friend Mrs Elton that she wanted to go home!

Emma spurned

After her consideration, Emma's behaviour with Frank on Box Hill must devastate Jane. Then Emma is rude to Jane's aunt. This pain, on top of knowing the offensive ideas that

Emma has harboured about Mr Dixon, makes it small wonder that Jane succumbs to searching out Mrs Elton.

Mrs Elton as moral model

Indeed, Mrs Elton, like Miss Bates, has things to teach Emma. She *claims*, at least, that 'I always take the part of my own sex' (vol. 2, ch. 18). The notice that she takes of Jane also ought to put Emma to shame. Then on the occasion when Emma speaks so heedlessly to Miss Bates, she declares: 'I really must be allowed to judge when to speak and when to hold my tongue.' (vol. 3, ch. 7) The *reason* for her declaration is because she has nothing clever to say, but the remark is a timely reproach.

Emma rebuffed

Emma's heart has long been growing kinder towards Jane and she regrets her injustice in the past. She also wishes to make amends to Jane's aunt.

As Anne Elliot tries to show the Musgroves in *Persuasion*, life requires that we make allowances for one another. Instead of baulking at her duty to old family friends, Emma seems at last to be embracing it.

Emma now wants to lavish regard and sympathy on the previously neglected Jane. She feels pity for her condition and situation. She knows her own intentions are good and is saddened to be 'given so little credit for proper feelings' (vol. 3, ch. 9).

When news of Frank and Jane's engagement bursts upon Emma, though, she understands why Jane has avoided her. 'She must have been a perpetual enemy' (vol. 3, ch. 12). It has been a matter of misplaced loyalty. Emma has trusted her salacious fantasies to a man who has deceived her and led her to be unkind to and about one of the worthiest of her sex.

Emma welcomed

However, when Emma visits Jane after news of the engagement is out, Jane meets her on the stairs with great warmth. They cannot say much because Mrs Elton is present. Nevertheless, Jane sees Emma off and demonstrates in just what esteem she holds her. After this, Emma takes Jane warmly by the hand. Jane acknowledges how 'cold and artificial' (vol. 3, ch. 16) her manners have been to Emma. Emma begs of her:

> Pray say no more. I feel that all the apologies should be on my side. Let us forgive each other at once. We must do whatever is to be done quickest, and I think our feelings will lose no time there.

At the beginning of the novel Emma is not mature enough to appreciate Jane. She has been confined more or less to Hartfield and has hardly suffered vexation or distress. Jane has had a much broader education than Emma, seen more and had to adjust, like Fanny Price, to moving from life with one family to another. Moreover, she has developed a far stronger sense that 'Life is real! Life is earnest!' (Longfellow, 'A Psalm of Life') as a result of being brought up knowing that she has her own living to make. One cannot imagine Jane Fairfax wasting time over a riddle book. Throughout her ordeal her good sense and strength of character have shown her for the adult that she is.

During the course of the novel, however, Emma has grown morally and intellectually. She had many fine traits in the first place. But in the beginning she would rather be considered clever than *think through* what it means to be good. She can never be an Anne Elliot or a Mrs Weston but at times she is beginning to sound more like them. It is both ironic and revealing to hear Emma echo a sentiment of Mr Knightley's that for she and Jane runs deep: 'Oh! if you knew how much I love everything that is decided and open!' (vol. 3, ch. 16).

At last Jane and Emma are beginning to trust one another. Mr Knightley has taught Emma much, not least that Jane would make a suitable companion.

But it is Jane Fairfax herself, uncomplaining in her rapidly varying plight, who has brought home to Emma how much she is to be respected. Jane also points the way to the duty that woman owes to woman in their complicated lot.

20 Loves

20.1 Enthusiastic men

'hard at work upon the lower buttons of his thick leather gaiters' (vol. 2, ch. 15).

Fences and drains

In *Emma* there is an unusually full picture of male preoccupation, pursued with enthusiasm. Men move briskly in and out of Highbury. They ride and walk alone, manage and cultivate acres. They go to market where they bid for produce and have theirs bidden for.

Land-owner and magistrate, Mr Knightley is arguably the most fully developed male character in Jane Austen. He is active in a world which is not co-terminus with the central concerns of the novel; he runs parish meetings and an estate; he confers with local farmers and his steward. Mr Knightley says he would rather spend the evening going over his accounts with William Larkins than attend the ball at the Crown. His engagement to Emma disturbs the male world of master and man.

Male company

The men go to their comparatively non-discriminatory whist club at the Crown. We occasionally over-hear masculine conversation. The Coles give some all-male dinner parties. Perhaps this is where Mr Knightley gains insight into the vulgarity and indiscretion of Mr Elton?

Emma affords examples of male affection. Mr Cole and Mr Elton are very close, as are George Knightley and Robert Martin. The Knightleys' brotherly tie means 'either . . . would do anything for the good of the other' (vol. 1, ch. 12).

20.2 Marriage and independence

'the question of dependence or independence' (vol.1, ch. 1)

An establishment of one's own

Mr Knightley sees marriage as admirable because it gives women an establishment of their own.

In this, he contrasts with Mr Woodhouse. The latter sees it as a kind of death. Mr Knightley argues strongly for Miss Taylor's marrying. Similarly, he says that marriage to Robert Martin will give Harriet respectability, prosperity and happiness. He may disapprove of Frank, but would hardly wish Jane to be a governess. He would be the first to acknowledge that she deserves the independence Frank Churchill has to offer.

Sacrificing Donwell

Emma puts forward an excellent case for her own celibacy and we appreciate the argument that she makes for Mr Knightley's remaining single. Yet he chooses to marry a woman who, despite their similarities, is very different from himself. Emma reaches what she cannot approach rationally via her fancy; her intuitions can achieve a penetration that Mr Knightley lacks. She also brings a lightness of touch. Mr Knightley can be stolid; Emma renders him more airy. Perhaps he loves her for that?

Yet for much of the novel Emma, like her father, would reduce herself and Mr Knightley to fruitless atrophy. He must inhabit Donwell, solo, till he drops, but frequently visit her airless (pun intended?) place.

Once Emma and Mr Knightley reach their understanding, he is prepared to sacrifice Donwell, temporarily, extending the generosity which has always allowed Hartfield's claim to the John Knightleys. Although, Emma loves Donwell, she postpones it, too, for her father's sake.

Mr Knightley and Emma unite, in spite of a sturdy, mutual independence of every sort.

20.3 Love of mischief

'a source of high entertainment to you, to feel that you were taking us all in' (vol. 3, ch. 18)

Bifurcation

Emma is a carefully designed novel. It rests on a series of bifurcations.

To bifurcate is to have, or to divide into, two branches.

Bifurcation is the basis of irony. Emma reads 'truths' in one direction only to discover that they lie in another.

The central love story epitomizes bifurcation. Ronald Blythe quotes R. Liddell in *The Novels of Jane Austen* (Longman's, 1963):

> 'Highbury thinks Mr Knightley is . . . [Emma's] brother, but he is her future husband; Highbury thinks Frank Churchill is her future husband, but he is her brother.' Emma, the personification of Highbury, thinks so too, and so the magnificent central action of the novel, usually referred to as 'the intrigue' by its critics, is revealed.
> Introduction to the Penguin Library edition of *Emma,* (London: 1966) p. 22

Mild mischief

Emma's self-deception concerning Mr Elton's love for Harriet hinges on bifurcation.

Emma has plenty of evidence that she, not Harriet, is Mr Elton's object, but she misreads the clues.

Emma used to have 'a great passion for taking likenesses' (vol. 1, ch. 6). Regarding Mr Elton, she does not have her eye in at all!

Emma's Damascus road

When Emma appreciates the enormity of her error, she resolves never to interfere again. But she formulates a plan for Harriet and Frank Churchill which proves a greater travesty. That Emma and her protégée end up vying for the same man is ironic and inevitable.

> The fun of the novel lies in its portrait of a myopic detective, sure of her own investigative ability, but continually taken aback by the mysterious turn of events.
> I. Milligan, *Studying Jane Austen*, (London: Longman, 1988) p.105

When Emma thinks herself a little in love with Frank, she ponders symptoms. Frank senses that she does not love him. He knows what being in love feels like. Eventually Emma does too.

Love, Emma suddenly recognizes, is an imperative.

With the truth about Emma's feelings for Mr Knightley comes the truth about everything. Love renders Emma stricken with conscience in proportion to her blame. She acknowledges Mr Knightley's insight. 'With unsufferable vanity had she believed herself in the secret of everybody's feelings . . . She was proved to have been universally mistaken;' (vol. 3, ch. 11).

Bifurcation and Duplicity

A complex example of bifurcation is the duplicity practised on Highbury by Jane Fairfax and Frank Churchill.

When Jane and Frank step into Highbury two worlds exist simultaneously – the world in which each acts to avoid suspicion and the 'true' world which can only be acknowledged on rare occasions.

Jane Austen's maintenance of these two worlds in a long and complex novel discloses an important feature about the narrative.

The subtlety and the extravagance of the bifurcation can only fully be appreciated on a second reading.

Frank and Jane's duplicity is complicated by Emma's determination still to live in a world of her imagination. She deceives herself about Jane. Moreover, Frank deceives her about Jane *and* herself.

Jane is almost passive under the weight of her secret engagement. Frank courts subterfuge, manipulating Highbury with relish; he also manipulates Emma as she previously manipulated Harriet. Ronald Blythe pin-points the difference between Frank and Jane:

> He sees no harm in the secret. Bradbrook sees him as a bit of a dandy who has received an aristocratic education based on Lord Chesterfield's concept of the lesser truth being adequate when the whole truth is not expedient. For Jane it is the opposite; her culture rests on truth seen as absolute, as it must. Her love for Frank seduces her into agreeing to a short term suspension of the truth and this strikes at the roots of her self-respect.
> (Introduction to the Penguin English Library edition of *Emma*, 1966 p. 25)

Scandalous thoughts

Meanwhile, Emma hits on a preposterous notion. Only in Emma's febrile imagination could the essentially decorous Miss Fairfax be 'adulterously' involved. It is ironic that Emma suspects a young, *married* man from Weymouth days, not the single Frank Churchill.

Three in a bind

Emma is very taken by Frank; (she enjoys sporting him like a trophy.) But one wonders why Frank feels the need to make Emma his object. (He could have chosen to be civil, but non-committal, to a number of Highbury's young women.) Their circumstances render friendship almost inevitable, and parental expectations give him a good excuse, in his eyes, for flirtation. But he engages with Emma *regardless of Jane.*

Frank knows Jane is his, and, for him, she is the perfect woman. But Emma is exciting and fun, and he need not engage his heart. What is Jane supposed to think? Until they quarrel, Frank does not appear to explain to Jane that he uses Emma as a blind. She has not known Frank long, and although they met frequently at Weymouth, it would have been in others' company. She must wonder how far their secret 'understanding' goes. She surely feels envious? Emma is beautiful and, superficially, more Frank's type. Jane must also understand the Westons' special interest in promoting the match. Moreover, Emma, like Frank, is rich and prominent; Jane has nothing.

'This gallant young man, who seemed to love without feeling . . .' (vol. 3, ch. 5) sums up Frank. His decision to court Emma is a prime example of his impetuosity and his insouciance concerning both Emma and Jane. He later says that he was sure Emma did not love him, but how could he be certain?

Manipulations

Very soon there are multiple manipulations. Frank leads Emma to believe that he is romantically struck. He also manipulates his father, by confiding in him that he 'admired her extremely' (vol.2, chap. 7). Mr Weston manipulates Emma by passing on Frank's remark.

Frank appears continually to criticize Jane. Actually, his remarks skip in and out of 'truth'. He speaks with purity only when he speaks from the heart: 'I cannot keep my eyes from her' (vol. 2 chap. 8).

Emma's relationship with Frank demonstrates how greedy she is for discerning recognition. Mr Knightley mainly criticizes her.

The ambiguity of gifts

Frank's ordering of the pianoforte is an obtuse act. It makes Jane the gossip of Highbury.

Frank's is a rash, reckless love – one that springs surprises through impulse and passion.

The scene where Emma hears the new piano is the supreme example of Frank's duplicity. He manages to communicate with both Jane and Emma, but

Frank's *meaning* is for Jane alone, although Emma thinks he is being outrageous to entertain *her*. However, *Jane* cannot be sure about this.

Emma's preenings and blushings are in the dark. Frank, wickedly, is revealed working on a pair of spectacles. Jane is in the dark too. The scene is full of sexual, as well as narratorial, charge, and painfully puzzling for Jane. In the face of her potential rival Jane can be sure of nothing. Even as Frank kneels with her, 'fixing' her piano, she cannot know for certain that their object is his gift.

That this model of decorum, rationality, moral refinement and intellectual rigour should be irresistibly attracted to an erratic dilettante shows the enigmatic force of love.

But the above description sells Frank short. He tempts Emma with the best (baked) apple. He rides a 'blameless' (vol. 3, ch. 6) black mare. Things heat up when Frank visits Donwell and at Box Hill they get even hotter. He is Jane Austen's most intelligent, slippery and mysterious rogue. Yet Frank is in thrall to Jane's goodness as well as to her beauty, and there is a force that binds them – music.

The deceiver deceived

In a novel of 'double-think', there is an unexpected pleasure (again only experienced on second reading) of seeing the biter bit.

Frank can misread Emma as well as the other way round.

For some reason, he thinks that Emma may have suspicions about Miss Fairfax and him. It is amusing that Frank, like Harriet, credits Emma with being exceptionally clear-sighted when she is not. He nearly confides in her, but as ever she misreads his motive. Frank is as keenly aware as Mr Knightley of how clever Emma is. Moreover, he is fond of her. This is fertile ground for extravagant appraisal, as Harriet proves regarding Mr Knightley. He is 'five hundred million times . . . above me' (vol. 3, ch. 11).

Emma and Frank deserve one another. Both manipulators, they frequently manage to be at cross purposes.

Utter mischief

Continuous narratorial mischief, such as is hinted at above, is what makes reading *Emma* so exhilarating. It yields up different patterns, emphases, meanings with every fresh encounter. Even its apparently straightforward characters conceal as well as reveal. We are given the impression that none of the characters, Emma, Jane, Frank, even Mr Knightley, quite knows what they are, what they are saying or doing, or what they might mean by it.

Recovered?

Reading *Emma* generates for many an overwhelming desire to *re*-read it, in order, the second time, to pick up on the clues. But the first reading is, in a sense, the purest. It is the one that equates most closely with living a life. We can only *cover* life, we cannot *re*-cover it, any more than we can recover from it. We may inveigh against Jane Austen for hoodwinking us, in the tradition of the best mystery stories. But don't we, inevitably, hoodwink ourselves, and one another? To see the inherent absurdity of our situation given form in *Emma* is a curious relief.

20.4 Love and Mr Knightley

'How long had Mr Knightly been so dear to her . . . ?' (vol. 3, ch. 6)

Perhaps the most destabilizing irony in *Emma* is that it is a love story about two people who do not know they are in love. Emma views Mr Knightley as at odds with her because he points out her errors. Emma clearly enjoys verbal sparring and sets herself up in deliberate opposition.

The central attachment between Emma and Mr Knightley is subtly delineated but veiled. Emma is strangely unaware of herself and him as sexual beings but *is* conscious of his physical impact. She is energized by others' desire and by her sister's children.

In retrospect it is obvious what Emma and Mr Knightley share. They respect family harmony and adopt diversionary tactics when it is threatened. They cooperate instinctively. They work in partnership, separately running Hartfield's affairs. They prioritize one another in their thoughts though Emma *imagines* that Frank is 'Always the first person to be thought of!' (vol. 2, ch. 14). Emma, like Harriet, clings to irrelevancies: 'Stop; Mr Knightley was standing just here, was not he?' (vol. 3, ch. 4). Mr Knightley clings to Emma's book list!

The couple reach their understanding through mutual selflessness. Their love is based on tested friendship. In a highly plotted novel there proves to be no need to plot at all.

Emma provides her namesake with a series of tests which for a long time she fails. With neat inversion, this maiden has to win her Knight-ley. In return, Mr Knightley rescues *her*, lifting her beyond Highbury on the occasion of their honeymoon. He takes her to the ocean which Emma has never seen before.

20.5 Love of nature

'out of doors' (vol. 3, ch. 6)

Good shepherds

Jane Austen is not Wordsworth nor Rousseau but she perhaps shares some of their preoccupations. Both poet and philosopher were interested in people who live close to nature. The latter championed the role of the nursing mother.

Emma jerks Harriet away from 'what comes naturally', the first stirrings of love for a young farmer, simultaneously in love with Harriet and with his farm. Such an alliance Emma believes would be a 'degradation' (vol. 1, ch. 8). Yet Harriet is at her happiest in a farmer's parlour or communing with his cows.

Mr Knightley shares her enthusiasm for the byre and the midden. He counts Robert Martin among his closest friends, admitting to Emma that he could as ill dispense with him as he could with William Larkins.

Both his right hand men have names reminiscent of birds. House martin comes to mind for Robert. Did William bequeath himself to H. E Bates, whose irrepressible scrapdealer farmer bears his name in *The Darling Buds of May*?

Abbey Mill Farm, by its very name, suggests responsible cultivation and honourable toil. It is beautiful – 'sweet to the eye and sweet to the mind' with its apple orchards, 'meadows in front and the river making a close and handsome curve around it' (vol. 3, ch. 6). Emma causes Harriet temporarily to lose this earthly Eden.

20.6 Mother love

'baby was fetched' (vol. 3, ch. 8)

Emma aims to give Harriet more 'elegance' (vol. 1, ch. 3) and offers Hartfield as her second home. But it is Mrs *God*dard's (our italics) attention that Harriet craves when she is unwell. This motherly woman dresses her pupils' chilblains, gives them plenty of wholesome food and leaves them free to run around.

Elegance has a lot to answer for. Had it jerked Emma away from her mother's breast, as it had jerked Jane Austen and almost certainly Frank Churchill, placing them at the mercy of a wet nurse? Harriet was certainly wrenched away from her mother, and for ever. As in Shakespeare's plays, *Emma* abounds in absent mothers. Emma, Isabella, Harriet, Frank, Jane – all have been motherless since infancy.

It is Mrs Elton who draws attention to the centrality of mothering to the good life. She pinpoints the great attraction of Mrs Weston – 'there is something so motherly . . . about her' (vol. 2, ch. 14). Mrs Weston shares her name – Anne – with the Virgin's mother. One cannot help wondering whether she holds out against the conventions of gentility and is breast-feeding little Anna.

Mrs Elton's sister, Selina Suckling, (suckling: 'a young creature yet fed by the pap' Johnson) is also a mother, as her name so hilariously – doubtless misleadingly – suggests. So are Mrs Bragge, the impatient Mrs *Small*ridge (our italics) and (perhaps) Mrs Partridge. Surely Jane Austen chose their names mischievously? All, together with the former Miss *Hawk*ins, are puffed up: 'Wax-candles in the school room! You may imagine how desirable!' (vol. 2, ch. 7). But Jane Austen is serious, even at her funniest. Mrs Suckling and Mrs Bragge are patronesses of schools. One blanches, almost as much as one chills at the thought of Mr Elton's blessing Emma's and Harriet's wedding and Jane's turning from Frank to make a pact with Mrs Elton.

What kind of mother would Mrs Elton make? She wants 'everything to be as natural . . . as possible', and to *her* specification, at the Donwell strawberry picking. She wants to 'play at' gypsies (see 20.14), sporting a basket adorned with ribbon. She also wants to arrive with Jane Fairfax and Miss Bates on donkeys, like a burlesque of the flight from Egypt, with 'my caro sposo walking by' (vol. 3, ch. 6). It is Miss Bates who recognizes that there is something queen-like about 'Augusta'. She carries a gold and purple reticule.

20.7 Father love

'accountable to nobody but her father' (vol. 1, ch. 5)

Pastoral care?

And Mr Elton as father? He is sneering and unkind, but Mrs Elton is worse. Mr Elton lives, according to who is bearing witness, in a 'blessed abode' or 'an old and not very good house' (vol. 1, ch. 10). Mr *(H)el-ton* (our italics) and his wife could take a heavy toll on Highbury. Are we to infer that it could become a *Helltown* under Mr Elton's ministry? As vicar Mr Elton is almost certainly a magistrate too. We know he breaches priestly confidentiality. (But Perry also divulges professional information.)

Will it depend, perhaps, as with others in the novel, on how far the Eltons can 'get away with it'? At the ball at the Crown it is Mr Knightley who wins the day. As Mrs Elton puts it 'Mr E is Knightley's right hand man' (vol. 3, ch. 16). If this is the case, who is *supposed* to be the 'sinister' one?

Mr Woodhouse

Mr Woodhouse believes that Emma is a seer. She is not. He also believes her to be perfect. Others do too. The only person who dares find fault with her openly is Mr Knightley, the 'ideal' father whom Emma never had. It seems inevitable that Emma should marry someone sixteen years older than herself. It is almost Freudian that her husband-to-be agrees to live in her father's house. We are told that the only person who could handle Emma was her clever mother. Are contemporary psychologists right? Is this genetic attraction? Does Mr Knightley replace, not only for Emma but in a sense for Mr Woodhouse, the brilliant, all-reassuring mother whom Emma lost so young?

20.8 Self-love

'so very superior to all other pork' (vol. 2, ch. 3)

Narcissism

Narcissim blinds Emma. She is opinionated, and her opinions run away with her. Jane Austen recognizes that young opinion, like young love, has its tyrannical face.

Emma is impossible, but from the outset shows moral promise. She combines the perfectionism of a hostess, determined to impress, with '*the real good will* of a mind delighted with its own ideas' (vol. 1, ch. 3, our italics.)

Emma disconcerts because her weaknesses are her strengths. She is a questing creature. Unlike Harriet, she would never be content to 'hear and believe' (vol. 1, ch. 4). She may at times terrify, through her capacity to play at snake, but she seems prepared to try to learn by her mistakes. There is hope for Emma. She believes that living a life is the best investment for old age. Mrs Elton *claims* inner 'resources' (vol. 2, ch. 14); Emma *has* them.

Partiality

An extension of narcissism is partiality. Partiality to self will never concede Mrs Elton self-knowledge, and is Emma's initial bane. Partiality towards others is a blindness from which not even Mr Knightley and Jane are exempt.

Family partiality is shown to be both natural and dangerous. People tend to take others' offspring at their parents' evaluation. This is partly what makes Harriet such a poignant case. There is something lemming-like about Highbury's acceptance of Frank, sight unseen, as one of its 'boasts' (vol. 1, ch. 2). Like a family, a village is shown to demonstrate a naïve conceit which renders it gullible and vulnerable.

20.9 Love of ideas

'It is a very simple story.' (vol. 3, ch. 8)

Grounded

Highbury is a meticulously imagined Surrey village which forms the scaffold for the amatory, social and moral skirmishes of its inhabitants and new comers. Never was a novel more grounded (see 17).

Yet in no other Austen novel does the word 'idea' have such prominence. *Emma* is about the confidence and error of youth. It is also about shame, pain, suffering, guilt, treachery, betrayal, cruelty, misery, sin, temptation, sacrifice, repentance, judgement, justice and forgiveness. There might be some justification for calling *Emma* a novel of ideas.

Its implications are very dark. Yet it is a great comedy of manners and a compelling love story. For all the depths of its shadows, and the profundity of the questions it never answers, it seems an optimistic, even at times a downright happy, book. *Emma* grows slowly and painfully into a triumphant celebration of human compassion and forgiveness. Love is its ultimate force.

Nevertheless, the up-beat ending is only that; it is not the final resonance. *Emma* is a book that could induce nightmares if you think about it long enough.

Flawed

Emma's 'blessings' (vol. 1, ch. 1) prove curses. Far from being the genius of Surrey, she proves she is a part of struggling humanity, with all that implies for better or for worse. We may not like Emma, as Jane Austen predicted. Perhaps because she reminds us uncomfortably of ourselves?

We're all capable of 'doing an Emma'. She does not *know* what she's doing half the time, though she feels sure that she is right. She certainly doesn't know what her meaning implies. Pride and self-love make her cruel. She proves that she would, in her own words, 'rather have been merry than wise' (vol. 2, ch. 12). When proved wrong, she can never quite forgive herself. Emma, who 'could not forgive' Jane Fairfax (vol. 2, ch. 3), *is* forgiven, though.

Emma seems to triumph in the end more by moral luck than by good judgement, as does Frank. Are we even right to think of Emma as a heroine? Is she not rather Jane Austen's most intelligent villainess? She is chastened when she hurts Miss Bates and sacrifices the good opinion of Mr Knightley. But does she recover too fast? Does Mr Knightley forgive her too readily? Is she a temptress we can trust with the Donwell apples? And if she even remotely reminds us of ourselves, where does this leave *us*?

Jane Austen demonstrates in *Emma* that anybody's reading of any situation is taken from a terrifyingly limited, because egocentric, perspective. This applies both individually and on a global scale. 'I . . . have no self-command without a motive,' Frank says (vol. 3, ch. 7). *Emma* challenges all motivation. Is the final arbiter our own safety and pleasure, the novel might ask. Or is it something else? Above all, what might this *mean*?

20.10 Love of meaning

'What do you mean?' cried Emma . . . 'Good Heaven! what do you mean?' . . . Her voice was lost . . . in great terror. (vol. 2, ch. 14)

Sows' ears

Emma, like Frank, loves to talk, but she is naïve in her use of words. She holds out to Harriet the apple of 'a little more knowledge'. This, she believes, combined with a little more 'elegance' will make Harriet '*quite perfect*' (vol. 1, ch. 3, our italics).

Emma carelessly volleys moral absolutes. In her eagerness to form Harriet's opinions she reveals herself as an imperialist over meaning. She snatches language from her narrator, whose function is to grant her silk words loaded with moral and spiritual significance. Emma is impatient over most things. She works with passion, in a rush. In this she differs from Jane (except in extremis) and Mr Knightley. Both are more restrained and careful over words. They take their time to make decisions or draw conclusions.

Jane Austen cares about meaning. She opens to question what her characters 'mean by that' in almost every word they utter. She is aware that words may mean directly opposed things to different people. What Emma reads as 'useful' (vol. 1, ch. 4) behaviour towards Harriet Mr Knightley might read as dangerous. However, Emma deals out meaning with the thoughtless deftness with which she probably deals out cards. She is 'quick and assured' (vol. 1, ch. 5) in everything. She has had to be, to cope with a father who always procrastinates.

Through its scrupulous examination of meaning in the mouths and minds of flawed humanity, *Emma* draws attention to the inevitability of error in a world without absolutes - except as ideas – a 'fallen world', to put it emblematically. If Mr Knightley is Emma's hair shirt, *Emma* could be ours.

Unstable?

Ideas may proliferate, but story is all. Even a sense of the narrator in *Emma* is as cloaked, and recedes as elusively, as everything else. What Jane Austen gives us is a tale that bears witness, by her judicious, scrupulously placed words, quivering with suggestibility, to the essential unreliability of every narrative and every reading. She destabilizes meaning and defies interpretation. Characters shimmy in and out of getting it 'right', both in the sense of reading accurately and being morally aware. Words in an Austen novel, perhaps particularly in *Emma*, act like strobe lightning. They flicker in and out of absurdity; you might fear that they could induce a fit even as you think they might make 'sense'. One might be excused the idea, when reading *Emma*, that silence is the purest form of meaning, along with a blank page.

But Jane Austen does not advocate silence, even though silences in successive novels may increase. As far as we know, she continued writing and talking as long as she could. Rather than vaunting silence she seems to suggest: put your trust in the word. The word is mightier than we are, though its meaning may elude.

20.11 Love of place

'My heart was in Highbury.' (vol. 3, ch. 14)

Highbury

Frank Churchill loves Highbury. Emma despises it. It takes Frank's enthusiasm to make her reconsider. We can see there might be parallels between the narrowness of Highbury and Emma herself. Highbury endears and repels by turns.

Emma seems, at times, less a woman, more a way of life. *If* it is not stretching things too far to suggest that *Emma* is simultaneously a person and a universal condition of being, then perhaps 'Highbury' is everywhere? Everywhere where humans sink and soar, aspire and fail, at every turn?

England

When Emma is at Donwell she, along with others, appreciates England: 'English verdure, English culture, English comfort, seen under a sun bright without being oppressive' (vol. 3, ch. 6). Donwell reflects its owner, a man of courtly manners, direct and true. He shares a Christian name with England's patron saint.

Donwell

Donwell is a focus in the lives of all Highbury's inhabitants. Donwell: now owned by a rational, generous, kindly man, once a religious, then a desecrated, foundation. Emma looks forward to dwelling there with the keenest appreciation. But in the novel she never quite reaches it. (She visits it just once.) In fact, her ultimate horror is the dread of its loss: 'if to these losses, the loss of Donwell were to be added . . . How was it to be endured?' (vol. 3, ch. 12)

Hartfield

It is Hartfield that becomes the archetypal home, an earthly sanctuary for love, marital and cross-generational. It is simultaneously the 'field of the heart' (seat of love) and 'the field of the hart' (preserve of a male animal, the deer – pun intended?).

However, Hartfield is currently presided over by a *female,* the male having abnegated his responsibility. It will be inherited by a female too. There seems to be no threat of an entail hanging over Hartfield.

Flying to nowhere?

The very title, *Emma,* might invoke speculation. At Box Hill Mr Weston makes her name into a conundrum. 'What two letters of the alphabet . . . express perfection?' (This, after Emma has just demonstrated her capacity to be morally bereft!) Mr Knightley's response is 'gravely' laconic: 'This explains the kind of clever thing that is wanted, and Mr Weston has done very well for himself; but he must have knocked up everybody else. *Perfection* should not have come quite so soon' (vol. 3, ch. 7).

The novel is full of a longing for perfection. It starts with Emma's looking forward to Christmas. Eventually Emma weeps to be good. Robert and Harriet, Jane and Frank,

Emma and George Knightley – we see all of them wretched; all of them yearn. *Emma* is contained in the word 'enigma', with a doubling up appropriate to a novel that requires a double-take. *If* we see in *Emma* not only a woman but a way of being, might it also be, like *Utopia* or *Erewhon*, a seemingly impossible place?

20.12 Love of love

'which is very odd!' (vol. 1, ch. 4)

Romance

Emma is a wild romantic, though scared silly at the thought of love for herself. She proves a novice at reading love. But she is not the only one. The same can be said at least of Harriet, Mr Elton and the apparently impeccable Mr Knightley himself.

Hood-winked

Mr Knightley *seems* absurd in his final estimation of Emma: 'faultless in spite of all her faults' (vol. 3, ch. 8). He waives what was 'badly done indeed!' (vol. 3, ch. 7) because Emma shows remorse. Jane is as generous as Mr Knightey. The implication is that love *has* to be prepared to overlook our errors. That is what makes love love. *Love* is blind, as well as Emma. Cupid is the 'hood-wink'd boy' (vol. 1, ch. 9).

20.13 Love of laughs

'without our sighing out our souls over this charade' (vol. 1, ch. 9)

Jokes

Emma is full of hidden jokes. It is only when you start putting one and one together that you wonder whether Jane Austen might be tipping us the wink. Jokes doubtless lie undiscovered in *Emma.* In some ways Jane Austen seems like Jane Fairfax, admirably careless about whether she pleases or not.

What are you like?

Jane Austen writes comedy because comedy is built into the human condition. We try so hard, but we're hilarious. It's not only because we're mottled morally that 'motley is the only wear' (*As You Like It* Act 2, Sc. 7).

Goodness and absurdity reach their apotheosis in Miss Bates. Her spinsterhood is triumphant, for ever connected, for ever separate, universally loving. The same can be said of Mr Knightley, whether he embraces matrimony or not.

Miss Bates is a paradox. Her conversation is unadulterated autobiography, yet she never thinks of herself. She is poor, yet believes herself inexpressibly blessed. Like Emma, she enjoys 'all that' is 'enjoyable to the utmost' (vol. 1, ch. 14). She makes way for Mrs Elton. She loves all her neighbours, yet is incurably partisan when it comes to Jane.

20.14 Love of all

'Emma, I accept your offer.' (vol. 3, ch. 8)

A personist?

Jane Austen has been embraced by feminism but makes no claims to moral high-ground on behalf of either sex. She simply scrambles roles, substituting a female figure where tradition, including that of Christianity, has presupposed a male, and vice versa. It is Emma who offers Mr Knightley the friendship that both can then redefine as romantic love. It is Mr Knightley who offers childcare when Emma seems to have much on her plate, including the possible pursuit of romance via someone other than himself. It is Mrs Churchill who, by her death, saves Jane from having to serve the Elton set. This suggests the mysterious nature of chance. Earlier Frank, in the same boat as Jane, had failed her (unlike Mr Dixon).

Beyond the fringe

Not the least of *Emma*'s interest lies in its fringe characters, in those of humanity who breach space currently occupied by others, either by seizure or invitation.

Gypsies (see 20.6) infiltrate the parish and Mr Knightley has to cope with them. A child of the deserving poor is invited by Emma into Hartfield. Emma, more than any other Austen heroine, takes her charity work seriously, right into the houses of the poor. The fate of fricassée of chicken and asparagus, served up with delicious irony, is all the more tasty set against charity broth. Foreshadowed in the tale of Harriet and the gypsies, and the silent appeal of the hungry of *Emma* to be fed, are asylum seekers, freedom fighters, homicide bombers, all those who feel marginalized or who starve. Globalization is prefigured in Austen's work. The monstrous gap between rich and poor was as glaring then as now. Adult slavery has been abolished, but what about the child?

20 15 Love of forms

'the proper form' (vol. 1, ch. 9)

Love of virtue

Although there is nothing to suggest that Jane Austen read Plato, in *Emma* she arguably seems drawn towards what the philosopher called 'forms' in 'The Republic', for example, beauty, The Good.

Emma means well by matchmaking. She seems to grasp instinctively that if a couple is well suited, if their love is based in reciprocated spirit, which might include honour, respect, shared glee and the deep mystery of sexual attraction, their capacity to disseminate good to one another and beyond, and to bring up any children well, is incalculable. Emma wants to help others to find this love. She is groping after something which is way beyond her reach. Whereas Plato's 'forms' are not quite of this world, Emma tries to do good in the here and now. However, she is living demonstration, through her shameless meddling, that what we intend as love of others can so easily prove to be love of self.

Emma challenges our ideas about goodness. Mrs Weston is the embodiment of 'the Angel of the House' as defined by Virginia Woolf:

> She was intensely sympathetic. . . . She was utterly unselfish. She excelled in the difficult arts of family life. She sacrificed herself daily . . .
> Professions For Women: from *Collected Essays* vol. II edited by Leonard Woolf: (London: the Hogarth Press, 1931)

But Mr Knightley does not consider that Mrs Weston was a good governess and her author unflinchingly demonstrates her gullibility. Mr Knightley, her most discerning fan as well as her keenest critic, provides her complement. In Mr Knightley we see a goodness that has grits.

Love of beauty

Emma is hung up on looks. She crudely dismisses Robert Martin as 'very plain indeed'. Harriet is in possession of the riddle of such matters. Knowing Robert, she no longer thinks of him as 'so very plain...One doesn't, you know, after a while'. (vol. 1, ch. 4)

When Emma comes to sketch Harriet, she exaggerates her beauty and distorts the likeness. Mr Knightley points this out baldly: 'You have made her too tall, Emma.' Mrs Weston goes further: 'Miss Smith has not those eye-brows and eye-lashes. It is the fault of her face that she has them not'. (vol. 1, ch. 6).

Why does Emma exaggerate Harriet's image? Partly because she aspires to an 'Exactly so!' of a love match. But Emma is mesmerized by beauty. She admires it in Harriet and in the very different Miss Fairfax. She appreciates it in landscape and pursues it at Donwell.

Mr Knightley concedes *Emma's* beauty – 'I love to look at her;' (vol. 1, ch. 5) – but it doesn't *appear* to compel him in the same way. He doesn't forget, or over-look, everything else.

Emma seems in pursuit of an ideal form, something that is never quite before her eyes. Perhaps Emma has something in common with Yeats, who speaks in a woman's voice in his poem *Before The World Was Made* (1929)?

> If I make the lashes dark
> And the eyes more bright
> And the lips more scarlet,
> Or ask if all be right
> From mirror after mirror,
> No vanity's displayed;
> I'm looking for the face I [she] had
> Before the world was made.

Emma is an artist, after all. She is hasty in executing, and dismissive of, her portraits, but recognizes, with delight, when 'The corner of the sofa is very good'(vol. 1, ch. 6). She is never satisfied, but keeps returning to, and is absorbed by, the human form.

Love of truth

Emma's primal error – you can see it in her art – is that she assumes she will have access to the truth if only she tries hard and often enough. Frank, who is far from frank, aims for truth too: 'Then I will speak the truth – and nothing suits me so well' (vol. 2, ch. 6).

Emma grants the Knightley brothers 'penetration' (vol. 1,ch. 16) and aspires to it herself. Unwisely she attributes 'no penetration' (vol. 1, ch. 4) to Harriet. What she herself causes to happen in that quarter, of course, proves her agonizingly wrong.

20.16 Love of God

'between us, I am convinced there never can be any likeness' (vol. 1, ch. 10)

Baby

As *Emma* draws to a close we have a birth and a death – the death of Mrs Churchill and the birth of Anna Weston. In the mutual embarrassment of Frank's and Emma's reunion, a baby helps to save the day – Mrs Weston's baby girl. Earlier, Isabella's and John's baby daughter heals the breach between Emma and Mr Knightley. Children, as elsewhere in comedy, afford another opportunity, a fresh start.

'The wishes, the hopes'

Is *'Emma'* a 'religious', or a 'spiritual', book? Perhaps it depends what one means by religious and spiritual. It is the life that we share that is its subject. It may work itself out through images and ideas associated with Christianity more profoundly than is at first apparent. But what it seems concerned with is the unfathomable and chequered capacity that each human life has for what we call goodness and wickedness in the world. Whether the reader is theist, agnostic or atheist, perhaps we share a similar experience when reading *Emma*? That we are all 'in it together, and in a fog?

The novel ends with people being astonishingly compassionate towards one another. What we *are* assured of is that, in spite of 'deficiencies', 'the wishes, the hopes, the confidence, the predictions of the small band of true friends . . . were fully answered in the perfect happiness of the union' of Emma and Mr Knightley. (vol. 3, ch. 11). Earthly bliss for those two is realized. But we know that nothing has been resolved, and that they, and the whole of Highbury, still have everything to prove. Their burdens and responsibilities are awesome. Their heritage is all history, and beyond that, in space and time. They are creating the future for each other, as are we all.

Part VI

Persuasion

21 Anne and the other characters

21.1 Anne as romantic heroine

'Anne, with an elegance of mind and sweetness of character, which must have placed her high with any people of real understanding.' (vol. 1, ch. 1)

The centre of it all

Anne Elliot has the qualities that Captain Wentworth attributes to a nut: 'To exemplify, – a beautiful glossy nut, which, blessed with original strength, has outlived all the storms of autumn' (vol. 1, ch. 10).

The point of the narrative is that the heroine of *Persuasion* 'has outlived the storms' without losing her fortitude. This is what her former lover Captain Wentworth has to come to see.

Anne is the centre – the kernel – of *Persuasion* in at least two other ways.

Anne is the moral centre; other characters are measured against her sense, sensitivity and practicality.

She is also the centre in a formal sense:

Anne is the most fully realized and richly varied character.

This is a function of Jane Austen's narratorial strategy:

The reader is directly acquainted with Anne's thoughts and feelings; the other characters are largely known through Anne's perceptions of them.

In no other novel is the narratorial distinction so sharp. Compared to her, the others are conveyed in far less detail.

21.2 Thoughts and feelings

'She was deep in the happiness of such misery, or the misery of such happiness, instantly.' (vol. 2, ch. 11)

Anne 'had been forced into prudence in her youth', only to learn 'romance as she grew older – the natural sequel of an unnatural beginning' (vol. 1, ch. 4).

The intense concentration on the central character results in *Persuasion*'s being the most interior of novels.

It is Anne's introspections that we are aware of in the first volume rather than her voice.

She has lived, and lives still, on memories, and, when Captain Wentworth comes on the scene, on reflections. She has achieved only a fragile accommodation in the eight years they have been apart.

Body and mind

When Captain Wentworth first visits Uppercross Cottage (vol. 1, ch. 7), experience becomes a matter of simple but essential terms. The syntax reflects this: 'Mary talked, but Anne could not attend. She had seen him. They had met.' Mary's conversation implies a world at large; Anne's is narrowed to a 'she' and a 'he'. Anne feverishly tries to blot out feelings with reason. But her hurt is as raw as ever.

Anne sees her lot as a moral struggle. She tries to 'harden her nerves' (vol. 1, ch. 4).

Anne's endeavours to calm herself are seen *by the reader* to be always at variance with her physical state. The problem Anne encountered over Captain Wentworth eight years ago is repeated. She battles between overwhelming feeling and the right way to behave.

Jane Austen creates a distinction between exhibited and concealed emotions; when Anne meets Mr Elliot in Bath she merely blushes (we are a long way from *Pride and Prejudice* at this point – see 10.1), whereas Captain Wentworth makes her heart beat faster. The reader might forgive the other characters for thinking that Anne is favouring Mr Elliot. All the signs are that she does. Only the reader can see that, in a way special to *Persuasion,* the external is of little consequence compared to the (agitated) workings of the human heart.

Resolution

Anne's character is created, as it were, from the inside. It is only when she has come to an inner resolution that she can act. When Anne reaches Bath she has made this change in mental outlook – she allows her body to have more of a mind of its own and she stops berating herself so much.

Anne is determined that she will take the initiative with Captain Wentworth.

Her inner resolve makes her stronger and more defiant towards family and friends.

At the concert she literally (and thereby metaphorically) makes an advance towards Captain Wentworth. Anne seems to lose her body completely, whereas before it had intruded itself painfully. The material world loses its significance: 'Anne saw nothing, thought nothing of the brilliancy of the room' (vol. 2, ch. 8).

Anne is finally integrated: emotions, reason, desire and a certainty of right. This is inward, and only the reader knows of it.

Pride

The distinction between Anne and the far less realized characters is evident in the matter of pride. In English (unlike Italian and Spanish) there is only one word for both the *sin* of pride and that proper feeling of pleasure in what is ours. We only see the proud outward boast of the Elliots, but with Anne we know those feelings that value place, tradition and inheritance.

Sir Walter's pride is self-regarding; by contrast, Anne's pride is not self-invested. As a consequence of this Anne empathizes strongly with others.

The inwardness of the novel is seen in the way that it is Anne who mediates to the reader the anguish of Charles Hayter's longing (see 23.4). As the one who registers what others are going through, she approaches being a surrogate narrator.

21.3 Silence and conversation

'How eloquent could Anne Elliot have been.' (vol. 1, ch. 4)

Silence

Silence is a token of inwardness. One of the most striking aspects of Anne in the first volume is her silence. She is particularly quiet at Kellynch, where Mrs Clay seems to have more to say than she does. As J. Wiltshire points out:

> Anne is without power in her family circle as she is at first without dramatic prominence in the text, but the narrative gradually becomes suffused with her presence, idioms and approach. (*The Cambridge Companion to Jane Austen*, Cambridge University Press, 1997, p. 76).

At the centre of the novel we see Anne at Uppercross, having done everything she can to help the Musgroves off to Lyme. Anne imagines the room, now occupied only by 'her silent pensive self', filled with happy, chattering people, 'all that was glowing and bright in prosperous love, all that was most unlike Anne Elliot!' (vol. 2, ch. 1; see 22.4).
The company is indeed unlike Anne: only she in the design of the novel is able to imagine and picture.

Articulacy

One of Anne's functions is to serve as the moral centre of the novel. (It is Captain Wentworth who has to adjust to *her.*) She is the touchstone for our judgements. Given the manner in which the full rendering of her character dominates the novel and given Jane Austen's preoccupation in *Persuasion* with right-minded behaviour, Anne has to be morally reliable, for otherwise the reader would have no bearings. She is a very different heroine from Emma.
Anne's speech gives the novel moral stability.

In spite of her silences, Anne always speaks out for what she believes is right.

This is apparent from her first speech in the novel. When her father is grudging about what he might allow his tenants access to, Anne immediately challenges him. Her speech about what is due to naval men shows herself at variance with her father in a number of ways.

Anne is suggesting that merit should determine social hierarchy.

Anne also challenges Admiral Croft, who considers Captain Benwick 'rather too piano for me' (vol. 2, ch. 6). She is speaking up for *herself* too, wishing to oppose 'the too common idea of spirit and gentleness being incompatible with each other'.
A feature of the novel's formal and moral design is that

Anne becomes increasingly articulate as the plot unfolds.

In Bath when she joins her family she withdraws a little, and for a while her speech is only reported. However, we hear her voice directly when she picks Mr Elliot up on the meaning of 'good company' (vol. 2, ch. 4). Her definition would certainly incorporate herself. We are told that in the past Captain Wentworth and she could never stop talking to one another.

Short speeches

Jane Austen does not give Anne long reflective speeches; her moral concern is given a bracing urgency by her pithy imperatives.

When others are despairing in Lyme, she simply and emphatically gets her message across. She demonstrates the strength that Captain Wentworth comes to recognize and admire.

Anne's last words to Captain Wentworth in the novel, the last words she speaks to anyone, are similarly brief. He asks whether she would have renewed their engagement if he had written to her when he had made a few thousand pounds: '"Would I!" was all her answer; but the accent was decisive enough' (vol. 2, ch. 11).

Compatible conversation

Anne talks readily with people whom she likes. She sustains conversation easily with Admiral and Mrs Croft, Captain Benwick and, initially, Mr Elliot. She enjoys chatting with Charles and Mrs Musgrove. Her most animated and lengthy speech is reserved for two people, though – Mrs Smith and Captain Harville.

With both of them she engages in a kind of debate.

Anne's eloquence emerges in heightened language.

The debate she holds with Mrs Smith concerns the opportunities a nurse has to witness human nature. Anne takes an 'elevated' view (vol. 2, ch. 5); her imaginative discernment of the many qualities demonstrated in the narrow space of the sickroom – 'fortitude, patience, resignation' – is enacted in her ardent and wondering cadences.

The second debate (vol. 2, ch. 11), about the relative constancy of men and women, occurs when Anne has become prominent in both word and action. She commands the attention of Captain Harville and Captain Wentworth. Anne's powers of articulation, which have been kept more or less restrained, are gradually released.

It is as if Anne has been inwardly practising for this debate for eight years.

It starts tentatively and in lowered tones. Anne's responses increase in length as she becomes more engaged and decided. The debate develops through increasingly committed argument and counter-argument, until Anne has the wisdom to say that nothing can be proved.

With this established, Captain Harville cries out his personal testimony, and Anne responds eagerly that she would never wish to 'undervalue the warmth and faithful feelings of any of my fellow creatures'. Anne speaks from her heart.

Here Anne is rendered silent once more. But it is not the cowed silence of the opening of the novel. It is the silence of one who has opted for self-expression and is overcome. Anne must speak as she feels. Captain Harville does not know that she is speaking about herself. But Captain Wentworth does, and she has not dropped her voice.

Anne has used all her powers of articulation to declare herself to Captain Wentworth.

She has submitted to feelings she had rationalized away at nineteen. Through speech she becomes the heroine of her own story.

21.4 Negotiation

'Anne had everything to do at once.' (vol. 1, ch. 7)

Kellynch Hall

In a novel concerned with changes in economic circumstances, it is important that one character – in this case, the central one – shows an awareness of the financial world.

Anne is trying to do the right thing by her family, and she is appreciated for none of it. In time, Anne's plans would have assured the continuity of Kellynch and all it stands for.

But it was not to be. Her plan would have destroyed Sir Walter's dignity, by which *he* means ostentatious display. Anne knows the difference between her interpretation of the word 'dignity' (doing one's duty by one's debtors) and her father's.

Mediation at Uppercross

In the midst of others who are not not so minutely drawn – Mary snobbish, the Musgrove girls lightly flirtatious, Mrs Musgrove comical in her simple pathos – Anne registers and responds to need. She listens, she accommodates herself, she distracts and, when necessary, tries to reason. As a fully realized character, she has all the features and mental resources to allow her to do these things. Mary soon rallies with Anne's company and Anne finds herself in her usual situation of useful arbiter.

In charge

It is fitting that the still centre of the novel is, in scenes of panic, the one stable character. Anne remains controlled and – as she is in the narrative, so in the story – in control.

When little Charles Musgrove injures his back and dislocates his collar bone, Anne sees to everything, including tempering the potential hysteria of his mother. Significantly, the apothecary issues his instructions to Anne and Charles and not to Mary. Anne is as fearless as Captain Wentworth is at sea in a domestic crisis.

The accident at Lyme

The accident at Lyme shows Anne's being appreciated for what she does by those, unlike Mary, who do not take her competence for granted. Anne thinks rationally. Typically practical, she carries salts, which can be applied immediately. While Captain Wentworth reels against the wall, she gives instructions. He repines; she issues sound suggestions. She is instinctive in her endeavours to help Henrietta and, when she can, looks to comfort the others. Charles and Captain Wentworth both turn to her for what to do next. That Captain Wentworth recognizes Anne's outstanding qualities is manifest in the debate about who will remain to to nurse Louisa: 'if Anne will stay, no one so proper, so capable, as Anne!' (vol. 1, ch. 12; see 22.4).

21.5 Anne's significance in relation to the other characters

'What should they do without her?' (vol. 2., ch. 1)

Confidante

Is there, for the reader, a mismatch between the responsive, finely nuanced Anne and the sometimes painfully comical narrowness of the other characters' emotional lives?

Anne is trusted. She hears opinions that show gross self-deception. Thinking of her problematic, inadequate son who died young, Mrs Musgrove sighs to Anne that he would probably have been another Captain Wentworth. This makes Anne subdue a smile but she 'listened kindly' (see 22.3). Perhaps that is as far as communication can go between a full character and a caricature. The problem with the centrality of Anne, the reader might feel, is that some conversations are not possible.

Helpmate

Anne as a helpmate is an easier thing to achieve because the helper can always 'reserve' their life in attending to the needs of others. Yet such help issues in a kind of paradox:

the one full character, in attending to others, is, within the social dimensions of the novel, living on the periphery of her own life.

Challenge

It is worthwhile asking why Anne can engage with some characters.

In the case of Captain Benwick, communication is possible because the text shows a clear similarity between Anne and the melancholy sailor. He is broadened as a character, because the reader is encouraged to think of his emotional life in similar terms to Anne's.

Captain Benwick is believed to suffer greatly, 'uniting quiet, serious, and retiring manners, and a decided taste for reading' (vol. 1, ch. 11). Anne is in a position to compare their plights and be prophetic. She thinks that Captain Benwick 'will rally again, and be happy with another'.

Anne hopes to be of use to him in bringing her experience of affliction to bear. They share a knowledge of the extravagant sorrow of Byron and Scott, and Captain Benwick has committed to memory 'the various lines which imaged a broken heart, or a mind destroyed by wretchedness'. Presumably, he would quote only the lines reflecting the experiences of men, but one can see why Anne might have developed a taste for Scott. The authors mentioned are, indirectly, a means of further nourishing the reader's sense of Anne's inwardness. Her past by no means mirrors that of Sister Clare from *Marmion*, but there *is* something nun-like about Anne, shut away in Kellynch for years, allowing herself none of the customary pursuits of youth, such as dancing:

> Nought say I here of Sister Clare,
> Save this, that she was young and fair;
> As yet a novice unprofessed,
> Lovely and gentle, but distressed.
> She was betrothed to one now dead,

Or worse, who had dishonoured fled.
Her kinsmen bade her give her hand
To one, who loved her for her land:
Herself, almost heart-broken now,
Was bent to take the vestal vow,
And shroud, within Saint Hilda's gloom,
Her blasted hopes and withered bloom.
(*Marmion*, Canto 2)

Anne is 'lovely and gentle' and she is distressed because the one she [illegible] dead to her. 'Withered', of course, is a *Persuasion* word. (see 24.1).

The narrative at this point works as a judgement, as it frequently does. Anne, who knows sorrow, sees that Captain Benwick is tending to self-indulgence. She recommends a course of sympathetic but bracing prose.

21.6 The persuaders

'He, who had ever boasted of being an Elliot.' (vol. 2, ch. 3)

At the heart of *Persuasion* there is a difficulty about the literary status of the persuaders.

It is debatable whether the comparatively 'thin' characterization of Mr Elliot and Lady Russell is satisfactory. The difficulty can be located in the disparity between their plot function and their presence in the text as figures who are influential but have nothing of Anne`s textual substantiality.

The problem of Lady Russell

Lady Russell is limited in two quite different ways: her character is little more than sketched in. Moreover, such character as she does have is limited; she herself cannot discern character. She, far more than Anne, is wrongly persuaded.

We are perhaps supposed to find her right-minded but wrong-judging. However, she is a character upon whom it seems difficult for the reader to achieve a focus, not, as C. Rawson says, so much through 'a complexity of which the author has a comprehensive grasp, as an uncertainty as to which of her characteristics is to be approved or disapproved' (Introduction to the Oxford World Classics edition of *Persuasion*, Oxford University Press, 1990, p. xxxvii).

Like Sir Walter, Lady Russell is preoccupied with the material world. She is engaged in studying 'the handsomest and best hung' drawing room curtains in Bath when Anne believes she is transfixed by Captain Wentworth. This is, of course, less reprehensible than Sir Walter's reduction of Admiral Croft to 'stuff', sight unseen: '"Then I take it for granted," observed Sir Walter, "that his face is about as orange as the cuffs and capes of my livery"' (vol. 1, ch. 3).

The allure and the test

Mr Elliot and Lady Russell have much in common:

Both are 'hinderer' figures, bent on a second formidable persuasion.

rs all of Lady Russell's aspirations for Anne. Here at last is someone with ment to value her. Lady Russell is determined to press his allure.

iot appears to pose a serious alternative to Captain Wentworth, both for himself d his peculiar position regarding Kellynch.

Mr Elliot's chief plot function is to test Anne. Jane Austen presents his choosing subjects to please her – he praises Lady Russell, and they find that they have a common distrust of Mrs Clay.

Anne is not impervious to Mr Elliot's advances; he cheers her up, entertains her and makes her feel appreciated.

Jane Austen artfully uses him both as a potential threat to Captain Wentworth and as a signaller that he is no threat at all.

He is a means to Anne's enjoying the indulgence of occasionally reminiscing about Lyme and one cannot but suspect that Mr Elliot's greatest appeal is that he is thus a link with Captain Wentworth.

Anne finds him as slippery a character as the reader does. He *apparently* has many of the best qualities, but Anne feels that she cannot get to know his true character. She would not like to answer for his past. He is too universally agreeable and too controlled. Anne still prizes eagerness and warmth. She equates a tendency to impetuosity with sincerity. So

Anne uses a comparison with Mr Elliot to verify what she most appreciates in a man.

It is the function of Mr Elliot and Lady Russell to hold out to Anne the possibility of reuniting indirectly with her beloved mother and directly with Kellynch. Lady Russell draws a picture of Anne's being, perhaps, the future Lady Elliot, 'presiding and blessing' in her mother's spot (vol. 2, ch. 5)

For a few moments Anne has to subdue the emotion that picture excites: to take her mother`s place and be restored to Kellynch! This is a crisis in the novel both for Anne and the reader, because we can see that there is only Anne who deserves to be Lady Elliot.

Later, when Mr Elliot's true nature is revealed, the reader shudders retrospectively with Anne. Even with Anne as Lady Elliot, Kellynch could have become a moral ruin.

The problem of William Elliot

Two distinct features make William Elliot a problematic character. The first is moral. He appears to appreciate and love Anne. He apparently honours her for helping Mrs Smith, yet he uses the Mrs Smith *he* knew to woo Anne, to awaken her curiosity and flatter her.

The second is a matter of plot: his relationship with Mrs Clay is opaque. If it is, as it looks, a convenient way of getting him out of the plot, the reader is left with the problem of motive.

Had Mr Elliot been more fully drawn, he might have been more of a challenge for Anne, and the reader might have had a sharper sense of what was evil about him. The trouble is that the reader is made to feel that he is more evil than he actually appears.

Jane Austen was not in the best of health when she wrote *Persuasion*, and compared with *Mansfield Park* and *Emma* it is very short. The end seems rushed and one wonders whether she had broader plans for it than she could realize. The horror, disappoint-

ment and disgust that Lady Russell must have felt on learning the tr
is not shown, merely reported in a very understated half-sentenc
Lady Russell must be suffering some pain in understanding an
Elliot' (vol. 2, ch. 12).

Was there to be a second more dangerous 'persuasion' from La

Anne's inconsistency?

Anne appears to regret Lady Russell's persuasion until the novel's end when she says that she would have suffered more by withstanding it, because of her conscience. Is it, as Jane Austen said, that Anne was 'almost too good' for her? Yet Anne's inconsistency might be more interesting than an object lesson in duty. Is this a case, as Claude Rawson argues, of Jane Austen's moving away from stable characterization to 'a more open and destabilized perception of human personality and behaviour'? (Introduction to the Oxford World Classics edition of *Persuasion*, 1990, p.xxxvii)?

21.7 Compatible company

'They were people whom her heart turned to very naturally.' (vol. 2, ch. 6)

There is an asymmetry in the characterization. Anne is fuller and more open than other characters, yet those less realized characters are the means by which her character is extended.

Anne encounters and re-encounters a number of people in the novel who draw her out and encourage her to assume charge of her own destiny.

The tenants

The Crofts have a number of functions, all in relation to Anne.

Admiral and Mrs Croft serve Anne with her model of what a couple should be: good-humoured, and loving being together.

Mrs Croft is of particular interest to Anne, being Captain Wentworth's sister. Like her brother, she is practical, knowledgeable and gutsy. The Crofts are the kind of couple that Anne and Captain Wentworth might become. (On a trivial level, when Anne and Captain Wentworth come to their understanding, they echo their favourite couple by driving around in 'a very pretty laudalette' (vol. 2, ch. 12) to complement the Crofts' gig.)

The Crofts have a function in relation to the future of Anne's home.

Admiral and Mrs Croft lead Anne to sober reflections on the fate of Kellynch.

Anne believes that the Crofts deserve to live at Kellynch more than the Elliots. She knows that they will set a good example to the parish and the poor will be looked after. Perhaps, in time, Anne and Wentworth will succeed the Crofts at Kellynch (see 23.6).

The example of Uppercross

The Musgroves of Uppercross function similarly to the Crofts in that they can live the life of the rural gentry without implicating themselves in financial difficulties. They are y different from Sir Walter and Elizabeth and, consequently, are an affirma- Anne. Their 'respectable forms in the usual places' (vol. 1, ch. 6) give her a of stability and the continuation of family, which (in poignant contrast) her own ple cannot supply. Sir Walter and Elizabeth take no interest in Mary's children, hereas Mrs Musgrove has them with her often, even though she finds them hard work.

Mrs Musgrove, like Mrs Croft, has a horror of long or uncertain engagements. The strong implication is that if Anne's parents had been the Musgroves, her engagement to Captain Wentworth would have been accepted with joy, and the couple would have been encouraged to marry as soon as was feasible. The example of the Musgroves might have been behind Anne's reflections: 'How eloquent could Anne Elliot have been . . . on the side of warm early attachment, and a cheerful confidence in futurity' (vol. 1, ch. 4).

Henrietta and Louisa

The Musgrove girls are shallow, popular, high-spirited, self-confident, pleasure-loving and accomplished; they are literal-minded, living on life's surface, with no idea that Anne is ever in turmoil or pain behind her outstanding capability.

Louisa is slightly older than Anne had been when she became engaged to Captain Wentworth. Louisa functions as a contrast; she is much more childlike than Anne, running, skipping, dancing and wanting to be jumped off stiles.

The impression of Louisa's and Henrietta's superficiality is the corollary of the lack of detail in their characterization. They serve as a foil to the meditative Anne, and, as part of that function, they distract Captain Wentworth. But because the reader knows Anne's worth, it is inconceivable that Captain Wentworth should ever find either sister appealing for long.

Charles Musgrove

Anne is very fond of Charles and he of her. One wonders what could have possessed him to marry Mary when Anne turned him down.

Like Captain Benwick and Mr Elliot, Charles Musgrove is one of the alternative men in Anne's life, who demonstrate that they are no substitute for Captain Wentworth.

Charles continues to feel concern for Anne and will insist on walking her home when the letter from Captain Wentworth makes her feel faint. The very circumstances in which Anne is rescued is almost an illustration of the different levels of their characterization; certainly it underlines their incompatibility. Anne feels, yearns and longs: Charles is glad that he is able, after all, to visit the gunsmiths. His zeal for country sports is one of his few distinguishing characteristics. How appropriate, and yet how surreal, is the juxtaposition of the gun shop and the lovers' intimate exchanges!

21.8 Contrasting lives

'"Westgate-buildings!" said he; "and who is Miss Anne Elliot to be visiting in Westgate-buildings?"' (vol. 2, ch. 5)

The invalid

Because Mrs Smith is important in the novel`s moral design and plot resolution, we should like to know more of her. She is the image of what Anne might become. To survive as she does, Mrs Smith (is there meaning in her deliberately common name?) must have a tenacious inner strength. What gives it to her? The hint is that it is the gift of Heaven. If so, is there an important story which she does not tell us? Our frustration is not that of contradiction but of teasing incompleteness.

Sir Walter Elliot, Elizabeth and Mary

Sir Walter, Elizabeth and Mary are constituted of a few boldly drawn features. They are all closed characters: Sir Walter and Elizabeth will never be woken out of their snobbery, and Mary will always give way to lassitude. Their function is, in part, moral; they contrast with Anne in their attitudes – to status, for example.

It is difficult for characters as different as Anne and the rest of the family to coexist in the novel. In the case of Mary, the comedy of her self-regarding littleness makes for amusing contrasts, but the sketchiness of her characterization compared with Anne's means that it would be hard to maintain more scenes between them than we have.

Jane Austen's move in making Anne decide to suit herself and thereby distance herself from her family in Bath is a brilliant one. Anne is thus engaged by characters who at least have a plot function – Mr Elliot and Mrs Smith.

While Elizabeth and Sir Walter are ingratiating themselves in Laura-place, Anne is visiting Mrs Smith in Westgate-buildings. Through her, Anne – and Jane Austen – considers the plight of those merely surviving on the peripheries of Bath – the poor who are there for the waters alone. Her father, who has no idea of the interrelationship of the world, mocks Anne for her visits.

The Harvilles

Like the Crofts, the Harvilles have more distinguishing features than Sir Walter, Elizabeth and Mary. If Captain Harville were merely an assemblage of two or three features that had useful plot functions, it would be difficult for the reader to regard as significant the debate with Anne on the nature of male and female love.

Possibly because he has to engage in the debate, Captain Harville, of the characters other than Anne and Wentworth, has the claim to be the most fully presented. This is partly necessity – to engage with Anne he has to have a mind and case of his own – and partly a matter of the novel's ideology (see 23.7).

Anne recognizes that the Harvilles did what she and Captain Wentworth could have done. They risked all and married. Indeed, Captain Harville made money side by side with Captain Wentworth, so in time both couples would have been secure. The Harvilles are partly present to make Anne regret that she has missed out on these people whom she finds so compatible and who would have been her friends.

Captain Harville is as tender as Anne herself. His lips tremble as he remembers his sister, Fanny.

Captain Harville is the only character in the novel to give expression to the sanctity of family life. He has a depth which is completely lacking in Anne's own family.

He manages to convey how acutely a man suffers, knowing that it is in the hands of God whether he will ever see his family again. He speaks too of 'the glow of his soul' when he sees them even earlier than expected 'as if Heaven had given them wings' (vol. 2, ch. 11).

Captain Harville impassions Anne so that she speaks from her heart, and so he acts as the bridge between Captain Wentworth and her.

He also recognizes Anne's goodness *before* he learns that she will become a second sister to him.

21.9 A determined man

'He had not forgiven Anne Elliot.' (vol. 1, ch. 7)

As a character Captain Wentworth is in a crucial position. First, he has to be worthy of Jane Austen's most worthy heroine. Second, he has to be open to change. For the plot to work, the reader must see him as an impulsive, romantic individualist who comes to recognize that he was wrong in despising Anne for want of courage.

Captain Wentworth has determined views. It must strike him as ironic that reversals in the Elliot family mean that he is under the roof of those who denied him welcome eight years ago. But it means nothing to him now. He has fulfilled everything that he had promised Anne Elliot before she spurned him. But eight years ago she had lost her chance. He is still stubbornly angry; he is determined to be silent in her presence. She is silent in turn.

Anne is silent because she finds love overwhelming; Captain Wentworth is silent, because he refuses to allow that love can overwhelm.

Captain Wentworth's personal declaration that Anne's 'power with him was gone for ever' (vol. 1, ch. 7) shows he has built a carapace around himself. Is he aware of this? He is not an introvert like Anne; he opted for action rather than self-understanding. This does not mean that he is in harmony with his deepest desires, just that he has a capacity for self-delusion. He is a man apparently without self-doubt, courageous, industrious and full of energy. He is an excellent naval officer, with real concern for his men – generous and respected.

A true friend

Captain Wentworth does realize that life provokes thought. He is as uncertain as Anne has been on how to balance feeling and principle. On principle, he will not allow women on board ship because he believes they deserve high levels of personal comfort. He is not consistent, though – his sister points out that he brought female members of the Harville family, together with three children, 'from Portsmouth to Plymouth' (vol.1, ch. 8). He declares that he would 'assist any brother officer's wife that I could, and I would bring any thing of Harville's from the world's end'.

Friendship

The sign that he is a character who, in his inner complexity, can be worthy of Anne in both moral and literary terms is given in the strength of his various attachments to his colleagues. Captain Wentworth is capable of warm friendships.

His tenderness for his friends and his joining in with the Harvilles' family life makes him, as Lady Russell claims for Anne, 'peculiarly fitted by...warm affections and domestic habits' (vol. 1, ch. 4) for marriage.

A second chance?

And his determination *is* now to marry. He believes that he knows what he is doing. He is happy to bring into play a 'quick taste' and 'a clear head' (vol., ch. 7). However, if he is honest with himself, he knows that there are not many Anne Elliots and that his requirements this time are just as demanding. It could take years to find what he is wanting. But for all that his sister can tell that he is still 'nice' (vol. 1, ch. 7), he seems to launch on his quest for a bride hastily and under a certain amount of pique.

It appears that Captain Wentworth thoughtlessly looks to a possible attachment to one of the Miss Musgroves. Has he forgotten that he has a social responsibility and that women have feelings? Making himself agreeable to two sisters at once is sailing close to the wind!

It is not at all clear whether Captain Wentworth prefers the liveliness of Louisa or the gentleness of Henrietta. Actually, 'sweetness of manner' (vol. 1, ch. 7) is one of his two criteria in the woman he seeks, but Henrietta removes herself from the calculation when she resumes her attachment to Charles Hayter.

On a walk to Winthrop, Captain Wentworth believes that he has found his other criterion for marriage – 'firmness' – (vol. 1, ch. 10) – in Louisa. But we can see her 'firmness' may be another word for self-interest (see 23.2).

Anne's character is the model of what Captain Wentworth seeks in a wife. Yet impulsively, he attributes all kinds of extravagant qualities to Louisa: 'decision', 'powers of mind', 'spirit' and 'resolution'. (vol. 1, ch. 10) The reader can see where such characteristics *can* be found. Is Captain Wentworth trying to convince himself that he has found a viable substitute for Anne? He and Louisa walk together down a 'rough, wild sort of channel'. He is going wildly about his business, satisfied with a rough approximation to what he wants.

Morever, Captain Wentworth is apt to use and interpret words roughly too. He has attributed to Anne 'feebleness of character' (vol. 1, ch. 7). The firmness that he is so quick to associate with Louisa becomes, in another light, heedless obstinacy.

When he realizes that his interpretation of people is misguided, Captain Wentworth has to reinterpret the meaning of the words that he has used too hastily both recently and in the past.

As a result, he decides that he was unjust to Anne.

Captain Wentworth reappraises his *own* character. He perceives the weakness in himself that he has attributed to Anne. He has also suffered from pride as unintelligent as Elliot pride.

Through reappraisal he becomes worthy to be Anne's hero in both the romantic and the literary sense. A man who has himself experienced great vicissitudes in fortune, he takes his decisive step towards Anne, fittingly in changing times, amid the shifting population of an inn, the touchingly named White Hart. His laconic humour is not misplaced as he says to her with a smile (vol. 2, ch. 11):

> Like other great men under reverses, I must endeavour to subdue my mind to my fortune. I must learn to brook being happier than I deserve.

22 On being persuaded

Persuasion Notes

22.1 The exposition

'She was persuaded to think the engagement a wrong thing.' (vol. 1, ch. 4)

Establishing the theme

The exposition makes clear that a persuasion has occurred before the beginning of the novel. An exposition is an explanatory account which establishes everything a reader needs to know to understand the workings of the plot.

The literary use of the term is akin to its usage in music, for in musical terms exposition is the part of a movement in which the themes are presented. This is true of *Persuasion.*

The passages of exposition reveal the clash that human beings face between feelings and duty, emotion and reason. They also underline the care characters should exercise in attributing meaning to the words and actions of others.

Passages of exposition

There are three major passages of exposition, all concerned with the difficult question of the right way to behave.

The first is about the parlous condition Sir Walter has allowed Kellynch to slump into since the death of his well-regulated wife (vol. 1, ch. 1).

The second concerns Lady Russell's persuasion of Anne to break off her engagement to Captain Wentworth (vol.1, ch. 4).

The third concerns Captain Wentworth's conclusions about Anne after she broke off their engagement (vol. 1, ch. 7). After eight years: 'He had not forgiven Anne Elliot.' The novel will explore the justice of his reading of Anne`s character.

22.2 The ubiquity of persuasion

'It had been the effect of . . . persuasion.' (vol. 1, ch. 7)

There are many attempts to persuade in the novel besides the key persuasions of the hero and heroine.

Persuasion and marriage

The prudential marriage, the marriage that preserves rank, marrying above and below oneself and the outrageously unsuitable marriage all play variations on the theme of whether Anne and Frederick Wentworth should have married. Before the beginning, there was probably an act of persuasion that has given rise to the anomalies of the early chapters – the very different characters and attitudes of Anne and the rest of her family.

An 'excellent woman, *sensible* and amiable' (vol. 1, ch. 1; our italics) became, surprisingly, Lady Elliot. Anne takes after her mother in sense and virtue and, as became her mother's fate, suffers for it.

Unsuccessful attempts

Sir Walter did not rule out the idea of remarrying when his wife died. Unfortunately for him, he suffered 'one or two private disappointments in very unreasonable applications' (vol. 1, ch. 1). Miss Elliot, Sir Walter's eldest daughter, had hoped to persuade the heir presumptive to the baronetcy into marriage to keep Kellynch Hall in the immediate family.

Louisa Musgrove tells Captain Wentworth how her parents had great hopes that their son Charles would marry Anne Elliot. When she refused him, it was believed to be the result of Lady Russell's persuading Anne that Charles was not 'learned and bookish enough' (vol. 1, ch. 10).

In fact, Lady Russell had advised *in favour of* Charles, but this time 'Anne had left nothing for advice to do' (vol. 1, ch. 4).

Mary – unsuccessful and successful persuader

Mary Musgrove, née Elliot, plays Lady Russell's role in relation to Henrietta Musgrove's wish to marry Charles Hayter. However, fortunately for her, Henrietta has a counter persuader (unlike Anne) in Louisa.

A complex of persuasions

In Bath, as at Kellynch, Mrs Clay makes herself extravagantly agreeable to Sir Walter in the hope of becoming Lady Elliot. She also continues to flatter Elizabeth. Mrs Clay may be trying to convince Mr Elliot of her charms too.

Another complex of persuasions involves Mr Elliot and Colonel Wallis. The plausible Mr Elliot, in trying to insinuate his way back into the Elliot fold, uses his friend Colonel Wallis. Colonel Wallis discloses circumstances concerning Mr Elliot's first marriage which prove persuasive with Sir Walter. His wife had been a very fine woman, with a great deal of money, but most importantly she was 'excessively in love with his friend' (vol. 2, ch. 3). She had pursued and persuaded *him* into marrying *her*. Sir Walter is assured that 'Without that attraction, not all her money would have tempted Elliot'.

Persuasions over money

The lawyer Mr Shepherd is keen to have Sir Walter reform his finances. Presumably, he is fearful that otherwise he may not be paid; but there could be a more far-reaching motive.

The oily Mr Shepherd as well as his unctuous daughter would like the latter to marry Sir Walter. Doubtless Mr Shepherd relishes the thought of a grandson's becoming a baronet and inheriting Kellynch.

That Sir Walter has lost a great deal of money is his own fault. Mrs Smith's position is very different. She hopes to use Anne's influence with Mr Elliot to win back her husband's West Indian property. She has discovered that her own persuasions are hopeless.

Persuasion concerning rank

In Bath, Sir Walter, whose own rank and looks have sustained him for years, insinuates himself among those with even higher status. On hearing that cousins of the Elliots, Irish nobility, are in Bath, Sir Walter endeavours to persuade them to accept his family again after an unfortunate lapse. This proves successful, and the Elliots have an entrée into the first drawing rooms in Bath.

Persuasions concerning Mr Elliot

Lady Russell, on hearing that Mr Elliott wants to reunite with the family, is willingly persuaded to meet him. She has 'prejudices on the side of ancestry' (vol. 1, ch. 2). Anne is more sceptical than her friend. She listens to her family's account of the reconciliation, but cannot be persuaded that what they have heard is all there is to tell.

Lady Russell is soon entirely convinced by him.

Mr Elliot is able to persuade Lady Russell that he is everything which she considered, in her prejudice, that Captain Wentworth was not.

It is not surprising that Anne, however, given her increasing scepticism, is persuaded by Mrs Smith's account of Mr Elliot's character, melodramatic as it is. It confirms all her suspicions.

22.3 Self-deception or persuading oneself

'to enjoy the sight of a dead young lady, nay, two dead young ladies, for it proved twice as fine as the first report' (vol. 1, ch. 12)

Mirrors of the self

Sir Walter's self-deception is reflected in his mirrors – the numerous mirrors that adorn his bedroom at Kellynch, the mirrors that he has doubtless added to his drawing room in Bath and that most satisfying mirror of all, the Baronetage, in which he can happily gaze upon his own glory.

In a novel that uses mirroring effects to suggest the reciprocity of love (see 22.4), the mirror, in Sir Walter's case, is narcissistic, reflecting the image of the self's own glory. The mirror, traditional image of mimetic art, does not, in Sir Walter's case, reflect the world as it really is. He deceives himself by accepting his self-image as the only reality.

Self-interest and sore throats

Mary is an arch manipulator with no self-knowledge, hence her capacity for self-deception.

Most of Mary's self-delusions have their basis in jealousy or in a vastly overrated sense of Elliot importance.

Mary persuades herself that she is often ill, that it is Anne's duty to nurse her, that her illness can be brought on by being squashed into a carriage with the Musgroves and that her sore throats are worse than anyone else's. She believes she misses out on every exciting project. Mary's most wilful and distressing self-delusion is that she is more fitted than Anne to nurse Louisa. That she goes into hysterics every time there is a problem does not seem to register with her.

The plain and the personable

Both Anne and Lady Russell endeavour to persuade Elizabeth that Mrs Clay is a dangerous companion because of her father's possible predilection. Elizabeth will not hear a word of it. She convinces herself that Mrs Clay's freckles, protruding tooth and clumsy wrist cannot over-ride her efforts to make herself agreeable.

Lady Dalrymple is obsessed with appearances, just as her cousins are. She is much taken with the fine figure of Captain Wentworth and indulges in a little self-deception, declaring him: 'Irish, I dare say' (vol. 2, ch. 8).

Self-persuasion

Anne, in the first half of the novel, is a self-persuader. She interprets Captain Wentworth as being hostile to her.

Public deceptions

The fall on the Cobb provides a climax to the repeated pattern of self deception

A report of the accident soon circulates, resulting in many people gathering around.

However, the catastrophe that the spectators think that they are witnessing is an illusion.

Louisa is not dead. Her accident serves as a climax to the first volume because it brings into focus the real nature of Captain Wentworth's feelings for Louisa and for Anne.

After the fall on the Cobb Captain Wentworth begins to realize that he has been deceiving himself for eight years.

22.4 Captain Wentworth

'Tell me not that I am too late, that such precious feelings are gone for ever.' (vol. 2, ch. 11)

It might be said that the novel rests on a fourfold persuasion.

Anne has been persuaded that it is wrong to marry Captain Wentworth. The trajectory of the plot is a persuasion that Captain Wentworth is right to marry Anne. This entails Anne's being persuaded that Captain Wentworth still loves her, and then her persuading him that the feeling is mutual.

Persuasion requires the reader to supplement the narrative by a reconstructive empathy. There is an implicit invitation to imagine Captain Wentworth's inner state. We have indications of what he does during and after the episode at Lyme and we have reported to us the substance of the change he undergoes. It is up to us to feel our way into the stages by which he comes to be persuaded.

In volume 1 he has made significant progress towards re-recognizing Anne's worth without realizing it. The climax of volume 1, the accident at Lyme, proves a turning point and prepares us for a very different climax to volume 2.

The Cobb

Louisa Musgrove's fall from the Cobb is one of the most dramatic moments in Jane Austen's fiction. Although the scene is witnessed through Anne's eyes, there are moments when we see only Louisa. Louisa could be a figure from Catherine Morland's preferred fiction as her supposed lover kneels with her in his arms: 'her eyes were closed, she breathed not, her face was like death' (vol. 1, ch. 12).

But this is not an extravagant romance; it is a real emergency, and Captain Wentworth is not equal to it. Only Anne is. (See 21.3 and 21.4.)

Perhaps the reader is put in mind of words spoken in praise of Louisa on the hill near Winthrop but far more applicable to Anne in Lyme:

> and woe betide him, and her too, when it comes to things of consequence, when they are placed in circumstances, requiring fortitude and strength of mind, if she have not resolution enough. (vol. 1, ch. 10)

It is *Louisa's* resolution that brought the party to Lyme, that clinched the walk to the Cobb and insisted on the second jump in spite of Captain Wentworth's advice. It is her way of wooing. She is a literal-minded young woman, and once she has been praised for her determination, she is determined by rule. She is an Eve who tempts Adam. But Adam has said no, hers is the sin of disobedience and the result is not a 'sensation' which is 'delightful' (vol. 1, ch. 12) but a literal fall!

Because the drama at Lyme is interpreted through Anne's eyes and mind, the reader is encouraged to adopt her reading of Captain Wentworth's actions and words.

But the reader should be independent. After the surgeon has issued his opinion: 'The tone, the look, with which "Thank God" was uttered by Captain Wentworth, Anne was sure could never be forgotten by her'. She interprets it as gratitude for the life of one who is becoming beloved.

The reader might see that Captain Wentworth may be realizing Anne`s worth and his own self-deception.

Has his admiration unwittingly encouraged Louisa into foolhardiness? Is it that he is longing for Anne again?

Silence

At the very centre of the novel there is a deep silence. Anne thinks of Captain Wentworth, and Captain Wentworth thinks of Anne, and neither reads the other correctly.

Anne, on her own at Uppercross, believes that Captain Wentworth will soon marry Louisa (see 21.2). She thinks back over her time at Uppercross. Such memories would always be dear to her, but she still believes that Captain Wentworth thinks her weak and yielding. As the November rain almost blots out a monochrome afternoon and darkness comes early, she cannot believe that there will ever be a spring of spirit for her again.

In retrospect, the reader infers that Captain Wentworth has been forced into reflection.

The incident on the Cobb has persuaded him of his unremitting love for Anne. This recognition requires a re-reading of the immediate and the long-gone past.

Regrets

At first Captain Wentworth stays at Lyme, with plenty of time for thought. The comparison of Louisa's mind with Anne's alerts him to other truths:

> he had learnt to distinguish between the steadiness of principle and the obstinacy of self-will, between the darings of heedlessness and the resolution of a collected mind. (vol. 2, ch. 11)

He finds he reveres the woman who in the 'pride, the folly, the madness of resentment' he has rejected. He accepts what he had always known – Louisa Musgrove had never meant anything to him and never could.

He realizes, though, that he is not a free man. He cannot act upon his insights, for Harville and his wife believe he is engaged. If *they* are under this misapprehension, then possibly Louisa's family and Louisa herself are too. He realizes that he has been 'grossly wrong'. It is now that Captain Wentworth goes to his clergyman brother's home on what can best be seen as a kind of retreat.

Retreat

Captain Wentworth needs to 'weaken . . . speculations' (vol. 2, ch. 11) and endeavour to reconcile himself to the consequences of his thoughtlessness.

We do not know what Captain Wentworth thinks about during his six weeks of quiet in Shropshire. The most important 'events' of the book take place in silence and off-scene.

We are told that even before Captain Wentworth goes to Shropshire 'his penance had become severe'. He now has to go through a period of mortification and suffering such as Anne has long gone through. He speaks of his situation at this time as 'waiting only for evil' (vol. 2, ch. 11).

What Wentworth might think

We can imagine that Captain Wentworth is delighted to see his brother again. He had intended visiting Shropshire soon after arriving at Kellynch, but the charms of Uppercross had caused him to postpone the visit. He may have considered how differently things might have turned out had he visited when he intended.

But would he, under different circumstances, have come to know and appreciate Anne once more? Perhaps through the connection with Kellynch? He must recognize that this is unlikely.

One of the reasons why Captain Wentworth had wanted to visit his brother was to meet his wife whose 'charms and perfections' (vol. 1, ch. 9) had been much vaunted. It must have been painful for him to witness a happy marriage when he thinks of the mistake he has made.

That Edward, his brother, seems to hope that Anne and Frederick may still come to an understanding is strongly hinted at by the way that 'He enquired after' Anne 'very particularly'. (vol. 2, ch. 11). This he surely would not have done – out of tact for his brother's feelings – if he did not consider that Anne and his brother had been particularly well-suited. He is intimate in his enquiries, 'asked even if [Anne] were personally altered'. It is hard to resist speculating about when this conversation took place – after evensong, over a glass of wine? Would Edward's wife be present?

In any case, it is likely to make Captain Wentworth ponder on what Edward would make of Louisa. As he says: 'I was six weeks with Edward . . . and saw him happy. I could have no other pleasure. I deserved none.'

From this state of penance and regret, Captain Wentworth is released by news of Louisa's engagement to Captain Benwick. His old impetuosity is immediately to the fore: 'Within the first five minutes I said, 'I will be at Bath on Wednesday,' and I was' (vol. 2, ch. 11).

Constancy challenged

But before Captain Wentworth leaves, he has reason for more serious reflection. He wonders at Captain Benwick. Fanny Harville had been another Anne. Yet his friend had recovered enough within half a year to wish to marry again. Captain Wentworth knows Louisa's mind to be inferior to Fanny's. He realizes now why *he* is still single after eight years. This recognition of constancy in himself is a further persuasion back to Anne.

However, Captain Wentworth wonders whether there is any point in going to Bath, though he has determined upon it.

This shows how remarkably well Anne has concealed her feelings – he has no idea of her pain over the past weeks nor of the pleasure that his relenting attitude has afforded her.

But he knows that she has refused at least one man who would have suited the Elliot family and Lady Russell, and he wonders if this was for his sake.

Captain Wentworth's realization of Anne's excellence and her hold over his heart begin to make him worthy of being Anne's hero.

Being tested

His hope that he might yet regain Anne has come from thought, not action, but it is through relentless action that he has allowed himself to believe that he has forgotten her. He must now combine the two and, in doing so, undergo the ultimate test.

Captain Wentworth now has to undergo the trials that Anne has undergone. To become more like her, he suffers as she has done.

Mirror, mirror

At the centre of the novel, without either of the characters being in a position to know about it, a crossover has taken place. Captain Wentworth will become as tentative and uncertain as Anne has been in volume 1. News of the engagement of Louisa Musgrove proves to be the liberation for Anne that it is for Captain Wentworth. In volume 2 she will become the compelling figure he was in volume 1.

In the second volume, Captain Wentworth's experience mirrors Anne's in the first volume. Anne will be admired by another. This will be a painful process for Captain Wentworth, until Mr Elliot is revealed as a distraction, just as Louisa was revealed as one in volume one.

Captain Wentworth has to suffer embarrassment and jealousy. He must blush and feel all the discomfort of a body at variance with his mind. He is full of doubt and low in spirits. He has to avert his eyes. He replicates Anne's silences – gone is the exuberant favourite who was at the hub of every social gathering. He is as marginalized as she was. It is his turn to look and listen. He has to suffer the tug of emotions that she has gone through. He struggles to compose his feelings – and is less successful than she is. He misreads her thoughts, interpreting them negatively, as she has often misread his. When she mentions how much, in spite of everything, she enjoyed Lyme, she blushes, and he attributes this to her first meeting Mr Elliot. He even misinterprets the radiance that he himself has caused. He imagines it is as the glow of an engaged woman.

The tables turned

Anne is in Molland's when she first sees Captain Wentworth. Her self-bestowed licence to do what she pleases makes her go to the door 'to see if it rained' (vol. 2, ch. 7). She thus prepares herself before he sees her, so:

> For the first time since their renewed acquaintance, she felt that she was betraying the least sensibility of the two.

Mr Elliot comes to collect Anne. Captain Wentworth recognizes him immediately and witnesses the eagerness with which he approaches. He has the pain of seeing Anne walk off on his arm, just as Anne had felt pain watching Captain Wentworth walk with Louisa on the hill near Winthrop.

Anne is allowed off-scene momentarily (almost the only time in the book) so that Captain Wentworth has it confirmed that the man from Lyme *is indeed* Anne's cousin. He has to listen to the convictions of his party as to 'what will happen there', just as Anne had to listen to Admiral Croft's wishing that Captain Wentworth would bring one of the Miss Musgroves home to Kellynch.

How it must seem to Captain Wentworth

The match between Mr Elliot and Anne must seem far more likely than ever his and Louisa's had been. Captain Wentworth is fully aware of what he is up against. Everyone who knows Anne must think it the perfect arrangement. Her family will approve of it. The formidable Lady Russell will glory in it. Anne has been persuaded before. The pressure on her now will be enormous, even if her feelings were to admit any doubt. A lesser man or a man less deeply in love would have instantly left Bath. What Captain Wentworth has witnessed must persuade him that his hopes of a reconciliation are dim.

Fortunately, however, Anne and Captain Wentworth are to meet at the concert. Captain Wentworth's word choice to describe the experience is perhaps one more traditionally associated with a woman than a man. Does this suggest that he is becoming more like Anne?

That evening seemed to be made up of exquisite moments. The moment of her stepping forward in the octagon room to speak to him, the moment of Mr Elliot's appearing and tearing her away. (vol. 2, ch. 11)

On the evening of the concert Captain Wentworth gives vent to his jealousy in a way that Anne never did: 'there is nothing worth my staying for', he declares melodramatically (vol. 2, ch. 8), demonstrating some of his former pique. Anne attributes this outburst to its rightful cause. She uses the word that Captain Wentworth had used about the prospect of a loveless marriage with Louisa to describe the attentions of Mr Elliot: 'Their *evil* was incalculable' (vol. 2, ch. 8; our italics).

Captain Wentworth will continue to be tested until almost the end of the novel but Anne now has a better knowledge of his feelings than he has of hers. She senses that he has persuaded himself back to her, though as yet she does not know why or how. This means that she can continue to show what her true feelings are, in the hope that they eventually reach a mutual understanding.

22.5 How *Persuasion* endeavours to persuade

'Dare not say that man forgets sooner than woman.' (vol. 2, ch. 11)

Persuasion endeavours to persuade the reader in two fundamental ways: (1) into believing that Captain Wentworth *is* gradually persuaded back to Anne; (2) into believing that constancy in love *can* be achieved by both man and woman.

The artistry of the novel makes the persuading of Captain Wentworth convincing. The two-volume construction, with its mirroring pattern, requires Captain Wentworth's volte-face at the very centre of the book.

An exploration of the theme of obedience and disobedience, plus the fall at the heart of the novel, lends an emblematic feel to the story. Captain Wentworth has to become obedient to the true promptings of his heart. He also has to obey his reason and discriminate between what is just and unjust. Through the delicacy of its allusions to a larger story and a greater love, *Persuasion* convinces that it is possible for human beings to recognize delusion and to win through to *their* truth about love.

To honour and obey

Although Anne breaks her engagement, she lives her life for almost eight years as if she has taken marriage vows and is a widow. She continues to honour all Captain Wentworth's virtues. No one else she meets can measure up to him. She continues to hold dear in her heart Captain Wentworth's 'powers', 'conversation' and 'grace' (vol. 1, ch. 6). 'Quiet and confined', as she says in her debate with Captain Harville (vol. 2, ch. 11), she does dwell on her feelings. This is what fuels her argument that women are more constant than men when all hope is gone.

Captain Wentworth, on the other hand, goes to sea as quickly as he can, full of resentment. As Louisa Musgrove will do later on the Cobb, he acts precipitantly. He dishonours Anne when he clings only to the memory of her breaking their engagement. He appears to forget Anne's virtues, because she has 'deserted and disappointed him' (vol. 1, ch. 7). All he carries with him are hastily attributed faults, and meanwhile he pursues his career. He is most successful; as Anne claims, it takes a man's mind off things.

We *can* believe that Captain Wentworth remains constant to Anne. Because of her, without even realizing it, he lives for eight years vicariously, through his profession. There are balls on ship, there will be balls in the places he visits abroad, he has had leaves – there *have* been plenty of opportunities for him to meet women, though he tells his sister the reverse. It is credible that he is won back by Anne because he is clearly ripe for it.

But with what looks like being a prolonged period of peace it seems he cannot get married to someone else fast enough. Is it that his buried feelings for Anne make his single life intolerable? He claims that he has 'a clear head' (vol. 1, ch. 7), but this is doubtful. He has never seen Anne Elliot's like, and yet he will no longer admit to her virtues. He was heartbroken when the engagement ended, but he will not acknowledge that deep down he is hurting still.

For the past eight years Captain Wentworth has harboured a disobedient heart.

The first fall

We have seen how Louisa's fall from the Cobb, prompted by disobedience, led to Captain Wentworth's falling in love with Anne again, appropriately by the sea.

Perhaps the most telling scene in the first volume, apart from the scene on the Cobb, is the occasion when the disobedient Walter tries to tease little Charles who has innocently sustained a fall. Anne, appropriately, is kneeling, tending him, while Captain Wentworth stands, in the ascendant, but hovering uncertainly by the window.

Anne stops the child from interfering with his brother, but Walter clambers on Anne's back with his hands around her neck. He defies all orders to get down until Captain Wentworth relieves Anne. He unlocks the child's hands and carries him away:

> it is almost as if the boy's unruly attachment to her is an incarnation of Wentworth's still childish rage against, and therefore conflicted involvement with, Anne. His release of the boy thus figures as an initial movement towards his own relinquishment of a disabling psychological attitude. (J. Wiltshire, *The Cambridge Companion to Jane Austen,* Cambridge University Press, 1997, p. 79).

Or, in our terms, the disobedient two-year-old helps to reclaim Captain Wentworth's disobedient heart by prompting this initial move towards Anne.

A steady gaze

We have noted how Anne's experience is later replicated in Captain Wentworth's (22.4) and how the two appear in diametric opposition from volume 1 to volume 2. Jane Austen persuades the reader that the two are moving closer together by the way their behaviour gradually mirrors one another's *directly* as they move through volume 2.

For example, in the octagon room Anne brings Captain Wentworth to her by *her* determined 'How do you do?' (vol. 2, ch. 8). They talk politely until they begin to run out of conversation, whereupon Captain Wentworth shows *his* determination to stay on. They then move on to topics of mutual interest, in particular Captain Benwick's engagement. Captain Wentworth seems bent on giving 'His opinion of Louisa Musgrove's inferiority' (vol. 2, ch. 8). Moreover, he makes it clear what he feels about strong attachments, almost faltering as a result of his emotion: 'A man does not recover from such a devotion of the heart to such a woman! – He ought not – he does not.'

This is mirrored later by Anne's determination that Captain Wentworth should know of her indifference to her family's party and therefore to Mr Elliot. She, too, almost falters when she indirectly makes it clear that she loves Captain Wentworth. She certainly has no breath left by the end: 'All the privilege I claim for my sex . . . is that of loving longest, when existence or hope is gone' (vol. 2, ch. 11).

It is not a matter of words alone.

Anne's and Captain Wentworth's body language mirrors one another as well.

Gone are the days when by chance they sit on the same sofa, completely blocked from one another by the substantial bulk of Mrs Musgrove, Captain Wentworth's potential mother-in-law! They literally make room for one another in volume 2 or occupy adjacent space. Anne subtly but deliberately manoeuvres herself so that there is a place next to her at the concert. Later, at the inn, Captain Wentworth leaves his seat to approach the fireplace in order to walk away from it soon afterwards and stand, 'with less bare-faced design' (vol. 2, ch. 10) next to Anne.

As it becomes more apparent that each is reaching out towards the other, Anne and Captain Wentworth become increasingly agitated. The debate between Captain Harville and Anne is crucial to this. Just as precipitant *action* by Louisa Musgrove brought volume 1 to its climax, so rational *argument* and deeply felt *passion* do the same for volume 2. Captain Wentworth, as he strains to hear Anne's and Captain Harville's conversation, drops his pen. When he leaves the room in great haste, only to return and draw out his letter, Anne collapses into the chair that he has just vacated as onto his knee.

Her story

When Captain Harville is arguing his case, he observes that 'all *his*tories are against you, all stories, prose and verse' (vol. 2, ch. 11; our italics). However, he has the grace to add: 'But perhaps you will say, these were all written by men.'

Persuasion is not written by a man. It is most fitting and most equitable that this, Jane Austen's last completed novel, should make a case for constancy as the potential of both woman *and* man. Indeed, to redress the inbalance of examples of woman's inconstancy in fiction, Anne is far more consciously constant than Captain Wentworth. This is not really the point, though. What Jane Austen wants to persuade us of is what Mozart and his librettist may have believed, namely that: 'Man and woman, woman and man / *Together* make a Godly span' (*The Magic Flute*; our italics).

Jane Austen has given us, in passing, some memorable examples of constancy – Admiral and Mrs Croft, Captain and Mrs Harville, Mr and Mrs Musgrove, Lady Russell, who, it would seem, has not considered marrying again, Mrs Smith who stays loyal to 'My poor Charles, who had the finest, most generous spirit in the world' (vol. 2, ch. 9).

But it is on Anne and Captain Wentworth that Jane Austen finally rests her case.

Fittingly, it is when they are both once more reduced to silence that we feel most persuaded of their love.

The explanations on the gravel path are necessary but love is ultimately too complex for the spoken, perhaps even for the written, word.

Captain Wentworth's feelings become so overwhelming that they burst from him onto paper. So Captain Wentworth first breaks through to fulfilled love with Anne by silently breaking his own silence: 'I must speak to you by such means as are within my reach' (vol. 2, ch.11). He gives Anne the opportunity to accept or reject him by a word or a look. She chooses a look and 'He walked by her side'.

The profundity of their relationship, resumed after a period of eight years, is perhaps best expressed by Anne when she speaks of the impossibility of doing justice to an Italian love song, either in translation or in its native tongue.

'"This," said she, "is nearly the sense, or rather the meaning of the words, for certainly the sense of an Italian love song must not be talked of"' (vol. 2, ch. 8).

But the lovers have a life to live and they have to talk. Yet perhaps something of the eternal is suggested in their love for one another as they talk of past and present and 'of yesterday and today there could scarcely be an end' (vol. 2, ch. 11).

Captain Wentworth also has a career to pursue, and they both have a home to run. The conclusion of the novel pays tribute to the possibility of the naval profession's 'domestic virtues' (vol. 2, ch. 12) being even more 'distinguished' than 'its national importance'. We may remember Captain Harville, improving on 'netting needles and pins' for his wife, fashioning toys for his children and defending his family against the weather. (It seems most appropriate that in addition to being a sailor, Captain Harville is a carpenter.) Perhaps we may be persuaded that he and Captain Wentworth, as much as Mrs Harville and Mrs Wentworth, deserve Coventry Patmore's accolade, later endorsed by Virginia Woolf (though both reserved the designation only for women), of being angels in the house.

Argument

Another way in which *Persuasion* persuades is by the sheer intelligence of its argument. Not the least potent legacy of the debate between Captain Harville and Anne is the difference that it highlights between men's and women's lives. Here Jane Austen demonstrates, not for the first time, how far she was ahead of her time. She recognizes the difference that gender can make to how fast or slowly time goes by and how much we grieve.

Anne is right that life at sea is arduous and dwelling on feelings would make it impossible. Captain Wentworth found it easier to relegate Anne because he was busy. Anne has no problem in holding her own in debate with a man, of course. If, like Jane Austen, she had had novels to write, she would still have been constant, but the eight years might not have seemed so painful or so long.

The last of the canon

Captain Wentworth expresses his love on paper, just as Jane Austen commits her deepest convictions about human love to words. Through her artistry, Jane Austen manages in every novel to suggest that life, like couples, friends and books, add up to something greater than the sum of their parts. There is a consistent rationality that runs through her work but, as Virginia Woolf observed, she seemed to intimate as she grew older that the world is more romantic and more mysterious than she had even hitherto believed.

Jane Austen is the great proponent of the potency of words, of the crucial importance of refined meaning and of meticulous reading. But the suggestion that words themselves may be holding up a mirror to something far more immense is perhaps hinted at by the importance she also attributes to silence. We never see that moment of avowal of love.

The variety, strength and ultimate constancy of all Jane Austen's central lovers perhaps help to persuade the reader of this, her last completed novel, of two possibilities. First, that Captain Wentworth *is* genuinely persuaded back to Anne, because he, like she, has eventually remained true through faith. Second, that constancy *is inevitable* in those who recognize and win through to true love because they have succeeded in mirroring the constancy of a greater love that inevitably prevails.

23 Summer 1814

23.1 The case of Charles Hayter

'Charles Hayter was the eldest of all the cousins, and a very amiable, pleasing young man.' (vol. 1, ch. 9)

A cousin and curate

Charles Hayter is a minor character whose marginal position reveals something important about the world presented in *Persuasion.*

The interest the reader is invited to take in him is of two kinds:

Charles Hayter is a young man with ambitions and romantic hopes. Moreover, his life supplies the traditional material of literature – the struggle between love and social class.

Charles's position is reminiscent of Captain Wentworth's, with Mary Elliot is playing the role of Lady Russell. But the resolution is different.

Charles Hayter's education

Indeed, Charles Hayter's plot enacts the themes that have frequently dominated Jane Austen's novels. She is interested in the relationship between social class (which includes, though is not the same as, wealth) and romantic attachments.

Charles is a cousin of the Musgroves, but his family are poor relations of the Uppercross dynasty. However, Charles has the advantage of being the eldest son, and he is, like Wentworth, what the Victorians would have called 'a self-improver'.

The Hayters are not cultivated people, so their children 'have been hardly in any class at all' (vol. 1, ch. 9). But Charles has acquired an education and a profession. He has 'chosen to be a scholar and a gentleman' (vol. 1, ch. 9).

We may deduce that he went to university and that he had mastered the complex business of being civil. Jane Austen knows that:

education is a social commodity that can be used to the advantage of the person who has received it.

23.2 The uncertainties of love

'Charles Hayter had met with much to disquiet and mortify him in his cousin's behaviour.' (vol. 1, ch. 9)

Charles in love

Charles Hayter's problem is that he is in love with a young woman who is more socially elevated than he. We are told that her parents, 'without any disapprobation' (vol. 1, ch. 9), can see that Charles takes an interest in Henrietta.

The difficulty for Charles is that there is another man. Henrietta '*did* seem to like him . . . before Captain Wentworth came' (vol. 1, ch. 9).

Charles, however, realizes that he cannot compete with the attractive newcomer. Anne can see that 'Henrietta had sometimes the air of being divided between them'. (vol. 1, ch. 10) But Charles appears to think that he has lost.

The country walk

Charles Hayter's story ends happily, but the way it works out is left an intriguing mystery. The Musgrove girls call at the Cottage to announce 'that they were going to take a *long* walk' (vol. 1, ch. 10). Did they call in the hope of being accompanied by Captain Wentworth?

The direction of the walk is also a puzzle. Anne asks: 'Is not this one of the ways to Winthrop?' The reply might be significant: 'But nobody heard, or, at least, nobody answered her.' Was there no answer because Henrietta was trying not to advertise that not only was Winthrop the destination but that she had a reason for going there?

Yet there might be another factor in the resolution. Captain Wentworth is walking with both Musgrove sisters. The conversation is playful, and from Louisa's side almost suggestive. Captain Wentworth wonders whether the walking party will meet the Crofts in their gig. He describes how his sister is constantly being pitched out (vol. 1, ch. 10). Louisa's reply is 'spoken with enthusiasm':

> If I loved a man . . . I would rather be overturned by him, than driven safely by anybody else.

This is lively stuff. The conditional 'If I loved a man' elicits the question 'What man?' and the talk about her rather being turned over than driven safely can, in context, easily be read as erotic solicitation. Captain Wentworth, 'catching the same tone', responds gallantly with a word central to the marriage service: 'I honour you!' Might this be the point at which Henrietta decides that she had better stick with Charles Hayter?

Winthrop

There is indecision and, frustratingly for the reader, conversations that are not heard. Mary, anti-Charles Hayter, wants to turn back, and

> Henrietta, conscious and ashamed, and seeing no cousin Charles walking along any path, or leaning on any gate, was ready to do as Mary wished.

Is Henrietta 'conscious and ashamed' for her past treatment of Charles or because she thinks Mary has found out the purpose of the walk? Did she really expect to find Charles Hayter in the pose of the disconsolate lover 'leaning on any gate'? Does Charles Musgrove see more in the event than the claims of politeness to his relatives? And what is Louisa saying, and, more importantly, why? Has Henrietta disclosed to her sister she would like to make it up with Charles but now lacks the courage, or is Louisa making it clear that Henrietta should be content with Charles, because Captain Wentworth is hers?

Louisa sees the need to encourage (?), cajole (?), persuade (?). All Anne can conclude is that 'there had a been a withdrawing on the gentleman's side, and a relenting on the lady's' but that now they were 'very glad to be together again'.

From here the Charles Hayter plot is resolved by his gaining preferment. The income is sufficient for the couple to marry, so Charles Hayter ends enjoying a good living with the woman he loves. Thus, given different attitudes, could Anne and Captain Wentworth's difficulty also have been soon, and easily, resolved.

23.3 The debate about Charles Hayter

'It suited Mary best to think Henrietta the one preferred, on the very account of Charles Hayter, whose pretensions she wished to put an end to.' (vol. 1, ch. 9)

The dispute

The significance of the Charles Hayter plot emerges in the dispute Mary has with Charles. A marriage into the Hayters would be an undesirable connection. Charles sees things differently. He likes his cousin 'and he saw things as an eldest son himself' (vol. 1, ch. 9). He points out that Charles Hayter has connections – the Spicers – so might be 'getting something from the Bishop in the course of a year or two'. (Was Spicer the person who offered him the Dorset living?)

Charles Hayter also has prospects as the heir of the Winthrop estate: he will be a substantial landowner and may also be a prominent ecclesiastic.

Charles, Mary and the changing world

What is significant about the dispute between Mary and Charles is the different attitudes they take to change:

Charles sees the world as relatively stable and can therefore be optimistic about what will happen to Charles Hayter. He accepts the patronage system in the Church and fully expects that it will work in favour of Charles Hayter.

He has no worries about its continuance; debates in Parliament concerning it have presumably not come to his notice. Likewise, he sees no change in the workings of primogeniture. To Charles all is safe. Charles Hayter probably also thinks this way. His disinclination to talk to Captain Wentworth might, at least symbolically, stand for his unwillingness to recognize that the world *is* undergoing profound changes.

Mary Musgrove is not articulate enough to frame an argument about the rupture of tradition; her attitudes, like those of her father and eldest sister, are shaped by class considerations. She wishes, therefore, to end the 'pretensions' of the Hayters. Yet she might be aware of factors that make her opposition to Charles Hayter all the stronger.

In a world in which her father has to relinquish the family home, it might seem to her all the more important to maintain those social distinctions that gives importance to a family such as hers.

23.4 Changing traditions: the Elliots

'any unwelcome sensations, arising from domestic affairs, changed naturally into pity and contempt, as he turned over the almost endless creations of the last century' (vol. 1, ch. 1)

Two things console Sir Walter in his change of fortunes.

The dignity of a baronet

The first is that his is an ancient family. The entry in 'the book of books' (vol. 1, ch. 1) shows that the Elliots were elevated to the 'the dignity of baronet' during the early years of the reign of Charles II.

Being a gentleman

His second comfort can be discerned in the tone with which he uses the word 'gentleman'. He cannot comprehend Mr Shepherd's use of the term for Mrs Croft's brother, formerly a curate: 'Mr Wentworth was nobody, I remember; quite unconnected; nothing to do with the Strafford family' (vol. 1, ch. 3).

A gentleman is not just anybody; he must be from an established family and have property of his own.

Disturbing times

Both Sir Walter's consolations have this in common:

Sir Walter's family and his argument about being a gentleman are associated with the English Civil War or the events prior to it.

Sir Walter's family might have remained loyal to the Stuarts during the Commonwealth, that period (1649–60) when there was no monarch and no established Church. The above reference is to Wentworth, the Earl of Strafford (1593–1641), a faithful minister of Charles I who was executed, largely because Parliament pressed for his death.

The young Jane Austen wrote a playfully provocative piece called *The History of England*. This is a defence of Mary, Queen of Scots. Because of this it is also a defence of the Stuarts. The story finishes with Charles I, who is defended from the accusation that he was a tyrant with the simple assertion that 'he was a STUART'.

We might tentatively conclude two things from this association with the Elliots and the Civil War, or, as Sir Walter might have called it, following Clarendon, the Great Rebellion.

First, at the very least,

Jane Austen draws a parallel between the disturbing times, which brought the reward of a baronetcy to the Elliot family and the period of history through which Sir Walter Elliot is living.

There had been revolutions in America and France, and in the wake of these there had been wars between both of those nations and England.

Second, we might speculate that an author who in her youth wrote with such enthusiasm about the Stuarts might still regard the Civil War as an undoubted calamity.

It is hard to imagine Jane Austen approving of a regime, which executed a legitimate monarch and abolished the bench of bishops.

This is how she sums up the activities of the leaders of Parliament: 'Cromwell, Fairfax, Hampden, and Pym may be considered as the original causers of all the disturbances, distresses, and civil wars in which England for many years was embroiled'.

If we think the testimony of one piece of juvenilia insecure, *Mansfield Park* may be appealed to as evidence that Jane Austen valued the continuities of tradition. May we then discern a note of regret in her presentation of the Elliots? Anne was at hand to rescue her family with her plan – 'on the side of honesty against importance' (vol. 1, ch. 2) – but the others were unfaithful to their heritage.

It might be argued that since Charles II was profligate in his bestowal of honours, the Elliots of the seventeenth century might not have been rewarded for their fidelity. To imagine, however, that they were a loyal family dramatizes the sad decline in family pride that led Sir Walter to value the trappings of gentility more than an English estate.

23.5 Leaving home

'No, he would sooner quit Kellynch-hall at once, than remain in it on such disgraceful terms.' (vol. 1, ch. 2)

Hard times

Sir Walter Elliot is short of money. Had the novel been narrated differently, there would have been irony and pathos in his situation. The proud Sir Walter, head of an ancient family, falls victim to an increasingly prosperous class of professionals and shopkeepers.

But it is his inflated self-estimation that has led to the financial crisis:

> The Kellynch property was good, but not equal to Sir Walter's apprehension of the state required by its possessor. (vol. 1, ch. 1)

Jane Austen is clear-eyed about money. She knows that status is a matter of having money sufficient to maintain one's position. And more: Anne is the means by which this insight is sustained. To be an Elliot is to be part of a society. Hence, if Kellynch is to be quitted, Anne's preference is a smaller house in the vicinity. The irony is that it is Anne who is the true inheritor of Kellynch; she values its beauties and its place in the family and the neighbourhood. Kellynch is valued by Sir Walter solely as an emblem of *his* respectability.

Leaving home

The disruption with which *Persuasion* opens is a variant of the motif found throughout Jane Austen – displacement. Formally, it is the rupture in the fabric of a hitherto secure life that makes the convolutions of the plot possible.

The reader might feel for Sir Walter in his disquiet about having others in his home and grounds. But when it comes to leaving, Sir Walter does not feel the loss acutely; he enjoys condescendingly bowing 'for all the afflicted tenantry who might have had a hint to show themselves' (vol. 1, ch. 5). Anne and Lady Russell feel keenly the loss of Kellynch. Later, Anne remembers the date – 29 September, Michaelmas, the day on which the rents start – and thinks of a 'beloved home made over to others; all the precious rooms and furniture, groves, and prospects, beginning to own other eyes and limbs' (vol. 1, ch. 6).

Choice

Sir Walter's apparent unconcern and Anne's anguish reveal an important difference. The facts of Sir Walter's case are not exactly like those in the earlier novels, where dispossession is an emblem of loss. Sir Walter's action is emblematic, but emblematic of pride and vanity:

Sir Walter is not ejected; he chooses to abandon Kellynch because he can no longer live in it as he wishes.

There is little pain, because the traditions of his home mean almost nothing to him.

Bath

As long as his house in Bath is one that fits his status, Sir Walter is content. We hear his voice in 'a very good house in Camden-place, a lofty, dignified situation, such as becomes a man of consequence' (vol. 2, ch. 3). Those who know Bath will appreciate the euphemism of 'lofty'; Camden-place (now Camden Crescent) is off the very steep Lansdown-hill. Did such an awkward position affect the rents? Camden-place is also built on 'shaky ground'. Maggie Lane, *A Charming Place: Bath In The Life And Novels Of Jane Austen* (Millstream Books, 1988 p. 38.) Sir Walter wasn't to know this, but Jane Austen, who had house hunted in Bath, certainly did (see p. 40 of above).

Sir Walter and Elizabeth have no regrets. In their enquiries 'Uppercross excited no interest, Kellynch very little, it was all Bath' (vol. 2, ch. 3). The reason for their satisfaction is that 'Their house was undoubtedly the best in Camden-place' and 'Their acquaintance was exceedingly sought after'.

Bath spaces

To be responsive to space is a sign of discernment. Anne cannot ignore how confined the space of the Bath house is. Her father sees 'no degradation in his change'. The same is true of Elizabeth: Anne

> must sigh, and smile, and wonder too . . . at the possibility of that woman, who had been mistress of Kellynch Hall, finding extent to be proud of between two walls, perhaps thirty feet asunder. (vol. 2, ch.3)

The fate of the Elliots

Perhaps it is just as well that neither Elizabeth nor her father are aware of how great their fall has been. Another aspect of Bath life that they also seem unaware of is just how narrow their circle of acquaintances is: it consists chiefly of Mr William Elliot, Colonel Wallis and Lady Dalrymple. By contrast just one paragraph (vol. 2, ch. 6) shows the Crofts have many friends.

Sir Walter and Elizabeth Elliot are representative figures.

They represent those who lose when the world changes, and because they do not recognize change, they cannot come to terms with it.

The Elliots and Charles Hayter

The Elliots strongly contrast with Charles Hayter. In Charles's case, he has to hope for luck in a system that smoothly continues in an established pattern. The Elliots are already caught up in a series of changes that are reshaping England.

23.6 The end of the war

'this present time (the summer of 1814)' (vol. 1, ch. 1)

The date

Unlike her other novels, Jane Austen chose to give a quite specific date to *Persuasion.* The action begins in the summer of 1814 and ends in either late February or early March of 1815 (either date would fall in Lent).

It seems likely that Jane Austen hoped that the reader would see the year of the novel's action as relevant to its plot and themes.

Two wars

In 1814 two wars came to an end: the European war against Napoleon and one in North America in defence of Canada. It was in 1814 that Britain found itself at peace, a peace it had not truly experienced since 1793, when Pitt took the nation into the war with France.

The European war

In 1812 Napoleon and his depleted army retreated from Moscow. The Russians pursued him and occupied much of what is now Germany in 1813. Napoleon recruited a new army and fought a successful campaign. But the countries he fought were beginning to form alliances, which by the summer included Britain.

Meanwhile, Wellington succeeded in driving the French from Spain. The story of his success encouraged the allies in Germany. There were initial setbacks, but by October Napoleon was retreating westwards.

In January 1814 Castlereagh, the Foreign Secretary, arrived in Europe to attempt a coordination of the allies' policy. On the field of battle, things moved quickly. Wellington, entering France from the south, sent an advanced party to Bordeaux, where the people proclaimed the Bourbons as, once again, the legitimate kings of France. The allies drank to the health of Loius XVIII and pushed on to Paris, which fell on 31 March. Napoleon was sent to Elba and, under Talleyrand, the Bourbon dynasty returned and France was restored, more or less, to the boundaries of 1792. In the autumn the Congress of Vienna confirmed the terms.

Canada

The war in North America had begun in 1812, when the House of Representatives voted that a state of war existed between Britain and America. Persuaded by Henry Clay, the Americans believed that a successful expansion westwards required the destruction of

British power in Canada. The Americans attacked to the north, but the British forces under Brock and Sheaffe successfully resisisted. There was fighting by sea; the American frigate *The Constitution* was successful in an encounter with the *Java*, and the British destroyed the *Chesapeake* by the Boston lighthouse. (Encounters fit for a Wentworth.) In 1814 Ross marched into Washington and burned the presidential house, subsequently named, after a coat of paint, the White House. Peace negotiations started in late 1814 and the treaty was signed on Christmas Eve.

Dates

Persuasion is a postwar novel. Jane Austen started the novel on 8 August 1815 and finished it on 6 August 1816. She therefore wrote it after the peace of 1814 and the final victory of Waterloo (against Napoleon, who had escaped from Elba) in June 1815. It is, like *Mansfield Park*, a 'condition of England' novel. It ponders the nation in the wake of long years of war and considers national identity in the light of the peace.

Three elements of the postwar world are evident in the novel.

The mood of victory

Anne speaks on behalf on the navy. When Mr Shepherd proposes that a naval man might be a suitable tenant for Kellynch Hall, Sir Walter is uncertain. It is left to Anne to commend their contribution to the national victory (vol. 1, ch. 3). Subdued as is her tone, we should read her words as an expression of national pride and gratitude. The ends of war are causes of rejoicing, and there is very often a renewed sense of the importance of national traditions and an appreciation of those who secured the continuance of those traditions for the future generations.

Anne's pride and gratitude are judgements on her family:

Sir Walter Elliot has no regard for those who fought for England, and his decision to abandon Kellynch rather than curtail his pleasures shows him oblivious of those traditions of English life that the navy (represented by Admiral Croft and Captain Wentworth) has ensured for the future.

If, like Mansfield, Kellynch in some ways stands for the nation, then the novel is pointedly asking whether the (e)state is in good hands.

The future of the nation

The fact that the future of Kellynch is uncertain is Jane Austen's way of provoking the question about the future of the nation. Again, like *Mansfield Park*, the novel asks who will guide and nurture the state. Will Kellynch devolve upon the designated heir, William Walter Elliot, or will Sir Walter find it convenient to sell it to the Crofts? The choice is sharpened by the postwar setting:

is the novel suggesting that the 'rightful heir' is no longer the worthy inheritor and that the future of Kellynch, and therefore of the nation, should be placed in the hands of those who have proved themselves worthy of shouldering responsibilities?

There is another alternative. If Elizabeth does not marry, and the estate is not entailed upon a male heir, then Sir Walter might leave it to the children of Anne and

Captain Wentworth. Such an arrangement would combine Anne's respect for tradition and Captain Wentworth's enterprizing spirit.

Bringing home the troops

Enormous numbers were engaged in the war. With the cessation of hostilities, most of them would have no further place in the armed services. There are no discharged soldiers in Jane Austen, but there are in *Persuasion* a number of naval officers who are adjusting to the peace. They have not been equally successful. Admiral Croft and Captain Wentworth have done well, but Captain Harville can only afford 'a small house, near the foot of an old pier of unknown date', because 'his health, and his fortune' direct 'him to a residence unexpensive' (vol. 1, ch. 11). Implicitly, the novel asks what will happen to those who fought for England. What will the England be like that they have helped to preserve?

23.7 The navy

'Ay, this comes of the peace.' (vol. 1, ch. 10)

Captain Harville's furniture

Captain Harville is a carefully drawn figure – a man of deep feeling who values his family and friends. He embodies more acutely than the richer naval officers the plight of those who have served their country in a recently finished war. When, after their visit to the Cobb, the Uppercross party return to the Harvilles' house, they find 'rooms so small as none but those who invite from the heart could think capable of accommodating so many' (vol. 1, ch. 11). What in this confined space delights Anne, who has grown up in the generous spaces of Kellynch, is the ingenuity of Captain Harville. She is pleasantly struck by

> the sight of all the ingenious contrivances and nice arrangements of Captain Harville, to turn the actual space to the best possible account, to supply the deficiencies of lodging-house furniture, and defend the windows and doors against the winter storms.

In Captain Harville the reader sees a man adapting to new circumstances with the ingenuity that he learned in his previous calling. This ingenuity extends to construction: 'He drew, he varnished, he carpentered, he glued'. In the rooms, Anne notes the contrast between the owner's furnishings and 'some few articles of a rare species of wood, excellently worked up, and with something curious and valuable from all the distant countries Captain Harville had visited'.

There is a new world in this scene. Here is a man who has had to adapt to changed circumstances and does what few English gentlemen would consider doing – make his own furniture.

Captain Harville is a new kind of man: 'a perfect gentleman, unaffected, warm, and obliging'. Yet he is a different kind of gentleman from, say, William Walter Elliot. Captain Harville has seen the world, so brings a breadth of experience into parochial English life. That experience makes his house an emblem of his adaptability and of a larger world, knowledge of which might transform England.

The reader is prompted to speculate. Has he selected the woods himself and does he explain about the different kinds to his guests? What are the 'curious and valuable' things from the remote regions? Are they inlays in stone or pieces of carving? Is there the beginning here of Captain Harville, the naturalist or the anthropologist? Has Captain Harville's naval life given him an insight into the richness of the natural world and the variety of human cultures?

New wealth

Captain Harville's permanant guest, the melancholy Captain Benwick, has, eventually, thrived financially: 'Fortune came, his prize-money as Lieutenant being great, promotion, too, came at *last*; but Fanny Harville did not live to know it' (vol. 1, ch. 11).

This is not the world of the Elliots. Captain Benwick follows a profession which might, through promotion, bring him wealth and status. Moreover, his particular profession, the navy, offers him a way of becoming rich.

Prize money

Roger Sales draws attention to the importance to the navy of prize money (*Jane Austen and Representations of Regency England*, Routledge, 1994, p. 182f). Prize money was a system of rewarding those who braved the dangers of the sea. If a ship, either a merchantman or one from the Royal Navy, captured an enemy vessel, its value was divided among the crew. It was an established system by the time of the Napoleonic war. Admiral Croft, Captain Benwick and Captain Wentworth have served their country and have had the luck of being rewarded for the capture of enemy ships.

Sir Walter is self-absorbed but he does know what goes on in the world; he lightly talks about a naval man finding Kellynch a 'prize' (vol. 1, ch. 3). One of his objections to the navy is that it is 'the means of bringing persons of obscure birth into undue distinction' (vol. 1, ch. 3). If by 'distinction' he means money he is right.

The war brought wealth to a small group of people who, hitherto, could have expected neither financial nor social success.

The war meant that an adjustment was being made between the landed gentry and the professional classes. It is a world in which profligate gentlemen lose out to hard-working sailors. Mary Elliot will only envy Anne if Captain Wentworth is made a baronet.

Danger

The Royal Navy ensured that its men were rewarded because life at sea was very hard. Again, Sir Walter is right in his second objection to the naval profession: 'it cuts up a man's youth and vigour most horribly' (vol. 1, ch. 3). There was also danger.

Captain Wentworth appreciates that over the capture of a French frigate he was particularly fortunate; no sooner had he brought the captive ship into Plymouth than a four days' gale 'which would have done for poor old *Asp* blew up' (vol. 1, ch. 8). Men died or were wounded. Poor Dick Musgrove dies while in service (we do not know how), and Captain Harville 'had never been in good health since a severe wound which he received two years before' (vol. 1, ch. 11).

Living a life of uncertainty alters one's outlook.

***Persuasion* shows that the emotional texture of life – its fears, expectations and sense of values – is materially affected by the experience of war.**

With the easy assurance of someone who is accustomed to a way of life that he knows others are unfamiliar with, Admiral Croft says that Captain Wentworth should have made up his mind about which of the young Miss Musgroves to choose: 'Ay, this comes of the peace . . . We sailors, Miss Elliot, cannot afford to make long courtships in time of war' (vol. 1, ch. 10).

The pleasurable companionship of marriage might not last long. When Captain Wentworth relates the story of the gale that would have ended the *Asp*, no one notices Anne's 'shudderings'. Had they married she would have joined the band of war widows and might have looked back to the few weeks of marriage she had shared with her beloved. 'Shudderings' is disturbingly apposite; when a ship breaks up the whole frame shudders.

The navy and romance

It is a social and literary tradition that sailors are particularly attractive to young women. Captain Wentworth's account of his capture of the frigate is alluringly debonaire. No wonder the Musgrove sisters search the navy lists for references to the dashing captain's ships.

Admiral Croft and Captain Wentworth also speak romantically about vessels. The Admiral's liking for the *Asp* plays on the custom of applying gender terms to ships: 'Lucky fellow to get her. He knows there must have been twenty men better than himself applying for her at the same time' (vol. 1, ch. 8). This is the language of young men competing for the hand of a particularly attractive young woman.

Naval officers are new, they are wealthy and they bring dash and romance to a world which, by contrast, is beginning to look stale.

23.8 The Crofts

'He was in the Trafalgar action.' (vol. 1, ch. 3)

The Crofts at Kellynch

The Crofts enjoy their new life as a country squire and lady. Reports of their activities at the Hall show them as responsible and charitable. They bring to Somerset the enterprise of explorers:

> the Admiral and Mrs Croft were generally out of doors together, interesting themselves in . . . their grass, and their sheep . . . or driving out in a gig, lately added to their establishment. (vol. 1, ch. 9)

Grass and sheep

The late eighteenth century saw significant changes in the growing of crops, the treatment of land, the breeding of livestock and the improvement of agricultural machinery. A representative figure was Robert Bakewell (1725–95) of Leicestershire. He improved his pastures by digging a canal, designed to flood the grasslands. This enabled him to cut the grass four times a year rather than the usual common practice of two cuts. By selective breeding he improved the yield of both meat and wool in his sheep. Admiral Croft, therefore, is taking an interest in the right areas of country life. The wealth of an estate depends upon the yield of its land. Significantly, there is nothing in the text about Sir Walter taking an interest in his grass and sheep. Had he done so, the Elliots might have remained at Kellynch.

Charity

The Crofts' management of the Kellynch estate has the approval of Anne; she 'felt the parish to be so sure of a good example, and the poor of the best attention and relief'. Her conclusion, encapsulated in elegantly balanced syntax, states in a neat polarity that 'they were gone who deserved not to stay' (vol. 2, ch. 1). The passage implicitly gives an answer to the question: who should inherit the (e)state of England?

The Crofts fulfil the duties of the squire – they meet the needs of the poor. This was a duty that probably fell to Anne. She tells Mary that when she left Kellynch she went 'to almost every house in the parish, as a sort of take-leave' (vol. 1, ch. 5). She does not say that she distributed charity on these visits, but then, bearing in mind Christ's teaching on almsgiving, she would not advertise this fact in a conversation.

The gig

The Crofts buy a gig and drive themselves about the country in it. A gig is small (two-wheeled), practical and unpretentious. It was pulled by a single horse. (The Elliots kept two pairs of horses for their carriages.) The passages about the couple driving, not too expertly, around the lanes of Somerset are perhaps the most endearing in the novel.

Mrs Croft at sea

Perhaps the sense that the navy introduces a new note into the world of 1814 is at its strongest in Mrs Croft. She has followed her husband to sea so brings back to England experiences unknown to the women of Somerset.

Is there the implicit suggestion that those who are given the power to rule, as the Crofts now rule at Kellynch, should have a perspective on the world made possible by the war that has recently finished – and not only the men; the women too?

Nelson

Might we imagine that behind the figure of Admiral Croft we should see the man under whom he served at Trafalgar – Lord Nelson? Croft does not stand for Nelson; rather, it is a case of the 'company' of Nelson providing a context and a lustre for Admiral Croft. Nelson was very much a man whose fortunes were made by the war; he is therefore the epitome of the new kind of man that was formed by the navy.

Sir Walter could not possibly have approved of Nelson. When he speaks of the navy 'bringing persons of obscure birth into undue distinction' (vol. 1, ch. 3), it is hard not to think that Jane Austen was hoping that the reader would see that Nelson – the son of a north Norfolk parson – was such a person. He had those qualities that the narrative of *Persuasion* invites us to applaud; he was purposeful, resourceful and recognized and utilized the abilities of others. At Trafalgar he made it clear that the aim of the battle was the destruction of the French and Spanish fleets. His men were not to think of prize money.

23.9 The new people

'Mr Shepherd was completely empowered to act.' (vol. 1, ch. 3)

A professional

Mr Shepherd has power. It is clearly in his financial interest to move Sir Walter out of Kellynch, and he acts quickly. He sees that 'This peace will be turning all our rich Navy Officers ashore'. All he requires is flattery to hide his contrivings from Sir Walter (vol. 1, ch. 3).

Mr Shepherd does not point out that it is through such a person as himself that Sir Walter's decision to leave will become known. Hence, later in the chapter, the sardonic remarks of the narrator:

> It seemed as if Mr Shepherd, in this anxiety to bespeak Sir Walter's goodwill towards a naval officer as tenant, had been gifted with foresight.

Falling 'into company' with a prospective candidate while one is about one's business, which Mr Shepherd goes on to speak of, is the assured talk of the professional. His casual words about Admiral Croft 'accidentally hearing of the possibility of Kellynch Hall being let' convinces the materialistic but not worldly Sir Walter.

Mr Shepherd is a member of the class that is eroding the hitherto stable world of Kellynch. His forebears might have tended the sheep on the very estate that he is in the process of transferring to other hands. Mr Shepherd is still a shepherd: he supervises the movement of one flock out of the fold and prepares to move another in. He makes sure that Sir Walter is unaware that it is persons such as himself who now have power.

Mrs Clay

His daughter is equally skilful at securing influence. Mrs Clay knows how to survive in the world of 1814. She attaches herself to the Elliots and moves to Bath, and when she sees a prospect more promising she abandons them. Furthermore, she may inherit what the Elliots have given up. The text leaves the future unresolved, but if Sir William is 'wheedled and caressed at last into making her' his wife (vol. 2, ch. 12), the novel closes with the possibility that Mrs Clay will return to Kellynch as the lady of the manor and oust Elizabeth.

Individualism

Mr Shepherd, Mrs Clay and Sir William represent what for Jane Austen are the discomforting aspects of 1814.

What is most distressing for an author whose sympathies still seem to lie with the social cohesion of the old order and its public values of charity, duty and responsibility is that the heroes of 1814 are not in their attitudes fundamentally different from the individualistic self-seekers.

There *is* a difference, however: in order to be successful at sea there must be a communal sense arising out of the traditions of the navy and a sense of responsibility for the nation. The doctrines of Adam Smith (1723–90, author of *The Wealth of Nations* 1776) and advocate of economic individualism do not exactly apply to a country at war. But with the peace, can we be sure that rich sailors will not become calculating individualists?

The summer of 1814 sees a fracturing of the old order. The best – as Sir Walter and Elizabeth should be – lack all conviction, while the worst are uncomfortably like those whom we must recognize as the new heroes. It is to be hoped that in their rapidly approaching middle years Anne and Captain Wentworth can be like the Crofts. It is also to be hoped that if they do have children, theirs will be a family in more than name.

The Elliots hardly work as a family; they are more like an Adam Smith society of enterprising individualists. It is not just that Sir Walter and Elizabeth ignore Anne; she too ceases to think of them: 'She had lately lost sight even of her father and sister and Bath' (vol. 2, ch.1). The landlord in Lyme says that Mr Elliot 'did not mention no particular family' (vol. 1, ch. 12). Only in the Harvilles is there a family that unreservedly enjoys its own company and nurtures the young in the joyful responsibilities of being members of a larger society. *Persuasion* is a dark world. The childlessness of the Crofts is a significant and poignant feature. If the reader seeks consolation, it is again Captain Harville who might supply some; in the list of his crafts we read 'he made toys for the children' (vol. 1, ch. 11).

24 Changes and chances

24.1 Autumn

'the last smile of the year upon the tawny leaves and withered hedges' (vol. 1, ch.10)

Jane Austen and autumn

Sense and Sensibility, *Pride and Prejudice* and *Emma* all begin in September. *Persuasion* opens in the summer of 1814. Yet none of the novels is as rhythmically autumnal as *Persuasion*.

The walk to Winthrop

The walk to Winthrop is a key event (vol. 1, ch. 10). The pictures of the autumn countryside evoke the sense of time passing and the loss of happiness. Anne does not wish to intrude herself upon the others:

> Her *pleasure* in the walk must arise from the exercise and the day, from the view of the last smiles of the year upon the tawny leaves and withered hedges, and from repeating to herself some few of the thousand poetical descriptions extant of autumn, that season of peculiar and inexhaustible influence on the mind of taste and tenderness.

The poets

Jane Austen's language is in the tradition of the poets whom we may suppose Anne recalls. 'Tawny' and 'withered' are used by Spenser, Shakespeare, Milton and Dryden, though not, necessarily, in relation to autumn. Significantly, it is in Cowper's *The Task*, the most quoted poem in Jane Austen, where both words occur. For instance, it is not difficult to imagine Anne recalling

> The sycamore, capricious in attire,
> Now green, now tawny, and ere autumn yet
> Have changed the woods, in scarlet honours bright.
> (*The Task*, Book I, lines. 318–20)

or this about the redbreast in winter:

> he shakes
> From many a twig the pendent drops of ice,
> That tinkle in the withered leaves below.
> (*The Task*, Book VI, lines 80–2)

Autumnal Anne

It is difficult for the reader not to connect Anne with the word 'withered'. As she keeps company with her brother and sister on the separating field paths, the dashing Wentworth is behaving gallantly to the young Louisa. Neither *of them* has withered. The juxtaposition of the faded Anne and the still youthful Wentworth recalls to Anne his remark that she was 'Altered beyond his knowledge!' Anne, 'in silent, deep mortification', had reflected: 'he was not altered, or not for the worse' (vol. 1, ch. 7).

Captain Wentworth has lost none of his vital or active qualities; he is engaged in a sexually enticing discourse with a lively young woman. Anne's feelings are not beyond the consolations of art, but what she finds blessing in is the analogy between the passing of the year and the fading of her youth and hope:

> Anne could not immediately fall into quotation again. The sweet scenes of autumn for a while put by – unless some tender sonnet, fraught with the apt analogy of the declining year, and the images of youth and hope, and spring, all gone together, blessed her memory. (vol. 1, ch. 10)

The text here brings out what was before implicit. 'Fraught', meaning full and stored, applies to the densely written poems she recalls and her poor, aching heart, stored with faded hopes. It is up to the reader to apply the word to Captain Wentworth. In naval terms, it refers to the cargo a ship carries: in Captain Wentworth's case, the cargo that has made him rich.

24.2 The lessons of time and place

'changes, alienations, removals' (vol. 1, ch. 7)

Political readings?

Those who favour political readings of Jane Austen might easily turn her picture of an England undergoing social change and dominated by individual ambition into a political agenda.

It is possible to combine a political reading with others that give a place to literature's traditional subjects, in particular, the passing of time.

***Persuasion* can be understood as dealing with the inevitable fading of youth, strength, love and beauty.**

This theme is present in little things from Mary Musgrove 'lying on the faded sofa' (vol. 1, ch. 5) to Anne at her piano never knowing 'since the loss of her dear mother . . . the happiness of being listened to' (vol. 1, ch. 6).

Places prompt thoughts within the long perspective of time. When Anne returns to Kellynch, she wants to avoid 'ever seeing Captain Wentworth at the hall; those rooms had witnessed former meetings which would be brought too painfully before her' (vol. 1, ch. 11).

The land

There is one moment in *Persuasion* when we catch a glimpse of time passing on a grander scale than that of human life. This occurs when the Uppercross party first arrives in Lyme. The narrator speaks of the attractions of nearby Charmouth, its high ground and sweeps of countryside,

> and still more its sweet retired bay, backed by dark cliffs, where fragments of low rock among the sands make it the happiest spot for watching the flow of the tide, for sitting in unwearied contemplation; the woody varieties of the cheerful village of Up Lyme, and, above all, Pinny, with its green chasms between romantic rocks, where the scattered forest trees and orchards of luxuriant growth declare that many a generation must have passed away since the first partial falling of the cliff prepared the ground for such a state. (vol. 1, ch. 11)

The landscape reminds one of Coleridge's 'Kubla Khan', published the year that *Persuasion* was written:

> But oh! That deep romantic chasm which slanted
> Down the green hill athwart a cedarn cover!
>
> (lines12–13)

What Jane Austen adds is the sense of time passing. The many generations must be generations of trees rather than people, so the time span must, at least, be estimated in hundreds of years. Against this backgound of the long years of natural history the little perturbations of humankind are viewed.

And, furthermore, by an accident of history beyond the text, there is the frisson that it was in Lyme and the nearby 'fragments of low rock among the sands' that Mary Anning started collecting fossils, and thereby helped to open up vistas of history, geological as well as natural. She found what proved to be an ichthyosaurus in 1811, and took ten years to dig it out of the cliffs. With the sort of impudence that not all contemporary critical practice decries, we can imagine the local girl walking out of Lyme to work at her fossils while Louisa Musgrove is behaving irresponsibly – parodying the First Fall – on the Cobb. We might also imagine the author, had she known about Mary Anning, seeing that human folly appeared all the more pathetic against the backdrop of geological time.

Time passing

In English literature autumn is the season most associated with the passing of time. The Winthrop walk can be seen in the context of an England changing politically (Mary does not get her way). There is evidence too that the farmer is active:

> the ploughs at work, and the fresh-made path spoke the farmer, counteracting the sweets of poetical despondence, and meaning to have spring again. (vol. 1, ch. 10)

This too can be given a political reading: all around is activity aimed at achieving a prosperous future. Moreover, the party 'gained the summit of the most considerable hill'. In terms of time passing, Anne cannot expect another spring (another youth) so will not gain the summit of the hill of achievement. She may only retain 'the sweets of poetical despondence'.

From Kellynch to Uppercross

Anne's move from Kellynch to Uppercross brings home to her something which she already knew but now feels with a forceful immediacy: our 'conversation, opinion, and idea' alter from place to place (vol. 1, ch. 6).

This relativity of outlook and value is something she wishes her family could experience. Jane Austen has always made observation, perspective and judgement central to her thought; this passage takes the need to get things clear even deeper:

> yet, with all this experience, she believed she must now submit to feel that another lesson, in the art of knowing our own nothingness beyond our own circle, was become necessary for her.

There is a gravitas about those words which a reader might feel is in excess of the issue that has prompted Anne's thoughts. 'Submit' is very strong; the self must be schooled in tractability. The word 'nothingness' falls with a weight that is almost religious. Knowledge of how little we matter is the ground of religious humility, a humility that makes us sense how little 'our own' (a phrase repeated to alert us to the narrowness of our concerns) sphere of life is.

It is significant that such a note is struck early, for it puts into perspective not just the Elliots' pride but, even, the concerns of the heart that the book so plangently addresses. In the perspective of time, enforced by the sense of a world undergoing change, do our little feelings matter? And beyond time, when our nothingness can truly be known, our febrile anxieties will be of no account. This is, of course, a dangerous moment for a novelist, who wants to engage the reader in the concerns of his or her characters, but there is art, such as Chaucer's *The Parson's Tale*, which almost abandons what we usually find of interest in fiction to direct us to the relativizing sublimities of Eternity.

The heart might change

Anne does not like Bath, and the offer of Lady Russell to delay her removal is welcome because she will avoid, at least for 1814, 'the possible white heats of September in all the white glare of Bath' (vol. 1, ch. 5). Yet on her arrival after Christmas, she is not disconsolate. In fact, she is inclined to take a romantic interest in characters other than Captain Wentworth. The human heart is never entirely fixed in its choices and destiny.

Other heroes?

The heroine who, it seems, is destined by the plot for the hero, but who, usually after setbacks, encounters another potential husband is a feature of other Jane Austen novels. So, Anne, her heart sore from the past and troubled in the present, meets the melancholic Captain Benwick, with whom a rapport is established. Others notice. Charles Musgrove sees promise in it, whilst his wife, conscious of the dignity of her family, thinks the young man unsuitable and appeals to Lady Russell for support. Anne's contribution is to say that Lady Russell 'would be so much pleased with his mind' (vol. 2, ch. 2). She might want to prepare Lady Russell for a possible outcome.

Of course, Captain Benwick does have a plot function, but not the one the reader might expect: his engagement to Louisa removes two obstacles to the eventual union of Anne and Captain Wentworth.

Having arrived in Bath, Anne encounters, once again, the charming Mr Elliot. Anne thinks that the future might bring about his marriage with Elizabeth. She does not even think of Mr Elliot as possibly desirous of herself, but the reader will see two features apart from the obvious Kellynch connection that would make their marriage appropriate: they enjoy conversing and share a common interest in Lyme.

These two 'possible' romances draw attention to two things: the place of the unexpected in our lives (had Louisa not been injured, Captain Benwick might have pursued Anne), and the capacity of the human heart to change. In *Persuasion* it is implied that second attachments are possible, because even the strongest affections can fade and those who have deeply loved one person might, later, settle for another.

Mrs Smith

Mrs Smith is 'not one and thirty' (vol. 2, ch. 5) yet she is 'a poor, infirm, helpless widow' (vol. 2, ch. 5). She epitomizes the changes and chances of this fleeting world. Although Mrs Smith's life is in some respects the reverse of Anne's, her experience is, like Anne's, measured against the movement of time. Anne moves from prudence to romance. Of her early life, Mrs Smith says:

> I was very young, and associated only with the young, and we were a thoughtless, gay set, without any strict rules of conduct. We lived for enjoyment. I think differently now: time and sickness, and sorrow, have given me other notions. (vol. 2, ch. 9)

The 'other notions' that govern Mrs Smith's thought are set out in a lengthy passage in which the narrative viewpoint shifts from the narrator to Anne.

The narrator says that Anne 'could scarcely imagine a more cheerless situation' – a beloved husband in his grave, affluence gone, neither children nor relations to comfort her, health impaired and lodgings noisy, dark and confined:

> Yet, inspite of all this, Anne had reason to believe that she had moments only of langour and depression, to hours of occupation and enjoyment. (vol. 2, ch. 5)

'Yet' has considerable force, it might be regarded as one of the crucial words in *Persuasion*.

What follows is an interesting passage in which the expected reasons for such resilience are reviewed and qualified. Anne 'watched – observed – reflected and finally determined' that Mrs Smith's peace of mind is not just a matter of 'fortitude or of resolution only':

> A submissive spirit might be patient, a strong understanding would supply resolution, but here was something more; here was that elasticity of mind, that disposition to be comforted, that power of turning readily from evil to good, and of finding employment which carried her out of herself, which was from Nature alone. It was the choicest gift of Heaven.

We must remember that this is Anne and not the narrator, but even so, is there anything in the text that requires a reader to diverge from the interpretation?

In a world in which nothing is secure – in which events are unpredictable and the passing of time, with all that that brings, the only certainty – a recognition that there is a grace that will help the human spirit to bear up – is an insight that, indirectly, the author commends.

At this point *Persuasion* feels close to *Mansfield Park*; both point to the workings in human lives of powers that Jane Austen would have considered providential. Reflecting on her harsh experiences of what elsewhere in the text is called 'changes, alienations, removals' (vol. 1, ch. 7), Anne feels that she could be eloquent 'on the side of early warm attachment' and against 'that over-anxious caution which seems to insult exertion and distrust Providence' (vol. 1, ch. 4).

24.3 The fading of beauty

'the rapid increase of crow's foot about Lady Russell's temples' (vol. 1, ch. 1)

The first chapter

The first chapter of *Persuasion* has a burdened and discontented tone. Characters are unhappy with their lot and find little consolation. The opening passage about Sir Walter's favourite reading brings before the reader the passing of time. There might even be a sombre irony in Sir Walter's stillborn son entering the world on 5 November. The date reminds us of an aborted attempt to change history. So the history of the Elliots would have been changed had Sir Walter's son survived.

To contemplate the history of a family is to be aware of wider vicissitudes and the brevity of individual lives. However, though the reader might feel this, in his proud self-absorption Sir Walter's contemplation of his and other families' histories induces not a renewed sense of the One before whom the generations rise and fall but 'pity and contempt' for families not as ancient as his.

Elizabeth

His eldest daughter is more sensitive to the passing of time. At 29 she knows herself to be 'as handsome as ever, but she felt her approach to the years of danger'. When she is thus afflicted, 'the book of books' offers no consolation (the implication is that the real Book of books is the only book that does) for it reminds her of what might have been if the heir presumptive had not failed to honour her with the attentions of courtship. Her pushing away of the book, open at the page of her birth and recording no marriage but that of her younger sister, is, to adapt a phrase of Philip Larkin's, an aversion of the eyes from death.

Elizabeth, when she 'was in her first bloom', had entertained hopes of Mr Elliot, but all that remains of that is her 'wearing black ribbons for his wife'. Nevertheless, she is still attractive. The word Jane Austen frequently uses is 'bloom'. Elizabeth is 'as blooming as ever, amidst the wreck of the good looks of every body else'. Sir Walter, preoccupied with his own still remarkably handsome face, can

> plainly see how old all the rest of his family and acquaintance were growing. Anne haggard, Mary coarse, every face in the neighbourhood worsting; and the rapid increase of the crow's foot about Lady Russell's temples had long been a distress to him. (vol. 1, ch. 1)

Sir Walter's position is, ironically, central to the novel:

***Persuasion* explores the passing of time, the fading of beauty and the failure of persons of influence to learn from the lessons time teaches.**

Anne's faded bloom

In the opening chapter the narrator says of Anne: 'A few years before, Anne Elliot had been a very pretty girl, but her bloom had vanished early'. Her father never did find much to admire in her, but any esteem dies when she becomes 'faded and thin'.

The narrator insists that the fading of her bloom is due to the thwarting of her romantic hopes: 'an early loss of bloom and spirits had been' the 'lasting effect' (vol. 1, ch. 4). The narrator is making a point about the fading of Anne's beauty in the word 'early'. Elizabeth, two years older than Anne, is 'as blooming as ever' (vol. 1, ch. 1).

There are, therefore, significances in the placing of Anne in the autumn landscape. The tawny leaves and withered hedges are natural, because fading, as well as flourishing, is part of the cycle of life. This is poignant: the leaves will begin afresh, whereas beauty is like the rose of a single summer. The gradual fading of our looks is part of the cycle of nature, too. But because Anne has lost her bloom early, there is something premature in the juxtaposition of her in the autumn landscape of Somerset. Further, there is something unnatural about her loss of bloom; something other than the course of nature has caused her looks to fade.

Neglect

The text points to a further cause of Anne's premature loss of youth:

Anne is neglected by her father and two sisters.

This is brought out in the opening chapter. Even at the height of her beauty, her father found little in her to admire, and in the business of re-trenching and removal, her voice is unheeded. The narrator's summary is:

> but Anne . . . was nobody with either father or sister: her word had no weight, her convenience was always to give way; she was only Anne.

Youth relinquished

In Jane Austen dancing stands for youthful pleasure. It is, therefore, significant that Anne gives it up. To give up dancing is a sign that one is relinquishing youth.

When she plays and Captain Wentworth dances, Anne wonders whether he is trying 'to trace in them [her looks] the ruins of the face which once had charmed him'. She plays mechanically, and at one point realizes that he must have asked about her, because his dancing partner gives this reply: 'she has quite given up dancing' (vol. 1, ch. 8).

Recovery?

The drift of the narrative is that Anne regains something of her youth. This regaining is, however, an area of the text that is problematic. It is not clear whether she does recover her looks to any important degree, and if she does, the text is unclear about the cause.

The difficulty occurs in a passage comparing the invalid Mrs Smith with Anne. The narrator says that

> Twelve years had changed Anne from the blooming, silent, unformed girl of fifteen, to the elegant little woman of seven and twenty, with every beauty excepting bloom. (vol. 2, ch. 5)

Anne is clearly no longer the haggard girl whom her father sees in the first chapter, but the passage is hardly consistent with the account of her at Lyme, in which the narrator comments that her 'bloom and freshness of youth ([had been] restored by the fine wind' (vol. 1, ch. 12).

The text makes it clear that there is a change in Anne, or, rather, that others see a beauty in her that those who know her seem unaware of. The incident at Lyme referred to above comes after a gentleman, who turns out to be Mr Elliot, looks 'at her with a degree of earnest admiration' (vol. 1, ch. 12). In Bath the ladies of Captain Wentworth's party compare her favourably with Elizabeth:

> She is pretty, I think; Anne Elliot; very pretty when one comes to look at her. It is not the fashion to say so, but I confess I admire her more than her sister. (vol. 2, ch. 7)

In view of what was said above about how her faded beauty is, in part, the result of family neglect, it cannot be ruled out that the recovery of her looks owes something to the interest people start to take in her. Mr Elliot notices her looks, but is the implication that the fact that he notices her also helps to bring out what has been latent for too long? Furthermore, can the little attentions of Captain Wentworth – lifting the child off her, helping her into the carriage, praising her practicality – have helped to restore her?

The issue of the recovery of Anne's beauty is a difficult one to get into focus. Perhaps there is one thing we can be sure about:

one of the distinctive features of *Persuasion* is that the central figure is, by the standards of her day, no longer young and, for some time and in some eyes, no longer attractive.

24.4 Suffering

'suffering under severe and constant pain' (vol. 2, ch. 5)

Ill health

Sickness and ill health have a place in all of Jane Austen's novels. Illness and the uses to which it is put in the narrative increase from her early to later work.

Mrs Smith, at only thirty, has become infirm and virtually housebound.

In an autumnal novel, suffering, sickness and health are congruent with the themes, textures and tones of the work. *Persuasion* uses sickness to provide material for the plot. On Anne's first visit to Mrs Smith (vol. 2, ch. 5), there is a lengthy account of an invalid's life. Mrs Smith sums up what she owes to Nurse Rooke in the following words:

> Call it gossip if you will; but when Nurse Rooke has half an hour's leisure to bestow on me, she is sure to have something to relate that is entertaining and profitable, something that makes one know one's species better.

Is a purpose of a novel to enable us to know our species better and is it part of *Persuasion*'s purpose to put it in perspective?

Gossip

Jane Austen is playing on the different meanings of the word 'gossip'. Johnson's first definition of the word as a verb is 'To chat; to prate; to be merry.' His third defintion of the noun is 'One who runs about tattling like women at a lying-in.' A gossip therefore was one who chatted and one who was a midwife. Nurse Rooke is both: she brings Mrs Smith interesting gossip but she practises midwifery (she attends the lying-in of Mrs Wallis).

It is in both roles that Nurse Rooke contributes to the plot. She discovers the plans of Mr Elliot. As a midwife, Nurse Rooke's status is low. Hence there is an irony in the fact that she, along with Mrs Smith, is the source of the news that ultimately thwarts a high-status rogue.

Accidents

If ill health is a change in the circumstances of life, accidents are one of its chances.

There is a subtle piece of dramatic irony at work in the case of little Charles's fall. All responsibilities devolve upon Anne (vol. 1, ch. 7). Later, when Louisa falls, she takes control again. Had the accident happened to the Musgrove child when Anne and Mary had arrived at Uppercross House, Captain Wentworth would have witnessed Anne's calm and sensible disposition tested in domestic circumstances. And that is the point:

in coping with the accident, Anne shows that she will be an excellent wife, because all that she does – send messages (for which she has to control the servants) and, in different ways, comfort the distressed – are the tasks of one who is required to run a large household.

But would Captain Wentworth have appreciated Anne's presence of mind so much as when his own guilt was activated?

The happy fall

Something of Jane Austen's quiet preoccupation with the workings of Providence is evident in the treatment of Louisa's accident on the Cobb. The accident reveals to Captain Wentworth what he has lost in losing Anne and it brings together the woman he might have married (Louisa) and the man who might just have come round to proposing to Anne (Benwick).

When the accident happens on the Cobb, the writing does not prompt readers to search for emblematic analogies. It is, perhaps, only when surveying the configurations of the plot that a reader might be tempted to think of the primal fall – the loss of Eden – and how in the Christian imagination this is seen as a benefit, because without the loss of the apple there would have been no salvation nor, in the words of a medieval carol, a Queen of Heaven.

In a novel concerned with the passing of time, the incident on the Cobb has a double function: it stands for the uncertainty of life, and it shows that even in a world where time's ravages are all too evident, not everything that is chancy proves an evil.

24.5 Loss

'mourning her loss' (vol. 1, ch. 11)

The passing of time is poignantly evident in references to the dead. Perhaps this is a response to the ending of a war.

Poor Richard

Jane Austen is often said to idealize the navy. But Dick Musgrove, as the narrator calls him, is no naval hero. His name and his life are abbreviated, and not even an early death from unspecified causes (presumably not a naval action) can elevate him to the dignity of his baptismal name. The description of him as 'thick-headed, unfeeling, unprofitable' (vol. 1, ch. 6) identifies him as a feckless, thoughtless somewhat wild young man.

Because the narrator is so decisively negative about 'poor Richard', we feel that if so much grief is prompted by such a one, then are we not prompted to recognize the nameless numbers (of many worthy young men) who also perished abroad in the service of their country?

Fanny Harville

Fanny Harville dies before the narrative opens, yet she is a character who calls forth deep feelings. Hers is a story full of pathos. She and Benwick waited 'for fortune', but the fortune that is eventually sent is two-fold: wealth comes to Benwick, but fortune – the disposer of our fates – intervenes to take Fanny from him.

The pathos is increased by the delay in the news of Fanny's death reaching Benwick. Moroever, with the urgency associated with heroic action, Wentworth left his ship at Plymouth, characteristically without waiting for permission, 'and never left the poor fellow for a week' (vol. 1, ch. 12). We need to note the parallel: both Anne and Captain Wentworth can respond in emergencies and are adept at 'nursing' the ailing.

Fanny only appears as a memory but is eternally constant. As such she is a reminder of what Anne might have been if Captain Wentworth had not returned. Like Anne too she provides the measure of Louisa. Her death is also a matter of regret, a sign that we live in an uncertain world, where 'Carpe diem' seems the best advice.

On the other hand, is Captain Benwick's new-found love an indication that the losses of the past are not irremediable? That happy outcome, as well as making the reconciliation of Anne and Wentworth possible, might be said to foreshadow it. Time can heal the broken heart and a broken attachment. Wentworth's is the voice of experience and hope (vol. 2, ch. 8). The losses of the past might be recovered in a renewed love.

Remembrance

Other losses are recalled. Like *Hamlet*, *Persuasion* starts with a family in mourning – wearing black ribbons for Mr Elliot's wife. Anne also looks back to the happy days when her mother was alive. Now, for Anne, music is a reminder only of loneliness. The narrator makes a bleak summary of her practice of what contemporary society regarded as an essentially communal art: 'In music she had been always used to feel alone in the world' (vol. 1, ch. 6).

Men and women remembering

The close of the novel turns on the issue of male and female remembrance. Both hero and heroine make a case for their sex but the subject as an argument is not resolved. What does emerge is emotionally ambivalent. Remembrance has for much of the novel been a matter of regret, but it is the mutual regret of Anne and Wentworth that brings them together. Perhaps the novel dwells on the ancient idea, discussed in Dante, that the nearer we are to perfection the greater will be both our pain and pleasure. Anne and Wentworth, as the representative figures to whom the nation must look in the future, feel the pain of separation and the joy of reconcilation all the more keenly because they are essentially sensitive and honourable.

24.6 Literature and love

'she ventured to recommend a larger allowance of prose in his daily study' (vol. 1, ch. 11)

Poetry

Poetry is present in *Persuasion* to accompany private musings. As she walks though the autumn fields, Anne repeats 'to herself some few of the thousand poetical descriptions extant of autumn' (vol. 1, ch. 10). The ones she remembers are like the few leaves that hang upon the boughs that shake against the cold of the dying year. But not even poetry can immure her against pain.

Benwick wallows in poetry. In both the amorous and the cultural sense, Benwick approaches the romantic archetype: he has a 'melancholy air' (vol. 1, ch. 11), he likes churches and, so Anne assumes, has fallen in love with Louisa 'over poetry' (vol. 2, ch. 6).

Prose

Captain Benwick clearly needs rousing and fortifying. Anne, aware of the dangers of poetry for one so susceptible to it, suggests appropriate prose. It is prose, the prose of our moralists and religious writers, that provides both the precepts and the examples that she believes will help. Frustratingly for the reader, the narrator does not follow Anne in naming individual authors. Did the list include Butler, Johnson and Bishop Sherlock, whose sermons, we know, Jane Austen read?

Drama

If a critic wants to play intellectual games with the literature alluded to and worked on in *Persuasion*, there is a sort of Hegelian dialectic at work. Thesis: the poetry that Anne remembers and Captain Benwick reads; antithesis: the prose Anne recommends to allay Benwick's overindulgent romanticism; synthesis: Shakespeare, who provides a model for the crucial debate between Anne and Captain Harville on love, men, women and memory (vol. 2, ch. 11).

The debate, crucially overheard by Captain Wentworth, has something of the ritualized design of Renaissance discourse. Something of this formality is present in the intimate scene in *Twelfth Night*, when the Duke, Orsino, talks to a young courtier, Cesario (actually Viola in disguise) about the relative strengths of women's and men's love. Viola has fallen in love with Orsino. Orsino thinks that no woman can love with the intensity that he does. Viola fictionalizes her 'apparent' self to express what she feels for him:

My father had a daughter loved a man
As it might be perhaps, were I a woman
I should your lordship.
(Act II, Scene iv, lines 105–9)

In *Persuasion* the issues at stake are memory and the strength of love. Captain Harville shows Anne a miniature (a small portrait) of Benwick, drawn originally for Fanny. This is familiar territory to those who know *Twelfth Night*, in which there is debate about pictures and their originals. Meanwhile, like Viola, Wentworth is working under a fiction – that he is writing about the miniature - when really he is expressing his love for Anne. In Shakespeare's words from the same scene, both Anne and Wentworth have had to sit in patience until both, in their different ways, declare themselves.

24.7 The years between

'so many, many years of division and estrangement' (vol. 2, ch. 11)

A happy past

Persuasion is novel of in-between years. The narrative commences as the long period of separation is coming to an end. The past has so followed the conventional contours of a tale of young romance that the reader can see that in spite of very strong mutual feelings there was unlikely to be a quick and happy resolution for Anne and Wentworth. But before the snobbish prejudices of family and friends brought the attachment to a disabling close, there was 'A short period of felicity'. The narrator's insistence on this romantic golden age prepares the reader for one of the chief questions the novel raises:

is *Persuasion* a novel of recovering a vanished Eden or does the narrative rather insist on highlighting the lost years in between first love and final happiness?

Eight years

The narration brings forcefully home to the reader the time that has passed since Anne and Wentworth first met. The gap in their lives is referred to throughout the book.

The Musgroves, 'puzzling over past years', wonder whether the Wentworth who is to visit Kellynch is the same 'very fine young man' they once met; nor can they be certain 'whether it was seven or eight years ago' (vol. 2, ch. 6). When Anne and Captain Wentworth meet again, these 'eight years' haunt Anne's thought:

> Eight years, almost eight years had passed, since all had been given up . . . What might not eight years do? Events of every description, changes, alienations, removals, all, all must be comprised in it; and oblivion of the past – how natural, how certain too! It included nearly a third part of her own life. (vol. 1, ch. 7)

The language of seeing things at a distance – a language close to that used to discuss landcape painting – provides the terms for understanding Anne's thinking.

Wentworth's thinking

Persuasion is mediated almost exclusively through Anne's consciousness, so the reader cannot be sure what Captain Wentworth is thinking. Towards the close, as the reader might expect, it becomes clear that he, too, has been brooding on the lost years. He comments to Anne that she 'did not used to like cards; but time makes many changes'. Anne's reply is one of those responses that says more than she intended: 'I am not yet so much changed'. He waits a few moments and then, 'as if it were the result of immediate feeling, 'It is a period, indeed! Eight and a half years is a period!' (vol. 2, ch. 10). 'Period' seems equivalent here to a long time. Captain Wentworth not only feels that too many years have passed but he may be picking up on one of the meanings of 'period' given by Johnson: 'A stated number of years; a round of time, at the end of which the things comprised within the calculation shall return to the state in which they were at the beginning.' A long time, but . . . .

Blighted lives

Captain Wentworth was not thought good enough for Anne Elliot because he did not come from a family of gentlemen. In material terms, he was not, at the time of their first meeting, a wealthy man. Lady Russell did not wish Anne, 'so young; known to so few, to be . . . sunk . . . into a state of most wearing, anxious, youth-killing dependence' (vol. 1, ch. 4).

The meanings obtrude with something approaching aggression. It is the sailor, not Anne, who will make or mar his life by sinkings, and time reveals that it is because Anne did *not* marry Wentworth that her life is one of 'wearing, anxious, youth-killing dependence'. In case the reader misses the irony, the narrator spells it out: 'Her attachments and regret had, for a long time, clouded every enjoyment of youth'. (The language of landscape is again present: all her views are clouded.)

Moreover, Anne had to face alone 'the additional pain of opinions, on his [Wentworth's] side, totally unconvinced and unbending, and of his feeling himself ill-used by so forced a relinquishment'. As Mrs Musgrove says: 'There is nothing so bad as a separation' (vol. 1, ch. 8).

Options

Anne is like Wordsworth's Lucy, who, not unlike the obscurity of Anne, 'dwelt among th'untrodden ways':

> A Maid whom there were none to praise
> And very few to love.
> ('Song' from *Lyrical Ballads*, 1800)

Anne's refusal of Wentworth might have ended Anne's chances of marriage. Did those who desired the severance wonder whether they had acted wisely? There is no indication that her immediate family pondered this issue, but Lady Russell feels vindicated by the fact that:

> the man who at twenty-three had seemed to understand somewhat of the value of an Anne Elliot, should, eight years afterwards, be charmed by a Louisa Musgrove. (vol. 2, ch. 1)

She does, though, begin to despair of Anne's ever marrying although she sees her as most suited to the state.

Wentworth

Marilyn Butler sees Wentworth as central to the ideology of *Persuasion*.She opens her chapter with: 'In Captain Frederick Wentworth *Persuasion* has a classic case-study of a modern-minded man from the conservative point of view' (*Jane Austen and the War of Ideas*, Clarendon Press, 1975, p. 275). Her case is that he is the self-confident individualist, who blames Anne for heeding the advice of her friends.

That he changes is the substance and also the challenge of the novel, for it can be questioned whether the indirect account of his feelings, poured out as he and Anne walk the 'quiet and retired gravel-walk' (vol. 2, ch. 11), sufficiently convinces the reader that a real change, or realization, has taken place. However, regardless of whether Wentworth's change satisfies, the showing of those events in the autumn of 1814 that drew Anne and him together entails a bleak judgement upon the years in between:

if it took meeting Anne again to convince Wentworth of her worth, then it follows that the eight years since their first meeting and severance have, in so far as they have not led to healing, been a waste.

It says much for Anne, faded physically, that she can still convince Wentworth that she is superior to anyone else whom he has met, but this involves writing off, so to speak, those eight years. Writing off, as Anne thinks, nearly a third of her life. In this area of the novel, nothing can make up for that loss.

Syntax and cadence

The sad contemplation of the passing of time can sometimes be felt in the syntax and cadences of *Persuasion*'s lyrical prose, just as lament is heard in the 'dying fall' and receding past tenses of Viola's 'My father had a daughter loved a man'.

Persuasion is a novel of long sentences. Would it be pushing the idea of transience too far to say that the reader is thus made more aware than usual of time's passage? Certainly, the syntax sometimes *marks* time, so the reader is held in suspense until the full meaning is disclosed. When Anne and Captain Wentworth start to meet again, there is a past/present sentence that is concerned with Anne's reflections on the differences between then and now:

> With the exception, perhaps, of Admiral and Mrs Croft, who seemed particularly attached and happy, (Anne could allow of no other exception even among the married couples) there could have been no hearts so open, no tastes so similar, no feelings so in unison, no countenances so beloved. (vol. 1, ch. 8)

The suspensive movement increases expectation, and because time is taken reaching the point where the thought of the sentence is clear, there is the feeling that we (both reader and characters) have come a long way. And where we have reached is the past, not the present. The haunting past tenses, as in Viola's speeches in *Twelfth Night*, make what has been felt seem very distant. This sensation of being way back in the past as well as achingly in the present is the experience of reading *Persuasion*.

Occasionally we catch a lilting yet falling little tune, sadly epitomizing loss. It is heard in the first chapter when the narrator speaks of the neglect of Anne: 'her convenience was always to give way; she was only Anne'.

When Lady Russell decides that Bath would be good for Anne, there is a tonal inflection which expresses an almost Wordsworthian regret: 'Anne had been too little from home, too little seen' (vol. 1, ch. 2). That sounds like the Lucy poem quoted in 24.6.

The reader who has a taste for the beauty of melancholy will always find *Persuasion* appealing. In this novel Jane Austen shows an acute feeling for the transient. Lovers will come and lovers will go, and some will connect and some will not. There will, for the time being, always be 'green chasms' between 'romantic rocks'. But in time even the rocks will erode.

The occasional falling modulation of the style echoes the sense of loss, the feeling that the text occasionally induces that nothing can ever quite make up for lost years. The silences in Jane Austen's novels increase as she grows older. They give straight out onto eternity. The sounds we hear in *Persuasion* are like the dripping November rain on Mary's verandah at the soberly named Uppercross. They are those which Wordsworth in the lines he wrote above Tintern Abbey called 'The still, sad music of humanity'.

Index

D

E

F

G